HANDBOOK OF INNOVATION INDICATORS AND MEASUREMENT

Handbook of Innovation Indicators and Measurement

Edited by

Fred Gault

Professorial Fellow, UNU-MERIT, The Netherlands and Professor Extraordinaire and Member, TUT Institute for Economic Research on Innovation (IERI), Tshwane University of Technology (TUT), South Africa

Edward Elgar
Cheltenham, UK • Northampton, MA, USA

Published by
Edward Elgar Publishing Limited
The Lypiatts
15 Lansdown Road
Cheltenham
Glos GL50 2JA
UK

Edward Elgar Publishing, Inc.
William Pratt House
9 Dewey Court
Northampton
Massachusetts 01060
USA

Paperback edition 2014

A catalogue record for this book
is available from the British Library

Library of Congress Control Number: 2012953530

This book is available electronically in the ElgarOnline.com
Economics Subject Collection, E-ISBN 978 0 85793 365 2

ISBN   978 0 85793 364 5 (cased)
       978 1 78254 517 0 (paperback)

Contents

v

Contributors

Esko Aho, Senior Fellow, Harvard University. Former Prime Minister of Finland. esko.aho@hks.harvard.edu.

Mikko Alkio, Partner, Avance Attorneys. Former State Secretary responsible for innovation policy in Finland. mikko.alkio@avanceattorneys.com.

Anthony Arundel, Australian Innovation Research Centre, University of Tasmania. Anthony.Arundel@utas.edu.au. UNU-MERIT, Maastricht, The Netherlands, a.arundel@maastrichtuniversity.nl.

Carter Bloch, Danish Centre for Studies in Research and Research Policy, Department of Political Science and Government, Aarhus University, Denmark. Carter.Bloch@cfa.au.dk.

Jeroen P.J. de Jong, RSM Erasmus University, Rotterdam, The Netherlands. jjong@rsm.nl.

Frank Foyn, Statistics Norway, Oslo, Norway. Frank.Foyn@ssb.no.

Konstantin Fursov, National Research University 'Higher School of Economics', Moscow, Russia. ksfursov@hse.ru.

Fernando Galindo-Rueda, Directorate for Science, Technology and Industry, Organisation for Economic Co-operation and Development (OECD), Paris, France. fernando.galindo-rueda@oecd.org.

Fred Gault, UNU-MERIT, Maastricht, The Netherlands. gault@merit.unu.edu. The Institute for Economic Research on Innovation (IERI), Tshwane University of Technology, Pretoria, South Africa. fred@ieri.org.za.

Leonid Gokhberg, National Research University 'Higher School of Economics', Moscow, Russia. lgokhberg@hse.ru.

Nathalie Greenan, Centre d'Etudes de l'Emploi and TEPP (CNRS), France. Nathalie.Greenan@cee-recherche.fr.

Christopher T. Hill, Center for Science, Technology and Economic Development, SRI International, Arlington, VA, Technology Policy International, Boston, MA, George Mason University, Arlington, VA. Chill2@gmu.edu.

Hugo Hollanders, UNU-MERIT (Maastricht University), Maastricht, The Netherlands. h.hollanders@maatrichtuniversity.nl.

Tomohiro Ijichi, National Institute of Science and Technology Policy (NISTEP), Tokyo, Japan. ijichi@nistep.go.jp. Faculty of Innovation Studies, Seijo University, Tokyo, Japan. ijichi@seijo.ac.jp.

Norbert Janz, FH Aachen University of Applied Sciences, Aachen, Germany. janz@fh-aachen.de. UNU-MERIT, Maastricht, The Netherlands. janz@merit.unu.edu.

Kippy Joseph, The Rockefeller Foundation, New York. jjoseph@rock found.org.

Ilkka Lakaniemi, Senior Advisor, Future Internet, CONCORD, Aalto University, Finland. Programme Chair, Future Internet, Public–Private Partnership, CONCORD, European Commission. Senior Advisor, Finland Chamber of Commerce. ilkka.lakaniemi@aalto.fi.

Edward Lorenz, Research Group in Law, Economics and Management, University of Nice and CNRS, France. Edward.lorenz@gredeg.cnrs.fr.

Dirk Meissner, National Research University 'Higher School of Economics', Moscow, Russia. dmeissner@hse.ru.

Ian Miles, University of Manchester, Manchester UK and National Research University 'Higher School of Economics', Moscow, Russia. Ian. miles.manchester@gmail.com.

Geoff Mulgan, National Endowment for Science Technology and the Arts (Nesta), London, UK. Geoff.Mulgan@nesta.org.uk.

Will Norman, The Young Foundation, London, UK. Will.Norman@ Youngfoundation.org.

Kieran O'Brien, Australian Innovation Research Centre, University of Tasmania. Kieran.Obrien@utas.edu.au.

Giulio Perani, National Institute of Statistics, Rome, Italy. perani@istat.it.

Bettina Peters, Centre for European Economic Research (ZEW), Mannheim, Germany. B.Peters@zew.de.

Christian Rammer, Centre for European Economic Research (ZEW), Mannheim, Germany. Rammer@zew.de.

Keith Smith, Imperial College, London, UK. Keith.Smith@imperial. ac.uk.

Alexander Sokolov, National Research University 'Higher School of Economics', Moscow, Russia. sokolov@hse.ru.

Ann Torugsa, Australian Innovation Research Centre, University of Tasmania. Nuttaneeya.Torugsa@utas.edu.au.

Eric von Hippel, Massachusetts Institute of Technology, Cambridge, MA. evhippel@mit.edu.

Andrew W. Wyckoff, Directorate for Science, Technology and Industry, Organisation for Economic Co-operation and Development (OECD), Paris, France. Andrew.Wyckoff@oecd.org.

Acknowledgements

The principal acknowledgement goes to the authors who contributed to this handbook, for the content of their chapters and their willingness to make changes requested by the editor. All the contributors produced their chapters while doing many other things, and their work represents a sacrifice on their part from which the reader will benefit.

During the two years of gestation of the handbook the editor sat on a number of panels dealing with subjects related to those in the book. None of that material can be used here, but the meetings and discussions did provoke thoughts that would not otherwise have occurred, and acknowledgement is made to the Council of Canadian Academies (CCA), the US National Academies of Science (NAS), and the Canadian Science, Technology and Innovation Council (STIC).

Inputs also came from discussions at four committees on which the editor served: the Advisory Steering Committee for the Centre for Science, Technology and Innovation Indicators (CeSTII) of the Human Sciences Research Council in South Africa, the Scientific Council of the Observatory of Science, Technology and Qualifications in Portugal, the Comité scientifique et de prospective of the Observatoire des Sciences et des Techniques in Paris and the Social, Behavioral and Economic Sciences Advisory Committee at the US National Science Foundation.

At the Organisation for Economic Co-operation and Development (OECD), the editor chairs the NESTI Board, providing advice to the Bureau and Secretariat of the OECD Working Party of National Experts on Science and Technology Indicators (NESTI). The many contributions of NESTI members, observers and the Secretariat are acknowledged. The OECD is also acknowledged for permitting OECD material to be reproduced in the handbook.

Eurostat, the statistical office of the European Union (EU), has been very helpful and has permitted the reproduction of the English version of the questionnaire of the EU Community Innovation Survey (CIS) for 2010. Special thanks go to Veijo Ritola of Eurostat for answering many questions.

Thanks also go to colleagues at UNU-MERIT in Maastricht in the Netherlands and at IERI at the Tshwane University of Technology in South Africa for discussions as the book evolved, and also to former colleagues at Statistics Canada and Canada's International Development Research Centre (IDRC).

Producing a chapter or a book is a collective process with many, not named here, helping to deliver the final product. Erika Rost is thanked for her constructively critical reading of all the material in the book.

The idea of the book came from Matthew Pittman and was approved by Edward Elgar. Without their support, and that of the staff at Edward Elgar, this book would not have seen the light of day.

Abbreviations

AIDS	acquired immunodeficiency syndrome
AMT	advanced manufacturing technology
ANBERD	Analytical BERD (OECD database)
APE	average partial effect
ARRA	American Recovery and Reinvestment Act (2009)
ATP	Advanced Technology Program
AU	African Union
BACO	best available charitable option
BBC	British Broadcasting Corporation
BDI	Bundesverband der Deutschen Industrie
BERD	business enterprise expenditure on research and development
BMBF	Federal Ministry of Education and Research (Germany)
BRDIS	Business R&D and Innovation Survey (USA)
BRICS	Brazil, Russia, India, China and South Africa
CABE	Commission for Architecture and the Built Environment (UK)
CAD	computer aided design
CATI	computer assisted telephone interview
CBA	cost–benefit analysis
CCA	Council of Canadian Academies
CDM	Crépon, Duguet and Mairesse (model)
CEC	Commission for the European Communities
CIS	Community Innovation Survey
CMU	Carnegie Mellon University (CMU NISTEP Survey)
CO_2	carbon dioxide
CPA	Consolidated Plan of Action (NEPAD)
CSTP	Committee for Scientific and Technological Policy (OECD)
CSTP	Council for Science and Technology Policy (Japan)
DALY	disability-adjusted life years
DG	Directorate-General
DNA	deoxyribonucleic acid
DOC	Department of Commerce (USA)
DSTI	Directorate for Science, Technology and Industry
EC	European Commission or European Community

ECE	Economic Commission for Europe
ECR	*European Competitiveness Report*
ECS	European Company Survey
EE	employee survey
EEA	European Economic Area
EET	emerging and enabling technologies
EFILWC	European Foundation for the Improvement of Living and Working Conditions
EIMS	European Innovation Monitoring System
EIS	European Innovation Scoreboard
EPO	European Patent Office
ER	employer survey
ESES	European Structure of Earnings Survey
EU	European Union
Eurostat	statistical office of the EU
FAQ	frequently asked question
FMM	Foresight Maturity Model
FOS	Fields of Science and Technology
FTE	full-time equivalent
FY	fiscal year
GBAORD	Government Budget Appropriations or Outlays on R&D
GCI	Global Competitiveness Index
GCR	*Global Competitiveness Report*
GDP	gross domestic product
GEM	Global Entrepreneurship Monitor
GERD	gross domestic expenditure on research and development
GII	Global Innovation Index (INSEAD)
GPRA	Government Performance and Results Act (1992)
GPT	general-purpose technology
GSM	Global System for Mobile communications
HERD	higher education expenditure on research and development
HIV	human immunodeficiency virus
HRDC	Human Resources Development Canada
HRM	human resource management
HRST	human resources for science and technology
ICT	information and communication technology
IERI	Institute for Economic Research on Innovation
IFO	Institut für Wirtschaftsforschung (Germany)
IIT	Illinois Institute of Technology (Research Institute)

ILO	International Labour Organization
IMF	International Monetary Fund
INSEAD	Institut Européen d'Administration des Affaires (France)
IP	intellectual property
IPC	International Patent Classification
IPR	intellectual property rights
IRAP	Industrial Research Assistance Program
IS	innovation strategy
ISCED	International Standard Classification of Education
ISCO	International Standard Classification of Occupations
ISIC	International Standard Industrial Classification
ISO	International Organization for Standardization
ISP	Internet service provider
ITIF	The Information Technology and Innovation Foundation (USA)
IUC	Innovation Union Competitiveness
IUS	Innovation Union Scoreboard
J-NIS	Japan-National Innovation Survey
KAM	knowledge assessment methodology
KAU	kind-of-activity unit
KBE	knowledge-based economy
KEI	Knowledge Economy Index
KI	Knowledge Index
KIBS	knowledge-intensive business sector
LEI	The Conference Board Leading Economic Index®
LKAU	local kind-of-activity unit
MDGs	Millennium Development Goals
MEADOW	Measuring the Dynamics of Organisations and Work
MEPIN	Measuring Public Innovation in the Nordic Countries
MERIT	Maastricht University's Economic Research Institute on Innovation and Technology (now: UNU-MERIT)
MEXT	Ministry of Education, Culture, Sports, Science and Technology (Japan)
MFP	multi-factor productivity
MIC	Ministry of Internal Affairs and Communications
MII	most important innovation
MIP	Mannheim Innovation Panel (ZEW)
MN	market novelty
NABS	nomenclature for the analysis of science budgets
NACE	Statistical Classification of Economic Activities in the European Community

NAICS	North American Industry Classification System
NAO	National Accounting Office
NCP	National Classification of Products
NCSES	National Center for Science and Engineering Statistics (USA)
NEPAD	New Partnership for Africa's Development
Nesta	National Endowment for Science, Technology and the Arts (UK)
NESTI	OECD Working Party of National Experts on Science and Technology Indicators
NGO	non-governmental organization
NIS	national innovation system
NISTEP	National Institute of Science and Technology Policy (Japan)
NOK	Norwegian krone
NPCA	NEPAD Planning and Co-ordinating Agency
NPM	new public management
NR	non-response
NRC	National Research Council (USA)
NRC-IRAP	National Research Council, Industrial Research Assistance Program (Canada)
NSF	National Science Foundation (USA)
NSO	national statistical office
NSO	Norwegian Statistical Office
OECD	Organisation for Economic Co-operation and Development
PATSTAT	Worldwide Patent Statistics Database
PC	process innovation
PD	product innovation
PEA	partial (marginal) effect at the average value
PISA	Programme for International Student Assessment
PPP	purchasing power parity
PROM	Patient Reported Outcome Measurement
PRSPs	Poverty Reduction Strategy Papers
PSU	primary sampling unit
QALYS	quality-adjusted life years
R&D	research and development
REDF	Roberts Enterprise Development Fund
RICYT	Ibero-American Network on Science and Technology Indicators
RNA	ribonucleic acid
S&T	science and technology

SAM	social accounting matrices
SciSIP	Science of Science and Innovation Policy
SEO	socioeconomic objectives
SIBS	Survey of Innovation and Business Strategy
SITRA	Finnish Innovation Fund
SME	small and medium-sized enterprises
SNA	system of national accounts
SPRU	Science and Technology Policy Research (University of Sussex, UK) (formerly Science Policy Research Unit)
SROI	social return on investment
STAN	Structural Analysis (database)
STBP	Science and Technology Basic Plan
STEM	Science, Technology, Engineering and Mathematics (jobs)
STI	science, technology and innovation
STIC	Science, Technology and Innovation Council (Canada)
SYTA	Sosiaalisen Yrityksen/Yhteisön Toiminnan Analysointiin (Finland)
TBP	technology balance of payments
TEKES	Finnish Funding Agency for Technology and Innovation
TEP	Technology Economy Programme (OECD)
TFP	Total Factor Productivity
TPP	technological product and process (innovation)
TQM	total quality management
TUT	Tshwane University of Technology
UK	United Kingdom
UN	United Nations
UNESCO	United Nations Educational, Scientific and Cultural Organization
UNU-MERIT	United Nations University Maastricht Economic and social Research and training centre on Innovation and Technology, The Netherlands
WERS	Workplace Employment Relations Survey
WIPO	World Intellectual Property Organization
WPIA	Working Party of Industrial Analysis
WPIIS	Working Party on Indicators for the Information Society
ZEW	Centre for European Economic Research (Germany)

PART I

WHY INDICATORS MATTER

1 Innovation indicators and measurement: an overview
Fred Gault

1. INTRODUCTION

People want jobs, ideally good jobs, and some support when things go wrong. The fundamental policy question is how to deliver jobs and sufficient growth to provide the public services expected. Some would argue that innovation is part of the answer, if not the only answer, but innovation is a complex phenomenon and the implementation of an innovation policy is not straightforward. More needs to be known about innovation and how it connects to the economy and the society.

A step in this direction is learning how to measure the activity of innovation and its links to the innovation system. This handbook is a guide to how this is being done now and may be done in the future. It is written at a time when the domain of innovation studies is expanding and there are discussions about the definition of innovation for measurement purposes.

As the reader will find, the definition of innovation, for the purposes of statistical measurement, was codified 20 years ago in the *Oslo Manual*. Then, it included only technological product and process innovation in manufacturing. Over the years the technological restriction has been removed, recognizing that innovation can be achieved by changing business practices and the organization of the firm, and by finding new ways of developing markets or finding new ones. The coverage was extended from manufacturing to the entire market economy.

Now, there is a growing body of work on innovation in the public sector, in communities, and by individuals. Each of these developments is giving rise to calls for further examination of the definition of innovation for measurement purposes. The subject continues to grow and change, and this handbook is a guide for the reader who wants to understand, in practical terms, what is happening.

As this is a handbook on innovation, indicators and measurement, the next section discusses how those words are used. This is a short overview of the subject as the definition of innovation, its evolution and the legitimacy of the process are covered in Chapter 2. Chapter 3 examines the implementation of the definition through measurement activities, specifically the use of surveys, especially the Community Innovation Survey (CIS) of the European Union (EU), which measures the activity of innovation. The questionnaire for CIS 2010 is provided in the appendix. Other chapters deal with the production and use of indicators. However, here the meaning of the term 'indicator' is considered, along with the importance of the formal language (Chapter 2) needed for the discussion of indicators.

Section 3 is a short guide for the reader who wants to treat the handbook as a toolkit and seeks direction on which chapters to read first in order to participate in discussions about developing or using innovation indicators.

Section 4 looks at innovation indicators as a technology that changes the behaviour of those who work with it and the consequences of that both for indicator development and for the use of indicators.

2. INNOVATION, INDICATORS AND MEASUREMENT

This section looks at the process through which innovation is defined, the sources of data, including statistical measurement, and definitions of indictors.

Defining Innovation

For measurement purposes, innovation is defined in the third edition of the *Oslo Manual* (OECD/Eurostat 2005: 46; Chapter 2 in this volume) and that definition governs most of the five parts of the book. However, there are deviations. Chapter 5 raises a question about how to treat as innovators consumers who change or create goods and services for their own benefit, and Chapter 17 looks at definitional issues in public sector innovation. Chapter 18, which deals with social innovation, is the furthest removed from the *Oslo Manual* definition. The other chapters follow the rules.

'Rules' raise questions about how they are developed and used, and the openness of the process. Chapter 2 provides a history of the *Oslo Manual* but the question of rulemaking is discussed here as it is relevant to the entire book and, indeed, the book is part of the discourse that will influence such rulemaking.

The *Oslo Manual*, since the second edition, is a joint product of the OECD and Eurostat, the statistical office of the EU. The body that developed the manual and is responsible for its revision is the OECD Working Party of National Experts on Science and Technology Indicators (NESTI), where representatives of 34 member countries are present as well as the EU, including Eurostat, and observer countries and organizations.

As this is a working party, the participants are experts who are producers of innovation statistics and indicators, users of innovation indicators in the policy process, or who are active in the intersection of indicator production and policy use. The mix ensures that the indicators recommended for production and international comparisons are both feasible and relevant. NESTI is also a consensus organization, which means that the approval of the *Oslo Manual* has not been opposed.

NESTI members come from the governments of member or observer countries or from international organizations that participate. The statistics and indicators that are published by the OECD are produced by the participating countries, and the sources and methods are reviewed and documented by the OECD. Academics or interest groups are free to contact their national delegation if they wish to discuss any of the matters for which NESTI is responsible. That access can be arranged through the Permanent Delegation of member countries to the OECD.

In the case of the *Oslo Manual*, for non-EU member countries, there is no requirement to comply with the rules, but there is the incentive of having the statistics for their country reviewed and published by the OECD so that they can see how their country compares with others. For member states of the EU, not all of which are members of the OECD, the approach is different.

As discussed in Chapter 3, Commission Regulation (EC) No. 1450/2004 of 13 August 2004 implementing Decision No. 1608/2003/EC of the European Parliament and of the Council concerning the production and development of Community statistics on innovation, and its revisions, governs the provision of innovation statistics to Eurostat, the industrial coverage, the frequency of reporting of variables, the employment size classes of firms surveyed and various other breakdowns of variables. The provision of the innovation statistics 'shall be based on harmonized concepts and definitions contained in the most recent *Oslo Manual*'.

Countries are free to use sample surveys, administrative data and other sources to provide the required statistical data.

From the public law perspective, there are two quite distinct processes in place for the production of innovation statistics and indicators. Public law is used by von Bogdandy and Goldmann (2012) to develop a methodology for framing indicators and other information produced and disseminated by international organizations. Their example is another OECD project, the Programme for International Student Assessment (PISA). Additional material on indicators and their uses can be found in Davis et al. (2012).

One of the examples of von Bogdandy and Goldmann is the impact of the results of the PISA exercise on Germany. The first results were not good and there was an immediate reaction that transformed the education systems in the *Länder*. This raised questions about the power of the PISA indicators and the governance process leading to their production. By contrast, when the first official statistics on innovation in the USA were published (NSF 2010), and they were low compared with the results of many other countries, there was little or no reaction on the part of the federal or state governments. For state governments the lack of reaction may have reflected the absence of state-level statistics, but this was not the case at national level. Chapter 12 provides examples of indicators changing the behaviour of governments, but they are not indicators of the activity of innovation.

Indicators and Measurement

Many of the data used in the production of indicators come from sample surveys, of which the CIS is an example. The data can also come from administrative data, such as business registers or tax files. There are other sources.

For the purpose of this discussion, a 'statistic' is a numerical fact or datum, especially one computed from a sample. A statistic such as gross domestic product (GDP) can be discussed in the absence of data but when it comes to the use of the statistic it has to be populated with statistical data. 'Statistical data' refers to data from a survey or administrative source used to produce statistics (OECD 2008). Designing the survey or data acquisition process, including the control of the quality of the data produced, is part of 'statistical measurement'.

A 'statistical indicator' is a statistic or combination of statistics that provides information on the state of a system or its change over time. GDP or GDP/capita provides information on the economic state of a country and both can be considered statistical indicators along with their change over time. Negative growth of GDP for two consecutive quarters is considered by some as indicative of a recession. Of course, statistical indicators do not tell the whole story and should never be used in isolation. As an example, two countries may have the same GDP/capita but quite different income distributions. If GDP/capita is used as an indicator of welfare, the actual welfare of the people will be quite different in the two countries.

In this handbook, the terms 'indicator' and 'measurement' are used without the term 'statistical'.

Language

By now it should be clear that the terms used to discuss the subject of innovation indicators and measurement are well defined and the *Oslo Manual* is the lexicon for the users of the language. It also provides the grammar.

For example, a member of the community of practice that uses the *Oslo Manual* cannot write the sentence: 'The tax incentive was an innovation of the government' or 'Painting the product green was an innovation'. Neither sentence conforms to the agreed rules codified in the *Oslo Manual*. In the first case the tax incentive is a framework condition for innovation, it is not a product placed on the market. In the second, the product is not new and neither is it significantly improved. Neither example is an innovation.

As in the case of other technologies, indicators and their standards are converging and innovation is no different. The *Oslo Manual* uses the language of the system of national accounts (EC et al. 2009), a simple example of which is that a product is a good or a service. In discussion of these concepts, the use of 'goods and services', or 'products and processes', can occur, but not 'products and services'.

The determined reader, by reading the *Oslo Manual* (www.oecd.org/sti/oslomanual), and discussing the subject with members of the community of practice, will quickly become fluent in the language.

Next follows an introduction to the handbook chapters, with enough information to help the reader to choose a path through the handbook.

3.   THE HANDBOOK

This is a handbook of innovation indicators and measurement. The chapters are written by experts who make measurements and produce indicators, or by other experts who are users of the indicators, or are on the boundary between production and use. The chapters provide the reader with knowledge of what works, what does not, and what could, or should, work in the future. The knowledge provided should be sufficient for the reader to ask informed questions about both the production and the use of indicators, and to understand the answers. The chapters are grouped into five themes: definition of innovation and implementation of the definition; measurement practices; the development and use of indicators; using innovation indicators in innovation strategies; and chapters that address the future of the subject, some of which go beyond the definitions and guidelines used elsewhere in the book.

The Subject is Difficult

As mentioned in the introduction, innovation is a difficult subject and so is the study of innovation indicators. There are several reasons for this. The first is that innovation is not an isolated event. A firm may put a new product on the market, becoming, as a consequence, an innovative firm, but to understand that one event, there must be measures of sources of information, organization and business practices, production processes and market development that influence the activity of innovation. Questions should also be asked about whether the knowledge needed for the innovation was generated within the firm (or multinational enterprise), purchased, acquired by hiring people with the knowledge, or from outside the firm in other ways. For example, a user of the product of the firm could present to the firm a prototype of an improved product.

Time scale is an issue in understanding innovation. New software products can be conceived and produced in months, new biotechnology products for human health can take more than a decade to go through pre-clinical and clinical trials and there is no innovation until the product enters the market. Once products are on the market, they can have a rapid impact on users, or it could take decades before the impact is seen.

This leads to a systems approach to classifying the actors and activities in the system, the linkages between them and the outcomes and impacts of putting a new or significantly improved product on the market (Gault 2010).

Change is Happening

The very concept of the 'market' is an issue. The current state of innovation measurement is governed by an internationally agreed set of rules presented in the *Oslo Manual* (OECD/Eurostat 2005; Chapter 2 in this volume). The *Oslo Manual* makes clear that for there to be innovation, the product must be introduced to the market or changes made in how the firm functions to get the product to market in ways that serve better the business strategy of the firm. This approach to connecting to the market has governed innovation indicators and measurement for decades, but now questions are being asked about consumers who change goods or services to improve their own welfare (Chapter 5) or public sector organizations that improve service delivery, although this is not necessarily delivered to a market (Chapter 17), or communities that find ways of solving problems that improve the welfare of the community (Chapter 18). Where do these cases fit in the study of innovation indicators and measurement? The authors of these chapters review the most recent work and indicate where the subject is going and the implications for the *Oslo Manual*.

To prepare the reader for these discussions, Chapter 2 reviews the history of the *Oslo Manual*. This is only partially a historical exercise to provide context for the rest of the handbook. Many of the issues that were present in the early discussions of the *Oslo Manual* are reappearing as more experience is gained of measuring innovation and of developing and using indicators. Chapter 3, which provides a history of the EU CIS (Community Innovation Survey), also brings to the fore issues that were discussed in the past and are now being reconsidered. Change is indeed happening and the handbook offers a guide to the key issues to the point where the reader should be able to contribute to the debate.

The Rules must be Implemented

For measurement to be made and indicators to be developed, the rules must be implemented. Since 1992 the most extensive implementation of the rules in the *Oslo Manual* has been the CIS, along with similar surveys conducted in many other countries (Smith 2005). Chapter 3 provides a history of the CIS, which, like the *Oslo Manual*, now in its third edition, is an ongoing learning process of collecting data, using the data to populate statistics, and then selecting statistics or combinations of statistics to produce indicators, the subject of this handbook. More historical material is found in Smith (2005).

However, not all respondents understand the survey questions in the same way, and this becomes a larger problem when the questions are in different languages and asked in different countries. Chapter 4 looks at the evidence for the robustness of international comparisons of innovation indicators, derived from CIS or CIS-like questionnaires. Chapter 8 reviews the situation in Japan and Chapter 9 addresses the issue and discusses an OECD project on cognitive testing of questions to ensure comparable answers. Cognitive testing and survey design are not just issues for innovation surveys, but they are important at a time when the definitions and survey questions are evolving.

Approaches to Measurement are Different

Three chapters deal with measurement in the context of a CIS approach and, in addition to measurement issues, each chapter introduces a related topic: the role of panel surveys (Chapter 6); arguments for and against combining innovation surveys with R&D surveys (Chapter 7), also discussed in Chapter 3; and the differences resulting from conducting an innovation survey in a country with a non-European language and culture (Chapter 8).

When statistical surveys are conducted, decisions are made about the coverage (industry and geography) and the level of detail (see the appendix in Chapter 2). As innovation surveys are business surveys (but read Chapters 5, 17 and 18 for different approaches), a statistical sample is drawn from a business register and the survey is conducted. The result is a set of statistics that provides a cross-sectional view of the industries being studied for the reference period of the survey. For the CIS, this process is repeated, currently every two years, and the result is a series of cross-sectional observations. The resulting statistics can exhibit change over time, for example the propensity of firms in a particular industry in a particular region to innovate, which may or may not be correlated with other observables, such as economic recession, the presence of good universities or trade agreements. While trends are interesting, and have many uses, these statistics cannot be used to identify causal links between a policy intervention or an economic shock and the behaviour of a firm. For that, a panel survey is needed where the same firms remain in the sample year after year. An example of a panel survey, and its applications, is described in Chapter 6.

One of the more striking examples of the difference between repeated cross-sectional surveys and panel surveys is found in Saunders (2010). The author describes 'arrival cities' in various parts of the world where immigrants from villages come to seek work. Some thrive and move into the life of the city; others do not. However, if the arrival city were surveyed every year using a cross-sectional survey, the findings would reveal poverty and other related issues. A longitudinal survey, which followed a cohort, would show evidence for reduced poverty and a growing change in social status within the cohort. Clearly the policy implications following from the two sets of results are different. How measurement is made matters and how results are interpreted also matters.

Another issue is the combining of business R&D and innovation surveys. The argument in favour is that both are business surveys and the same approach can be used for both. Norway has done both separate and combined surveys, and Chapter 7 presents the problems involved. Combining these surveys could work in some countries where both the R&D and innovation survey were based on random samples drawn from a business register. In the USA, the National Science Foundation added innovation questions to their R&D survey as part of its redesign to become the Business R&D and Innovation Survey (BRDIS). The innovation results for reference year 2008 (NSF 2010) were low compared with CIS results for other countries and the reasons are still being discussed (Jankowski 2013). There are other statistical issues to consider, such as the fact that the performance of R&D is a rare event and the expenditures (and personnel) are highly concentrated in a few firms in an industry and in a few industries in the economy. Innovation is a more common event, less concentrated and more pervasive. These different distributions have to be taken into account in a combined R&D and innovation survey. In

Chapter 3, the concern is raised that a combined survey reinforces a link in the minds of analysts and respondents that innovation must be tied to R&D. This is an important issue as the empirical evidence is that more firms innovate than do R&D (OECD 2009), suggesting the need for more policy interest in innovation.

Combining innovation and R&D surveys is not a new issue, as paragraph 193 from the first edition of the *Oslo Manual* shows:

> Innovation surveys supplement the picture of R&D given by R&D surveys. Though it is conceivable that they might ultimately be combined, there are two arguments against this:
> (i)   A combined survey would be long and rather complicated, which might well reduce the response rate;
> (ii) Different people in the company may well be responsible for answering questions on R&D and questions on innovation. (OECD 1992: 47)

This quotation illustrates the dominance of R&D in the thinking about innovation 20 years ago, the concern raised in Chapter 3.

Chapter 8 provides the experience from Japan of conducting an innovation survey. The principal issues are the evolving understanding of the concept of innovation and the words needed to refer to it, the limited presence of innovation in government policy that treats innovation as an extension of science and technology policy and the consequences of using voluntary surveys. Chapter 8 also notes difficulties in using the data on innovation for analytical purposes, a point that is discussed further in Chapter 19.

Developing and Using Indicators

Whatever the measurement process used, whatever the other sources, such as administrative data, the end result is a set of statistics that can be used, or combined and used, as indicators for international comparison and comparison over time. Chapter 9, and Chapter 11, discuss the process for the collection of statistics and indicators and the validation and publication of internationally comparable results. As already mentioned, there is an OECD cognitive testing project, in consultation with Eurostat, to ensure that the data resulting from survey questions are indeed comparable (see Chapter 3 on this issue). Chapter 9 makes the point that not everything can be learned from aggregate statistics and there is much to be gained from analysing the data of individual firms (OECD 2009). One of the observations already made is that more firms innovate than do R&D, and this observation recurs both in Chapter 9 and in Chapter 12 on the OECD Innovation Strategy.

Data on individual firms, or microdata, are also necessary for analysing the link between innovation activities, such as R&D and investment in machinery and equipment, and the activity of innovation and productivity (Hall 2011; Mairesse and Mohnen 2010). Cohen (2010) provides a review of empirical studies over the last half-century and Verspagen (2005) reviews the link between innovation and economic growth.

With the third edition of the *Oslo Manual* (see Chapter 2) the definition of innovation was expanded beyond product and process innovation to include organizational change and market development. Chapter 10 looks at harmonized measures of organizational change and develops indicators for the activity. It is clear that it has taken time for organizational change to enter the measurement domain and this is not because the idea is novel. There were earlier projects on the overlapping subject of knowledge management (OECD 2003) that influenced the revision of the *Oslo Manual*, but organization and business practices are still not as prominent in CIS as product and process innovation (see Chapter 3 for more on this point).

Chapter 11 provides a comprehensive overview of the ways in which indicators are presented to users through reports, scoreboards and databases. It makes the distinction between the use of direct measurement of innovation and the use of proxy measures, and compares the rankings of the various scoreboards.

Innovation Strategy

Innovation indicators are produced to provide information to decision makers and, if used in context, they may provide knowledge and confer a capacity to act[1] to change the situation that gives rise to the values of the indicators. If indicators are not used, a question immediately arises why they are being produced, as innovation indicators and measurement are costly undertakings. Three chapters address the place of indicators in the policy process and Smits et al. (2010) provide contextual information on the theory and practice of innovation policy.

Chapter 12 covers the OECD, which is an international organization with a mission to 'promote policies that will improve the economic and social well-being of people around the world'. Innovation is linked to economic growth, and promoting innovation is part of improving economic and social well-being. The chapter presents key indicators, related to innovation, that form part of evidence-based policy advice consistent with the mission of the OECD. It also provides indicators on innovation activities such as R&D and the use of intellectual property instruments, as well as on the activity of innovation.

Chapter 13 looks at Finland, a small open economy that has used policy, including institutional change, to add to its resource-based activities a significant ICT (information and communication technology) sector and is now dealing with the next step. The example in the chapter is healthcare as a means of supporting an ageing population but also as a platform for developing new technologies and adding them to the product range of the country.

Chapter 14 reviews innovation policy from a US perspective and discusses the role of indicators. The chapter provides a historical perspective on the involvement of US researchers in indicator development, which is also discussed in Chapters 2 and 3. It goes on to explain the political and administrative difficulties of introducing new policies and indicators into the activities of the US government. Political and administrative difficulties are also discussed in Chapter 8 for the case of Japan.

Going Further

The handbook, in Parts I to V, keeps to its objective of showing the reader what works and what does not for innovation indicators and measurement, including the use of indicators to support public policy. However, the point has been made that this is an evolving subject so the next step is to look at what is being done to move the subject forward, to look at other actors and other sectors of the economy, and at the consequences of these activities. There are four chapters on new directions, of which two would fit within the definitions of the current *Oslo Manual* and two would not.

Chapter 15 deals with how emerging and enabling technologies can be measured. These may be rare events, but the objective is to give rise to indicators that can be used to influence policy related to these new technologies. This chapter links to discussions of measuring technologies and practices in Chapter 2 and Chapter 5, and its objective is to promote a standard practice for technology measurement, building on work done over the years on ICT, bio- and nanotechnologies.

While Chapter 15 deals with what is present but is difficult to measure, Chapter 16 addresses what is going to happen and the role of indicators of innovation in the foresight process. Foresight has never been part of the *Oslo Manual*, but there is much empirical work (e.g. Miles et al. 2008) and the OECD has engaged in foresight studies (OECD 1997, 1998, 1999). In keeping with the purpose of the handbook, Chapter 16 discusses what is working in foresight. The chapter is included to provoke thought about indicators and the future, and where foresight belongs in discussions about innovation indicators and measurement.

Public sector organizations can do most, if not all, of the activities of innovation described in the *Oslo Manual* and in Chapter 2, but the resulting good or service is not necessarily delivered to the market, but to potential users of the good or service. This point is discussed in Chapters 2 and 5. Chapter 17 shows what has been done to measure public sector innovation and to provide guidelines for measurement that give rise to indicators. The question for the rulemakers is whether public sector innovation should be incorporated into the next revision of the *Oslo Manual*, treated separately as the first new member of an 'Oslo' family of manuals, or left to others to deal with.

Chapter 18 deals with social innovation. This is as far from the *Oslo Manual* definition of innovation that the handbook gets, but it merits serious consideration as part of the development of the subject. In social innovation, communities solve problems that increase the welfare of the members, in some ways like a firm (community) that improves its production process, organization or use of business practices, or market development in order to achieve the objectives of its business strategy (welfare) discussed in Chapter 2. The firm does not sell processes; it sells products. It uses, as a user innovator, the innovation it produces, just as a community uses the 'innovation' it has produced to improve its own welfare. There is also a parallel with the individual (community) that changes a good or a service (solves a problem) for his or her own benefit (welfare) discussed in Chapter 5, and there are links with Chapter 17 in public sector innovation.

Finally, Chapter 19 lays out a work programme for those engaged in innovation indicators and measurement. This is the only chapter in the handbook that does not present what works or what does not. It goes directly to what could work and why it should. It should be seen as providing topics for discussion as only the OECD, in consultation with Eurostat, can revise the *Oslo Manual*.

4.   INDICATORS AS TECHNOLOGY AND AS INTERVENTIONS

This section examines two topics: indicators as a technology; and indicators as interventions that have economic and social consequences. The first is based on Gault (2010, 2011a, 2011b, 2011c) and the second on Davis et al. (2012). The intention is to make clear that the development of measurement and indicators is a social process, with social and economic consequences. While this is a more general discussion than in Section 2, it matters for the broader understanding of what the handbook is about and suggests both pitfalls and benefits of ways of moving forward.

Indicators are a Technology

Innovation indicators are developed as a result of a perceived need of the community that wants to use them, and both the development process and the eventual use of the indicators have social impacts. The development process involves consensus building and the establishment of a common language, with an agreed vocabulary and grammar, that facilitates the discourse that is part of the development and evolution of the indicators. These activities have an impact on the community of practice that sets the standards as it learns to use the language and to advance the subject. Once the indicators are produced, their use and the use of the language that describes them have economic and social impacts. This is not just a unidirectional activity. Feedback from the users of the indicators to the producers contributes to further evolution of the indicators.

There is a similarity in these activities with those in an organization, or firm, that produces new or significantly improved products (goods or services) or processes (transformation or delivery processes, organizational processes or those resulting from the use of business practices, or market development). The producer of indicators for public use is usually an international organization or supranational organization such as the OECD or the EU in the case of innovation indicators. There are also organizations that seek international impact through the production of indicators on various subjects and their use in ranking (Chapter 11).

Users of indicators are just about every organization in society, including individuals. As a result of using the indicators, users may change their behaviour and may provide a motivation for revision of the indicators. It is in this sense that indicators act as a technology or practice (Gault and McDaniel 2002). Consider the impact of the iPhone, the social insurance number, or the web.

The role of the user is fundamental in this process and is similar to that of the user in any innovation system. The user can provide information that leads the producer to improve the product, the user can collaborate with the producer on new products, or the user can create a new product and transfer it to the producer. The user can also produce the new product independently or publish the methodology for any organization to use.

In the case of user innovation involving consumers (Gault 2012; Chapter 5 in this volume), there is a fourth possibility, which is that the user who has created a new product or modified an existing one does nothing but benefit from its use and the knowledge is not transferred to the broader community of practice. This fourth case does not arise in indicator development for public use, as indicators are developed to be used by a community. Indicators that are not used are not indicators.

Measurement and indicators of innovation are governed by sets of rules in manuals, which are the guidelines for the collection and interpretation of data and for international comparisons of data, statistics and indicators. They are codified knowledge, knowledge that can be written, learned and applied. This is discussed further in Chapter 2 in the case of the *Oslo Manual* (OECD/Eurostat 2005). Cowan et al. (2000) warn of the possibility of 'lock-in' to obsolete conceptual schemes as a result of codification, but this is avoided by regular revision of the manual.

This is the view from the perspective of innovation indicators, but there are other approaches to indicators, and Davis et al. (2012) provide examples of indicators that are not necessarily the result of user–producer collaboration. Examples are the Doing Business Indicators, The Control of Corruption and the Rule of Law, the Millennium Development Goals (MDGs) indicators, the Corruption Perceptions Index, the Human Development Index and the Trafficking in Persons indicators (Davis et al. 2012: 3). Davis et al. also treat indicators as a technology, but the sense is different from that discussed earlier. They regard a means or mechanism of governance as a technology of governance. They also adopt a more elaborate definition of an indicator (Davis et al. 2012: 6), which focuses on the use of indicators for comparison and evaluation, and fits with the applications of indicators that they wish to examine.

They go on to discuss the economic and social results of using indicators to rank countries, or law schools, and then consider the regulation of indicators that exert considerable influence on decision making. As with the meaning of indicators as a technology, this is a different approach from the development of innovation indicators by NESTI, which is an open process, governed by consensus, leading to published guidelines. Nonetheless, Davis et al. (2012) provide interesting examples and useful thoughts on what happens when indicators have a strong influence on the measured, on the policies that governed the measured, and on decisions by international organizations and firms. If the release of innovation indicators ever has the same impact as PISA indicators had on Germany, there may be more interest in how NESTI develops the rules for producing indicators of innovation.

Impacts

As the innovation indicators expand and policy makers recognize that innovation is not an isolated event, more attention is being given to the framework conditions and the policy mix that helps the system to work better. As more microdata analysis is done, the important result that the propensity to innovate in firms is higher than the propensity to do R&D will have more influence on policy. An R&D tax benefit is of no use to an innovative firm that does no R&D, but support for capital investment in ICTs may be, or a voucher or granting programme allowing the firm to access knowledge from universities and colleges to help in the solving of problems related to innovation. Such policies, based on the empirical evidence provided by the indicators, change the behaviour of people, and of firms, and how they learn.

Indicators as Interventions

Indicators are a technology and technologies change behaviour. Indicators described in this handbook are developed so that they can be used to change behaviour; the implicit assumption is that the behaviour will be beneficial to the economies and societies for which the indicators have been developed (see Chapter 9 and the mission of the OECD). However, there is a cost.

Statistical offices are aware of, and in some cases measure, the burden on the respondent of a survey. In this respect, a business survey is no different from a tax as it uses the resources of the respondent, and frequently highly skilled resources, and it can be seen as a policy intervention that justifies the collection of the data, the production of the resulting indicators and their use in the policy process. This public-good aspect is the justification for making many business surveys compulsory. Tax is also compulsory.

There are benefits. In developing a survey of the use and planned use of knowledge management practices, the team at Statistics Canada found that it was difficult to produce a survey instrument that would survive cognitive testing with respondents. Respondents tested could not understand the questions sufficiently well to answer them. When the testing team prepared to leave, there was more than one request for a clean questionnaire. This was a surprise in view of the less-than-successful testing exercise, and the response to why the questionnaire was wanted was that it contained a description of a number of practices that the firm should be looking at. It was clear that the survey team was an agent of knowledge transfer and a similar cognitive testing exercise six months later would yield a different result. In the end, after much revision, the testing worked, a successful questionnaire was used for the survey and the results contributed to an OECD project on knowledge management (OECD 2003).

This raises the question of surveys being used as a deliberate means of transmitting information or knowledge as part of a teaching initiative or as a promotion. For a statistical office that should be at arm's length from the policy process, these are difficult issues to resolve as all questionnaires have the capacity to teach. However, the deliberate use of a questionnaire to transfer information about a new government programme would raise ethical questions. Of course, not all statistical offices are at arm's length from government, and that raises another set of ethical problems.

Davis and Kingsbury (2011: 10) also suggest that 'Interventions that involve indicators should also be compared to interventions that go beyond providing data. If the ultimate purpose of intervention is to effect social change then indicators should be compared to familiar interventions, such as direct provision of money, goods or services, capacity-building, regulatory change, litigation etc.' Most official statisticians would agree. From the perspective of this handbook, the intended impact of the indicators is a consideration for the reader and for future revisions of the rules that govern the development of the indicators.

5.   CONCLUSION

This chapter provides definitions of key terms in the handbook and an introduction to the process of developing innovation indicators. There is a guide to reading the book and treating it as a toolbox for practitioners or would-be practitioners. To provide a broader context, there is a section on indicators as technology and as interventions. The other chapters in the handbook, with the exception of Chapter 19, are self-contained and can be read independently.

NOTE

1. 'Knowledge as a capacity for action' is a recurring theme in the business of developing indicators. It was the title of the opening address (Stehr 1996) for the 1996 OECD Blue Sky Forum (OECD 2001), which discussed the development of new indicators for science, technology and innovation and the importance of the systems approach to innovation. Knowledge fits into a hierarchy that begins with data and moves to information, which is data in context, and then to knowledge, which is information in context, and provides a capacity to act. This hierarchy has been in use for many years, as a review of T.S. Eliot's *Choruses from the Rock* (1934), will demonstrate (Eliot 1954: 107). Eliot and others continue the hierarchy to knowledge in context, which is wisdom. The subject of innovation indicators and measurement, and its communities of practice, may be moving towards wisdom. At the very least, it should be an objective.
    In the text, there is a discussion of data that populate statistics, which may be combined or used independently to provide information about the state of the system under review. That information, in the context of policy priorities, provides the policy maker with the capacity to act, to change the state of the system.

REFERENCES

Cohen, Wesley M. (2010), 'Fifty years of empirical studies of innovative activity and performance', in Bronwyn H. Hall and Nathan Rosenberg (eds), *Handbook of the Economics of Innovation*, Amsterdam: North-Holland, pp. 129–213.

Cowan, R., P.A. David and D. Foray (2000), 'The explicit economics of knowledge codification and tacitness', *Industrial and Corporate Change*, **9**, 221–51.

Davis, K. and B. Kingsbury (2011), *Indicators as Interventions: Pitfalls and Prospects in Supporting Development Initiatives*, New York: Rockefeller Foundation, http://www.rock efellerfoundation.org/news/publications/indicators-interventions.

Davis, K.E., A. Fischer, B. Kinsbury and S. Merry (eds) (2012), *Governance by Indicators: Global Power Through Quantification and Rankings*, Oxford: Oxford University Press.

EC, IMF, OECD, UN and the World Bank (2009), *System of National Accounts, 2008*, New York: United Nations.

Eliot, T.S. (1954), *Selected Poems*, London: Faber and Faber Limited.

Gault, Fred (2010), *Innovation Strategies for a Global Economy: Development, Implementation, Measurement and Management*, Cheltenham, UK and Northampton, MA, USA: Edward Elgar and Ottawa: IDRC.

Gault, Fred (2011a), 'Developing a science of innovation policy internationally', in Kaye Husbands Fealing, Julia Lane, John Marburger, Stephanie Shipp and Bill Valdez (eds) (2011), *Science of Science Policy: A Handbook*, Palo Alto, CA: Stanford University Press, pp. 156–82.

Gault, Fred (2011b), 'Impactos sociales del desarrollo de los indicadores de ciencia technologiae innovationcion', in Mario Albornoz and Luis Plaza (eds), *Agenda 2011: Temas de indicadores de Ciencia y Technologia*, Buenos Aires: REDES, pp. 19–34.

Gault, Fred (2011c), 'Social impacts of the development of science, technology and innovation indicators', UNU-MERIT Working Paper 2011-008, Maastricht: UNU-MERIT.

Gault, Fred (2012), 'User innovation and the market', *Science and Public Policy*, **39**, 118–28.

Gault, F.D. and S. McDaniel (2002), 'Continuities and transformations: challenges to capturing information about the "information society"', *First Monday*, **7** (2), Feb. 1–13.

Hall, Bronwyn H. (2011), 'Using productivity growth as an innovation indicator', Report for the High Level Panel on Measuring Innovation, Brussels: European Commission, DG Research and Innovation.

Jankowski, John (2013), 'Measuring innovation with official statistics', in A. Link and N. Vonortas (eds), *Handbook on the Theory and Practice of Program Evaluation*, Cheltenham, UK and Northampton, MA, USA: Edward Elgar, pp. 366–90.

Mairesse, Jacques and Pierre Mohnen (2010), 'Using innovation surveys for econometric analysis', in Bronwyn H. Hall and Nathan Rosenberg (eds), *Handbook of the Economics of Innovation*, Amsterdam: North-Holland, pp. 1129–55.

Miles, Ian, Jennifer Cassingena Harper, Luke Georghiou, Michael Keenan and Rafael Popper (2008), 'The many faces of foresight', in Luke Georghiou, Jennifer Cassingena Harper, Michael Keenan, Ian Miles, and Rafael Popper (eds), *The Handbook of Technology Foresight: Concepts and Practice*, Cheltenham, UK and Northampton, MA, USA: Edward Elgar, pp. 3–23.

NSF (2010), 'NSF released new statistics on business innovation', NSF InfoBrief 11-300, Arlington, VA: NSF.

OECD (1992), *OECD Proposed Guidelines for Collecting and Interpreting Technological Innovation Data: Oslo Manual*, OCDE/GD (92)26, Paris: OECD.

OECD (1997), *The World in 2020: Towards a New Global Age*, Paris: OECD.

OECD (1998), *21st Century Technologies: Promises and Perils of a Dynamic Future*, Paris: OECD.

OECD (1999), *The Future of the Global Economy: Towards a Long Boom?*, Paris: OECD.

OECD (2001), *Science, Technology and Industry Review: Special Issue on New Science and Technology Indicators*, No. 27, Paris: OECD.

OECD (2003), *Measuring Knowledge Management in the Business Sector: First Steps*, Paris: OECD.

OECD (2008), *OECD Glossary of Statistical Terms*, Paris: OECD.

OECD (2009), *Innovation in Firms: A Microeconomic Perspective*, Paris: OECD.

OECD/Eurostat (2005), *Oslo Manual: Guidelines for Collecting and Interpreting Innovation Data*, Paris: OECD.

Saunders, Doug (2010), *Arrival City: The Final Migration and Our Next World*, Toronto: Alfred A. Knopf.

Smith, Keith (2005), 'Measuring innovation', in J. Fagerberg, D.C. Mowery and R.R. Nelson (eds), *The Oxford Handbook of Innovation*, Oxford: Oxford University Press, pp. 148–77.

Smits, Ruud E., Stefan Kuhlmann and Philip Shapira (eds) (2010), *The Theory and Practice of Innovation Policy*, Cheltenham, UK and Northampton, MA, USA: Edward Elgar.

Stehr, Nico (1996), 'Knowledge as a capacity for action', Science Technology Redesign Project Research Paper 02, Ottawa: Statistics Canada, http://www.statcan.gc.ca/pub/88f0017m/88f0017m1996002-eng.pdf

Verspagen, Bart (2005), 'Innovation and economic growth', in J Fagerberg, D.C. Mowery and R.R. Nelson (eds), *The Oxford Handbook of Innovation*, Oxford: Oxford University Press, pp. 487–513.

von Bogdandy, A. and M. Goldmann (2012), 'Taming and framing indicators: a legal reconstruction of the OECD's programme for International Student Assessment (PISA)', in K.E. Davis, A. Fischer, B. Kinsbury and S. Merry (eds), *Governance by Indicators: Global Power Through Quantification and Rankings*, Oxford: Oxford University Press, pp. 52–85.

APPENDIX: CIS 2010

The final English text for the Community Innovation Survey 2010 is reproduced with the permission of Eurostat.

The Community Innovation Survey 2010
(CIS 2010)

THE HARMONISED SURVEY QUESTIONNAIRE

The Community Innovation Survey 2010   FINAL VERSION July 9, 2010

This survey collects information on your enterprise's innovations and innovation activities during the three years 2008 to 2010 inclusive.

An innovation is the introduction of a new or significantly improved product, process, organisational method, or marketing method by your enterprise. The innovation must be new to your enterprise, although it could have been originally developed by other enterprises.

Sections 5 to 8 only refer to product and process innovations.

Please complete **all** questions, unless otherwise instructed.

Person we should contact if there are any queries regarding the form:

Name: _____
Job title: _____
Organisation: _____
Phone: _____
Fax: _____
E-mail: _____

1. General Information about the Enterprise

Name of enterprise _____

Address[1] _____

Postal code _____   **Main activity**[2]_____

1.1   **In 2010, was your enterprise part of an enterprise group?** (A group consists of two or more legally defined enterprises under common ownership. Each enterprise in the group can serve different markets, as with national or regional subsidiaries, or serve different product markets. The head office is also part of an enterprise group.)

Yes ❏   In which country is the head office of your group located?[3] _____

No ❏

If your enterprise is part of an enterprise group: Please answer all further questions about your enterprise only for the enterprise for which you are responsible in [your country]. Exclude all subsidiaries or parent enterprises.

1.2   **In which geographic markets did your enterprise sell goods and/or services during the three years 2008 to 2010?**

	Yes	No
A. Local / regional within [your country]	❏	❏
B. National (other regions of [your country])	❏	❏
C. Other European Union (EU), EFTA, or EU candidate countries*	❏	❏
D. All other countries	❏	❏

Which of these geographic areas was your largest _____
market in terms of turnover during the three years
2008 to 2010? (Give corresponding letter)

*: Include the following countries: Austria, Belgium, Bulgaria, Croatia, Cyprus, Czech Republic, Denmark, Estonia, Finland, France, Germany, Greece, Hungary, Iceland, Italy, Ireland, Latvia, Liechtenstein, Lithuania, Luxembourg, Macedonia, Malta, Netherlands, Norway, Poland, Portugal, Romania, Slovenia, Slovakia, Switzerland, Turkey, Spain, Sweden and the United Kingdom.

---

[1]   NUTS 2 code.
[2]   NACE 4 digit code.
[3]   Country code according to ISO standard.

2. Product (Good or Service) Innovation

A product innovation is the market introduction of a **new** or **significantly** improved **good or service** with respect to its capabilities, user friendliness, components or sub-systems.

- Product innovations (new or improved) must be new to your enterprise, but they do not need to be new to your market.
- Product innovations could have been originally developed by your enterprise or by other enterprises.

A **good** is usually a tangible object such as a smart phone, furniture, or packaged software, but downloadable software, music and film are also goods. A **service** is usually intangible, such as retailing, insurance, educational courses, air travel, consulting, etc.

2.1 During the three years 2008 to 2010, did your enterprise introduce:

	Yes	No
New or significantly improved goods (*exclude the simple resale of new goods and changes of a solely aesthetic nature*)	❏	❏
New or significantly improved services	❏	❏

If no to all options, go to section 3, otherwise:

2.2 Who developed these product innovations?

Tick all that apply

	Goods innovations	Service innovations
Your enterprise by itself	❏	❏
Your enterprise together with other enterprises or institutions*	❏	❏
Your enterprise by adapting or modifying goods or services originally developed by other enterprises or institutions*	❏	❏
Other enterprises or institutions*	❏	❏

*: Include independent enterprises plus other parts of your enterprise group (subsidiaries, sister enterprises, head office, etc). Institutions include universities, research institutes, non-profits, etc.

2.3   Were any of your product innovations (goods or services) during the three years 2008 to 2010:

		Yes	No
New to your market?	Your enterprise introduced a new or significantly improved product onto your market before your competitors (it may have already been available in other markets)	❑	❑
Only new to your firm?	Your enterprise introduced a new or significantly improved product that was already available from your competitors in your market	❑	❑

Using the definitions above, please give the percentage of your total turnover[4] in 2010 from:

New or significantly improved products introduced during the three years 2008 to 2010 that were **new to your market**   %

New or significantly improved products introduced during the three years 2008 to 2010 that were **only new to your firm**   %

Products that were **unchanged or only marginally modified** during the three years 2008 to 2010 (include the resale of new products purchased from other enterprises)   %

Total turnover in 2010 | 1 | 0 | 0 | %

2.4   Were any of your product innovations during the three years 2008 to 2010:

	Yes	No	Don't know
A first in [your country]	❑	❑	❑
A first in Europe	❑	❑	❑
A world first	❑	❑	❑

---

[4]   For credit institutions: interests receivable and similar income; for insurance services: gross premiums written.

3.   Process Innovation

A process innovation is the implementation of a **new** or **significantly** improved production process, distribution method, or supporting activity.

- Process innovations must be new to your enterprise, but they do not need to be new to your market.
- The innovation could have been originally developed by your enterprise or by other enterprises.
- Exclude purely organisational innovations – these are covered in section 9.

3.1   During the three years 2008 to 2010, did your enterprise introduce:

	Yes	No
New or significantly improved methods of manufacturing or producing goods or services	❏	❏
New or significantly improved logistics, delivery or distribution methods for your inputs, goods or services	❏	❏
New or significantly improved supporting activities for your processes, such as maintenance systems or operations for purchasing, accounting, or computing	❏	❏

If no to all options, go to section 4, otherwise:

3.2   Who developed these process innovations?

Tick all that apply

Your enterprise by itself	❏
Your enterprise together with other enterprises or institutions*	❏
Your enterprise by adapting or modifying processes originally developed by other enterprises or institutions*	❏
Other enterprises or institutions*	❏

*: Include independent enterprises plus other parts of your enterprise group (subsidiaries, sister enterprises, head office, etc). Institutions include universities, research institutes, non-profits, etc.

3.3   Were any of your process innovations introduced during the three years 2008 to 2010 new to your market?

Yes	❏
No	❏
Do not know	❏

4.   Ongoing or Abandoned Innovation Activities for Process and Product Innovations

Innovation activities include the acquisition of machinery, equipment, software, and licenses; engineering and development work, design, training, marketing and R&D when they are *specifically* undertaken to develop and/or implement a product or process innovation. Also include basic R&D as an innovation activity even when not related to a product and/or process innovation.

4.1   During the three years 2008 to 2010, did your enterprise have any innovation activities that did not result in a product or process innovation because the activities were:

	Yes	No
Abandoned or suspended before completion	❏	❏
Still ongoing at the end of the 2010	❏	❏

If your enterprise had no product or process innovations or innovation activity during the three years 2008 to 2010 (no to all options in questions 2.1, 3.1, and 4.1), go to section 8.
Otherwise, go to section 5

5.   Innovation Activities and Expenditures for Process and Product Innovations

5.1   During the three years 2008 to 2010, did your enterprise engage in the following innovation activities:

		Yes	No
In-house R&D	Creative work undertaken within your enterprise to increase the stock of knowledge for developing new and improved products and processes (include software development in-house that meets this requirement)	❏	❏

	If yes, did your enterprise perform R&D during the three years 2008 to 2010:	❏	❏
External R&D	Same activities as above, but performed by other enterprises (including other enterprises or subsidiaries within your group) or by public or private research organisations and purchased by your enterprise	❏	❏
Acquisition of machinery, equipment and software	Acquisition of advanced machinery, equipment (including computer hardware) or software to produce new or significantly improved products and processes	❏	❏
Acquisition of external knowledge	Purchase or licensing of patents and non-patented inventions, know-how, and other types of knowledge from other enterprises or organisations for the development of new or significantly improved products and processes	❏	❏
Training for innovative activities	Internal or external training for your personnel specifically for the development and/or introduction of new or significantly improved products and processes	❏	❏
Market introduction of innovations	Activities for the market introduction of your new or significantly improved goods or services, including market research and launch advertising	❏	❏
Design	Activities to design, improve or change the shape or appearance of new or significantly improved goods or services	❏	❏

Other   Other activities to implement new or   ❏   ❏
                   significantly improved products and
                   processes such as feasibility studies,
                   testing, routine software development,
                   tooling up, industrial engineering, etc.

5.2 Please estimate the amount of expenditure for each of the following four innovation activities in 2010 only. (Include personnel and related costs)[5]

If your enterprise had no expenditures in 2010, please fill in '0'

In-house R&D (Include capital expenditures on buildings and equipment specifically for R&D)

Purchase of external R&D

Acquisition of machinery, equipment, and software (Exclude expenditures on equipment for R&D)

Acquisition of external knowledge

Total of these four innovation expenditure categories

5.3 During the three years 2008 to 2010, did your enterprise receive any public financial support for innovation activities from the following levels of government? Include financial support via tax credits or deductions, grants, subsidised loans, and loan guarantees. Exclude research and other innovation activities conducted entirely for the public sector under contract.

	Yes	No
Local or regional authorities	❏	❏
Central government (including central government agencies or ministries)	❏	❏
The European Union (EU)	❏	❏
If yes, did your enterprise participate in the EU 7th Framework Programme for Research and Technical Development?	❏	❏

---

5   Give expenditure data in 000's of national currency units to eight digits.

6. Sources of Information and Co-operation for Product and Process Innovation

6.1 During the three years 2008 to 2010, how important to your enterprise's innovation activities were each of the following information sources? Please identify information sources that provided information for new innovation projects or contributed to the completion of existing innovation projects.

Degree of importance

Tick 'not used' if no information was obtained from a source

	Information source	High	Medium	Low	Not used
Internal	Within your enterprise or enterprise group	❏	❏	❏	❏
Market sources	Suppliers of equipment, materials, components, or software	❏	❏	❏	❏
	Clients or customers	❏	❏	❏	❏
	Competitors or other enterprises in your sector	❏	❏	❏	❏
	Consultants, commercial labs, or private R&D institutes	❏	❏	❏	❏
Institutional sources	Universities or other higher education institutions	❏	❏	❏	❏
	Government or public research institutes	❏	❏	❏	❏
Other sources	Conferences, trade fairs, exhibitions	❏	❏	❏	❏
	Scientific journals and trade/technical publications	❏	❏	❏	❏
	Professional and industry associations	❏	❏	❏	❏

6.2 **During the three years 2008 to 2010, did your enterprise co-operate on any of your innovation activities with other enterprises or institutions?** Innovation co-operation is active participation with other enterprises or non-commercial institutions on innovation activities. Both partners do not need to commercially benefit. Exclude pure contracting out of work with no active co-operation.

Yes   ❑
No   ❑ **(Please go to question 7.1)**

6.3 **Please indicate the type of innovation co-operation partner by location**

(Tick all that apply)

Type of co-operation partner	[Your country]	Other Europe*	United States	China or India	All other countries
A. Other enterprises within your enterprise group	❑	❑	❑	❑	❑
B. Suppliers of equipment, materials, components, or software	❑	❑	❑	❑	❑
C. Clients or customers	❑	❑	❑	❑	❑
D. Competitors or other enterprises in your sector	❑	❑	❑	❑	❑
E. Consultants, commercial labs, or private R&D institutes	❑	❑	❑	❑	❑
F. Universities or other higher education institutions	❑	❑	❑	❑	❑
G. Government or public research institutes	❑	❑	❑	❑	❑

*: Include the following European Union (EU) countries, EFTA, or EU candidate countries: Austria, Belgium, Bulgaria, Croatia, Cyprus, Czech Republic, Denmark, Estonia, Finland, France, Germany, Greece, Hungary, Iceland, Italy, Ireland, Latvia, Liechtenstein, Lithuania, Luxembourg, Macedonia, Malta, Netherlands, Norway, Poland, Portugal, Romania, Slovenia, Slovakia, Switzerland, Turkey, Spain, Sweden and the United Kingdom.

6.4 Which type of co-operation partner did you find the most valuable for your enterprise's innovation activities? (Give corresponding letter)

————

7. Objectives for your Product and Process Innovations during 2008 to 2010

7.1 How important were each of the following objectives for your activities to develop product or process innovations during the three years 2008 to 2010?

If your enterprise had several projects for product and process innovations, make an overall evaluation

	High	Medium	Low	Not relevant
Increase range of goods or services	❏	❏	❏	❏
Replace outdated products or processes	❏	❏	❏	❏
Enter new markets or increase market share	❏	❏	❏	❏
Improve quality of goods or services	❏	❏	❏	❏
Improve *flexibility* for producing goods or services	❏	❏	❏	❏
Increase *capacity* for producing goods or services	❏	❏	❏	❏
Reduce labour costs per unit output	❏	❏	❏	❏
Reduce material and energy costs per unit output	❏	❏	❏	❏
Reduce environmental impacts	❏	❏	❏	❏
Improve health or safety of your employees	❏	❏	❏	❏

8. Factors Hampering Product and Process Innovation Activities

8.1 **During the three years 2008 to 2010, how important were the following factors in preventing your enterprise from innovating or in hampering your innovation activities?**

		Degree of importance			
		High	**Medium**	**Low**	**Factor not experienced**
Cost factors	Lack of funds within your enterprise or group	❏	❏	❏	❏
	Lack of finance from sources outside your enterprise	❏	❏	❏	❏
	Innovation costs too high	❏	❏	❏	❏
Know-ledge factors	Lack of qualified personnel	❏	❏	❏	❏
	Lack of information on technology	❏	❏	❏	❏
	Lack of information on markets	❏	❏	❏	❏
	Difficulty in finding co-operation partners for innovation	❏	❏	❏	❏
Market factors	Market dominated by established enterprises	❏	❏	❏	❏
	Uncertain demand for innovative goods or services	❏	❏	❏	❏
Reasons not to inno-vate	No need due to prior innovations by your enterprise	❏	❏	❏	❏
	No need because of no demand for innovations	❏	❏	❏	❏

9. Organisational Innovation

An organisational innovation is a new organisational method in your enterprise's business practices (including knowledge management), workplace organisation or external relations that has not been previously used by your enterprise.

- It must be the result of strategic decisions taken by management.
- Exclude mergers or acquisitions, even if for the first time.

9.1 During the three years 2008 to 2010, did your enterprise introduce:

	Yes	No
New **business practices** for organising procedures (i.e. supply chain management, business re-engineering, knowledge management, lean production, quality management, etc)	❏	❏
New methods of **organising work responsibilities and decision making** (i.e. first use of a new system of employee responsibilities, team work, decentralisation, integration or de-integration of departments, education/training systems, etc)	❏	❏
New methods of **organising external relations** with other firms or public institutions (i.e. first use of alliances, partnerships, outsourcing or sub-contracting, etc)	❏	❏

If no to all options, go to section 10.
Otherwise, go to question 9.2

9.2 How important were each of the following objectives for your enterprise's organisational innovations introduced during the three years 2008 to 2010 inclusive?

If your enterprise introduced several organisational innovations, make an overall evaluation

	High	Medium	Low	Not relevant
Reduce time to respond to customer or supplier needs	❏	❏	❏	❏
Improve ability to develop new products or processes	❏	❏	❏	❏

Improve quality of your goods or services	❑	❑	❑	❑
Reduce costs per unit output	❑	❑	❑	❑
Improve communication or information sharing within your enterprise or with other enterprises or institutions	❑	❑	❑	❑

10.   Marketing Innovation

A marketing innovation is the implementation of a new marketing concept or strategy that differs significantly from your enterprise's existing marketing methods and which has not been used before.

- It requires significant changes in product design or packaging, product placement, product promotion or pricing.
- Exclude seasonal, regular and other routine changes in marketing methods.

10.1   During the three years 2008 to 2010, did your enterprise introduce:

	Yes	No
Significant changes to the aesthetic **design** or **packaging** of a good or service (*exclude changes that alter the product's functional or user characteristics – these are product innovations*)	❑	❑
New media or techniques for **product promotion** (*i.e. the first time use of a new advertising media, a new brand image, introduction of loyalty cards, etc*)	❑	❑
New methods for **product placement** or sales channels (*i.e. first time use of franchising or distribution licences, direct selling, exclusive retailing, new concepts for product presentation, etc*)	❑	❑
New methods of **pricing** goods or services (*i.e. first time use of variable pricing by demand, discount systems, etc*)	❑	❑

If no to all options, go to section 11.
Otherwise, go to question 10.2

10.2 How important were each of the following objectives for your enterprise's marketing innovations introduced during the three years 2008 to 2010 inclusive?

If your enterprise introduced several marketing innovations, make an overall evaluation

	High	Medium	Low	Not relevant
Increase or maintain market share	❏	❏	❏	❏
Introduce products to new customer groups	❏	❏	❏	❏
Introduce products to new geographic markets	❏	❏	❏	❏

11. Creativity and Skills

11.1 During the three years 2008 to 2010, did your enterprise employ individuals in-house with the following skills, or obtain these skills from external sources?

Tick both 'Employed in-house' and 'Obtained from external sources' if relevant.

	Employed in-house	Obtained from external sources*	Skills not used /not relevant
Graphic arts / layout / advertising	❏	❏	❏
Design of objects or services	❏	❏	❏
Multimedia (combining audio, graphics, text, still pictures, animation, video etc)	❏	❏	❏
Web design	❏	❏	❏
Software development	❏	❏	❏
Market research	❏	❏	❏
Engineering / applied sciences	❏	❏	❏
Mathematics / statistics / database management	❏	❏	❏

: Include freelancers, consultants, other independent enterprises, other parts of your enterprise group, etc.

11.2 **During the three years 2008 to 2010, did your enterprise use any of the following methods to <u>stimulate new ideas or creativity</u> among your staff? If yes, was the method successful in producing new ideas or increasing creativity?**

	Method used and:			
	Success-ful	Not Successful	Don't know if successful	Method not used
Brainstorming sessions	❑	❑	❑	❑
Multidisciplinary or cross-functional work teams	❑	❑	❑	❑
Job rotation of staff to different departments or other parts of your enterprise group	❑	❑	❑	❑
Financial incentives for employees to develop new ideas	❑	❑	❑	❑
Non-financial incentives for employees to develop new ideas, such as free time, public recognition, more interesting work, etc	❑	❑	❑	❑
Training employees on how to develop new ideas or creativity	❑	❑	❑	❑

12.   Basic Economic Information on your Enterprise

12.1 **What was your enterprise's total turnover for 2008 and 2010?[6] Turnover is defined as the market sales of goods and services (Include all taxes except VAT[7]).**

2008	2010
☐☐☐☐☐☐☐☐☐	☐☐☐☐☐☐☐☐☐

---

[6]   Give turnover in '000 of national currency units. *Leave space for up to nine digits.*

[7]   For Credit institutions: Interests receivable and similar income; for Insurance services give gross premiums written.

12.2 What was your enterprise's average number of employees in 2008 and 2010?[8]

2008	2010
□□□□□□	□□□□□□

12.3 Approximately what percent of your enterprise's employees in 2010 had a university degree?[9]

0%	□
1% to 4%	□
5% to 9%	□
10% to 24%	□
25% to 49%	□
50% to 74%	□
75% to 100%	□

---

[8] If administrative data are used and the annual average is not available, give results for the end of each year. Leave space for up to six digits for question 12.2.

[9] National translation: This includes ISCED 5a and 6. If administrative data are used, use the same time period as for question 12.2.

PART II

DEFINING INNOVATION AND IMPLEMENTING THE DEFINITIONS

2 The *Oslo Manual*
Fred Gault

1. INTRODUCTION

Rules are needed to guide the measurement of innovation in ways that are reproducible over time and that give results comparable across jurisdictions. The *Oslo Manual* provides these rules. The *Oslo Manual* is used in countries belonging to the OECD, the EU, the African Union and in others. This chapter provides a history of the development of the *Oslo Manual* and reviews some of the consequences of its use.

Experts at the OECD have been discussing innovation, its place in policy, and the need to measure it and its impacts, for more than 30 years (OECD 1992a: 3, 1992b). In the 1990s, experts in the working groups of Eurostat, the European statistical office, joined in the discussion as part of managing the EU Community Innovation Survey (CIS), described in Chapter 3. While the policy imperatives change from day to day, the need to measure and understand the activity of innovation remains. Over the years of discussion, a common vocabulary and grammar have emerged that facilitate the discussion, and the rules for measuring innovation have been codified in manuals on three separate occasions.

As mentioned in Chapter 1, indicators are like technologies and practices;[1] they are produced and adopted, they diffuse and they can be changed by users or the users can communicate the need for change to the producers of the manuals. Users of manuals who feel that the manual does not solve their problem can develop a new manual. In this chapter, there are examples of all three activities.

The Role of Experts

The OECD Working Party of National Experts on Science and Technology Indicators (NESTI), as a group of experts, pre-dates the OECD. It goes back to the first meeting of experts in 1957 that gave rise to the first edition of the OECD *Frascati Manual* in 1963 (OECD 2002: 151). The *Frascati Manual* dealt with the collection and interpretation of data on R&D but, over the years, NESTI gave rise to the 'Frascati' family of manuals (OECD 2002: 16) of which the *Oslo Manual*, dealing with innovation, was one.

The OECD working party's membership consists of delegates from the 34 OECD member countries and the European Commission. There are also observers, such as Brazil, China, India, the Russian Federation and South Africa (BRICS), and other international organizations such as the UNESCO Institute of Statistics, the Latin American Ibero-American Network on Science and Technology Indicators (Red Iberoamericana de Indicadores de Ciencia y tecnologia (RICYT)) and the African Union and the NEPAD Planning and Co-ordinating Agency (NPCA). Delegates and observers are a mix of official statisticians or researchers, responsible for the development of statistical indicators, and policy analysts, responsible for the development of policy and for its evaluation once it is implemented. The mix of users and producers ensures that any outcomes of NESTI are grounded in the worlds of statistical measurement and the application of the results.

The OECD is a consensus organization, which means that the case must be argued until delegates are convinced or, at least, will not oppose a decision. Establishing consensus ensures peer learning, which is reinforced by OECD country peer reviews of innovation policy, managed by the OECD at the request of the countries under review. Recent examples are Slovenia (OECD 2012), Peru (OECD 2011a) and the Russian Federation (OECD 2011b). Peer learning, consensus building and peer review are characteristics that make the OECD unique as an international organization and they ensure that products of the committees and working parties are used by the countries that contributed to their creation. Chapters 9 and 12 discuss the role of the OECD in greater detail and Chapters 3 and 4 review measurement issues. This chapter deals with the history of the *Oslo Manual*.

2.   THE *OSLO MANUAL* AND DEFINITIONS OF INNOVATION

The first *Oslo Manual* was prepared with support from the Nordic Fund for Industrial Development and presented to NESTI in November 1989, reviewed in 1990 and sent to the Committee for Scientific and Technological Policy (CSTP) for approval in 1991.[2] It appeared in 1992 (OECD 1992a) and it was used to guide the first European Community Innovation Survey (CIS) for reference year 1992. The Community Innovation Surveys, as means of implementing the *Oslo Manual*, are the subjects of Chapters 3 and 4. Those surveys and similar innovation surveys in other countries provided ongoing testing of the definitions and guidelines in the first edition and demonstrated the need for revision, giving rise to the second edition (OECD/Eurostat 1997). The current manual (OECD/Eurostat 2005) is the third edition.

The review of the progress from the first to the third edition that follows illustrates the growth and importance of the common language introduced in Chapter 1, the role of statistical measurement, policy needs, peer learning in developing the language, and the need to go on developing the language and expanding the community of practice. The work began with technological product and process innovation in manufacturing and expanded to include non-technological innovation, and organizational and market development innovation. The *Oslo Manual* is the set of rules that guides the collection of innovation statistics in 34 OECD member countries, 27 EU member states and a number of other countries, including those that are NESTI observers.

The First Edition

All definitions of innovation in the Oslo manuals require a connection to the market. This has implications for innovation by consumers (Chapter 5), public sector innovation (Chapter 17) and social innovation (Chapter 18). These will be discussed after the third edition has been presented.

The definitions of technological innovation in the first edition were the following:

> 90.[3] Technological innovations comprise new products[4] and processes and significant changes of products and processes. An innovation has been implemented if it has been introduced to the market (product innovation) or used within a production process (process innovation). Innovations therefore involve a series of scientific, technological, organizational, financial and commercial activities. (OECD 1992a: 28)

> 92. *Product Innovation* can take two broad forms: – substantially new products: we call this *major product innovation*; – performance improvements to existing products: we call this incremental *product innovation*. (Ibid.: 29)

> 97. *Process innovation* is the adoption of new or significantly improved production methods. These methods may involve changes in equipment or production organization or both. The methods may be intended to produce new or improved products, which cannot be produced using conventional plants or production methods, or essentially to increase the production efficiency of existing products. (Ibid.)

The following were considered as a non-exhaustive list of innovative activities: R&D; tooling up and industrial engineering; manufacturing start-up; marketing for new products; acquisition of disembodied technology; acquisition of embodied technology; and design. The point was made that not all innovative activities lead to innovation, as the definition of innovation requires a connection with the market. In addition, not all innovation activities have been measured by surveys, such as the CIS. Design, for example, has been in the *Oslo Manual* from the beginning, but it took some years to enter the CIS.

The manual went on to discuss topics to be probed by surveys, including sources of information for innovation, objectives of the firm, barriers to innovation, impacts and cost. It reviewed survey methods and classifications and observed that 'the population of innovation surveys usually consists of enterprises in manufacturing industry' (OECD 1992a: 57), but suggested that 'it may also be useful to include parts of the service sector, particularly those working directly with manufacturers'. This is a precursor to the revision leading to the second edition of the manual, which included the service sector and other goods-producing industries but not agriculture.

The first revision was also in process at a time when there was a debate about how productive the service sector was and whether its impact, such as it was, was due to manufacturing firms outsourcing some of their innovation activities, such as R&D and industrial design. This may be an explanation for the preoccupation with service firms working directly with manufacturers.

The first CIS, CIS 1, was carried out in Europe for reference year 1992 using the *Oslo Manual* guidelines. This was the beginning of the interaction between official surveys and the Oslo manuals, and it brought Eurostat and the OECD closer together. The second and third editions were joint productions of the two organizations.

Novelty and technology use
The first edition contained topics that would change or vanish in future editions. Examples are novelty of innovation and technology use surveys.

As the first edition dealt with technological innovation, it provided a classification of novelty based on aspects of technology in the innovation. It also provided the classification that would be retained in the third edition: new to the firm, the country or the market, or the world (OECD 1992a: 41), although its implementation in the CIS has been just new to the firm or to the market and the relevant questions have been revised over the years. Most recently, CIS 2012, approved in November 2012 and mandated in Commission Implementing Regulation (EU) No. 995/2012 of 26 October 2012, has a novelty question about innovations being 'A first in [your country]', 'A first in Europe', 'a world first'. The measurement of novelty continues to develop.

Technology use surveys, especially in manufacturing, were appearing while the manual was being developed (Ducharme and Gault 1992) and a section of the manual was devoted to them. These surveys consisted of a list of 'advanced' technologies (Statistics Canada 1987, 1989, 1991; US Department of Commerce 1989) and respondents were invited to say whether they were using or planning to use any of the technologies in the list provided. In the Canadian surveys there were questions initially on user modification of the technologies and later (Arundel and Sonntag 2001; Statistics Canada 2008a) on adoption of the technology by developing it in house. These questions followed the work of von Hippel (1988) and were a first probe by official statisticians of user innovation by firms. User innovation by firms and by consumers is discussed further in Chapter 5 and in Gault (2012).

The *Oslo Manual* took a producer perspective and presented technology use surveys as measures of the diffusion of technologies produced as products by other manufacturing firms. It would take some years before user innovation would become a research question in the measurement community. However, the seed was there in the first manual in paragraph 185 in the sentence: 'Questions about whether the technology was modified to improve productivity or ease of use give insight into the propensity to innovate on the factory floor'.

Before going on to the second edition of the *Oslo Manual*, and before the reader goes to the next chapter, the point is made that the definition of product innovation in all three editions of the *Oslo Manual* required only that the product be introduced to the market. The product did not have to 'generate a return on investment' (Chapter 3) and neither did it have to be 'good'. The introduction of new or significantly improved debt-based financial products by the US financial services industry in 2006 was a classic example of innovation that led to the most significant recession in 70 years from which the world is still recovering.

To discuss toxic financial products as innovations requires a review of the framework conditions in place at the time. Framework conditions, in this case the regulatory environment, can support or prevent innovation. However, this is a handbook on innovation indicators and measurement, not on the innovation system and long-term and shorter-term framework conditions that influence the activity of innovation in the firm. An introduction to the subject can be found in Gault (2010).

The Second Edition

While the first CIS focused on manufacturing, it soon became evident that understanding innovation in service industries was at least as important.

In most industrialized countries, 70 per cent of GDP comes from services and less than 20 per cent from manufacturing. The significant statistic is that half, or more, of GDP comes from marketed services and the remaining 20 per cent or so is in the public sector, education, government and health. Innovation, to be innovation, has to connect to the market, although work is being done on public sector innovation (OECD 2006a; Chapter 17 in this volume) and is being called for on consumer innovation (von Hippel 2005; Chapter 5 in this volume). These initiatives, which could have affected the definition of innovation, were not an issue for the innovation measurement community in 1995 when the revision of the *Oslo Manual* began.

Discussions on measuring innovation in services had been going on for years and reference to such measurement had already been made in the first edition of the *Oslo Manual*. However, there was not the same depth of experience to draw upon as had been built up for manufacturing. This required a widening of the community of discourse and led to the inclusion of innovation in services in the agendas of Eurostat committees and of the UN City Group working at the time on service industry statistics, the Voorburg Group (Gault and Pattinson 1994, 1995). In the revision of the *Oslo Manual*, innovation in services had its own working group, co-chaired by Australia and Canada.

The second edition was an improved version of the first edition, informed by survey experience and policy debate. It continued to deal with technological innovation and confined itself to product and process innovation. However, it had broader economic coverage, including construction, utilities, manufacturing and marketed services. It took advantage of new international classifications, such as the 1993 revision of the system of national accounts (EC et al. 1994), and it recognized the importance of a systems approach to innovation (OECD/Eurostat 1997: 15) and of learning in the transfer of knowledge for innovation (ibid.: 34). Both would have a larger role in the third edition.

While the definitions remained fundamentally the same as those in the first edition, they emphasized the technological aspect of innovation. This may have reflected a view that removing or weakening the reference to technology would admit an uncontrollable flood of non-technological innovations for which the community was not ready. Here is the summary definition, which can be compared with that used in the first edition.

130.   *Technological product and process (TPP) innovations* comprise implemented technologically new products and processes and significant technological improvements in products and processes. A TPP innovation has been *implemented* if it has been introduced to the market (product innovation) or used within a production process (process innovation). TPP innovations involve

a series of scientific, technological, organizational, financial and commercial *activities. The TPP innovating firm* is one that has implemented technologically new or significantly technologically improved products or processes during the period under review. (OECD/Eurostat 1997: 47; emphasis in original)

The definition provides an excellent example of why survey questionnaires should never take their definitions uncritically from the *Oslo Manual*. This should not be seen as a criticism of the sometimes arcane language used. It results from lengthy debate at the end of which the use of a word, or the position of the word, may be the only way consensus is achieved. When the questions are put into surveys, the language is, or should be, tested and revised before subjecting respondents to the questions. This is the subject of the cognitive testing project at the OECD (Chapter 9) and it is a practice for introducing new CIS questions (Chapter 3).

Reference to surveys of technology use appears in the second edition, again from a producer perspective as a measure of diffusion. The text is essentially unchanged from the first edition, including the reference to user modification of technologies, which is present in paragraph 259. The importance of learning, of knowledge, and of a systems approach to understanding innovation, reflected the academic literature of the time and the outcomes of the first OECD Blue Sky meeting on new science and technology indicators in 1996 (OECD 2001a).

Following the adoption in 1997 of the second edition of the *Oslo Manual*, and its use in the CIS, the research community worked a great deal on service industries and on innovation in services (Metcalfe and Miles 2000; Boden and Miles 2000; Gadrey and Gallouj 2002; Gallouj 2002). This was not a causal relationship. This was at a time when it was becoming clear that if marketed services accounted for over half of the economy, they should be better understood, and an important aspect of this understanding was how innovation in services worked.

The OECD was also engaged in innovation in services in this period, from a productivity perspective (OECD 2001b), and from the perspective of knowledge intensity and the importance of knowledge in service industries (OECD 2006b). In fact, knowledge (Foray 2007, 2004) attracted much attention in the period before the next *Oslo Manual* edition.

In particular, there was work on knowledge management in the business sector and its relation to innovation. A group working on this, as part of an OECD project, developed a questionnaire (OECD 2003) that had similarities to questionnaires dealing with the use and planned use of technologies. The point to make in this chapter is that the questionnaires used in the countries participating in the project worked. That is, they demonstrated that information on the use of knowledge management practices could be collected, analysed and used to improve the understanding of firm activity. As a specific example, the use of knowledge management practices was shown to be correlated with innovation (Kremp and Mairesse 2002). This work influenced the second revision of the *Oslo Manual*; the development of innovation indicators and measurement for organizational practices is ongoing (Chapter 10).

By 2002, with the publication of the sixth edition of the *Frascati Manual* (OECD 2002), Eurostat and the OECD were ready to undertake the three years of work needed to produce the third edition of the *Oslo Manual*, although it was not foreseen that it would take as long as it did and be such a challenging process. The hope had been that the new manual could be used by Eurostat to guide the CIS 4. One of the lessons learned from this process was that it was difficult, if not impossible, for a consensus-based organization, with its expert group chaired by a delegate from a member country, to work to a timetable required by a supranational organization where the expert groups are chaired and directed by the Secretariat. As in all such things, it was the good will on both sides that ensured a positive outcome.

The Third Edition

The first thing to notice about the third edition is its title, *Oslo Manual: Guidelines for Collecting and Interpreting Innovation Data* (OECD/Eurostat 2005) and its comparison with the title of the second edition, *Proposed Guidelines for Collecting and Interpreting Technological Innovation Data – Oslo Manual*, (OECD/Eurostat 1997). The word 'technological' has gone and 'proposed' no longer appears in front of 'guidelines'. Both changes are important as non-technological innovation had now been admitted for the purposes of measurement and the *Oslo Manual* provided the guidelines for that measurement. Another influence, given that this was a joint OECD/Eurostat undertaking, was the European Commission Regulation 1450/2004, introduced in August 2004, amended in 2009, which made CIS compulsory for member states of the EU. The language had acquired new vocabulary.

The definition had been expanded.

> 146.   An *innovation* is the implementation of a new or significantly improved product (good or a service), or process, a new marketing method, or a new organization method in business practices, workplace organization or external relations.

It was still linked to the market through 'implementation'.

150.   A common feature of an innovation is that it must have been *implemented*. A new or improved product is implemented when it is introduced on the market. New processes, marketing methods or organizational methods are implemented when they are brought into actual use in the firm's operations.

The definition of an innovative firm remained the same.

152.   An *innovative firm* is one that has implemented an innovation during the period under review.

The systems approach[5] and knowledge management activities were incorporated in a new chapter on linkages that also addressed networks and network capital. Network capital[6] describes the knowledge stored in the networks that contributed to innovation. While the linkages chapter was a major step forward in providing guidance for the measurement of innovation, it could not deal with the dynamics of change, but it could situate the change in an innovation system.

The classification of novelty in the third edition had nothing to do with technology but was new to the firm, to the market, or to the world (OECD/Eurostat 2005: 57). There was a reference to disruptive innovation (ibid.: 17), as developed by Christensen (1997), but also recognition that it was an impact measure that could not be measured easily by an innovation survey. Disruptive innovation was not a category used for classification in the manual.

Diffusion of innovation was treated in the chapter on linkages and questions were suggested on the developer of the innovation. Was it developed by: the firm; the firm in cooperation with other firms or institutions; or mainly by other firms or institutions (OECD/Eurostat 2005: 84)? This is a very important question when it comes to user innovation and it can be found in CIS 4, CIS 2006 and CIS 2008. In CIS 2010 the question was revised to add a question about whether it was developed by adapting or modifying processes originally developed by the firm or other institutions.

With the modification, three of the questions mirrored the same three questions used in surveys of use and planned use of technologies (next subsection), but there they were about the adoption of a technology and whether the firm adopted by developing the technology itself, by purchasing and modifying the technology or by purchasing an available technology and using it, which would be process innovation if the purchased technology were new to the firm. The collaboration question was not present in the technology use surveys, of which Schaan and Uhrbach (2009) provide an example.

Surveys of technology use

The third edition made no reference to surveys of technology use and planned use or the adoption of technologies by purchase (an innovation, if new to the firm), by purchase and modification (a user innovation by the firm), or by developing the needed technology in the absence of its being available on the market (user innovation by the firm).

This did not mean that technologies were neglected at the OECD. In 1997 the precursor of a new working party, the Working Party on Indicators for the Information Society (WPIIS), was established, under the chairmanship of a NESTI vice chair, to define the ICT sector for statistical purposes and there followed the collection of internationally comparable data on ICT use, but the question of user innovation was not pursued (OECD 2009a).

In the case of biotechnology, an *ad hoc* group established by NESTI produced definitions to support the collection of internationally comparable data (OECD 2009b) and was then dissolved. Definitions and statistics for nanotechnology have moved in the same direction (OECD 2009c).

The history of these initiatives is reviewed in Chapter 15, leading to a discussion of how to generalize the process of identifying emerging and enabling technologies.

However, measurement of the use and planned use of technologies was continued by Statistics Canada (Schaan and Uhrbach 2009) for the 2007 Advanced Technology Survey (Statistics Canada 2008a, 2008b; Chapter 5 in this volume) and a similar measurement was made in 2009 as part of the Survey of Innovation and Business Strategy (SIBS) (Industry Canada 2011). Schaan and Uhrbach found that about 20 per cent of firms adopted by developing their own technologies and another 20 per cent adopted by purchasing and modifying technologies. The finding from SIBS for adoption by developing the technology was comparable. The Schaan and Uhrbach figures suggest that about 40 per cent of firms in the Canadian manufacturing sector are user innovators. This is discussed further in Chapter 5.

User innovation in innovation surveys

CIS captures, in its measures of innovation, all of the user innovation by the firm but it does not identify explicitly that it is user innovation. That is a point discussed in Chapter 5. The situation is different for the individual consumer or end user (von Hippel 2005).

In the third edition of the *Oslo Manual*, the only place for the individual consumer, or end user, is as a source of information for the firm that engages in product innovation or perhaps as a collaborator with the producing firm. Users as sources of information and as co-producers are significant in the findings of CIS, but this is user-driven innovation, not 'user innovation'. A user could provide a prototype of a new or improved product to a producer. If the user was a firm, the recipient of the product, if it was later introduced to the market, would report that it was developed by 'other enterprises or institutions'. If the user was a consumer, it is not clear what the answer would be to the question. Identifying consumers as 'innovators' remains an open question, which is discussed in Chapter 5.

3.   USING THE *OSLO MANUAL* IN DEVELOPING COUNTRIES

Innovation is not the prerogative of developed countries. It happens in the developing world and it can be a driver of economic growth there as elsewhere. While it may be more incremental than radical and make more use of knowledge from sources other than R&D, it is still innovation.

Discussions took place in Latin America and in Africa about how best to measure innovation and how to produce guidelines to support the process. In Latin America, RICYT developed and published the *Bogotá Manual* (RICYT/OEC/CYTED 2001) and in Africa there were discussions about how to approach the need for guidelines for measuring innovation (NEPAD 2006). Returning to indicators as a technology, RICYT developed its own technology, while NEPAD decided to follow the path of acquiring and modifying the technology for its own benefit.

Experience with the *Bogotá Manual* gave rise to a proposal to the OECD to add an annex to the third edition of the *Oslo Manual* to interpret it for use in developing countries. This was accepted and the preparation of Annex A of OECD/Eurostat (2005) was coordinated by the UNESCO Institute of Statistics. The advantage of adding the annex to the *Oslo Manual* was that it could be revised, along with the rest of the manual, as experience was gained in developing countries of using both the manual and the annex. This ensured an ongoing dialogue within a broader community of practice.

In Africa, the first meeting of the African Intergovernmental Committee on Science, Technology and Innovation Indicators in Maputo in 2007 adopted the Oslo and the Frascati manuals for use in surveying innovation and R&D activities (NEPAD 2007) in Africa. The idea was that, over time, as experience was gained, African manuals could be developed to support the use of OECD manuals in African contexts (Ellis 2008; Gault 2008; Kahn 2008).

In developing countries, as in the developed, the innovation systems approach plays a role in classifying and interpreting statistics on innovation activities and on the activity of innovation itself. Lundvall et al. (2009) provide an introduction to innovation systems in developing countries. There is also the World Bank (2010) guide to innovation policy for developing countries and a discussion of innovation and the development agenda by Kraemer-Mbula and Wamae (2010).

4.   CONCLUSION

The last 30 years have seen considerable progress in the definition, measurement and interpretation of data on the activity of innovation as a result of the revisions of the *Oslo Manual* and its implementation through CIS. However, Chapters 3 and 4 make the point that measurement is still a work in progress and other chapters show that there is work to be done to understand the activity of innovation and the factors that influence it.

While the third edition adopted more of a systems approach and introduced organizational change and business practices, and market development, to the definition, there is more to be done to provide guidance on dealing with framework conditions that have long- and short-term effects on firms, on understanding the dynamics of the innovation process, especially the multiple time scales that are present, and a need to work more with microdata than with macro-aggregations. These issues are discussed in Chapter 9 and again in Chapter 19.

Finally, the *Oslo Manual* is not an isolated set of rules. The rules are set within the context of the guidelines for the system of national accounts (EC et al. 2009) and the business surveys, such as CIS, that measure innovation use common classifications that are part of the international infrastructure for business surveys. Some of these tools are presented in the appendix.

NOTES

1. In Chapter 1, the reference was to technologies, here it is to technologies and practices; the point is that practices are equivalent to technologies. In future references, technologies are assumed to include practices, such as knowledge management practices, or just-in-time delivery of inputs for production.
2. A more detailed history of the first edition of the *Oslo Manual* is given in the Preface by Robert Chabbal, then the Director of the OECD Directorate for Science, Technology and Industry (OECD 1992a: 3–4).
3. In all quotations from the Oslo manuals, the paragraph number is included. The page number is given in the citation.

4. Oslo manuals use vocabulary taken from the system of national accounts (EC et al. 2009). Product refers to a good or a service. The phrase 'products and services' should never appear in *Oslo Manual*-based discourse.
5. The systems approach is just that, the identification of actors (business, education, government etc.), engaged in activities (R&D, acquisition of knowledge, training, design etc.), linked by flows of data, information and knowledge, energy, material and finance, and people, giving rise to short-term outcomes and longer-term impacts. Classification and analytical devices such as national systems of innovation, local clusters, or global value or supply chains are applications of the systems approach.
6. Paragraph 260 of the third edition of the *Oslo Manual* states that 'building social capital may be a vital part of an enterprise's innovation strategies' and then goes on to observe that 'The term *social capital* has many meanings outside of economic analysis and this can lead to confusion. *Network capital* has been used as an alternative.' This does not mean that social capital is not important in the study of innovation, and the reader is referred to Ostrom and Ahn (2003) and Svendsen and Svendsen (2010) for an introduction to the subject.

REFERENCES

Arundel, A. and V. Sonntag (2001), *Patterns of Advanced Manufacturing Technology (AMT) Use in Canadian Manufacturing: 1998 AMT Survey Results*, Catalogue no. 88F0017MIE, no. 12, Ottawa: Statistics Canada.

Boden, Mark and Ian Miles (eds) (2000), *Services and the Knowledge-Based Economy*, London: Continuum.

Christensen, C.M. (1997), *The Innovators Dilemma: When New Technologies Cause Great Firms to Fail*, Boston, MA: Harvard University Press.

Ducharme, L.M. and F.D. Gault (1992), 'Surveys of manufacturing technology', *Science and Public Policy*, **19**, 393–9.

EC, IMF, OECD, UN and World Bank (1994), *System of National Accounts, 1993*, New York: United Nations.

EC, IMF, OECD, UN and World Bank (2009), *System of National Accounts, 2008*, New York: United Nations.

Ellis, Simon (2008), 'The current state of international science statistics in Africa', *African Statistical Journal*, **6**, 177–89.

Foray, D. (2004), *The Economics of Knowledge*, Cambridge, MA: The MIT Press.

Foray, Dominique (2007), 'Enriching the indicator base for the economics of knowledge', in OECD, *Science, Technology and Innovation Indicators in a Changing World, Responding to Policy Needs*, Paris: OECD, pp. 87–100.

Gadrey, Jean and Faïz Gallouj (eds) (2002), *Productivity, Innovation and Knowledge in Services, New Economic and Socio-Economic Approaches*, Cheltenham, UK and Northampton, MA, USA: Edward Elgar.

Gallouj, Faïz (2002), *Innovation in the Service Economy: The New Wealth of Nations*, Cheltenham, UK and Northampton, MA, USA: Edward Elgar.

Gault, Fred (2008), 'Science, technology and innovation indicators: opportunities for Africa', *African Statistical Journal*, **6**, 141–62.

Gault, Fred (2010), *Innovation Strategies for a Global Economy: Development, Implementation, Measurement and Management*, Cheltenham, UK and Northampton, MA, USA: Edward Elgar and Ottawa: IDRC.

Gault, Fred (2012), 'User innovation and the market', *Science and Public Policy*, **39**, 118–28.

Gault, Fred and William Pattinson (1994), 'Model surveys of service industries: the need to measure innovation', Voorburg Conference Paper, Sydney, Australia.

Gault, Fred and William Pattinson (1995), 'Innovation in service industries: the measurement issues', Voorburg Conference Paper, Voorburg, The Netherlands.

Industry Canada (2011), *Business Innovation and Strategy: A Canadian Perspective*, Ottawa: Government of Canada.

Kahn, Michael (2008), 'Africa's plan of action for science and technology and indicators: South African experience', *African Statistical Journal*, **6**, 163–76.

Kraemer-Mbula, Erika and Watu Wamae (2010), *Innovation and the Development Agenda*, Paris: OECD and Ottawa: IDRC.

Kremp, E. and J. Mairesse (2002), *Le 4 Pages des statistiques industrielles*, No.169, Décembre, Paris: SESSI.

Lundvall, Bengt-Åke, K.J. Joseph, Christina Chaminade and Jan Vang (eds) (2009), *Handbook of Innovation Systems and Developing Countries: Building Domestic Capabilities in a Global Setting*, Cheltenham, UK and Northampton, MA, USA: Edward Elgar.

Metcalfe, Stanley J. and Ian Miles (eds) (2000), *Innovation Systems in the Service Economy: Measurement and Case Study Analysis*, Norwell, MA: Kluwer Academic Publishers.

NEPAD (2006), 'African Science, Technology and Innovation Indicators (ASTII): towards African indicator manuals – a discussion document', www.nepadst.org/doclibrary/pdfs/iastii_jun2006.pdf.

NEPAD (2007), Decisions of the First Meeting of the African Intergovernmental Committee on Science, Technology and Innovation Indicators', September 18, 2007, Maputo, Mozambique, Pretoria: NEPAD.

OECD (1992a), *OECD Proposed Guidelines for Collecting and Interpreting Technological Innovation Data – Oslo Manual*, OCDE/GD (92)26, Paris: OECD.

OECD (1992b), *Technology and the Economy: The Key Relationships*, Paris: OECD.

OECD (2001a), *Science, Technology and Industry Review*, Special Issue on New Science and Technology Indicators, No.27, Paris: OECD.

OECD (2001b), *Innovation and Productivity in Services*, Paris: OECD.

OECD (2002), *Frascati Manual: Proposed Standard Practice for Surveys on Research and Experimental Development*, Paris: OECD.

OECD (2003), *Measuring Knowledge Management in the Business Sector: First Steps*, Paris: OECD.

OECD (2006a), *Economic Policy Reforms 2008: Going for Growth*, Paris: OECD.

OECD (2006b), *Innovation and Knowledge-Intensive Service Activities*, Paris: OECD.

OECD (2009a), *Guide to Measuring the Information Society*, Paris: OECD.

OECD (2009b), *OECD Key Biotechnology Indicators*, Paris: OECD.

OECD (2009c), *Statistical Framework for Nanotechnology*, Paris: OECD.

OECD (2011a), *OECD Reviews of Innovation Policy: Peru*, Paris: OECD.

OECD (2011b), *OECD Reviews of Innovation Policy: Russian Federation*, Paris: OECD.

OECD (2012), *OECD Reviews of Innovation Policy: Slovenia*, Paris: OECD.

OECD/Eurostat (1997), *Proposed Guidelines for Collecting and Interpreting Technological Innovation Data – Oslo Manual*, Paris: OECD.

OECD/Eurostat (2005), *Oslo Manual: Guidelines for Collecting and Interpreting Innovation Data*, Paris: OECD.

Ostrom, E. and T.K. Ahn (2003), *Foundations of Social Capital*, Cheltenham, UK and Northampton, MA, USA: Edward Elgar.

RICYT/OEC/CYTED (2001), *Standardization of Indicators of Technological Innovation in Latin American and Caribbean Countries: Bogotá Manual*, Buenos Aires: RICYT.

Schaan, Susan and Mark Uhrbach (2009), *Measuring User Innovation in Canadian Manufacturing, 2007*, Catalogue 88F0006X, no.3, Ottawa: Statistics Canada.

Statistics Canada (1987), 'Survey of Manufacturing Technology – June 1987', *The Daily*, 15 October, Ottawa: Statistics Canada.

Statistics Canada (1989), 'Survey of manufacturing technology – the characteristics of the plants', *Science Statistics*, **13** (10), Ottawa: Statistics Canada.

Statistics Canada (1991), *Indicators of Science and Technology 1989: Survey of Manufacturing Technology – 1989*, Catalogue 88-002, vol. 1, no.4, Ottawa: Statistics Canada.

Statistics Canada (2008a), 'Survey of Advanced Technology 2007', *The Daily*, 26 June, Ottawa: Statistics Canada.

Statistics Canada (2008b), 'Follow-up to the Survey of Advanced Technology 2007', *The Daily*, 27 October, Ottawa: Statistics Canada.

Svendsen, G.T. and G.L.H. Svendsen (2010), *Handbook of Social Capital: The Troika of Sociology, Political Science and Economics*, Cheltenham, UK and Northampton, MA, USA: Edward Elgar.

US Department of Commerce (1989), *Manufacturing Technology 1988*, Current Industrial Reports, Washington, DC: US Department of Commerce.

von Hippel, Eric (1988), *The Sources of Innovation*, New York: Oxford University Press.

von Hippel, Eric (2005), *Democratizing Innovation*, Cambridge, MA: MIT Press.

World Bank (2010), *Innovation Policy: A Guide for Developing Countries*, Washington, DC: World Bank.

APPENDIX: CLASSIFICATION AND REGISTERS

This appendix provides a brief introduction to classification systems, starting with the system of national accounts. It then reviews business registers and industry classifications. These classifications are used for the business surveys and administrative data that provide the statistics that populate innovation indicators. Registers, classification systems and survey techniques are the tools used by statistical offices and research institutes that run surveys as a principal activity. This is meant to complement the material in Chapter 4, Institutional Classifications (OECD/Eurostat 2005: 64) and Chapter 8, Survey Procedures (ibid.: 117) of the third edition of the *Oslo Manual*. Following the discussion of business registers and classifications, other classifications are introduced that are used in current analysis related to innovation and which may be used more as the subject evolves.

System of National Accounts (SNA)

The current version of the system of national accounts is SNA 2008 (EC et al. 2009), which provides a framework for statistics in all parts of the economy, including the market economy, the public sector and households. In the EU, this is accomplished by the European system of national and regional accounts of 2010, referred to as ESA 2010.

Business Registers and Business Classifications

A business survey starts with the drawing of a statistical sample from a 'frame', which is a list of firms that are in scope for the survey. That list is found in a business register maintained by statistical offices or other government departments and the firms are assigned a standard industrial classification. It is the industrial classification that permits the scope of the sample to be specified.

There are many challenges in building a business register and all influence statistical measurement. Finding new firms and adding them to the register is important because, if they are not present in the sample, the survey cannot reflect current activities in the economy. Business registers make use of tax data, or other registration requirements, to note the appearance of new firms. Removing firms that are no longer active is also important, especially in an industry where firms are being created and terminated rapidly. If inactive firms are not removed, the survey sample will contain these firms and costs will be incurred as a result of identifying and removing them from the sample so that a realistic response rate can be reported.

For larger firms, there are questions of the unit of observation, and the business register should provide a profile of the structure of the firms so that the survey manager can draw a sample at the firm or enterprise level or at the 'establishment' level. The issue here is that a large firm may have many establishments that produce different goods and services and are classified under different industries. These establishments may be present in different regions of the country and their location is needed for geographical distribution of the statistics resulting from the survey. However, the recommendation in the *Oslo Manual* is that the enterprise is the most appropriate statistical unit (OECD/Eurostat 2005: 65, para. 234).

As business registers are important to all economic statistics, not just those for innovation, they are under constant review by statistical offices and they are the subject of a UN City Group, the Wiesbaden Group on Business Registers,[1] which meets regularly to discuss common problems.

Industry classifications

There are three main industrial classifications. They are the International Standard Industrial Classification (ISIC), the Statistical Classification of Economic Activities in the European Community (NACE) and the North American Industry Classification System (NAICS), which is used in Canada, the USA and Mexico. Countries may maintain separate industrial classification systems but for reporting to international organizations they will use ISIC or, to the supranational EU, NACE.

As economies change, and can change rapidly, these classifications are regularly revised by the UN (ISIC), Eurostat (NACE) or the statistical offices of Canada, Mexico and the USA (NAICS). Statistics Canada provides an overview of these classification systems.[2] The most recent versions are ISIC Rev. 4, NACE Rev. 2; NAICS, while providing a North American standard, is revised to reflect country issues at lower levels of aggregation. The current version in Canada is 2012, in the USA 2007 and in Mexico 2007.

Industrial classifications are not neutral activities, as they are, like any technology, used for purposes not originally intended and give rise to interest groups that influence their revision. For example, there is no biotechnology industry as biotechnology consists of a number of technologies that are used in production in some industries and are products in others. Biotechnology appears in bioremediation in environmental activities, human and animal health, plant research and food production. However, in the US version of NAICS there is a Research and Development in Biotechnology Industry, but not in Canada. This is found in Sector 54, Professional, scientific and technical services, Subsector 541, Professional, scientific and technical services, Industry Group 5417, Scientific research and development services, Industry 54171, Research and development in the physical, engineering and life sciences, and then Canadian industry 541710, Research and development in the physical, engineering and life sciences. The US NAICS is the same until US industry level, where there are two entries, 541711, Research and Development in Biotechnology, and 541712, Research and Development in the Physical, Engineering, and Life Sciences (except Biotechnology). International comparisons can be made at the industry level but not at the country level.

Coverage and industry classifications

The *Oslo Manual* makes specific recommendations for industrial coverage (OECD/Eurostat 2005: 68) based on ISIC Rev. 3.1 and NACE Rev. 1.1. It is clear that the *Oslo Manual* in its next revision will have to take account of the changes in the industrial classifications already made by the European Commission for the classification of business statistics. However, as it is 'the most recent version of the *Oslo Manual*', it will continue to provide the definition of innovation used to govern the collection under Regulation (EC) No. 1450/2004, 13 August 2004, amended 22 June 2009.

Size classification

Innovation, like R&D, is very dependent on the size of firm measured by turnover or revenue. The *Oslo Manual* recommends that size be measured on the basis of number of employees and that the employment cut-off be ten or more employees. A size classification is proposed, 10–49, 50–249, 250 and above, for the presentation of the statistics. Some countries use a cut-off of 20 employees (Canada) and others five (USA). A common cut-off for the presentation of the data is important for international comparisons.

Other Classifications

Classifications of the functions of government (COFOG)[3]

Chapter 17 introduces COFOG as part of the analysis of public sector innovation.

Education and occupation classifications

As more work is done on employee–employer relations as part of examining innovation arising from organizational change and use of business practices (Chapter 10), there will be more applications in innovation research of international classifications of education and of occupations. These are supported by different parts of the UN system.

The International Standard Classification of Education (ISCED), supported by UNESCO, has completed a revision, resulting in ISCED 2011.

The current International Standard Classification of Occupations (ISCO), supported by the International Labour Organizations (ILO), is ISCO-08.

NUTS – Nomenclature of Territorial Units for Statistics

The NUTS classification is a hierarchical system for dividing up the economic territory of the EU. For this handbook, the principal application of NUTS is its use in the collection, development and harmonization of EU regional statistics. See http://epp.eurostat.ec.europa.eu/portal/page/portal/nuts_nomenclature/introduction.

Most countries have a similar geographical classification system for their territories.

Notes

1. http://unstats.un.org/unsd/methods/citygroup/wiesbaden.htm.
2. http://www.statcan.gc.ca/concepts/industry-industrie-eng.htm.
3. http://unstats.un.org/unsd/cr/registry/regcst.asp?Cl=4.

3 History of the Community Innovation Survey

Anthony Arundel and Keith Smith

1. INTRODUCTION

The Community Innovation Survey (CIS) was first developed in the early 1990s. It arose from a shared view by researchers and policy makers that understanding the extent and distribution of innovation activity required direct and economy-wide indicators of innovation inputs and outputs at the firm level.[1] These included tangible and intangible investments in innovation, outputs in terms of sales of new or changed products, plus data on such topics as collaboration, and knowledge flows.

The first CIS has evolved into the largest innovation survey in the world based on the number of participating countries and the number of responding enterprises. It is conducted in the 27 member states of the European Union (EU) plus Norway and Iceland, and is used in many of the candidate states to the EU, such as Croatia and Turkey. The 2008 CIS, the most recent survey for which data are available, obtained responses from 196 000 enterprises in the EU-27 countries. The CIS has influenced the design of innovation survey questions in other countries, including Australia, Canada, China, Japan, New Zealand, Russia, South Africa, Switzerland and the USA. The frequency of the CIS was increased after 2004 from every four years to every two years. The last completed survey at the time of writing, CIS 2010, was implemented in 2011 and a proposed version of the questionnaire for the next survey, CIS 2012, was produced in July 2012.

The CIS survey produces policy-relevant indicators that are used in Europe's Innovation Union Scoreboard (IUS) and by the OECD. Six out of 25 indicators in the 2011 IUS are obtained from the CIS, including indicators for innovation expenditures as a share of turnover, the percentage of SMEs that develop innovations in house, and the percentage of turnover from new-to-market and new-to-firm innovations. In addition, the survey provides a rich data source for academic research. As shown in Figure 3.1, the number of academic papers, in English, that use CIS data has increased from fewer than ten per year before 2000 to over 50 per year after 2008. Academics also continue to be interested in each version of the

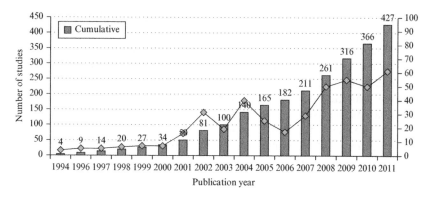

Source: N. Es-Sadki and A. Arundel, UNU-MERIT.

Figure 3.1   Academic papers (in English) using CIS data (1994–2011)

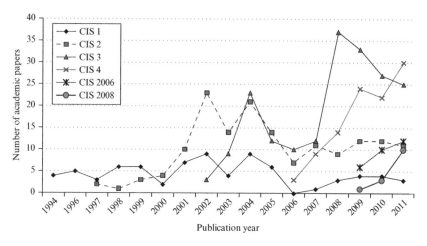

Source: N. Es-Sadki and A. Arundel, UNU-MERIT.

Figure 3.2   Use of each CIS version over time

CIS, due to different questions included in each survey and variations in data access. For example, in 2011, three academic papers were published using CIS 1 data and 11 were published using CIS 2 data (see Figure 3.2).

The CIS has its origins in the OECD's *Frascati Manual* on how to measure R&D, where it was recognized that R&D covered only a part of all innovation expenditures and innovation activities. This provided the motivation for a series of studies, dating back to the late 1950s, that sought to measure non-R&D innovation activities as well as innovation outputs. The types of questions included in the CIS were initially driven by academics involved in the design of innovation surveys, but over time the greatest influence on the CIS has gradually shifted from academics to the interest of policy analysts in innovation indicators and the interest of national statistical offices in obtaining comparable and reliable data while at the same time reducing the time required for respondents to answer the survey. The use of the CIS to produce indicators has been established in European law, with Commission Regulation 1450/2004 requiring all EU member states to provide Eurostat with a number of innovation indicators derived from the survey.

The CIS questionnaire is not static, with both minor and substantive changes to the questions made for every CIS. Some of the changes are driven by efforts to improve data quality or to solve problems with the interpretation of the data. Many of these issues date back to the period of experimentation with innovation measurement, from the 1950s to the first CIS survey (CIS 1) in 1993. For example, researchers active before and after the first CIS have grappled with how to improve the accuracy of data on innovation expenditures and how to improve the comparability of data derived from questions that use subjective definitions of innovation. Other changes to the CIS have been made to ensure that the questionnaire remains relevant for its main users, policy analysts and academics. This includes the 2008 decision to alternate questions between each consecutive CIS in order to create space for a module of one-off questions of interest to policy. Other changes have been made to improve the usefulness of the questionnaire for academic research. For example, the 2012 questionnaire includes a number of changes to support econometric research on the linkages between innovation and growth.

In this chapter we examine the history of the CIS, starting with its origins in the period of experimentation before the first CIS, followed by an evaluation of the changes to the survey questionnaire since CIS 1. Our focus is on the CIS questionnaire instead of the survey methodology, since the questionnaire determines the research questions that can be addressed using CIS data and the types of indicator that can be constructed from the data. The concluding section discusses some of the challenges for the future.

2.   EXPERIMENTATION WITH INNOVATION MEASUREMENT: THE 1950S TO 1993

Early survey research on innovation was initially limited to R&D, with R&D surveys conducted in Canada, the UK and the USA from the 1920s.

These developed into larger-scale surveys in the 1950s, with the NSF (National Science Foundation) conducting a survey of industrial R&D in 1953. The next major step in the development of R&D surveys was the work by the OECD in the early 1960s to develop standard definitions of R&D for use in surveys by OECD countries (Godin 2001a, 2001b). The definitions were published as the *Frascati Manual* (OECD 1963) and were used in the first attempt to conduct an internationally comparable R&D survey in 1963, with 16 participating countries.

The *Frascati Manual* has gone through six editions, with the most recent version from 2002 (OECD 2002). From the start, the contributors to the different editions of the *Frascati Manual* recognized that R&D was one of many inputs to innovation and that there was a need both to measure other inputs for innovation and to obtain output measures for innovation itself. This recognition increased with successive versions of the *Frascati Manual*, with the fourth edition from 1981 noting that R&D did not include many activities and steps to bring a product to market. Instead, the fourth edition states that innovation 'consists of all those scientific, technical, commercial and financial steps necessary for the successful development and marketing of new or improved manufactured products, the commercial use of new or improved processes or equipment or the introduction of a new approach to social service' (OECD 1981: 15–16).

The limitations of R&D as a measure of innovation created an interest in measuring innovation outputs, which began with measuring the innovation itself. Until the 1980s, the most common methodology for collecting innovation data was an object-based approach that gathered data on specific innovations, which constitute the 'object' of the study. Innovations were identified by technology experts or from advertisements or announcements in trade publications. Additional information on the innovation was obtained from follow-up questionnaires sent to the firm that developed each innovation. This information included the date of introduction, whether or not the innovation was a world-first development, the sources of ideas behind the innovation and the amount of investment in money or time to develop it (Hansen 1987).

According to Godin (2009), the earliest reported object-based innovation survey pre-dates the first *Frascati Manual* and was conducted in the late 1950s by Carter and Williams (1957). The study evaluated 201 innovations developed by 116 firms in the UK. Godin (2009: 9) also cites several object-based studies from the 1960s, including studies by Arthur D. Little (1963), the IIT Research Institute (1968) and a study by Myers and Marquis (1969) that was supported by the National Science Foundation. Hansen (1987) refers to an object-based study in the 1970s by Gellman

Research Associates and several other object-based studies funded by the NSF in the USA.

One of the largest object-based studies was conducted by academics from the Science Policy Research Unit (SPRU) in England. The survey was first conducted in the 1960s and later repeated in the 1970s and 1980s, with the final data set including information on 4378 innovations introduced between 1945 and 1983 (Townsend 1981; Pavitt et al. 1987). The relevance of this study to the CIS was due to its influence on the design of a research project in the early 1980s by de Bresson and Murray (1984) on innovations in Canada, which also covered innovations since 1945 and was funded by the Science Council of Canada. Instead of relying only on experts or trade journals to identify innovations, as in previous object-based research, de Bresson and Murray introduced several novel methods that influenced future research on innovation. First, they conducted a stratified random sample of all firms, including firms that were not previously identified as innovative, and asked the respondents to briefly describe their three most important innovations. Second, they provided a definition of innovation to guide the respondents' answers. The definition was as follows:

> By innovation we mean any new or improved product which has withstood the trial of the market and generated a return on investment, or a new or improved process for commercial production. By new we intend new to Canada.

This definition contains several features that were used in innovation surveys during the 1980s and consequently influenced the definition of innovation used by the CIS. First, it defined innovation as either a 'new or improved' product or process. Second, the innovation had to be implemented (it generated a return on investment), and third, there was a novelty requirement, although in this case the innovation did not need to be new to the world, but only 'new to Canada'. A follow-up telephone survey to respondents that reported at least one innovation requested additional information, including on the users of the innovation and on who developed the innovation. Response options for the latter included the firm itself, an affiliated firm, or a different firm. This question introduced the concept that a firm could innovate without having developed the innovation itself.

A few object-based innovation surveys were conducted after 1984, but the focus of innovation survey research shifted to a subject-based methodology where the unit of analysis was the firm (or product division) instead of the innovation. An early pioneer of this methodology was Humphrey Stead of Statistics Canada, who conducted surveys in the early 1970s in order to examine the R&D share of total innovation expenditures by firms (Stead 2001). Stead's work influenced Lothar Scholz of the German Institut für Wirtschaftsforschung (Ifo), who used the subject-based method in a 1979 survey. The questionnaire was sent to the product divisions of German industrial firms, rather than to the head office (Hansen 1987). The Ifo questionnaire defined innovation as 'new products or significant improvements of products as well as production and strategic technologies including the information techniques in administration'. The Ifo survey continues to be conducted on an annual basis.

The subject-based methodology has a major advantage over the object-based approach for measuring innovation: it can obtain information on all types of innovations from all firms, regardless of whether or not the firm innovated or if a particular innovation was successful. In contrast, the object-based approach, when based on experts or trade journals to identify innovations, is biased towards successful product innovations (Smith 1992). By contrast, subject surveys can also collect information on 'innovation outputs that are "routine", incremental, part of the normal competitive activity of firms, yet not strikingly new enough to be reported in trade journals' (ibid.: 385). This can include innovations that are new to the firm only, rather than being new to a market or even to the world. Subject-based surveys, at least for national statistical offices with access to a business register, are also less costly to implement because they do not require a lot of work to identify innovations in advance.

In addition to the Ifo survey, six other subject-based innovation surveys in Germany, the USA, the Netherlands, France, Italy and the Nordic countries were conducted in the 1980s and had a significant influence on the first CIS. These surveys tested a range of questions on innovation and often conducted pre-testing, either pilot surveys or interviews with respondents, to determine if respondents were able to answer the questions. Testing often resulted in extensive changes to questions, with researchers from the Fraunhofer Institute changing almost half of their proposed questions, but it is not known how many of the interviews in the different studies were conducted using best-practice standards for cognitive interviewing.[2] According to Smith (1992), the interviews found that respondents understood the questions, were able to answer them with reasonable precision, but rarely read detailed definitions – instead they worked with intuitive understandings derived from their readings of the question itself. The implications of this finding were not fully implemented until the fourth CIS was developed in 2004.

Most of these surveys asked similar questions on whether or not the firm innovated over a defined time period (usually five years), the number of innovations, the type of innovation, the source of ideas or other knowledge for innovation, collaboration, innovation objectives or effects, innovation barriers, and the sources of finance for innovation. Of particular interest are the treatment of key questions for expenditures on innovation and innovation outputs in terms of the percentage of sales from innovation (the innovation sales share), and questions on innovation novelty, non-technological innovation and the source of innovations. These key questions have been central to ongoing discussions on how to improve the CIS questionnaire and experimentation with these questions in the 1980s continues to be relevant.

The methodologies and key questions used in six of these surveys are summarized in Table 3.1, using the information gathered by Hansen (1987). Hansen interviewed the leading researchers for each of the surveys and consequently was able to obtain information on the survey methodology and pre-testing that was not available in published reports.

All six studies covered industrial or manufacturing firms or product divisions, with two studies limited to firms or divisions that performed R&D. Several studies that included non-R&D performers also found that considerably more firms than in the official R&D surveys reported R&D (Sirilli 1998). All of the survey questionnaires contained extensive questions on R&D activities, although many of the questions on innovation processes (information sources, barriers, objectives etc.) could apply to either R&D or non-R&D innovative activities.

All but one of the surveys included questions on innovation expenditures, including investments on activities other than R&D, and three surveys included a question on the innovation sales share. Most of the questions on expenditures requested the percentage of total innovation expenditures for each category, while the questions on innovation sales shares provided categorical response categories.

Several reviews have linked the definition of an innovation that is used in innovation surveys to Schumpeter's five types of innovation: new products, production methods, exploiting new markets, new methods for organizing business activities, and new sources of supply (Godin 2009; Smith 1992). Schumpeter also noted that innovations could be incremental or involve radical, disruptive new technologies (Schumpeter 1934). The innovation surveys of the 1980s consistently appeared to follow Schumpeter by including new products and production methods (processes) in their definitions of innovation, but only the surveys by Ifo and the 1984 survey by the National Institute of Statistics in Italy (Istat) included a reference to organizational innovation (although only in the 1984 scoping survey) and none of the surveys examined new markets and sources of supply or attempted to collect data on radical innovations.

The roots of innovation surveys in the *Frascati Manual* created an important ambiguity over the definition of innovation and consequently

Table 3.1 Subject-based innovation surveys in the 1980s

Country & year	Question pre-testing	Sampling unit and Definition of innovation	Number of respondents	Questions
Germany (Ifo), 1979	Interviews with firms, but no details provided	Unit: product divisions within firms Definition: 'new products or significant improvements of products as well as production and strategic technologies including information techniques in administration' Reference period one year	400 in 1979, up to 1500 units in mid-1980s	*Expenditures*: percentage of total innovation expenditures in 8 categories, including 'preparation for selling new products' *Innovation sales share*: not asked *Innovation novelty*: questions on the underlying technologies behind product and process innovations *Non-technological innovation*: process innovations related to administration *Who developed*: not asked
Germany (Fraunhofer), 1980 and 1983	10 interviews with firms using cognitive testing principles; half of questions changed as a result	Unit: R&D-performing SMEs (fewer than 1000 employees) participating in government R&D subsidy programmes Definition: None provided, but survey limited to R&D-performing SMEs. Some of the questions refer to R&D projects. Reference period of five years	700 in 1980 and 780 in 1983	*Expenditures*: distribution of total innovation expenditures over past 5 years for R&D up to prototype stage, gearing up production, and market introduction costs *Innovation sales share*: categories for share from products introduced in the last 5 years that were new to the enterprise and those that were 'entirely new technological applications' *Innovation novelty*: 'entirely new technological applications' *Non-technological innovation*: not asked *Who developed*: not asked as focus on in-house R&D projects

Table 3.1 (continued)

Country & year	Question pre-testing	Sampling unit and Definition of innovation	Number of respondents	Questions
MIT, USA, 1984	Discussion of questions with potential respondents and pre-testing with 9 firms followed by 60 firms; 12 in-person follow-up interviews with respondents to 1984 survey	Unit: *Business Week* list of firms that performed R&D and with more than US$30 million in sales Definition: none provided, but survey limited to R&D performing firms	300 to 1984 survey	*Expenditures*: 5 categories of non-R&D expenditures, including equipment purchases and marketing *Innovation sales share*: percentage categories for products introduced in previous 5 years *Innovation novelty*: limited to R&D-performing firms *Non-technological innovation*: not asked *Who developed*: not asked
France, 1984	Tested with experts, but not with potential respondents	Interviews with stratified sample of firms with 50 to 2000 employees in 10 industrial sectors Definition: none; firms asked to provide their own definition Reference period of possibly 5 years, but not always specified	302, of which 146 did not report R&D	*Expenditures*: total cost of innovation activities plus expenditures by 7 categories, including investment in new production equipment and on marketing *Innovation sales share*: not asked *Innovation novelty*: level of change from previous products, three-point scale for level of technology, and questions on first to world, first to France, first to firm; main novel features of their recent innovations; time to develop three principal innovations from beginning of

| Netherlands, 1983 and 1984 | 10 firms sent a questionnaire to determine if respondents could answer the questions; interviews with respondents to 1983 survey, resulting in some questions being dropped | Unit: 1984 survey sent to a sample of 2900 manufacturing firms drawn from the Dutch Chamber of Commerce
Definition: a product innovation is 'the market introduction of products that in your opinion are entirely new for your enterprise, or which show considerable technical improvements with regard to former products'. A process innovation is 'the introduction of production techniques which in your opinion are entirely new for your enterprise or which are considered technically improved with regard to former production techniques'
Reference period: not given | 130 in 1983, 1842 in 1984 | R&D to commercialization (less than a year, 1 to 2 years, over 2 years)
Non-technological innovation: not asked
Who developed: in-house or external development of process innovations
Expenditures: not asked
Innovation sales share: not asked
Innovation novelty: number of new-to-firm and new-to-the-Netherlands product innovations; categories for average time required to develop product, process and combined product–process innovations
Non-technological innovation: not asked
Who developed: not asked |

Table 3.1 (continued)

Country & year	Question pre-testing	Sampling unit and Definition of innovation	Number of respondents	Questions
ISTAT, Italy, 1984 and 1987	Interviews with 25 firms for preparation of 1987 survey	Unit: for 1984 survey manufacturing firms with 20 or more employees; for 1987 survey limited to 16000 innovative firms that replied to the 1984 survey Definition for 1987 survey: 'a product that allows the firm to enter a new market, a product substantially new from a technological point of view when compared to products previously produced'; 'a process designed to produce new or improved products otherwise not producible using existing systems. Also the application of new techniques' Reference period: 3 years	24 500 in 1984, 8220 in 1987	*Expenditures*: total investment in new processes; average share of total innovation expenditures by development stage (R&D, engineering, pilot projects, and marketing) *Innovation sales share*: categorical percentage response options for share of sales in 1985 from innovations introduced over 3 years *Innovation novelty*: average time between the start of an innovation project and the beginning of production; novelty of research; number of new-to-firm, new-to-region, and new-to-Italy product innovations *Non-technological innovation*: asked about organizational innovation in 1984, but not included in 1987 survey *Who developed*: not asked

Note: The leading researchers in each of the above studies include Lothar Scholz (Ifo), Frieder Meyer-Krahmer (Fraunhofer), John Hansen and Christopher Hill (USA), Andre Piatier (France), Alfred Kleinknecht (Netherlands) and Giorgio Sirilli (Italy).

Source: Hansen (1987).

what innovation surveys were designed to measure. The perspective of the *Frascati Manual* is that innovation is a supplementary activity to R&D, in that R&D-performing firms must make other investments to develop an R&D project into a commercially useful product or process. Pavitt supported this perspective in a 1976 paper for the OECD (Godin 2009: 6). The MIT and Fraunhofer studies took this approach by limiting the surveyed population to R&D-performing firms. The alternative perspective is that innovation is a unique activity that may or may not be combined with R&D. This perspective was partly supported by Kline and Rosenberg's (1986) chain link model of innovation, where the inspiration and source of information for an innovation can come from many sources other than the R&D department. However, Kline and Rosenberg's model can also be interpreted as largely applying to R&D-performing firms, with management choosing between several strategies for developing an innovation.

De Bresson and Murray (1984), by defining 'new to Canada' products and processes as an innovation, had widened the definition of innovation to include technologies that the firm may not have developed. In effect, this combined the concept of technology production with the concept of technology diffusion, as a firm that implemented a pre-existing technology obtained from another firm was the recipient of a diffusion process. Most previous research on innovation tended to separate the production of innovations from their diffusion and study them as two distinct processes (David 2011).

Only the French survey directly asked if the firm had introduced innovations that were developed by other firms, although this option was only provided for process innovations. Otherwise, many of the six surveys summarized in Table 3.1 were ambiguous on this issue. The Dutch, French and Italian surveys asked if the firm had introduced an innovation that was only new to the firm or its local region, implying that these innovations could have been obtained from external sources, but this possibility was not explicitly recognized in the definition of an innovation. This ambiguity in most of the surveys from the 1980s over who developed the innovation could have been due to the importance given by academics to in-house R&D, with the assumption that R&D-performing firms developed at least some of their innovations through their own in-house activities. This ambiguity also continued with the first *Oslo Manual* and the first CIS.

Three of the six surveys provided definitions of a product and a process innovation. Two surveys that were limited to R&D-performing firms did not include a definition of innovation, presumably because responding firms were assumed to innovate, and the French survey allowed firms to provide their own definitions of an innovation. The three surveys that defined innovation included both entirely new products or processes and improved products or processes.

Including in the definition innovations that are only new to the firm creates substantial problems of comparability across firms because it includes as innovative both firms that only buy in new technology and firms that invest considerable financial resources to develop an innovation. Several of the questionnaires provided an opportunity to address the subjective element of these definitions by including other questions to establish the novelty of the firm's innovations. As shown in Table 3.1, two methods were commonly used to do so. The first was to ask if the firm had introduced innovations that were new to its country, while the second asked for the average amount of time required to develop an innovation from the initial stages to commercialization.

Other surveys in the late 1980s also contributed to innovation measurement and influenced the CIS. The Nordic Innovation Indicators Group conducted a survey of innovation in manufacturing firms located in Finland, Norway, Sweden and Denmark. Its main contribution was to implement a coordinated survey of innovation in four countries. The survey included questions that were similar to those used in the earlier studies in Germany, France, the Netherlands, Italy and the USA (Smith 1992). In respect to 'who developed' the innovation, the Nordic survey provided conflicting definitions of an innovation. A wide definition of product innovation was offered early on in the questionnaire as 'new products and substantial improvements of old products', but a later definition stressed in-house R&D, with product innovations defined as deriving from 'R&D projects that have resulted in marketable new products or essential improvements in existing products' (Smith 1992: 388). Finally, an American survey in the mid-1980s of R&D-performing firms examined appropriation strategies, technological opportunities and technological advance (Levin et al. 1987). The survey influenced the design of a question in CIS 1 on the importance of several appropriation strategies.

3.   THE SYNTHESIS: THE FIRST *OSLO MANUAL* AND CIS 1

The OECD actively encouraged research on the measurement of innovation from the early 1980s, holding a conference in September 1980 on S&T indicators (OECD 1992). One of the goals was to 'reach a consensus on R&D output indicators', which essentially required indicators of innovation. A paper on 'New innovation indicators: conceptual basis and practical problems' was prepared by Keith Smith and presented to an OECD meeting of the National Experts on Science and Technology Indicators (NESTI) in November 1989. It drew on the results of the six surveys summarized in Table 3.1 plus the experience of the Nordic Indicators Group.

The need for better innovation indicators was translated into action by the efforts of the OECD's Technology Economy Programme (TEP), which ran between 1992 and 1994. The TEP was an extraordinarily wide-ranging networking initiative led by Robert Chabbal of the Directorate for Science, Technology and Industry (DSTI) in the OECD, bringing in researchers from around the world to discuss innovation and growth, the innovation research agenda, indicator needs (to do with human resources as well as innovation) and policy implications. On the indicators issue, a small working group met on a number of occasions, especially in Oslo, to discuss the definitional and collection issues and eventually to draft a set of guidelines for data collection. This group included Lothar Scholz, Giorgio Sirilli, Alfred Kleinknecht, John Hansen, Chris de Bresson and Keith Smith. The group provided the impetus for the draft *Oslo Manual,* or *Proposed Guidelines for Collecting and Interpreting Technological Innovation Data,* which was written by Keith Smith and Mikael Akerblom of the Finnish Statistical Office, and approved by the OECD's NESTI Working Party in 1992.

The first *Oslo Manual* identified six core issues for innovation survey research that included both the production of output indicators and the collection of process-oriented data on corporate strategies such as diffusion, the sources of innovative ideas and obstacles to innovation, the role of public policy and innovation inputs. The manual set out several basic concepts that continue to influence the design of the CIS and ongoing innovation research. For example, the manual, although focused on technological product and process innovation, noted that innovation can occur anywhere, including the public sector and the services sector (OECD 1992: para. 84). Research on service sector innovation expanded in the 1990s and in the first decade of the 2000s several exploratory surveys of innovation in the public sector were conducted that replicated the history of innovation surveys of private sector firms. The early surveys used the object-based method (Borins 2001; NAO 2006), while the later surveys, inspired by the *Oslo Manual,* adopted the subject-based method (Arundel and Hollanders 2011; Bugge et al. 2011; Hughes et al. 2011; APSC 2011).

Unfortunately, the manual was not completely clear on the relationship between R&D and innovation. The first *Oslo Manual* notes that 'the core task is to integrate an understanding of the R&D contribution with an account of the non-R&D inputs to the innovation process' and that we need an 'overview of the balance which firms strike between R&D and non-R&D activities' (OECD 1992: para. 71). The paragraph suggests that innovation is a supplementary activity to R&D, although the definition of a technological innovation in paragraph 90 describes a process that does not necessarily require R&D. The ambiguity over the relationship between R&D and innovation continued through the first three CIS surveys.

In respect of the subjective nature of the definition of innovation, the first *Oslo Manual* suggests that the distinguishing factors that differentiate an innovation from a change that is not an innovation are 'elements of novelty and significance', but gives little further assistance other than to note that these elements are 'difficult to specify'. The reliance on 'elements of novelty' is similar to the definition of R&D in the *Frascati Manual*, which defines the difference between R&D and other problem-solving activities as based on an 'appreciable element of novelty and the resolution of scientific and/or technological uncertainty, i.e. when the solution to a problem is not readily apparent to someone familiar with the basic stock of common knowledge and techniques for the area concerned' (OECD 2002: 34). In paragraphs 146 and 147 the *Oslo Manual* suggests several questions to identify novelty, such as on the use of new materials or new production techniques.

The *Olso Manual* would have remained nothing more than a set of guidelines had it not been for the intervention of the European Commission. The Commission had at that time a programme in DG-XIII (later DG Enterprise) known as the European Innovation Monitoring System (EIMS), which undertook a wide range of analytical projects on innovation policy. EIMS was led by a visionary official, Gerhard Bräunling, who decided to implement the *Oslo Manual* as a Europe-wide survey, funded by the EIMS and organized and coordinated by Eurostat. The relevant Eurostat official, Werner Grünewald, saw the opportunity to create a much-needed set of policy indicators, and gave the project strong support. This led directly to the Community Innovation Survey (the title was Bräunling's contribution).[3]

The development of the first CIS, according to Smith (1997: 20), 'required a long process of discussions to seek a consensus on what types of firms should be included and what types of questions should be asked'. Many of the first *Oslo Manual's* recommendations for questions on innovation were not included in CIS 1. These include questions on the number of product and process innovations, the number of new-to-the-world innovations in order to give an 'impression of the originality of innovations' (para. 149) and an open question asking for a description of an innovation (para. 176). Similarly, not all recommendations in the second and third *Oslo Manual* were implemented in later versions of the CIS.

In several respects, CIS 1 was a large-scale pilot survey for innovation measurement, with 14 participating countries using different survey methods, survey units (establishment or enterprise) and follow-up protocols (Archibugi et al. 1997). The lack of a standard survey methodology and the absence of consistent participation by official statistical agencies led to large differences in response rates and the complete failure of the survey in the UK, where the survey was implemented by the Confederation of British Industry and the response rate was lower than 5 per cent. The standard questionnaire was based on the experience of the surveys of the 1980s, many of which had undergone some testing, but CIS 1 included many new questions and changes that had not been fully tested. But it laid the groundwork for what was to come.

The EIMS did not confine itself to coordinating the first CIS. It also funded over a dozen academic analyses of the CIS 1 data, with the results presented to a major 1996 conference in Luxembourg titled 'Innovation Measurement and Policies' (Arundel and Garrelfs 1997).

Godin (2009) argues that the main goal of the OECD and Eurostat for innovation surveys was to produce output indicators, a goal that arguably was not satisfactorily met because the surveys only produced two output indicators, the innovation sales share and the percentage of firms that innovated. The comparability of the latter indicator across sectors and countries was reduced by the highly subjective definition of product and process innovation that was used in the CIS. An examination of the history of innovation surveys, however, shows that the primary driver of innovation research was not statistical agencies but academics, although often with the support of government agencies interested in indicators, such as the NSF, Statistics Canada or the European Commission. Academic involvement ensured that innovation surveys collected microdata of value for research into four areas of economic theory: interactive models of innovation; evolutionary economics; the role of learning in innovation; and national systems of innovation (Smith 1997). The use of innovation surveys to produce indicators was not compulsory for the CIS until the implementation in 2004 of European Commission Regulation 1450/2004.

4.   CIS 2 TO CIS 4

Each CIS questionnaire since CIS 1 has been altered, either to improve respondent understanding and consequently the quality of responses, or to obtain new information on innovation. Eurostat has coordinated changes to the standard CIS questionnaire, for use by all member states of the EU, with the assistance of an expert responsible for collecting proposals and drawing up different draft versions of the questionnaire. Countries may add questions to the standard CIS and several countries have also altered the wording or response categories of some of the standard questions. Of note, this history is limited to changes to the standard questionnaire.

Up to and including CIS 2006, changes to the questionnaire were suggested and discussed by a committee that included all participating national statistical offices (NSOs). Due to the increasing number of participating NSOs, Veijo-Ismo Ritola of Eurostat replaced the full committee with a smaller CIS task force, consisting of approximately ten volunteer NSOs. Since CIS 2008, the Task Force has been responsible for developing a draft questionnaire that is presented to a meeting of all participating NSOs for discussion. As before, the final decision on which changes to accept or reject is made by consensus.

From CIS 4, Eurostat has required the external expert responsible for coordinating the changes to the CIS to produce a comprehensive final report that documents the reasons for all changes to the CIS questionnaire and the results of any pilot or cognitive testing. The reports also include other material of interest, such as the results of surveys of NSOs, academics and policy analysts on their use of CIS data.

Using the Eurostat reports and other documents, the history of the CIS after CIS 1 can be divided into two periods. Up until the fourth CIS (implemented in 2005 and referring to innovation activities between 2002 and 2004), the CIS underwent several substantial changes to some of the main concepts and definitions in order to address the ambiguity over who developed the innovation and the role of R&D. In addition, the coverage of innovation was expanded to include non-technological organizational and marketing innovation. By CIS 4, the main questions and questionnaire structure had crystallized. The need for consensus resulted in resistance to further substantial changes, with several NSOs preferring to maintain continuity over time in the indicators. For instance, a proposed CIS 4 questionnaire that gave equal treatment to product, process, organizational and marketing innovation was rejected in a meeting of representatives from all NSOs because it would destroy comparability with earlier CIS results for product and process innovation (Arundel and Bordoy 2005). Later attempts to develop a questionnaire that did not give preferential treatment to product and process innovation were also unsuccessful. Consequently, changes to the questionnaire after CIS 4 have been minor, with some exceptions discussed below. Table 3.2 provides an overview of the main changes to the CIS questionnaire, from CIS 2 to CIS 2012.

The largest changes to the CIS questionnaire were made for CIS 2. Mikael Åkerblom (1996), as the coordinating expert, proposed several substantive changes in a paper circulated to the participating NSOs and

Table 3.2 Overview of the CIS questionnaires

Survey	Observation period	Main changes or additions compared to the previous survey
CIS 1	1990–1992	–
CIS 2	1994–1996	Added questions on who developed product and process innovations
		Cooperation question extended from R&D only to include 'joint R&D and other innovation projects'
		Deleted questions on sources of new technology, technology transfer outside the enterprise, appropriation methods and product life cycles
		Separate questionnaire developed for service sector firms
CIS 3	1998–2000	Only one questionnaire for service and manufacturing firms, with improved relevance for service innovations by no longer referring to 'technological' product and process innovations
		Changed question on the innovation sales share from the share of sales from new products, improved products and unchanged products to the share of sales from unchanged, new-to-firm and new-to-market products
CIS 4	2002–2004	Added questions on three types of organizational innovation and two types of marketing innovation, plus questions on the effects of organizational innovation
		Under product innovation included separate questions for goods and services. Asked about three types of process innovations
		Cooperation question removes reference to 'active participation in joint R&D'
CIS 2006	2004–2006	Frequency increased to every 2 years
		Implemented cognitive testing for all question changes and additions
CIS 2008	2006–2008	Increased coverage of organizational and marketing innovation
		Introduced a rotating one-page module for questions of high policy interest, with the first module on environmental innovation
CIS 2010	2008–2010	Separate question on expenditures for design
		Module on creativity and skills
CIS 2012	2010–2012	Module on strategies and obstacles to growth, plus minor changes throughout the questionnaire to support econometric research on the link between innovation and growth
		Reintroduced a modified version of the CIS 1 appropriation question
		Added questions on the effect of the public sector and public procurement on innovation

Source: Authors.

77

to several external experts. One of the changes was to develop a modified questionnaire to be sent to service sector firms in order to meet the second *Oslo Manual's* (OECD/Eurostat 1997) recommendation to extend innovation surveys to cover selected service sectors. Other suggestions included reducing the lower bound for firm size from 20 to 10 employees, considerably reducing the length of the questionnaire to improve response rates and including an open question on the firm's most important innovation.

Åkerblom proposed deleting several questions in CIS 1 to reduce the questionnaire length: two questions on technology acquisition and technology transfer on the grounds that it was difficult to interpret the results to these questions; a question on appropriation; a question on product life cycles that accordingly produced unusable results due to very low response rates (Young 1997); and a question on exports from new or changed products that was very similar to the innovation sales share question and consequently added little additional information. The questionnaire length was also shortened by reducing the number of sub-questions on information sources, objectives and hampering factors, with the latter reduced from 18 to nine.

In addition to the question on the firm's most important innovation, Åkerblom proposed several new questions that were not included in the final version of CIS 2, for example questions on the factors that caused an increase in productivity, the frequency of introduction of new products or processes, the firm's main supplier of information and main customer, the time required to develop innovations, the expected pay-off period and the total budget. Conversely, several of Åkerblom's suggestions for new questions were accepted, including a question on incomplete or abandoned innovations, the use of government support, and if the firm had applied for at least one patent.

In addition to the major deletions and simplifications made to the CIS 2 questionnaire, significant changes were made up to and including CIS 4 to: (1) build all definitions into the question; (2) reduce the CIS emphasis on R&D; (3) improve the output questions on innovation expenditures and the innovation sales share; and (4) add questions on organizational and marketing innovations.

Definitions

CIS 1 and CIS 2 included lengthy definitions in preambles before questions, for instance to define product and process innovations and different types of innovation activities. The length of the definitions was reduced for CIS 3, but from CIS 4 all definitions were built into the question itself, wherever possible, to force respondents to read the question and to take advantage of the opportunity to collect additional data. For instance, CIS 4 used separate questions to determine if the firm introduced each of three types of process innovations, whereas CIS 3 used one question that referred to a lengthy definition of process innovation in a preamble.

Resolving the R&D Question

The CIS questionnaire's bias towards R&D was reduced by resolving the ambiguity over the status of innovative activities that did not require R&D. As a first step, CIS 2 added a question, proposed by Niels de Lanoy of the Dutch Central Bureau of Statistics, on 'who developed' product and process innovations. The options included 'mainly other enterprises or institutes', 'your enterprise and other enterprises or institutes' and 'mainly other enterprises or institutes'.[4] Respondents could tick one or more of these options, as relevant. The last option was designed to capture product and process innovations that firms primarily acquired from external sources. However, the definition of a product and process innovation in CIS 2 did not specify that an innovation only needed to be 'new to the enterprise', which was included as the minimum threshold for an innovation in the second edition of the *Oslo Manual* (OECD/Eurostat 1997). This change was made in the third CIS, which noted that a product or process innovation only needed to be 'new to your enterprise' and therefore could have been developed by 'your enterprise or by another enterprise'.

The question on cooperation for innovation was also changed over time to reduce the emphasis on R&D. In CIS 1 the question asked 'did your enterprise have any cooperation arrangements on R&D activities with other enterprises or institutions?' The requirement for R&D was reduced in CIS 2 and CIS 3, with innovation cooperation defined as 'joint R&D and other innovations projects' in CIS 2 and as 'active participation in joint R&D and other innovation projects' in CIS 3. In CIS 4 the reference to 'R&D projects' was finally removed, due to concerns that the inclusion of 'R&D' would still give a priority to R&D-based collaboration activities (Arundel and Bordoy 2005: 79).

Innovation Output Questions

The results for the CIS 1 survey showed that approximately 45 per cent of respondents by country did not answer the questions on the percentage of product sales by innovative novelty (unchanged, incrementally changed and significantly changed or new) and 37.5 per cent did not answer the questions on the percentage of total innovation expenditures for R&D

and other innovation activities (Arundel et al. 2007: Table B2). As these are the two main output questions for CIS, they have undergone extensive changes over time to improve response rates and data quality.

The structure of the innovation sales share question was changed for CIS 2 and changed again for CIS 3, with a shift in focus to the share of sales for products that were only new to the firm and the share from products that were new to the firm's market. Yet both CIS 2 and CIS 3 had made the question more complex than in CIS 1 by also attempting to obtain data on the innovation sales shares by level of novelty. CIS 4 reduced the complexity of the question by only asking for the percentage of sales in terms of the firm's market and by providing a definition of the firm's market (Arundel and Bordoy 2005: 74). Since then, the innovation sales share question has remained unchanged, except for a few minor changes in wording. Non-response rates to this question dropped to less than 3 per cent for CIS 4 (Arundel et al. 2007: Table B2).

The innovation expenditure question has undergone several changes in order to increase the reliability of the responses. One option that was considered for CIS 3 was to only ask for qualitative data on innovation activities (Foyn 2006). This option was rejected because of strong policy interest in expenditure data.

The basic format of the innovation expenditure question was reached for CIS 4, which made two substantive changes to the expenditure question compared to earlier versions of the CIS. First, the definitions of innovation activities were included in the question (instead of in a lengthy preamble as in CIS 2) and second, the question was split into two parts. The first part asked, on a yes-or-no basis, if the firm engaged in different types of innovation activities. The second part asked for expenditure data for four main activities: in-house R&D; external R&D; acquisitions of machinery, equipment and software; and acquisition of other external knowledge. These changes increased the response rate for the innovation expenditure question from an average of approximately 64 per cent for CIS 1 to 85 per cent for CIS 4 (Arundel et al. 2007: Table B2).

There are ongoing concerns over the comparability of the responses to the question on innovation expenditures across countries, although less so within countries. Only 3.2 per cent of 28 NSOs, surveyed in October 2010, gave a rating of 'poor' or 'moderate' for within-country comparability for the expenditure question on the acquisition of machinery, equipment and software (Arundel et al. 2010: 28). Some of the concerns over the expenditure question have been addressed by NSOs by adopting best-practice survey methods, such as contacting firms to verify unusually high or low expenditure data. In addition, alternative versions of the expenditure data question underwent cognitive testing as part of the preparatory work for

CIS 2012. One version asked for total expenditures by activity and then for the share of the total that was for innovation. For example, respondents were asked to give their firm's total expenditures for new machinery, equipment and software and then asked for the share of these expenditures that were related to innovation. None of the alternative versions of the question performed better in the cognitive tests than the version that has been in use since CIS 4.[5]

Organizational and Marketing Innovation

Annex 2 of the second *Oslo Manual* (OECD/Eurostat 1997) discussed the measurement of non-technological innovations, consisting of organizational and managerial innovations. The first questions on non-technological innovations were included in CIS 3 (developed in 2000). The question asked if the firm had introduced a new strategy, management technique, organizational structure, marketing concept or significant change to the aesthetic appearance or design of products. CIS 4 included questions on three types of organizational innovations and two types of marketing innovations, along with a question on the effects of organizational innovations. The questions on non-technological innovations were expanded for CIS 2008 to meet the requirements of the third *Oslo Manual* (OECD/Eurostat 2005), but the basic framework of these questions has remained the same, with questions on different types of organizational and marketing innovations followed by a question on their effects. A series of more ambitious questions on both organizational and marketing innovation and on knowledge management had been proposed for pilot surveys and cognitive testing as part of the work to develop CIS 2006, with Denmark testing these questions in pilot surveys. The questions on organizational and marketing innovation asked who developed the innovation, if the innovation was linked to product or process innovations, the effects of the innovation, and the reasons for not introducing an organizational or marketing innovation (Arundel et al. 2007: 54–8). Yet, for space reasons, the CIS has never included a full set of questions on non-technological innovation.

5.   CIS 2006 TO CIS 2012

The preparatory work for CIS 4 by UNU-MERIT included an evaluation of the use of CIS questions by academics (based on analysis of academic studies using CIS data) and a survey of the use of the CIS by policy analysts. The results found that academics rarely used CIS questions on innovation objectives and hampering factors, indicating that these questions did not need to be included in every CIS, and that policy analysts continued to rely on R&D and patent statistics. The main impact of the CIS on policy analysts had not been via indicators, but through academic research that showed that R&D and innovation were not the same. These CIS results 'had a diffuse effect on the innovation strategies of national governments and the European Commission, but rarely had a direct and identifiable impact on specific policy initiatives' (Arundel and Bordoy 2005: 109).

The CIS 4 report made 11 recommendations on how to improve the reliability and quality of CIS data and the value of the CIS to policy and academic users. Five recommendations were implemented by Eurostat: (1) improved data access for academics by means of a safe centre that provided secure data access; (2) the preparation of a quality report after each survey to collect data from all EU countries on question non-response rates and other information of value to the design of each CIS; (3) the implementation of field or cognitive face-to-face testing of all new questions or changes to existing questions; (4) basing all question changes on empirical evidence on data quality and the relevance of the question to users; and (5) the inclusion of policy users in the decision process for each CIS.

The third recommendation, for cognitive testing of all changes, had been strongly supported by Mark Pollard of the UK Office of National Statistics for several years. Since extensive testing for CIS 1, cognitive testing of changes to the CIS had been haphazard. France had conducted 34 cognitive interviews for CIS 2 and the Dutch Central Bureau of Statistics had tested several layouts for the CIS questionnaire (Foyn 1999), but there had been no organized method of conducting comparable testing in more than one country or sharing cognitive testing results between countries. In response to the recommendations of the CIS 4 report, pilot testing was implemented for CIS 2006 and since CIS 2008 all new and altered questions have undergone two rounds of cognitive testing in several countries.

Many proposed CIS questions that were cognitively tested failed, for instance if the question was interpreted differently by various interviewees or if several interviewees could not understand the question. Other questions passed testing, but were not used in the CIS due to space constraints. The UNU-MERIT reports for CIS 2006, CIS 2008 (Arundel et al. 2009) and CIS 2010 provide full details for the cognitive testing results. Annex A of the report for CIS 2010 provides a summary of tested questions that have not been used in the CIS (Arundel et al. 2010). This information can assist future research on innovation surveys by identifying the problems with tested questions and by providing a library of successful although unused questions on a range of topics.

As noted above, the main CIS questions have changed little since CIS 4, other than minor additions, deletions or wording changes. Nevertheless, several significant changes were included for CIS 2008 to ensure that the questionnaire remained flexible and relevant to changing policy interests. The CIS 2008 Task Force recommended including a one-page module of questions that could change every year in response to policy interest. To keep the questionnaire short, space for the module has been created by rotating questions that ask about factors that change slowly over time. These consist of the questions on hampering factors, intellectual property, information sources and innovation objectives. The first module for CIS 2008 covered environmental innovation, the second module for CIS 2010 asked about creativity and skills, and the module for CIS 2012 asks about the effects of strategies and obstacles for growth.

Flexibility can also be created by making minor changes throughout the CIS questionnaire. CIS 2010 improved coverage of the service sector by asking separate questions on goods and service innovations in the question group on product innovations. The proposed CIS 2012 questionnaire made several minor changes throughout the questionnaire to gather better data on the role of the public sector in private sector innovation. This included the addition of a question on the importance of 'clients or customers from the public sector' to the questions on information sources and cooperation and a new question on public procurement. These questions will complement ongoing work to measure innovation in the public sector.

Concern over the comparability of an innovation across sectors and countries has led to several additional changes after CIS 4 to identify the novelty of innovations. At the Blue Sky Forum in Ottawa in 2006, Svein Olaf Nas recommended adding a question on modifications and minor changes to existing processes and products obtained from other firms. This idea was picked up and included in a 'who developed' question in the 2007 Innobarometer Survey, designed to explore how non-R&D-performing firms innovate. The question was later added to the 2010 CIS. Extensive cognitive testing of questions on 'world-first' product innovations and new-to-market process innovations were conducted for CIS 2010 and CIS 2012, with a question on world-first product innovations and new-to-market process innovations added to CIS 2010. Cognitive testing for 2012 confirmed that respondents could answer an additional question on the share of total turnover from world-first product innovations.

Several perennial issues have been evaluated for almost every CIS survey since CIS 4 without reaching agreement. These include whether or not to provide equal coverage for organizational and marketing innovations, the

length of the observation period (two or three years), and if the questionnaire should be redesigned to avoid filter questions that currently send
non-innovators to the end of the questionnaire.

6.   CONCLUSION: FUTURE CHALLENGES FOR THE CIS

The future of the CIS depends on improving data quality and keeping the
survey relevant for policy and academic users. The addition of a question
module since CIS 2008 helps to maintain the interest of both sets of users,
as will questions on the role of the public sector, which can complement
current research on public sector innovation.

Other steps could also help to improve the relevance of the CIS. Eurostat
(2012) currently publishes over 90 types of innovation indicators drawn
from the CIS. However, all these indicators are based on one question, for
instance the percentage of small firms that collaborate with clients or customers. This does not solve the novelty problem for innovative firms as the
results combine highly innovative firms with weakly innovative firms. The
more recent versions of the CIS include data that could be used to classify
firms by innovative capability. For instance, indicators could be provided
for firms that are world-first product innovators or for firms that are both
world-first product innovators and active on global markets (Arundel
2007). These types of compound indicators could considerably improve
comparability across countries.

Another limitation is that the main CIS output indicator, the innovation sales share, is limited to product innovations. There are no output
indicators for process innovations or for organizational and marketing
innovations. An option is to collect data on the effects of these innovations on costs. Questions to collect output measures of process innovation have undergone preliminary cognitive testing (Arundel et al. 2010:
58), but 25 per cent of the interviewees could not answer the question.
Additional question development and testing would be required to reduce
this percentage.

An option for the CIS that has been supported by some countries,
including the USA, is to combine the innovation survey and the R&D
survey. This would create cost savings and possibly reduce respondent
burden. A concern expressed by many CIS Task Force members is that
combining the two surveys would give respondents the impression that
R&D is the dominant form of innovation, which if true would be a retro-
grade step, given the changes to the CIS over time to separate R&D from
innovation. So far, there is a lack of good empirical evidence on the effect

of combining the innovation and R&D surveys. An exception is a study by the Norwegian Statistical Office (Wilhelmsen 2012), which randomly assigned firms to two groups, one of which received the innovation survey by itself while the other received a combined R&D and innovation survey. The results are equivocal. The percentage of firms reporting product or process innovation was significantly lower in the combined survey compared to the separate innovation survey, but the differences were not statistically significant for the percentage of firms that introduced a marketing or organizational innovation (although for both the percentage was notably lower in the combined survey). Aggregated total innovation expenditures did not differ between the two surveys. Some of these results are a cause for concern, but similar studies would need to be conducted in other countries before concluding that a combined survey would be able to provide innovation data that are unbiased by proximity to a considerable number of questions on R&D.

NOTES

1. Most innovation surveys cover enterprises (the smallest legally defined business unit), but for simplicity this chapter uses the term 'firm'.
2. See Collins (2003), Noel and Prizeman (2005) and Qureschi and Rowlands (2004) for a discussion of cognitive testing methods and examples of applications.
3. Bräunling was also responsible for the creation of TrendChart, another major Commission innovation policy initiative.
4. The next four CIS asked respondents to select the most appropriate option of the 'who developed' question (CIS 3, CIS 4, CIS 2006 and CIS 2008), but from CIS 2010 the question reverted to asking respondents to select all relevant options. This was done to be able to calculate the percentage of firms that only innovated through acquiring product and process innovations (Arundel and Bordoy 2005).
5. The final report for CIS 2012 should be available from Eurostat in late 2012 or early 2013.

REFERENCES

Åkerblom, M. (1996), 'The second Community Innovation Survey: preliminary methodological considerations and first draft of revised core questionnaire', mimeo, 3 September.
APSC (Australian Public Service Commission) (2011), *State of the Service Report: State of the Service Series 2010–2011*, Canberra: Commonwealth of Australia.
Archibugi, D., P. Cohendet, A. Kristensen and K.-A. Schaffer (1997), 'Evaluation of the Community Innovation Survey', in A. Arundel and R. Garrelfs (eds), *Innovation Measurement and Policies*, Luxembourg: European Commission, EIMS publication 50, pp. 41–6.
Arthur D. Little (1963), *Patterns and Problems of Technical Innovation in American Industry*, Report c-65344 submitted to the NSF, Washington, DC: NSF.
Arundel, A. (2007), 'Innovation survey indicators: what impact on innovation policy?', in

OECD, *Science, Technology and Innovation Indicators in a Changing World: Responding to Policy Needs*, Paris: OECD, pp. 49–64.

Arundel, A. and C. Bordoy (2005), *The Fourth Community Innovation Survey: Final Questionnaire, Supporting Documentation, and the State-of-Art for the Design of the CIS*, Final report to Eurostat, Luxembourg: Eurostat, May.

Arundel, A. and R. Garrelfs (eds) (1997), *Innovation Measurement and Policies*, Luxembourg: European Commission, EIMS publication 50.

Arundel, A. and H. Hollanders (2011), 'A taxonomy of innovation: how do public sector agencies innovate? Results of the 2010 European Innobarometer survey of public agencies', Brussels: INNO Metrics, European Commission, http://www.proinnoeurope.eu/sites/default/files/page/11/12/IUS2010_A_taxonomy_of_innovation_How_do_public_sector_agencies_innovate.pdf, accessed 31 July 2012.

Arundel, A., C. Bordoy and A. van Cruysen (2009), *Community Innovation Survey 2008: Final Report*, report for Eurostat, Luxembourg: Eurostat, 19 March.

Arundel, A., C. Bordoy and A. van Cruysen (2010), *Community Innovation Survey 2010: Final Report*, report for Eurostat, Luxembourg: Eurostat, 24 January.

Arundel, A., C. Bordoy, A. van Cruysen and C. Huang (2007), *Community Innovation Survey 2006: Final Report*, report for Eurostat, Luxembourg: Eurostat, 11 September.

Borins, S. (2001), *The Challenge of Innovating in Government*, Innovation in Management Series, Arlington, VA: PricewaterhouseCoopers Endowment for the Business of Government.

Bugge, M., P.S. Mortensen and C. Bloch (2011), *Measuring Public Innovation in Nordic Countries: Report on the Nordic Pilot Studies, Analyses of Methodology and Results*, Oslo: MEPIN, NIFU.

Carter, C.F. and B.R. Williams (1957), *Industry and Technical Progress: Factors Governing the Speed of Application of Science*, Oxford: Oxford University Press.

Collins, D. (2003), 'Pretesting survey instruments: an overview of cognitive methods', *Quality of Life Research*, **12**, 229–38.

David, P.A. (2011), 'Zvi Griliches and the Economics of Technology Diffusion: Linking innovation adoption, lagged investments, and productivity growth', Stanford Institute for Economic Policy Research, Discussion Paper No. 10-029, Stanford, CA: Stanford Institute for Policy Research.

De Bresson, C. and B. Murray (1984), *Innovation in Canada: A Retrospective Survey: 1945–1978*, New Westminster, BC: Cooperative Research Unit on Science and Technology (CRUST).

Eurostat (2012), Community Innovation Survey database, http://epp.eurostat.ec.europa.eu/portal/page/portal/science_technology_innovation/data/database, accessed 14 August.

Foyn, F. (1999), 'Synthesis report from the national survey reports on CIS-II', Working Party of National Experts on Science and Technology Indicators: Joint Eurostat/OECD Workshop on Innovation Surveys, DSTI/EAS/STP/NESTI/RD(99)3, Paris: OECD.

Foyn, F. (2006), 'Using the Oslo methodology to measure innovation: the community innovation survey approach', in W. Blankley, M. Scerri, N. Molotja and I. Saloojee (eds), *Measuring Innovation in OECD and non-OECD Countries*, Cape Town, HSRC Press, pp. 111–22.

Godin, B. (2001a), 'Tradition and innovation: the historical contingency of R&D statistical classifications', Working Paper No. 11, Project on the History and Sociology of S&T Statistics, Montreal: INRS.

Godin, B. (2001b), 'The number makers: a short history of international science and technology statistics', Working Paper No. 9, Project on the History and Sociology of S&T Statistics, Montreal: INRS.

Godin, B. (2009), 'The rise of innovation surveys: measuring a fuzzy concept', Working Paper No. 16, Project on the History and Sociology of S&T Statistics, Montreal: INRS.

Hansen, J.A. (1987), *International Comparisons of Innovation Indicator Development*, Report for the National Science Foundation, Washington, DC: NSF.

Hughes, A., K. Moore and N. Kataria (2011), *Innovation in Public Sector Organizations: A Pilot Survey for Measuring Innovation Across the Public Sector*, London: Nesta.

IIT Research Institute (1968), *Technology in Retrospect and Critical Events in Science (TRACES)*, Washington, DC: NSF.

Kline, S.J. and N. Rosenberg (1986), 'An overview of innovation', in R. Landau and N. Rosenberg (eds), *The Positive Sum Strategy: Harnessing Technology for Economic Growth*, Washington, DC: National Academy Press, pp. 275–305.

Levin, R.C., A.K. Klevorick, R.R. Nelson and S.G. Winter (1987), 'Appropriating the returns from industrial research and development', *Brookings Papers on Economic Activity*, **3**: 783–831.

Myers, S. and D.G. Marquis (1969), *Successful Industrial Innovation: A Study of Factors Underlying Innovation in Selected Firms*, NSF 60-17, Washington, DC: NSF.

NAO (National Accounting Office) (2006), *Achieving Innovation in Central Government Organizations*, London: NAO.

Noel, V. and G. Prizeman (2005), *Using Cognitive Question Testing to Pretest a Questionnaire for a Large-Scale Postal Survey of Nonprofit Organizations*, School of Business Studies, Dublin: Trinity College Dublin.

OECD (1963), *Frascati Manual: Proposed Standard Practice for Surveys of Research and Experimental Development*, Paris, OECD.

OECD (1981), *Frascati Manual: Proposed Standard Practice for Surveys of Research and Experimental Development*, Paris: OECD.

OECD (1992), *Proposed Guidelines for Collecting and Interpreting Technological Innovation Data: Oslo Manual*, Paris: OECD.

OECD (2002), *Frascati Manual: Proposed Standard Practice for Surveys on Research and Experimental Development*, Paris: OECD.

OECD/Eurostat (1997), *Proposed Guidelines for Collecting and Interpreting Technological Innovation Data – Oslo Manual*, Paris: OECD.

OECD/Eurostat (2005), *Oslo Manual: Guidelines for Collecting and Interpreting Innovation Data*, Paris: OECD.

Pavitt, K., M. Robson and J. Townsend (1987), 'The size distribution of innovating firms in the United Kingdom: 1945–1983', *The Journal of Industrial Economics*, **35**, 297–316.

Qureschi, H., and O. Rowlands (2004), 'User satisfaction surveys and cognitive question testing in the public sector: the case of personal services in England', *International Journal of Social Research Methodology*, **7**, 273–87.

Schumpeter, J. (1934), *The Theory of Economic Development*, Cambridge, MA: Harvard University Press.

Sirilli, G. (1998), 'Old and new paradigms in the measurement of R&D', *Science and Public Policy*, **25**, 305–11.

Smith, K. (1992), 'Technological innovation indicators: experience and prospects', *Science and Public Policy*, **19**, 383–92.

Smith, K. (1997), 'Innovation measurement and the CIS approach', in A. Arundel and R. Garrelfs (eds), *Innovation Measurement and Policies*, Luxembourg: European Commission, EIMS publication 50, pp. 20–26.

Stead, H. (2001), 'The development of S&T statistics in Canada: an informal account', Paper No. 5, Project on the History and Sociology of S&T Statistics, Montreal: INRS.

Townsend, J. (1981), 'Science innovation in Britain since 1945', SPRU Occasional Paper Series No. 16, Brighton, UK: University of Sussex.

Wilhelmsen, L. (2012), 'The Norwegian innovation survey: combined with the R&D survey versus a separate CIS', presentation to the Eurostat CIS Workshop, Luxembourg, 2–3 July.

Young, A. (1997), 'Revising the *Oslo Manual*', in A. Arundel and R. Garrelfs (eds), *Innovation Measurement and Policies*, Luxembourg: European Commission, EIMS publication 50, pp. 92–8.

4 How firm managers understand innovation: implications for the design of innovation surveys

Anthony Arundel, Kieran O'Brien and Ann Torugsa

1. INTRODUCTION

Data on the innovation activities and outputs of firms have been collected through both object-based methods and subject-based surveys for several decades. Object-based methods collect information on specific innovations, generally through announcements in trade journals and other media (Kleinknecht and Reijnen 1993; Santarelli and Piergiovanni 1996). The advantage of this method is that the researcher can use the information in the media report and from other sources to classify the innovation by type. The fact that the innovation is advertised also ensures a level of novelty, since firms are unlikely to advertise minor differences in their products compared to competitors. The disadvantage of the object-based approach is that it collects little information on the innovation strategies used by firms and it is likely to miss many process and organizational innovations that the firm does not intend to sell and therefore does not advertise.

Subject-based innovation surveys, such as the EU Community Innovation Survey (CIS), can cover all types of innovations and collect a wide variety of information on innovation activities of use to both economic analysis and policy (Colecchia 2007; Freeman and Soete 2009; Bloch 2005; Arundel 2007). This includes information sourcing and collaboration strategies, revenues from innovative products, workforce characteristics, innovation investments, innovation objectives and factors that impede innovation. The *Oslo Manual* (OECD/Eurostat 2005) provides extensive guidelines on the types of questions that are worth asking. The disadvantage of subject-based surveys is that they usually obtain very little information on the characteristics of different categories of innovations. As an example, the CIS can show whether a firm has introduced both a good and a service innovation, but it provides only limited information on the characteristics of these innovations.

Data on the characteristics of specific innovations are of value because of the enormous differences in the effort required to develop innovations. The multiplex cinema and early versions of the ubiquitous roller suitcase required no research and development (R&D) and very little creative effort to develop, other than the initial idea. Conversely, the Trent jet engine and synthetic insulin required hundreds of millions of euros and many years to bring to the market. Object-based surveys can readily identify such differences in the creative effort, finance and capabilities required to innovate, but subject-based surveys are designed to provide general data, such as investments in all innovation activities.

The CIS has been criticized for a lack of consistency and comparability of data across countries, due to differences in survey methodology, survey questions and design, and to data quality problems associated with particular survey questions (Archibugi and Pianta 1996; Bordt 2008; Kleinknecht et al. 2002; Mortenson 2008). These concerns over the reliability and comparability of the CIS data have gradually been addressed through steps to improve survey methodology and questions. Many national statistical offices that are responsible for the CIS have implemented best practices in survey methodology, such as better follow-up of non-respondents and routines to contact enterprises to clarify unexpected responses, particularly for interval-level data on innovation expenditures. In addition, since CIS 2006, Eurostat has supported cognitive testing of all new or altered questions in the standard CIS questionnaire. The goal of cognitive testing is to ensure that each question is understood as intended, by all respondents, and that all respondents can provide a reasonably accurate answer to each question (Collins 2003; Willis 2005). These practices have improved the quality of the results for many of the CIS questions and reduced the percentage of respondents that do not answer specific questions.

However, there has arguably been insufficient research into how respondents interpret the basic concept of innovation itself. Innovation surveys based on the *Oslo Manual* (OECD/Eurostat 2005: 46) define innovation as products, processes, marketing methods or organizational methods that are, 'at the minimum, *new (or significantly improved) for the firm*'. It is often assumed that all survey respondents should understand each of the definitions of product, process, organizational and marketing innovation in the same way, even though interpretation of what is 'new or significantly improved' to the firm is subjective. Different respondent interpretations of this concept of novelty may be a source of variation in responses across countries, sectors or firm size.

A lack of data on the characteristics of innovations can produce curious and contradictory results for international comparisons. For example,

Arundel and Hollanders (2005) demonstrate the limitations of a simple interpretation of CIS results. They note that, between 1998 and 2000, 46 per cent of Portuguese firms are innovative compared to 45 per cent of Finnish firms, a questionable result given the superior innovation perform-ance of Finland across a number of other innovation indicators, including R&D expenditures and patenting activity. Some of these problems with comparability and interpretation can be improved through better analysis, for instance by developing indicators for how firms innovate (Frenz and Lambert 2009) and by improving the design of survey questions.

National differences in how firms interpret the concept of innovation could substantially affect comparability across countries. For example, it is known that the percentage of self-reported innovative firms varies by country in unexpected ways. For instance, CIS 2008 finds that between 2005 and 2007 the percentage of innovative firms was almost twice as high in Germany (78.9 per cent) compared to the Netherlands (44.9 per cent) and the UK (45.6 per cent). Although the pre-eminence of Germany might be expected if most CIS respondents were manufacturing firms, this is not the case, with the majority of respondents drawn from the service sectors. The recent 2009 NSF survey for the USA reports a much lower percent-age of product innovative firms compared to many European countries.[1] Although there are several possible causes for these differences, such as dif-ferent industrial structures, an alternative possibility is national and firm size differences in how respondents interpret the concept of 'innovation'.

In 2011 and 2012, the OECD and several countries that participate in the CIS Task Force conducted cognitive testing to determine how firm managers understand the basic concept of innovation. Preliminary results from the CIS Task Force interviews show that firm managers often view an innovation as requiring substantial creative effort by the enterprise or it must substantially increase sales. Managers from large firms also tend to reject the *Oslo Manual* definition of an innovation as needing only to be new to the firm. The result is that one interviewee's example of an innova-tion could be considered a minor change by another respondent.

The disadvantage of cognitive testing is that it is costly and therefore feasible only for a small number of interviews. An alternative approach to cognitive testing of the concept of innovation is to combine a feature of the object-based method with innovation surveys by including an open-ended survey question on the firm's most important innovation. This can provide useful data on how firms understand innovation for hundreds or thousands of respondents. The method is particularly useful when little is known about the types of innovation that are common. For this reason, open questions have been included in several of the recent subject-based exploratory surveys on innovation in the public sector (NAO 2006; Bugge et al. 2011). The description of the innovation can be used in several ways, for instance to determine the type of innovation that firms or public sector organizations consider their most valuable innovation or to assess the novelty of the innovation (how much creative effort was required). Once coded, this type of information can also be used to check if respondents are correctly interpreting the definitions of different types of innovations.

Open questions have been asked in several innovation surveys based on the *Oslo Manual*. A 2010 UNU-MERIT survey of national statistical offices from 32 countries that participate in the European CIS asked if they had ever included an open question on the enterprise's most important innovation in their CIS questionnaire (Arundel et al. 2010). The study also obtained similar information for Canada, New Zealand, Australia and South Africa, all of which conduct subject-based innovation surveys. National statistical offices from ten European countries responded that they had included such a question in at least one CIS survey.[2] In addition, Statistics Canada included an open-ended question on the firm's most important innovation in three innovation surveys.

Only three of these 11 countries have ever coded the responses for further analysis and of these three countries none has conducted a systematic analysis of the results. The open question has been used either as a focusing device to encourage the respondent to think of their most important innovation (Canada) or to assist the national statistical office to become acquainted with the variety of innovation activities within their country. One European country, if in doubt about the innovation status of the described innovation, would contact the enterprise for more information. Most national statistical offices do not code the results to this open question because of the high cost. As noted by a staff member from Statistics Canada, 'it takes considerable time [to code the results] . . . and analysis of this question was not a priority at the time and so resources were assigned to other activities'.[3]

In this chapter we provide the coded results of an open question on the respondent firm's most important innovation from a subject-based innovation survey in Australia. We first use the results to examine the importance of different types of innovations to the firm, and the relationship between creative effort and the firm's most important innovation. Second, we use the data to examine errors in the interpretation of the concept of innovation. The data do not provide information on differences across countries, but they do provide some clues as to how innovation can be interpreted differently across sectors and firm sizes. The results shed light on possible sources of respondent and measurement error that should help to improve innovation measurement, data quality, indicator development and related research and analysis.

2.   METHODOLOGY

The data are from a 2007 Innovation Census in the Australian state of Tasmania, which had a population of 500000 and a per capita state product of approximately €24000 in 2006 at the time covered by the census. The Tasmanian economy is more dependent on natural resources and manufacturing than other Australian states, with proportionally fewer firms from knowledge-intensive business services. Most manufacturing firms in Tasmania can be characterized as 'low tech', but there are also several clusters of advanced manufacturing firms.

The 2007 Tasmanian Innovation Census is a subject-based innovation survey that follows the *Oslo Manual*. All 2807 Tasmanian enterprises from the business sector with five or more employees were contacted by phone and asked to answer a series of questions on their firm's innovative activities in the previous three years, using a computer-assisted telephone interview (CATI) method. One advantage is that the definitions of innovation and of different types of innovation were read aloud to all respondents, avoiding the problem of respondents not reading instructions and definitions. Many of the questions are similar or identical to the standard fourth CIS questionnaire, but the Tasmanian question on process innovation did not provide full descriptions of three types of process innovations, as in the fourth CIS. Instead, the definition is limited to 'the use of new or significantly improved methods for the production or supply of goods or services'. This may have created problems for the correct interpretation of process innovations, as discussed below.

Responses were obtained from 1591 Tasmanian firms, for a response rate of 57 per cent. A follow-up survey of non-respondents found no statistically significant differences in the rate of innovation among survey respondents and non-respondents. As the study is a census with no significant differences between respondents and non-respondents, the statistical significance of differences in the results is not calculated.

Following the CIS structure, the interview began with questions on four types of innovations introduced by the enterprise (product, process, organizational and marketing), plus a range of other questions on the firm's innovative activities, expenditures and outputs. The final interview question was open-ended and asked respondents to 'briefly describe your most important innovation in the past three years'. The responses were recorded as text by interviewers and usually consisted of one or several sentences. The question was asked of both firms that replied elsewhere in the questionnaire that they had introduced an innovation (self-reported innovators) and of firms that did not report any innovations to other survey questions (self-reported non-innovators). The appendix provides the questions on innovation types that were used in the telephone interviews.

The open-ended text responses to the most important innovation question were analysed and coded independently by three experts and took four person-months. In order to prevent bias, the experts did not view other survey information on whether or not the firm had introduced a product, process, organizational or marketing innovation. Discrepancies in the coding were identified and discussed until a consensus was reached.

The coding assigned each most important innovation to one of five mutually exclusive innovation status categories:

1. Met the requirements for an innovation by implementing a new or significantly improved product, process, organizational or marketing method.
2. Not an innovation: the respondent stated that they had no innovations. This was most common for self-reported non-innovators.
3. Not an innovation because it was an extension of existing activities (purchase of more of the same type of equipment etc.) or the firm described something that did not meet the *Oslo Manual* definitions of an innovation.
4. Not an innovation because it was not yet on the market or in use by the firm.
5. Insufficient information was provided to determine innovation status.

If the example was an innovation, it was further classified into one of four types of innovations (product, process, organizational, marketing). These categories were not mutually exclusive. An innovation could be assigned to more than one category based on its characteristics. For example, it could be both a process and an organizational innovation.

The responses were also coded to three different levels of creative effort required by the firm to develop or implement the most important innovation: (1) mainly acquired externally or required minimal in-house effort to develop; (2) some in-house development likely; and (3) major in-house development likely. Although the amount of information provided can be used with a reasonable level of accuracy to determine innovation status, there is a much higher level of subjectivity in determining the level of creative effort required for valid innovations, largely due to the limited amount of information provided for these innovations.

Table 4.1   The innovation status of the most important innovation for
self-reported innovators and non-innovators

	Self-reported innovators		Self-reported non-innovators	
	Number	%	Number	%
The most important innovation is an innovation	1028	80.8	84	**35.3**
The most important innovation is *not* an innovation	245	**19.2**	154	64.7
Total	1273	100.0	238	100.0

3. RESULTS

Among the 1591 respondent firms, 55 did not provide enough details to code and classify their responses to the open-ended question on their most important innovation[4] and 25 reported activities to develop an innovation that had not yet been implemented. These respondents were excluded from the results. This left 1511 eligible firms for analysis. Of these, 1273 were self-reported innovators and 238 were self-reported non-innovators, based on other questions in the survey.

Table 4.1 provides the distribution of innovators and non-innovators by the innovation status of their most important innovation. Of 1273 innovators, 1028 gave a description of a valid innovation in response to the question on their most important innovation, while 19.2 per cent did not. For non-innovators, 64.7 per cent stated that they did not introduce an innovation or described something that was not an innovation. Conversely, over a third, 35.3 per cent, described a valid innovation.

Table 4.2 gives the distribution of the different types of most important innovations reported by self-reported innovators and non-innovators. The results are limited to valid innovations. Fifty innovations have the characteristics of more than one innovation type, resulting in 1212 observations. Among innovators, 39.4 per cent reported a product innovation as their most important innovation. Of these, service sector innovations were more frequently reported than goods innovations (22.4 per cent versus 16.9 per cent respectively). Process innovations were the second most frequently reported most important innovation (38.0 per cent), followed by marketing methods (11.4 per cent) and organizational innovations (11.2 per cent). These results confirm the importance of including survey questions on organizational and marketing innovations, as 22.6 per cent of innovators cited one of these as their most important innovation over the previous three years.

Table 4.2   Type of most important innovation reported by innovators and non-innovators

	Innovators, number	%	Non-innovators, number	%	Total number	%
Products	442	39.4	21	23.6	463	38.2
Goods	*(190)*	*(16.9)*	*8*	*(9.0)*	*198*	*(16.3)*
Services	*(252)*	*(22.4)*	*13*	*(14.6)*	*265*	*(21.9)*
Process	427	38.0	40	44.9	467	38.5
Organizational method	126	11.2	16	18.0	142	11.7
Marketing method	128	11.4	12	13.5	140	11.6
Total	1123	100.0	89	100.0	1212	100.0

Notes: Innovators and non-innovators identified on the basis of other survey questions. The counts exceed the total number of valid innovations reported by innovators (1028) and non-innovators (84) because several most important innovations were coded to more than one innovation type, for example both an organizational method and a process, or both a product and a process innovation.

The distribution of the reported most important innovations is very different for non-innovators, who consist of firms that erroneously reported that they did *not* innovate in other closed survey questions. These firms were much less likely to report a valid product innovation as their most important innovation, but were considerably more likely to report an organizational method (18 per cent versus 11.2 per cent for innovators), and more likely to report a marketing innovation (13.5 per cent versus 11.4 per cent) or a process innovation (44.9 per cent verses 38.0 per cent). Therefore one of the main causes for error among non-innovators appears to be a perception that changes to processes, organizational or marketing methods do not count as innovations. This will lead to under-reporting of these types of innovations.

Table 4.3 gives results for the amount of creative effort required for the firm's most important innovation for innovators and non-innovators. Of interest, 59 per cent of the most important innovations reported by innovators were mainly acquired from external sources, with little creative effort required by the firm itself. Only 8 per cent were likely to require major in-house development. Conversely, a much higher percentage of the most important innovations reported by non-innovators, 82.1 per cent, were mainly acquired from external sources. This suggests that an important confusion among non-innovators over what constitutes an

Table 4.3   Distribution of most important innovations by creative effort

Creative effort required	Innovators		Non-innovators	
	Frequency	%	Frequency	%
Mainly acquired externally	607	59.0	69	82.1
Some in-house development likely	339	33.0	14	16.7
Major in-house development	82	8.0	1	1.2
Total	1028	100.0	84	100.0

Table 4.4   Creative effort required for the most important innovation by R&D status: technological innovators only

Creative effort for the most important innovation	R&D status								Total	
	No R&D		R&D but no data on R&D intensity		Low R&D intensity ($< 1\%$)		High R&D intensity ($>= 1\%$)			
	N	%	*N*	%	*N*	%	*N*	%	*N*	%
Low (mainly acquired from external sources)	216	69.7	61	61.6	128	55.4	122	42.7	527	56.9
Medium (some in-house development)	82	26.5	30	30.3	81	35.1	125	43.7	318	34.3
High (major in-house development)	12	3.9	8	8.1	22	9.5	39	13.6	81	8.7
Total	310	100.0	99	100.0	231	100.0	286	100.0	926	100.0

Note: N = Number of MII innovators by level of creative effort and self-reported R&D status.

innovation could be due to these firms erroneously thinking that an innovation must require substantial in-house development.

Table 4.4 gives the distribution of the most important innovations by creative effort and by R&D intensity. The latter is an independent measure of each firm's creative capabilities using other innovation survey questions. The results are limited to firms that are self-reported technological innovators because the survey questions on R&D refer only to product or process innovations.[5] A higher percentage of firms that do not perform R&D report a most important innovation that was mainly acquired from external sources. For instance, 69.7 per cent of firms that do not perform R&D gave an example of a most important innovation that was probably acquired from external sources, compared to 42.7 per cent of firms with an R&D intensity of 1 per cent or higher. Conversely, the percentage of firms that report a most important innovation that was likely to require major in-house development increases with the R&D intensity of the firm.

Interestingly, 42.5 per cent of technologically innovative firms with an R&D intensity of 1 per cent or higher reported a most important innovation that was mostly acquired from external sources. If we assume that 'most important' to the firm equates to the most economically important (the evidence from the descriptions of the most important innovation suggests that this is in fact the case), then this result indicates that the innovations of most value to the firm are not always those with the highest level of creative effort on the part of the firm. This implies that it is very important for innovation surveys to capture these 'minor' innovations.

Errors of Interpretation

The results of Table 4.1 show that respondents can make two types of error when reporting their firm's most important innovation:

1. A respondent from an innovative firm reports a most important innovation that is *not* an innovation (e.g. an activity such as a refurbishment of existing premises or an extension of existing operations).
2. A respondent from a non-innovative firm reports a most important innovation that *is* an innovation. Or, a respondent from an innovative firm reports a specific type of most important innovation (product, process, marketing, organizational), but failed to report this specific type of innovation earlier in the interview.

Both Type 1 and 2 errors indicate that the respondent did not fully understand the concept of an innovation, as defined elsewhere in the questionnaire. As shown in Table 4.1, the Type 1 error rate is 19.2 per cent. Type 1 errors do not indicate that the firm failed to innovate, since it may have introduced other varieties of valid innovations.

Type 2 errors can be made by either non-innovative or innovative firms. In the former case (Type 2a), the firm does *not* innovate based on responses to other survey questions,[6] but it reports a valid innovation in response to the question on the most important innovation. Table 4.1 gives a Type 2a error rate of 35.3 per cent. This shows that innovation surveys could be

*Table 4.5   Type 2b error rates: percentage of innovators that report a
most important innovation that is not reported elsewhere in the
questionnaire*

Innovation type	MII Innovation	MII reported but this type of innovation is not reported elsewhere	% (row)
Products	442	32	7.2
Goods	*(190)*	*26*	*13.7*
Services	*(252)*	*31*	*12.3*
Process	427	69	16.2
Organizational method	126	20	15.9
Marketing method	128	29	22.7

Note: Only innovators were included in these calculations.

significantly underestimating the true rate of innovation, since 35.3 per
cent of respondents from non-innovative firms described a valid innovation in response to the question on their firm's most important innovation.

A Type 2b error occurs when a respondent from an innovative firm
reports a valid most important innovation, but fails to report this variety
of innovation elsewhere in the questionnaire. For instance, the respondent
describes a valid product innovation as the most important innovation,
but does not report a product innovation in the other closed survey questions. Table 4.5 provides the Type 2b error rate for innovative firms by the
type of innovation. For example, of 442 innovative firms reporting a most
important innovation that was a product, 32 (7.2 per cent) did not report a
product innovation previously in the questionnaire. The results show that
inaccurate reporting is lowest for product innovations such as goods or
services and highest for marketing (22.7 per cent) innovations, with intermediate error rates for process (16.2 per cent) and organizational innovations (15.9 per cent). These results suggest that innovation surveys could
lead to greater under-reporting of marketing, process and organizational
innovations by innovators.

The error rate for products in Table 4.5 is lower than for goods and
services separately, because each most important product innovation is
also classified as either a good or a service. For example, a firm could
report a goods innovation earlier in the questionnaire but not a services
innovation. If this firm then reported a services innovation as its most
important innovation, the results for services in Table 4.5 would be classified as an error. However, as both services and goods are classified as
products, this would not classify as an error for product innovators, so

Table 4.6   Type 2b error rates for innovative firms by sector

	Total innovators	Most important innovation is not a valid innovation	Error rate (%)
Industry	200	32	16.0
Manufacturing	267	30	11.2
KIBS	278	36	12.9
General services	528	147	27.8
Total	1273	245	19.2

Notes:
Limited to 1273 firms that reported, in response to other survey questions, that they had introduced an innovation between 2004 and 2006.
'Industry' includes agriculture, forestry and fishing, mining, electricity, gas, water and waste services, and construction. 'KIBS' includes information, media and telecommunications, financial and insurance services, rental, hiring and real-estate services, professional, scientific and technical services, and administrative and support services. 'General services' includes all services except KIBS.

Table 4.7   Type 2b error rates for innovative firms by number of employees

	Number of innovators	Most important innovation is not a valid innovation	Error rate (%)
5–9 employees	457	111	24.3
10–19 employees	364	67	18.4
20–49 employees	267	47	17.6
50+ employees	185	20	10.8
Total	1273	245	19.2

Notes: Limited to 1273 firms that reported, in response to other survey questions, that they had introduced an innovation between 2004 and 2006. Employment is in full-time equivalents.

the error rate for product innovators in Table 4.5 is much lower. The fact that the error rate for goods and services is higher than that for products shows that some firms find it difficult to differentiate between a good and a service innovation.

Table 4.6 gives the distribution of Type 2b errors among innovative firms by sector, while Table 4.7 gives error rates by firm size. The error rate is lowest for manufacturing firms, at 11.2 per cent, and for knowledge-intensive business sector (KIBS) firms, at 12.9 per cent. The highest error rate is for general services (retail, wholesale, accommodation etc.), where 27.8 per cent of innovative firms report a most important innovation that is not a valid innovation. These results indicate that the main survey questions on innovation are better understood by manufacturing firms than by general service sector firms. This has been a concern for innovation surveys since CIS 3, when service sector firms were added to the sample. In addition, as shown in Table 4.7, the error rate decreases with firm size, from 24.3 per cent for the smallest size class of firms (5 to 9 employees) to 10.8 per cent for firms with 50 or more employees. These results suggest that including firms with fewer than ten employees in innovation surveys will increase errors. Many surveys currently exclude these firms, though some countries such as Australia have recently widened the scope to include micro firms.[7]

Table 4.8 provides the Type 2b error rates for each type of innovation by sector, while Table 4.9 provides these results by firm size.[8] The error rate for service innovations is higher for manufacturing (15.8 per cent) and industrial firms (15.4 per cent) than for KIBS (12.7 per cent) and general services firms (11.3 per cent). Higher error rates for service innovations by manufacturing and industrial firms could be expected, as these firms focus on the production of goods and primary products. Knowledge-intensive business services and the industrial sector show the highest error rates for goods innovation (20 per cent and 19.4 per cent respectively). Industrial and manufacturing firms also have the highest error rates for marketing innovations (30 per cent and 29.2 per cent respectively), while general services has the highest error rate for organizational innovations (26.1 per cent).

The smallest error rates across sectors were for product innovation, indicating a more consistent understanding of this type of innovation. Knowledge-intensive business services have the lowest overall error rate (average across innovation types), indicating that respondents in this sector have a better understanding of the concept of innovation than respondents from other sectors.

The Type 2b error rate generally declines by firm size for product, goods, services and organizational innovations, as shown in Table 4.9. However, there is no notable trend for process or marketing innovations. Two of the largest declines in the error rate by firm size are for product and service innovations, with only 2.4 per cent of innovative firms with 50 or more employees describing a service innovation as their most important innovation failing to report service innovations elsewhere in the questionnaire. This suggests that larger firms may be more aware of these types of innovations because their relevance increases with firm size (e.g. with more product lines), with questions more often misunderstood by smaller firms.

Error rates do not show consistent differences by the categories of creative effort for the development of the most important innovation (no table

Table 4.8 Type 2b error rates for innovative firms by sector (MII = reported a most important innovation of this type)

Innovation type	Sector group											
	Industrial			Manufacturing			Knowledge-intensive business services			General services		
	MII reported	N	%	MII reported	N	%	MII reported	N	%	MII reported	N	%
Product	44	3	6.8	113	6	5.3	109	9	8.3	176	14	8.0
Goods	*31*	*6*	*19.4*	*94*	*9*	*9.6*	*30*	*6*	*20.0*	*35*	*5*	*14.3*
Services	*13*	*2*	*15.4*	*19*	*3*	*15.8*	*79*	*10*	*12.7*	*141*	*16*	*11.3*
Process	101	20	19.8	108	20	18.5	78	8	10.3	140	21	15.0
Organizational	19	2	10.5	14	2	14.3	47	4	8.5	46	12	26.1
Marketing	10	3	30.0	24	7	29.2	31	7	22.6	63	12	19.0

Note: N = number of firms for which an MII was reported but this type of innovation was not reported elsewhere in the questionnaire.

Table 4.9 Type 2b error rates for innovative firms by firm size (MII = reported a most important innovation of this type)

Innovation type	Firm size										
	5–9 FTE			10–19 FTE			20–49 FTE			50 + FTE		
	MII reported	N	%	MII reported	N	%	MII reported	N	%	MII reported	N	%
Product	153	14	9.2	126	11	8.7	83	5	6.0	80	2	2.5
Goods	*60*	*9*	*15.0*	*55*	*7*	*12.7*	*37*	*5*	*13.5*	*38*	*5*	*13.2*
Service	*93*	*13*	*14.0*	*71*	*12*	*16.9*	*46*	*5*	*10.9*	*42*	*1*	*2.4*
Process	132	19	14.4	123	18	14.6	104	22	21.2	68	10	14.7
Organizational	37	6	16.2	39	9	23.1	23	3	13.0	27	2	7.4
Marketing	53	10	18.9	31	8	25.8	32	8	25.0	12	3	25.0

Note: N = number of firms for which an MII was reported but this type of innovation was not reported elsewhere in the questionnaire.

provided). For example, the error rate for product innovations is 6.8 per cent for firms that acquired them from external sources, 7.8 per cent when some in-house development was likely and 6.7 per cent when major in-house development was likely. For process innovations, the error rates for these three categories of creative effort are 16.0 per cent, 15.9 per cent and 21.1 per cent, with the last rate based on data for only 19 firms.

4.   CONCLUSION

This chapter uses a unique data source on the most important innovation reported by firms. The results are of relevance both to research on the relative importance of different types of innovation and for how survey respondents interpret the concept of 'innovation'.

For all respondents, approximately 38 per cent reported that a product or process innovation was their firm's most important innovation, while 11.7 per cent reported that their most important innovation was an organizational method and 11.6 per cent a marketing method. This supports the inclusion of questions on these types of non-technological innovations in innovation surveys, which has been the subject of ongoing debate. The value of process innovations to firms suggests that a lack of questions on the outputs of process innovation is an important limitation of innovation surveys.

Of interest, 59 per cent of respondents from innovative firms reported that their most important innovation was mainly acquired externally, with little creative effort required by their firm. Furthermore, 42.7 per cent of technological innovators with a high creative capacity (as measured by an R&D intensity of 1 per cent or higher) reported that their most important innovation needed little creative effort by their firm. These results highlight the value of using a broad definition of innovation that includes 'minimal' innovations, rather than focusing only on innovations that require substantial creative effort.

An unexpected result was the high percentage of self-reported non-innovators, 35.3 per cent, that described a valid innovation in an open question. This suggests that innovation surveys could fail to correctly identify a substantial number of innovative firms. In addition, a notable share of respondents for innovative firms report a type of most important innovation that was not reported earlier in the interview. These errors appear to be caused by two factors. First, self-reported non-innovators could fail to correctly understand the questions on specific types of innovations or they could erroneously assume that in-house creative effort is required in order to be an innovator. This could be partly due to the problem, in all *Oslo Manual* innovation surveys, of defining an innovation as either new or 'significantly improved'. The highly subjective aspect of this definition could be leading to inconsistent responses.

Second, the results show that many innovative firms do not have a clear understanding of the definitions for specific types of innovation, particularly for non-technical marketing and organizational innovations. These problems are greatest among smaller firms, with respondents from larger firms having a better understanding of innovation. Innovative firms active in KIBS have the best understanding of the concept of innovation. However, a higher percentage of innovative firms that are active in industrial and general services sectors misunderstand differences in innovation types. Organizational innovation is misunderstood the most in general services, while marketing innovation is less well understood by firms in industrial sectors. Conversely, product innovations are relatively well understood by all types of firms, although there is some confusion over the difference between a good and services innovation for industrial firms and services innovations are least understood by firms in manufacturing.

The higher error rate for process compared to product innovations could partly be due to the short definition of a process innovation used in the Tasmanian Census. The more extensive definition of process innovations that was introduced in the fourth CIS questionnaire could reduce possible error rates.

These results have important implications for survey design and indicator interpretation. They suggest that careful attention needs to be given to the design of innovation survey questions on marketing, organizational and process innovations. Many firms might be misinterpreting the required level of novelty for an innovation, so the concept of 'new to the firm' needs to be carefully explained. If possible, it may be better to remove 'significant' from the definition of an innovation, and include other measures for capturing the creative effort expended by firms.

In addition, the results suggest that standard survey questions might be inadequate for capturing innovation in general services or industrial (low-tech) sectors, which showed higher error rates. A possible solution is to develop different question modules for specific sectors or for smaller firms, although this option faces practical constraints for the administration of large surveys.

With respect to international comparability, limiting the analysis to indicators with low error rates could provide a more accurate benchmark. For instance, a benchmark indicator could rely on product innovation rates among larger firms in the manufacturing sector, as these enterprises had the lowest error rates in our study.

In conclusion, this chapter demonstrates the value of including an open-ended question on the firm's most important innovation in innovation surveys. The results both provide valuable information on the types of innovations that firms find of value as well as data that can improve indicator reliability and usage. For larger surveys, this type of analysis could be limited to a sub-sample to reduce the time required to code textual information.

NOTES

1. See Boroush (2010). In the NSF BRDIS survey, covering activities between 2006 and 2008 inclusive, only 9 per cent of all companies with five or more employees reported a product innovation, although the percentage is higher for manufacturing companies, at 22 per cent. One explanation for the low percentage of innovators is because BRDIS includes firms with 5–9 employees, while the CIS only covers enterprises with 10 or more employees. However, it would be surprising if this were the only cause of the difference. The closest comparison group with the CIS is for SMEs with between 10 and 49 employees. Using the CIS 2008, 19.8 per cent of all German firms with 10 to 49 employees were product innovators.
2. Results of the November 2010 MERIT survey of 32 European NSOs.
3. Personal communication from Susan Schaan, Statistics Canada, in an email dated 13 April 2010.
4. This was most common for service sector firms, who would give an answer such as 'general improvement in quality of services'.
5. Technological innovators include all firms that reported implementing a new or significantly improved product (good/service) or process in the closed innovation survey questions. R&D intensity is calculated as 2005/2006 expenditure on R&D as the percentage of 2005/2006 turnover.
6. They did not report the introduction of any new or significantly improved product, process, organizational or marketing innovation over the survey period.
7. Since 2006–2007 the national innovation survey in Australia has included very small firms with zero or more employees, and debate has been ongoing regarding expanding the CIS scope to include firms with fewer than 10 employees.
8. Due to small counts, we do not provide the error rates by industry groups or firm size for non-innovators.

REFERENCES

Archibugi, D. and M. Pianta (1996), 'Measuring technological change through patents and innovation surveys', *Technovation*, **16**, 451–68.

Arundel, A. (2007), 'Innovation survey indicators: what impact on innovation policy?', in OECD, *Science, Technology and Innovation Indicators in a Changing World: Responding to Policy Needs*, Paris: OECD, pp. 49–64.

Arundel, A. and H. Hollanders (2005), *EXIS: An Exploratory Approach to Innovation Scoreboards*, Brussels: European Commission, DG Enterprise.

Arundel, A., C. Bordoy and A. van Cruysen (2010), *Final Report to Eurostat: Community Innovation Survey 2010*, Luxembourg: Eurostat, 24 January.

Bloch, C. (2005), 'Innovation measurement: present and future challenges', paper prepared for the Eurostat Conference 'Knowledge Economy – Challenges for Measurement', Luxembourg: Eurostat, 8–9 December.

Bordt, M. (2008), 'Response unit; new to firm, market and world; knowledge management', 32nd CEIES Seminar, 'Innovation indicators – more than technology?', Århus, Denmark, Luxembourg: Eurostat.
Boroush, M. (2010), 'NSF releases new statistics on business innovation', in *InfoBriefs*, National Science Foundation, Directorate for Social and Behavioural and Economic Sciences, NSF 11-300, October, Arlington, VA: NSF.
Bugge, M., P.S. Mortensen and C. Bloch (2011), *Measuring Public Innovation in Nordic Countries: Report on the Nordic Pilot Studies, Analyses of Methodology and Results*, Oslo: MEPIN, NIFU.
Colecchia, A. (2007), 'Looking ahead: what implications for STI indicator development?', in OECD, *Science, Technology and Innovation Indicators in a Changing World: Responding to Policy Needs*, Paris: OECD, pp. 285–97.
Collins, D. (2003), 'Pretesting survey instruments: an overview of cognitive methods', *Quality of Life Research*, **12**, 229–38.
Freeman, C. and L. Soete (2009), 'Developing science, technology and innovation indicators: what we can learn from the past', *Research Policy*, **38**(4), 583–9.
Frenz, M. and R. Lambert (2009), 'Exploring non-technological and mixed modes of innovation across countries', in OECD, *Innovation in Firms: A Microeconomic Perspective*, Paris: OECD, pp. 69–110.
Kleinknecht, A. and O.N. Reijnen (1993), 'Towards literature-based innovation output indicators', *Structural Change and Economic Dynamics*, **4**(1), 199–207.
Kleinknecht, A., K. van Montfort and E. Brouwer (2002), 'The non-trivial choice between innovation indicators', *Economics of Innovation and New Technology*, **11**(2), 109–21.
Mortenson, P. (2008), 'The regionalisation of CIS indicators: the Danish experience', 32nd CEIES Seminar, 'Innovation indicators – more than technology?', Århus, Denmark, Eurostat, European Commission.
NAO (National Accounting Office) (2006), *Achieving Innovation in Central Government Organizations*, London: NAO.
OECD (1992), *OECD Proposed Guidelines for Collecting and Interpreting Technological Innovation Data – Oslo Manual*, Paris: OECD.
OECD/Eurostat (2005), *Oslo Manual: Guidelines for Collecting and Interpreting Innovation Data*, 3rd edn, Paris: OECD.
Santarelli, E. and R. Piergiovanni (1996), 'Analyzing literature-based innovation output indicators: the Italian experience', *Research Policy*, **25**, 689–711.
Willis, G.B. (2005), *Cognitive Interviewing: A Tool for Improving Questionnaire Design*, Thousand Oaks, CA: Sage.

APPENDIX: TASMANIAN INNOVATION CENSUS 2007 QUESTIONS ON TYPES OF INNOVATION

The Next Section is about New or Improved Goods or Services at [Business Name]

When we say that, we are talking about the market introduction of a good or service that is new or significantly improved.

That could mean that the good or service is completely new and different to goods or services previously produced by the enterprise.

That can also mean that the good or service is significantly improved in terms of quality, functions or intended uses; or significantly improved through changes in materials, components, design, or other characteristics that enhance performance.

For example, we would exclude superficial changes (such as new colours or patterns on a label), but include new packaging that improves shelf-life, or reduces costs.

The new good or service does not need to be new to your market, only to your enterprise, and it does not matter if the new good or service was originally developed by your enterprise, or by other enterprises.

We don't include the simple resale of new goods purchased from other enterprises.

Q4. **During the past three calendar years, 2004, 2005 and 2006, did your enterprise introduce:**

	Yes	No
a. New or significantly improved goods	❏	❏
b. New or significantly improved services	❏	❏

The Next Section is about Process Change

*A New Process is the use of new or significantly improved **methods** for the production or supply of goods and services. Purely organizational or managerial changes should not be included – these will be covered shortly.*

The new process must be new to your enterprise, but it does not need to be new to your industry. Again, it does not matter if the new process was originally developed by your enterprise or by other enterprises.

Q8a.   During the three calendar years 2004 to 2006, did your enterprise introduce any new or improved processes for producing or supplying goods or services?

Yes   ❑
No   ❑   ⟶   Question 9

Organizational and Marketing Changes

In this next section we ask about new forms of organization, business structures or practices aimed at improving efficiency, or new approaches to markets and customers. The question asks for a 'yes' or 'no' response to a number of answer categories.

Q21.   During the three calendar years 2004 to 2006, did your enterprise make major changes in the following areas of business structure and practices?

Please cross one box for each category

		Yes	No
a.	Implementation of a new or significantly changed **corporate strategy**	❑	❑
b.	Implementation of **advanced management techniques** within your enterprise, e.g. knowledge management systems	❑	❑
c.	Implementation of major changes to your **organizational structure**, e.g. introduction of cross-functional teams, outsourcing of major business functions.	❑	❑
d.	Implementation of changes in **marketing concepts or strategies** *(e.g. packaging or presentational changes to a product to target new markets, or new activities to open up new markets)*	❑	❑

5 User innovation: business and consumers
Jeroen P.J. de Jong and Eric von Hippel

1. INTRODUCTION

Innovation is not only the domain of enterprises that seek to sell what they create. It is also done by firms and individual end users who wish to use what they create rather than sell it. User innovation is increasingly displacing producer innovation in many parts of modern economies, but official innovation indicators still do not capture the activity properly. This chapter discusses the distinguishing features of user innovation compared with traditional, producer-centered innovation, summarizes the empirical evidence, and reviews the state of the art in the measurement of user innovation.

Ever since Schumpeter (1934) introduced his theory of economic development, economists, policy makers and business managers have assumed that most important innovations originate from producers and are supplied to consumers through goods or services that are for sale. This view seems reasonable on the face of it; producers generally serve many users and so can profit from multiple copies of a single innovative design more than individual users would. In contrast, if individual users innovate, they could only depend upon their in-house benefits to recover their innovation investments. Presumably, therefore, a producer who serves many customers can afford to invest more in innovation than any single user could. From this, it follows that producer-centered innovation should dominate in most parts of the economy.

However, a second and increasingly important innovation model revolves around users who primarily innovate to satisfy their own needs, rather than to sell a product on the market (von Hippel 2005). Under this user-centered model, economically important innovations are developed first by users who divide up the tasks and costs of innovation development and then freely reveal their results. Users obtain direct use benefits from their efforts, and moreover, they may obtain benefits such as enjoyment, learning and enhanced reputations. User innovation is increasingly displacing producer innovation in many parts of modern economies (Baldwin and von Hippel 2011). A growing body of empirical work shows that users are the first to develop many and perhaps most new industrial and consumer products (von Hippel 2005). It has also been shown that substantial shares of users engage in innovation, and that their innovations are generally unconstrained by intellectual property rights, in samples of consumers (e.g. von Hippel et al. 2011) and user firms (e.g. de Jong and von Hippel 2009). Moreover, by diffusing to other economic actors, user innovation increases social welfare (Henkel and von Hippel 2005). Finally, the importance of good and service development by users is increasing over time (Baldwin and von Hippel 2011). This shift is being driven by two related trends: (1) the steadily improving design capabilities (innovation toolkits) that advances in computer hardware and software make possible for users; and (2) the steadily improving ability of individual users to combine and coordinate their innovation-related efforts through communication media such as the Internet.

The shift towards a user-centered mode of innovation has implications for innovation management and policy. In this contribution, the implications of the user-centered model for the measurement of innovation are examined. Researchers have recently begun to develop and test new methods for collecting data on user innovation (e.g. Schaan and Uhrbach 2009; Flowers et al. 2010; Gault 2012), and stock is taken of their efforts so far. The discussion begins with the main distinctions between the user- and producer-centered models (Section 2). Then the empirical evidence collected in the past five years is summarized, showing that user innovation is widespread, often left unprotected, and apparently valuable to others as many user innovations are adopted by other users and/or producers (Section 3). Subsequently, stock is taken of how user innovation can be measured, reviewing various survey methods that have been applied to measure user innovation by user firms and by individual consumers (Section 4). The chapter ends with conclusions and suggestions (Section 5).

2.   USER INNOVATION COMPARED WITH PRODUCER INNOVATION

Today, the dominant view of how innovation 'works' revolves around producers, here defined as anyone who would benefit from an innovative effort only if others adopted their innovation. In his early work, Schumpeter (1934) suggested that the economically most important and radical innovations are initiated by heroic entrepreneurs, and accordingly introduced by small and start-up enterprises. In his later work, he suggested that innovation takes place mainly in the R&D laboratories of large firms benefiting from a lack of competition (Schumpeter 1942). In both cases, however, innovations originate from producers and are supplied to intermediate and/or end users through products that are introduced to a market for sale.

After Schumpeter, a multitude of alternative models of innovation have been introduced. Thus the linear model of innovation revolves around fundamental knowledge production and its valorization, postulating that innovation starts with basic research, with commercially promising research output moving to applied research, development and production, while market adoption eventually follows (Bush 1945). The demand-pull version of this model argues that innovation is driven by the perceived demand of potential users, and producers develop products in efforts to respond to customer problems or suggestions, while basic research is much less significant (Rothwell 1992). The chain-link model of innovation (and its predecessors) stresses that relationships between science, development, production and diffusion are complex and interrelated (e.g. Price 1965; Kline 1985). The doing, using and interacting (DUI) model emphasizes that, beyond systematic or interrelated knowledge production, innovation in enterprises is more often concerned with informal processes of learning and experience-based know-how (Jensen et al. 2007).

What remains is that all these models regard producers as key actors in innovation. Typical producer innovators include commercial enterprises and individual inventors (who all primarily benefit from selling their innovations), and public research organizations and universities (needing others to adopt their innovative output). Producer-centered innovation is also still very much present in today's statistical indicators and innovation policy practices. An alternative line of research that emerged in the past three decades, however, shows that innovation can also be done by firms and individual end users who wish to use what they create rather than sell it (von Hippel 1976, 2005). User innovation differs from traditional, producer-centered innovation in three respects: (1) how the innovator benefits from innovation; (2) type of knowledge involved and resulting innovations; and (3) diffusion mechanisms.

Benefit from Innovation

The main distinction between user- and producer-centered innovation is rooted in how innovators benefit from their innovation effort. User innovators can be either firms or individual consumers that expect to benefit from *using* an innovative product. In contrast, producer innovators expect to benefit from *selling* an innovative product. Firms or individuals can be both producer and user innovators in specific situations. For example, Sony is a producer of electronic equipment, but it is also a user of machine tools. With respect to the innovations that it develops for its electronic products, it is a producer innovator, but if innovations in its machinery or production processes were investigated, the company could qualify as a user innovator. Users are unique in that they alone benefit directly from innovations. All others (here lumped under the term 'producers') must sell innovation-related products to users, indirectly or directly, in order to profit from innovations. Thus, in order to profit, producer inventors must sell or license knowledge related to innovations, and producers must sell goods or services incorporating innovations.

In line with this distinction, users innovate if they want something that is not available on the market, and are able and willing to invest in its development; expected benefits from in-house use is what primarily drives them. In practice, many users do not find precisely what they need on existing markets. Meta-analyses of market segmentation studies suggest that user needs for products are highly heterogeneous in many fields (Franke and Reisinger 2003). As a consequence, some of them will modify their products or have a high willingness to spend time and money to develop a personal version of a product that exactly satisfies their needs. In contrast, producers tend to follow product development strategies to meet the needs of homogeneous market segments. They are motivated by perceived opportunities to serve sufficiently large numbers of customers (users) to justify their innovation investments. This strategy of 'few sizes fit all' leaves many users dissatisfied with commercial products on offer (von Hippel 2005).

Type of Knowledge and Innovations

Users and producers tend to know different things and accordingly employ different knowledge in the innovation process. Users have the advantage of knowing precisely what they want: they possess superior information regarding their own needs. Producers must rely on market research to get a glimpse of those unsatisfied user needs, but in practice this is difficult. Estimates of failed product innovations range from 75 to 90 percent of all new product introductions (Cooper 2003). User innovators possess 'sticky information' about their needs – information that is costly to transfer from one individual to another because of differences in background knowledge, experience and context of use information (von Hippel 1994). Transferring this information to producers is expensive and tends to make user innovation more efficient than attempting to teach producers about user needs. A study of innovations in mountain biking equipment, for example, found that user innovations often depended on information that the inventors had obtained through their own cycling experience, reflecting their own unique circumstances and interests, such as a desire to bike in extreme weather conditions or to perform acrobatic stunts (von Hippel 2005). Producers, on the other hand, possess better capabilities to design and market innovations: they employ specialized engineers, have professional software and machines, and an infrastructure to develop and market innovations for larger numbers of users. In sum, producers are advanced in terms of 'solution information', while users are advanced in terms of 'need information'.

Users' and producers' differing stocks of local knowledge has an impact on the types of innovations that they develop. Due to information stickiness, innovators tend to rely on information they already have in stock (von Hippel 1994). Users are more likely to come up with functionally novel innovations, requiring a great deal of user-need information and use-context information for their development. In contrast, producers tend to produce incremental innovations that are improvements on well-known needs and that require a rich understanding of solution information for their development, including design, reliability and technical quality. Their innovations are more likely to be dimension-of-merit improvements, and not so much functionally novel innovations. In this context, Riggs and von Hippel (1994) studied the types of innovations made by users and producers that improved the functioning of two major types of scientific instruments. They found that users are significantly more likely than producers to develop innovations that enabled the instruments to do qualitatively new things for the first time. In contrast, producers developed innovations that enabled users to do the same things they had been doing, but to do them more conveniently or reliably.

Diffusion Mechanisms

A third important distinction is how producer and user innovations generally diffuse to other economic actors. As indicated, producers expect to benefit from their innovations by selling them to users, or alternatively, by selling or licensing their innovative knowledge to other producers who might do the job of commercialization. However, producers cannot capture all the profits their innovations engender; their profits will be reduced by knowledge that involuntarily 'spills over' to other innovating actors as a consequence of labor mobility, site visits of external actors and other reasons (Griliches 1992).

In contrast, users often achieve widespread diffusion by freely revealing what they have developed (Harhoff et al. 2003). This may seem strange, but it is often the best or the only practical option available to users, as hiding innovations with trade secrets is unlikely to be effective for long, and user innovators do not care much about direct economic benefits anyway. Other users may just pick what a user innovator has developed, or alternatively, a commercial producer may adopt his/her innovation to further develop it and introduce it to the market for general sale. Finally, some users may start their own businesses to commercialize innovations. They may find out that other users are interested, and become producers by themselves (Shah and Tripsas 2007).

3.　EMPIRICAL SCOPE OF USER INNOVATION

Early user innovation studies focused upon narrow categories of innovations, leaving room for criticism that this type of innovation is a marginal one. For example, early studies demonstrated the significance of users as a source of functionally novel innovations in scientific instruments, automated clinical chemistry analyzers and pultrusion processes (e.g. von Hippel 1976). Likewise, studies on the share of user innovators initially focused on specific products like printed circuit CAD software, pipe-hanger hardware, library information systems and surgical equipment, while samples of individual consumers dealt with outdoor consumers products, extreme sports equipment and mountain biking equipment (for an overview, see von Hippel 2005: 20).

In the past five years researchers have started to develop indicators to identify user innovators in broad samples of firms and consumers – beyond specific products or industries. From this work initial conclusions can be drawn regarding the frequency, openness and diffusion of user innovations in the general economy. Here, the empirical evidence is briefly reviewed, while a discussion of their survey methods follows in Section 4.

Frequency

Recall that user innovators can be either firms developing equipment or processes for in-house use, or individual end consumers primarily innovating for personal need. Table 5.1 offers an overview of empirical studies in chronological order.

Samples of firms
Surveys of small firms generally find that 15 to 20 percent can be considered user innovators (de Jong and von Hippel 2008; Flowers et al. 2010; Kim and Kim 2011). Those firms developed at least one innovation in the past three years that was primarily motivated by internal, process-related needs. After extrapolation, this concerns millions of companies across the globe. Moreover, survey evidence suggests that

Table 5.1 Frequency of user innovation in broad samples of firms and consumers

Source	Country	Year	Sample	Frequency (%)
Firm surveys				
Arundel and Sonntag (2001)	Canada	1998	3702 manufacturing plants with > 10 employees	41.0
Schaan and Uhrbach (2009)	Canada	2007	6478 manufacturing plants with > 20 employees and $250K revenues	39.8
de Jong and von Hippel (2009)	Netherlands	2007	498 high-tech SMEs with < 100 employees	54.0
de Jong and von Hippel (2008)	Netherlands	2008	2416 small firms (< 100 employees)	21.0
Flowers et al. (2010)	UK	2009	1004 SMEs with 10–250 employees	15.3
Kim and Kim (2011)	South Korea	2009	3081 manufacturers with > 10 employees	17.7
Consumer surveys				
von Hippel et al. (in press)	UK	2009	1173 individual end consumers ≥ 18 years	6.1
de Jong (2011a)	Netherlands	2010	533 consumers ≥ 18 years	6.2
Ogawa and Pongtanalert (2011)	USA	2010	1992 consumers ≥ 18 years	5.2
Ogawa and Pongtanalert (2011)	Japan	2011	2000 consumers ≥ 18 years	3.7

Note: Reported frequencies are population estimates, with the exception of de Jong and von Hippel (2009) and Ogawa and Pongtanalert (2011).

substantial investments are involved. Flowers et al. (2010) followed up on firms' most recent user innovations by documenting their time and money expenditures. They found that for every user innovation, companies spent on average 107 person-days and £44 500 out-of-pocket costs. When evaluated at the average salary for UK workers, this represented an annual spending on user innovation of £1.7 billion. It was also estimated that the annual R&D spending by similar firms was £2.6 billion, indicating that investments in user innovation are not marginal.

In more specific samples of manufacturers and high-tech small firms the share of user innovators is higher, that is, in the 40 to 60 percent range (Arundel and Sonntag 2001; Schaan and Uhrbach 2009; de Jong and von Hippel 2009). Arundel and Sonntag (2001), for example, analyzed data on the adoption, modification and development of specific technologies by Canadian manufacturing plants. From their findings it can be inferred that 41.0 percent modified existing technologies to better fit their internal needs, or developed their own technologies from scratch for application in their operations.

The empirical studies so far suggest that the frequency of user innovation is contingent on firm size, industry types and technical capabilities. Larger organizations are more process-intensive, which calls for in-house innovation, and indeed, studies report that the frequency of user innovation increases with size (e.g. de Jong and von Hippel 2008; Flowers et al. 2010). For industry types, generally manufacturers are more process-intensive and likely to innovate for their own process-related needs (e.g. de Jong and von Hippel 2009). For technical capability, it has been found that high-tech firms are more likely to innovate (e.g. de Jong and von Hippel 2009). Finally, it should be noted that user firm innovation partially overlaps with process innovation as defined by the *Oslo Manual* (OECD/Eurostat 2005). An important distinction, however, it that user innovation is limited to new creations and/or modifications of existing processes, while process innovation also includes adoptions of equipment or processes developed by other parties that are new to the firm. A further elaboration follows in Section 4 (Firm Surveys).

Samples of consumers

User innovation by individual consumers is not at all recorded in official surveys, and until recently it could be considered dark matter: unmeasured, and so impossible to include in economic or policy-making analyses. Consumers may innovate in their leisure time to create and/or modify everyday items like craft and shop tools, sports and hobby equipment, dwelling products, gardening equipment, vehicle and transport-related items, pet-related items and medical equipment (von Hippel et al., in press).

The evidence so far suggests that about 4 to 6 percent of all consumers created at least one user innovation in the past three years (Table 5.2). Von Hippel and colleagues (in press) found a share of 6.1 percent innovating UK consumers, equivalent to 2.9 million individuals. They also found that these innovators on average spent 7.1 days and £1098 out-of-pocket costs per year. At the macro-level and when evaluating person-days at average UK workforce salaries, total annual spending by consumers on innovation was estimated at £3.2 billion. (For comparison, estimated annual R&D expenditures by companies on consumer products were estimated at £2.2 billion.)

Results from the consumer surveys mentioned in Table 5.1 include that, across the globe, hundreds of millions of consumers are user innovators, with probably substantial investments involved (especially when consumers' time spending is taken into account). Moreover, it has been found that the frequency of innovation by consumers is higher for males, and for those with high educational attainment and/or technical training (von Hippel et al. 2011). Obviously, education and training reflect personal capabilities for innovation: highly educated engineers are most likely capable of developing fixes for their personal problems.

Openness

Producer innovators would generally protect their innovation-related knowledge with intellectual property rights (IPRs) to exclude others and/ or to facilitate licensing strategies. In contradiction, user innovators are not driven by profits that would result from selling their knowledge, and are often not rivalrous with potential users. Accordingly, users are less likely than producers to exclude others from adopting their knowledge. Moreover, the presence of innovating users does not always imply a big market of other users facing sufficiently similar needs. Producers generally employ product development strategies to meet the needs of homogeneous market segments, but user needs can be very diverse so that applying for IPRs is less useful. 'Open innovation' is here defined as innovation without claiming IPRs. In most of the surveys that were discussed above, researchers followed up by asking innovators if they had applied IPRs to protect their innovations – by patents, copyrights, trademarks and/or confidentiality agreements. See Table 5.2.

The share of innovating firms using IPRs for their user innovators ranges from 12.5 percent to 53.3 percent. In consumer samples this is much lower, ranging from 8.8 percent in the USA to even 0.0 percent in Japan. In general, user innovators are less inclined to protect their innovations with IPRs, most likely because they do not regard it as a source of profit. This becomes most evident when consumer samples are considered,

Table 5.2 Protection of user innovations with IPRs by firms and consumers

Source	Country	Year	Sample	Protection with IPRs (%)
Firm surveys				
de Jong and von Hippel (2009)	Netherlands	2007	364 user innovations developed by high-tech SMEs (< 100 employees)	12.5
Schaan and Uhrbach (2009)	Canada	2008	1277 user innovations developed by manufacturing plants with > 20 employees and $250K revenues	53.3
Flowers et al. (2010)	UK	2009	200 user innovations developed by SMEs with 10–250 employees	35.5
Kim and Kim (2011)	South Korea	2009	370 user innovations developed by manufacturers with > 10 employees	43.8
de Jong (2010)	Netherlands	2010	81 user innovations developed by high-tech SMEs (< 100 employees)	13.6
Consumer surveys				
von Hippel et al. (in press)	UK	2009	104 user innovations developed by consumers ≥ 18 years	1.9
Ogawa and Pongtanalert (2011)	USA	2010	114 user innovations developed by consumers ≥ 18 years	8.8
Ogawa and Pongtanalert (2011)	Japan	2011	83 user innovations developed by consumers ≥ 18 years	0.0

but also for high-tech small firms that are competing with differentiated products rather than unique production processes. In this context, de Jong (2010) presented data on 81 small high-tech firms that had engaged in both producer and user innovation in the past three years. While small high-tech firms were inclined to protect their new products (60.3 percent), the same firms did not bother about protecting their user innovations (only 13.6 percent applying for IPRs). For larger organizations, the findings are different. In the Canadian, UK and South Korean firm samples mentioned in Table 5.2, quite a few firms were eager to protect their knowledge. A possible explanation is that especially large manufacturers are more likely to operate in oligopolistic markets where competitive advantage revolves around unique production processes, and then it makes sense to exclude rivals from copying innovative processes. In general, however, user innovation seems more open than producer innovation.

Diffusion

From a social point of view, it is important that innovations diffuse across society. Knowledge spillovers appear when knowledge that is developed by one actor becomes available to others. When innovations are developed by producers, the pathway to diffusion is well known, as producers will sell what they have developed to all interested consumers and/or firms, or simultaneously, their knowledge may involuntarily spill over to other innovators and adopters.

User innovations should obviously diffuse too, or multiple users with similar needs would need to invest in similar innovations. This would be a poor use of resources from a social welfare point of view. In general, three mechanisms for the diffusion of user innovations include:

- peer to peer: users may reveal their innovations to others for inspection, copying and adoption, without charge, so that innovations diffuse peer to peer;
- producer adoption: commercial producers may adopt users' innovations to further improve and sell them as commercial products;
- new venture creation: innovating consumers may start a new business to introduce a commercial version of their innovation to the market, while innovating firms may further develop their user innovation into a new line of products which are then commercialized.

Free revealing
While many users do not bother about IPRs, some go further and actively reveal their innovations for free. They may do so hoping that commercial

producers will adopt and improve their innovations so that more robust and reliable solutions become available. Alternatively, free revealing can be driven by expected recognition of peers and reputation gains, communal norms of reciprocity (i.e. benefit from other users' contributions, as in open-source software) and desires to set informal standards (Harhoff et al. 2003).

After early studies demonstrated that users share their innovations, for example in medical equipment, open-source software, semiconductor process equipment, library information systems and mine-pumping engines (von Hippel 2005), recent studies find similar results in broad samples (e.g. Flowers et al. 2010).

Many innovations developed by users are of interest to the innovator only, or alternatively, the user does not bother about revealing the innovation for some reason (e.g. it is not considered of general interest, too much time is needed to reveal its design on the web etc.). However, in samples of firms about 10 percent of the user innovations are freely revealed. In consumer samples the share of innovations that are freely revealed is higher: in the 10 to 30 percent range (e.g. von Hippel et al. in press). Beyond this a subset of users reveals their innovations selectively, for example to their close social ties, and/or for non-monetary compensations such as promised discounts on future orders and other favors. For example, in a sample of user innovations developed by Dutch small high-tech firms, selective revealing applied to 13 percent (de Jong and von Hippel 2009).

Adoption by peers and/or commercial producers

Survey results regarding frequency of adoption are shown in Table 5.3. Note that most studies did not distinguish between adoption by producers and other users, but rather asked for adoption in a broad sense. In the samples of Dutch high-tech SMEs and Canadian manufacturing plants, adoption by commercial producers was around 25 percent of all reported innovations. Moreover, Schaan and Uhrbach (2009) found that another 25.3 percent was adopted by other users. For consumers these general adoption rates are lower, that is, 5 to 20 percent, but across the globe this still represents millions of innovations that are apparently useful to others. The only 'outlier' is the South-Korean sample, in which a few manufacturers reported that other businesses had picked up their inventions. Kim and Kim (2011) argued that this may be due to cultural reasons and the presence of hierarchically organized industry structures ('chaebols'). In summary, although most user innovations seem of interest to the innovator only and/or are known only to the innovator, it is generally found that 5 to 25 percent are adopted by others either in part or as a whole.

Table 5.3 Aadoption of user innovations by other actors (firms or consumers)

Source	Country	Year	Sample	Adoption (%)
Firm surveys				
de Jong and von Hippel (2009)	Netherlands	2007	364 user innovations developed by high-tech SMEs (< 100 employees)	24.7[a]
Schaan and Uhrbach (2009)	Canada	2007	1277 user innovations developed by manufacturing plants with > 20 employees and $250K revenues	26.3[a] ; 25.3[b]
Flowers et al. (2010)	UK	2009	200 user innovations developed by SMEs with 10–250 employees	19.5
Kim and Kim (2011)	South Korea	2009	370 user innovations developed by manufacturers with > 10 employees	3.2
Consumer surveys				
von Hippel et al. (in press)	UK	2009	104 user innovations developed by consumers ≥ 18 years	17.1
Ogawa and Pongtanalert (2011)	USA	2010	114 user innovations developed by consumers ≥ 18 years	6.1
Ogawa and Pongtanalert (2011)	Japan	2011	83 user innovations developed by consumers ≥ 18 years	5.0

Notes:
a. Adoption by commercial producers only.
b. Adoption by other users only.

New venture creation

If users develop an innovation that other people like, they generally receive requests from other users to build and provide them a copy. Users then sometimes decide to start their own business to commercialize their innovations, and accordingly become producers – although they were initially driven by personal need. Examples of entirely new industries that were born through such a process include juvenile products, rodeo kayaking equipment and dishwasher machines (Shah and Tripsas 2007).

Empirical studies demonstrating the relationship between user innovation and new venture creation include Shah et al. (2011) and de Jong (2011a). Shah et al. (2011) found that 46.6 percent of innovative start-ups in the USA which survived more than five years were founded by user innovators. De Jong, after an extensive screening procedure, obtained a sample of 33 Dutch consumers who had developed a user innovation in the past three years. Next, he analyzed how these innovators performed on various indicators adopted from the Global Entrepreneurship Monitor (GEM) (see Hartog et al. 2010). He found that user innovators are more likely to have entrepreneurial intentions and to engage in nascent entrepreneurship. Thus 15.2 percent expected to start a new business within the next three years, and 9.1 percent were actively involved in the process of business creation but had not yet received any income. Within the broad population of all Dutch consumers these percentages were 7.4 and 3.1, respectively. Both of these findings suggest that user innovation and entrepreneurship are correlated (obviously these findings do not prove causality). It may be that innovating consumers are more likely to recognize opportunities to build a business and then do so. Alternatively, user innovation and early-stage entrepreneurship may reflect people's general proactivity to take charge and pick up challenges and opportunities in life. More research is needed to explore how these concepts are related.

4.   MEASUREMENT OF USER INNOVATION

Researchers have applied a range of methods to survey user innovation in samples of firms and consumers. Here, an overview is provided, starting with firm surveys, and then for consumers. Next, the alternative perspective of the diffusion of user innovations is discussed, and how this can be better captured in official statistics.

Firm Surveys

Three methods have been applied in the past five years to document user innovation in samples of firms. First, surveys of advanced manufacturing technologies (AMT) have been done in Canada. The second method draws on telephone surveys and has been applied in the Netherlands and the UK. The third method is a follow-up to the Community Innovation Survey (CIS), which has been implemented in South Korea and Mozambique.

Method 1: AMT survey and follow-up
An early survey identifying user innovation in manufacturing plants revolved around the Canadian AMT survey (Arundel and Sonntag 2001). Back in 1998, Statistics Canada sampled thousands of Canadian manufacturing plants with at least ten employees, the continuation of a program begun in the 1980s following the publication of von Hippel (1988) (Gault 2012). Among other questions, data were collected on the adoption, modification and development of specific technologies. Respondents were offered a list of 26 technologies, ranging from computer aided design (CAD) to rapid prototyping systems. For each technology they indicated if they currently used it in their plant, and if yes, they were asked how the technology had been introduced: by licensing it or buying it off the shelf, by modifying an existing technology, or by developing a new technology from scratch. It appeared that more than half of the surveyed plants were either technology modifiers or technology developers (Arundel and Sonntag 2001: 27–9). Although the authors did not use the term 'user innovation', their definitions of technology modifiers and technology developers fit with the concept.

In 2007, the AMT survey was updated by Schaan and Uhrbach (2009). Again, a substantial share of the manufacturing plants had engaged in technology modification and/or technology development. Schaan and Uhrbach went on to organize a follow-up survey to collect data on the user innovation process, registering variables such as time and money expenditures, collaboration partners and more.

Obviously, all survey methods discussed here have their pros and cons. The AMT survey is an existing source of data, providing a quicker route to capture user innovation in official statistics. The survey is based on very specific cues, so that it is less likely that respondents would misunderstand any questions or overlook relevant innovations. A drawback is that the AMT is not as widespread as the CIS (see later). Many countries do not implement it, or only with substantial time gaps. Moreover, its questions deal only with technology modification and/or development, so the potential domain of user innovation in firms is not fully covered (e.g. consider organizational innovations for in-house use) and is probably most suitable for manufacturing industries. Finally, to collect detailed information on the innovation process, a follow-up survey is still needed.

Method 2: telephone survey

To more directly capture user innovation with specific indicators, de Jong and von Hippel (2009) piloted survey questions in a sample of high-tech SMEs. They utilized two indicators of the presence or absence of user innovation: (1) had the firm developed new process equipment or software for its own use; (2) had the firm modified existing process equipment or software for its own use within the past three years. Next, respondents were asked to select their most recent innovation and report what it was about (open-ended question).

This method gave rise to a second type of user innovation indicators that are collected by computer assisted telephone interviewing (CATI). Respondents first indicate whether they innovated in software or physical products, and if they created their innovation from scratch or by modifying an existing product. Next, the survey script follows up with open-ended questions to obtain a detailed description of what respondents have done, and why. These descriptions are then screened to eliminate 'false positives' – reported examples that are not in fact innovations. Finally, more false positives are eliminated through additional questions, for example if respondents know of equivalent products already available on the market, and if they developed their innovations for customers (which would make the example a product innovation). After being first applied in 2007 on small high-tech firms (de Jong and von Hippel 2009), this method has been further refined in broad samples of small and medium-sized enterprises (de Jong and von Hippel 2008; Flowers et al. 2010).

This method consists of a fully dedicated survey in which only user innovation data are collected, including process questions such as on collaboration, investments, application of intellectual property rights, free revealing of innovations and diffusion patterns. There is no need for follow-up surveys. Moreover, the CATI technique enables a rigorous screening procedure so that falsely reported innovations can be removed, making this method very suitable for academic purposes. A disadvantage is that any connection with official surveys (e.g. CIS) is lacking, making this method not an obvious candidate for the production of official statistics.

Method 3: CIS and follow-up

A third method is to use the CIS as a screening survey to trace potential user innovations. The usual question on the presence of process innovation can be considered a first indication. If the response is positive, then respondents are asked if their enterprise developed the process innovation (1) by itself, (2) together with other enterprises, (3) by adapting or modifying processes originally developed by other enterprises or institutions, or (4) entirely by other enterprises or institutions (Chapter 1: Appendix). Gault (2012) explains that positive answers to options 1 and 3 suggest the presence of user innovation, while the second option might. To gain more information on user innovation in firms, there can be follow-up surveys that start probing whether respondents to options 1–3 are really user innovators. These follow-up surveys could also record innovation process variables such as collaboration, intellectual property, investments and more, comparable with how researchers have done this when using the AMT or telephone survey methods.

This CIS-based method has been applied by Kim and Kim (2011) in a sample of manufacturing firms with more than ten employees in South Korea. More recently, Zita and Lopes (2011) did the same on a smaller scale in the Maputo province of Mozambique. A main advantage of this method is that the CIS is widespread, providing an opportunity to quickly capture user innovation indicators in official statistics. A drawback is that it is assumed that the first step (identifying potential user innovators with the CIS) captures all relevant user innovation activity, which still needs to be empirically demonstrated. Simultaneously, the first step has been shown to provide many false positives (Kim and Kim 2011), so a follow-up is indispensable in order to provide precise data on the frequency of user innovation. This is an area for future research.

Consumer Surveys

Official social surveys that capture the activity of consumers modifying or developing goods or services to suit their needs are still lacking. Researchers have so far been concerned with developing, testing and improving, a process that is still going on today.

A first attempt was made by Flowers and colleagues (2010) in the UK, based on computer-assisted telephone interviewing. While collecting data from 1173 UK consumers aged 18 and over, their survey method was inspired by the UK survey of 1004 small firms mentioned in Table 5.1. The survey started asking respondents whether they had created and/or modified software in the past three years, then the same for the creation and/or modification of hardware. For each of these options open-ended questions were asked to exclude false positives (e.g. 'I bought a piece of Ikea furniture and put it together myself'). Additional false positives were eliminated through analysis of responses to two screening questions. If respondents knew of equivalent products already available on the market, or if they had developed the innovation as part of their jobs, their claimed innovations were excluded. In effect, the survey was designed to identify only innovations with some kind of functional novelty that consumers had developed in their leisure time. After the UK survey, similar surveys were implemented among consumer samples in Japan and the USA, now using web survey tools instead of telephone interviewing (Ogawa and Pongtanalert 2011).

A next generation of consumer surveys was piloted in the Netherlands (de Jong 2011a) and Finland (de Jong 2011b). These pilots addressed some specific problems encountered in the UK. First, unlike business respondents, many consumers were not aware of what innovation may entail. As a consequence, more specific cues needed to be provided to support adequate recall. Drawing on six pilot surveys of 100 highly educated Finnish consumers each, de Jong (2011b) concluded that (rather than software versus hardware) eight specific cues provide more reliable data: (1) computer software; (2) household fixtures and furnishings; (3) transport and vehicle-related; (4) tools and equipment; (5) sports, hobbies and entertainment; (6) children and education-related; (7) help, care and medical; and (8) other (open-ended category). Second, it was found that in consumer samples the distinction between innovation modifications versus creations was less important. There is a gray area between the two, and asking respondents only for 'creations' gave nearly identical results. Third, web surveys were piloted to see if they would provide acceptable data, and they did. Although telephone surveys remain a 'gold standard', the possibility of web surveying is a potential cost saver in future data collection efforts.

De Jong (2011b) recommended five steps to identify user innovators in broad consumer samples. For each of the aforementioned cues, respondents first indicate if they have created it in the past three years (e.g. 'Did you create any computer software for personal need?'). If yes, up to four additional questions are asked to screen out false positives:

- Respondents indicate if they created it (e.g. computer software) for their job or business – to screen out job-related innovations.
- They then indicate if they could have bought a similar application on the market if they had wanted to – to screen out home-built versions of existing products.
- Next, they indicate if their primary motive was commercial rather than personal need – commercially driven innovations are discarded.
- Finally, respondents describe their innovation and its functional novelty (open-ended questions).

In conclusion, the measurement of user innovation by consumers is still in an early phase. State-of-the-art survey tools are currently helpful to inform academic studies, but they are not ready for adoption for the production of official statistics. One challenge is to reduce the number of questions, which may be done by asking extra advance screening questions. De Jong (2011b) identified two potential ones, related to tinkering and inventive activities. More specifically, he asked if respondents ever tinkered with machines, cars, computers or software in their leisure time, and if they ever spent their leisure time on inventions or developing new products, applications or concepts. If both answers were negative, the chances of being a consumer innovator became very small.

Diffusion of User Innovations

As the diffusion of user innovations is important for general welfare, the measurement challenge is to go beyond documenting the incidence of user innovation. While the aforementioned survey methods can include questions on diffusion, either directly (Method 2 and Consumer Surveys) or in a follow-up (Methods 1 and 3), the challenge can also be dealt with by modifying official surveys like the CIS.

Gault (2012) takes a different perspective by stressing the distinction between user innovation and user-driven innovation. User innovation, as discussed in Section 2, revolves around firms or consumers solving problems for personal need. User-driven innovation refers to the use by the producer of the flow of knowledge from the user as a result of using the product purchased. The producer may also collaborate with the user to co-innovate. These are cases of user-driven innovation, not of user innovation. In a recent contribution, Gault explained to what extent user-driven innovation is already present in official statistics.

While recalling that user innovations can diffuse through peer-to-peer sharing, producer adoption and new venture creation, Table 5.4 offers an overview of how the adoption of user innovations developed by firms and consumers is reflected in official statistics.

The left-hand column provides the case of user innovation by firms. If innovations are transferred to a producer (1a), or brought to the market by the user firm itself (1b), diffusion will sooner or later become evident in the frequency of product innovation as measured by the CIS. In the case of (1b), however, the source of innovation may be lost and additional questions and/or follow-up surveys would be needed to document if product innovations were first developed by users (Gault 2012). If user innovations are shared peer-to-peer (3a), process innovation numbers will go up.

Table 5.4   Diffusion of user innovation in official statistics

Diffusion mechanism	Type of user innovation	
	Firm modifies/develops a process (a)	Consumer modifies/develops product (b)
1. Producer adoption	Product innovation (user firm is source of innovation)	Product innovation (consumer is source of innovation)
2. New venture creation (or new product line)	Product innovation (user firm becomes producer)	Product innovation (consumer becomes an entrepreneur)
3. Peer-to-peer sharing	Process innovation in adopting firms (developed entirely by other enterprises or institutes)	Not yet visible in official statistics

Source: Derived from Gault (2012: 122).

Adopting firms would report a process innovation that is entirely developed by another enterprise or institute. Finally, in case the innovation is not transferred at all, the innovating firm itself would still report a process innovation (not in Table 5.4).

While official statistics are to some extent able to register the diffusion of firms' innovations, there are currently some serious shortcomings for user innovations developed by consumers. The right-hand column of Table 5.4 deals with this case. Again, in case of producer adoption (1b) and new venture creation (2b), statistics on product innovation should go up. But if consumers share their innovations peer to peer (3b), this is not considered innovation adoption according to the *Oslo Manual*. Gault (2012) suggests that the *Oslo Manual* definition of product innovation could be modified, that is, not limited to market introductions, but also include the situation when new products are made available to potential users, which does not necessarily happen through market mechanisms, but can also include sharing in a community of practice or peer group. It is suggested that paragraph 150 of the *Oslo Manual* should be modified to state: 'A new or improved product is implemented when it is made available to potential users', rather than 'when it is introduced on the market' (Gault 2012: 123), so that the CIS in the future could also capture the third mode of diffusion as far as diffusion to commercial enterprises is concerned.

5. CONCLUSION

User innovation is an alternative model of innovation, revolving around users who primarily innovate to satisfy their own needs, rather than for direct economic benefit. Recent evidence collected in broad surveys and in multiple countries shows that user innovation is present in large parts of the economy, practiced by millions of businesses and individual consumers. Substantial money and time investments are made by these innovators to satisfy their own process-related or personal needs, and this effort is not yet adequately recorded in official statistics (firms) or not recorded at all (consumers). Moreover, in consumer samples user innovation is very open (unconstrained by intellectual property), while early evidence for firms suggests that user innovation is at least more open than traditional producer innovation. Finally, user innovations appear to be useful to other economic actors. Diffusion mechanisms include peer-to-peer sharing (about 10 percent of the innovations developed by firms, and 10 to 30 percent of the innovations developed by consumers), new venture creation (user innovators are more likely to be occupied with early-stage entrepreneurship) and adoption by incumbent producers for further development and commercial sale.

In the near future user innovation will likely become even more important than it is today. Empowered by the Internet, specific types of user innovation, including open-source projects and other distributed forms of innovation, will be increasingly seen. Moreover, easy-to-use design tools such as CAD software and 3D printers will become more available, and as the average world education level is improving, an increasing share of world citizens will be able to innovate for themselves (Baldwin and von Hippel 2011).

This chapter suggests a research agenda. Researchers and policy makers could explore the implications of user innovation, starting with the current innovation measures. Today, the producer-centered model of innovation is still dominant in the thinking of both innovation researchers and policy makers, and current sources of innovation indicators do not yet (sufficiently) capture the concept of user innovation. Until the actual levels of user innovation and expenditures are made clear, researching and demonstrating its welfare implications and hampering factors will be complicated, and it will be difficult to get governments to take seriously any policy needs of innovating users.

In this vein, it has already been concluded that available indicators attract policy attention – think of the current focus in many countries on knowledge commercialization and continued interventions to stimulate R&D – and it has already been proposed repeatedly that current measures need modification (e.g. Jensen et al. 2007; Laestadius 1998).

To better capture user innovation in firms, more work could be done with the AMT and CIS-based methods, which would also include follow-up surveys to document how firms developed user innovations, and, more importantly, to what extent and how these innovations diffuse. Cognitive testing of the current questions in official surveys (e.g. process innovation questions in the CIS) is relevant and is the subject of a current OECD project (see Chapters 3 and 4). From the perspective of this chapter, the objective is that these questions more effectively serve as screening questions for detailed additional data collection, or may even be refined for this purpose. Finally, there are experiments with alternative survey designs to more directly measure user innovation in firms, using CATI methods. When doing so, the objective is to measure what hampers user innovation, and what parameters policy makers need to focus on so that the user-centered model can reach its full potential. The bottlenecks that user innovators encounter are still uncharted.

As for surveying consumers, the activity and the resulting information are absent, as far as official statistics are concerned. The authors are not aware of any official survey that has tried to measure innovation by individual consumers, so this would be a logical next step. First, however, the current survey procedures need to be further refined and simplified. Current methods used by researchers and reported here have proven capable of tracing and validating reported user innovations, but are still too complex and labor-intensive to be suitable for official surveys. In addition, consumer survey methods have not been developed that can capture services innovations by users – while services have been identified as another field in which users are active developers of innovations with a high degree of novelty (Olivera and von Hippel 2011). In the coming years interesting new measurement practices and results emerging from the work that is currently in progress are anticipated.

REFERENCES

Arundel, A. and V. Sonntag (2001), 'Patterns of advanced manufacturing technology (AMT) use in Canadian manufacturing: 1998 AMT survey results', Research Paper no. 12, Science, Innovation and Electronic Information Division, Ottawa: Statistics Canada.

Baldwin, C.Y. and E. von Hippel (2011), 'Modeling a paradigm shift: from producer innovation to user and open collaborative innovation', *Organization Science*, **22**, 1399–417.

Bush, V. (1945), *Science: The Endless Frontier*, Washington, DC: US Government Printing Office.

Cooper, R.G. (2003), 'Profitable product innovation: the critical success factors', in L.V. Shavinina (2003), *The International Handbook on Innovation*, Oxford: Elsevier Science, pp. 139–57.

de Jong, J.P.J. (2010), 'The openness of user and producer innovation: a study of Dutch high-tech small firms', paper presented at the User and Open Innovation workshop, Cambridge, MA, 2–4 August.

de Jong, J.P.J. (2011a), 'Uitvinders in Nederland' (Inventors in the Netherlands), Research Report A201105, Zoetermeer: EIM.

de Jong, J.P.J. (2011b), 'Identifying consumer innovators: a five-step survey procedure', Working Paper, Rotterdam: RSM Erasmus University.

de Jong, J.P.J. and E. von Hippel (2008), 'User innovation in SMEs: incidence and transfer to producers', Working Paper, Zoetermeer: EIM.

de Jong, J.P.J. and E. von Hippel (2009), 'Transfers of user process innovations to producers: a study of Dutch high tech firms', *Research Policy*, **38**(7), 1181–91.

Flowers, S., E. von Hippel, J. de Jong and T. Sinozic (2010), *Measuring User Innovation in the UK: The Importance of Product Creation by Users*, London: Nesta.

Franke, N. and H. Reisinger (2003), *Remaining Within Cluster Variance: A Meta Analysis of the Dark Side of Cluster Analysis*, Vienna: Vienna Business University.

Gault, Fred (2012), 'User innovation and the market', *Science and Public Policy*, **39**, 118–28.

Griliches, Z. (1992), 'The search for R&D spillovers', *Scandinavian Journal of Economics*, **94** (Supplement), S29–S47.

Harhoff, D., J. Henkel and E. von Hippel (2003), 'Profiting from voluntary information spillovers: how users benefit by freely revealing their innovations', *Research Policy*, **32**(10), 1753–69.

Hartog, C., J. Hessels, A. van Stel and J.P.J. de Jong (2010), 'Global entrepreneurship monitor 2009 the Netherlands: entrepreneurship on the rise', research report A201011, Zoetermeer: EIM.

Henkel, J. and E. von Hippel (2005), 'Welfare implications of user innovation', *Journal of Technology Transfer*, **30**(1/2), 73–87.

Jensen, M.B., B. Johnson, E. Lorenz and B.-Å. Lundvall (2007), 'Forms of knowledge and modes of innovation', *Research Policy*, **36**, 680–93.

Kim, J.B. and H.H. Kim (2011), *User Innovation in Korean Manufacturing Industries: Incidence and Protection*, Seoul: KAIST Business School.

Kline, S. J. (1985), 'Innovation is not a linear process', *Research Management*, **28**(2), 36–45.

Laestadius, S. (1998), 'The relevance of science and technology indicators: the case of pulp and paper', *Research Policy*, **27**, 385–95.

OECD/Eurostat (2005), *Oslo Manual: Guidelines for Collecting and Interpreting Innovation Data*, Paris: OECD.

Ogawa, S. and K. Pongtanalert (2011), 'Visualizing invisible innovation content: evidence from global consumer innovation surveys', Working Paper, June.

Oliveira, P. and E. von Hippel (2011), 'Users as service innovators: the case of banking services', *Research Policy*, **40**(6), 806–18.

Price, D.J.D. (1965), 'Is technology historically independent of science? A study in historiography', *Technology and Culture*, **6**(4), 553–68.

Riggs, W. and E. von Hippel (1994), 'The impact of scientific and commercial values on the sources of scientific instrument innovation', *Research Policy*, **23**, 459–69.

Rothwell, R. (1992), 'Successful industrial innovation: critical factors for the 1990s', *R&D Management*, **22**(3), 221–39.

Schaan, S. and M. Uhrbach (2009), *Measuring user innovation in Canadian manufacturing 2007*, Ottawa: Statistics Canada.

Schumpeter, J.A. (1934), *The Theory of Economic Development*, New York: Oxford University Press.

Schumpeter, J.A. (1942), *Capitalism, Socialism and Democracy*, New York: Harper and Row.

Shah, S.K. and M. Tripsas (2007), 'The accidental entrepreneur: the emergent and collective process of user entrepreneurship', *Strategic Entrepreneurship Journal*, **1**, 123–40.

Shah, S., S. Winston Smith and E.J. Reedy (2011), *Who are User Entrepreneurs? Findings on Innovation, Founder Characteristics & Firm Characteristics*, Kansas City, MO: Kauffman Foundation.

von Hippel, E. (1976), 'The dominant role of users in the scientific instrument innovation process', *Research Policy*, **5**(3), 212–39.

von Hippel, E. (1988), *The Sources of Innovation*, New York: Oxford University Press.

von Hippel, E. (1994), 'Sticky information and the locus of problem solving: implications for innovation', *Management Science*, **40**(4), 429–39.

von Hippel, E. (2005), *Democratizing Innovation*, Cambridge, MA: MIT Press.

von Hippel, E., J.P.J. de Jong and S. Flowers (in press), 'Comparing business and household sector innovation in consumer products: findings from a representative study in the United Kingdom', *Management Science*, doi: 10.1287/mnsc.1110.1508.

von Hippel, E., S. Ogawa and J.P.J. de Jong (2011), 'The age of the consumer-innovator', *MIT Sloan Management Review*, **53**(1), 27–35.

Zita, J. and A. Lopes (2011), 'User innovation in the Mozambican business enterprise sector for Maputo Province: presence of user innovation', Working Paper 2011-062, Maastricht: UNU-MERIT.

PART III

MEASUREMENT

6 Innovation panel surveys in Germany
Bettina Peters and Christian Rammer

1. INTRODUCTION

Surveying innovation activities of enterprises has a long tradition in Germany. The first large-scale survey instrument dates back to 1979 when the Munich-based Ifo Institute introduced its 'Ifo Innovation Test'. It used a methodology that was close to that later proposed in the *Oslo Manual*, distinguishing product and process innovation and collecting information on innovation activities and expenditure as well as some context information such as information sources for innovation, objectives of innovation activity and factors that hamper innovation. The survey is part of the Institute's wider activities to collect information on business climate and expectations in the manufacturing sector. The sample of the Ifo Innovation Test is drawn from Ifo's monthly business climate survey and is confined to the manufacturing sector (including mining and quarrying). Conducted annually since its start, the Ifo Innovation Test is probably the longest-lasting innovation panel survey in the world.[1] Although it has influenced the methodological work on innovation surveys, the Ifo Innovation Test does not fully apply the standards set by the *Oslo Manual* or those by the EU Commission's regulation on innovation statistics, which restricts international comparison. In addition, the survey's size is confined to about 1000 observations per year, which further limits its analytical potential in terms of sector breakdown.

In order to set up a survey that fully complied with the *Oslo Manual* (OECD 1992) and that could contribute to the then newly established Community Innovation Surveys (CIS), another innovation panel survey was introduced in Germany in 1993, the Mannheim Innovation Panel (MIP). This survey got its name from the city where the organization that conducts the survey is located, which is the Centre for European Economic Research (ZEW).[2] Commissioned by the Federal Ministry of Education and Research (BMBF), the MIP covers all production sectors (including mining, energy and water supply and construction) and a large number of service sectors, including trade, transportation, financial intermediation and business-related services. While the MIP shares many features of other national CIS, it holds some distinct characteristics that may make it worth discussing the experience gained from this survey instrument in more detail. First, and in contrast to most other CIS ventures, the MIP is an annual panel survey which provides more opportunity to analyse persistence of innovation activities and causal effects between innovation input and output, as well as between innovation and other firm activities such as firm performance, than repeated cross-sectional surveys can offer. Second, the survey goes beyond the standard CIS questionnaires and includes information on firm performance (e.g. profitability, gross value added) and a firm's market environment (including measures on competition). Third, the MIP has been attempting from its beginning to combine new approaches to measuring innovation discussed in the academic literature with the need for applying internationally harmonized concepts and keeping basic definitions constant over time to allow time-series analysis. Finally, firm data from the MIP have been merged with company data from other sources, including patent and trade mark data, credit rating data as well as data on public funding of R&D and innovation, which offers a multiplicity of new opportunities for empirical investigations.

Section 2 of this chapter considers methodological aspects of innovation panel surveys. It starts with an overview of the methodology of the MIP in terms of sampling, questionnaire and survey method. Subsequently, the panel structure of the data set is presented, followed by an analysis of the determinants of a firm's decision to participate regularly in the panel. Section 4 gives an overview of the development of various innovation indicators over time. In Section 5 an example is given of how the special virtues of the MIP have been exploited in empirical innovation research with the focus on one of the research questions sketched above; specifically, the analytical findings are discussed on the persistence of innovation activities. The chapter concludes with a discussion of the importance of longitudinal panel data for the analysis of the activity of innovation.

2.   THE MANNHEIM INNOVATION PANEL

Sample

The MIP sample is a stratified random sample that covers enterprises with five or more employees from a wide area of economic activities. The original sample drawn in 1993 included mining, manufacturing, energy and water supply, and construction as well as a few service sectors (wholesale trade, real estate, computer activities management consulting, engineering, sewage and refuse disposal). In 1995, the panel was expanded to cover retail trade, sale and repair of motor vehicles, renting activities and various business-related services, and in 2001, film and broadcasting (NACE Rev.

1.1 groups 92.1 and 92.2) have been added. In 2005, construction, retail trade, sale and repair of motor vehicles, real estate and renting activities were taken out of the random sample as there was little demand for analyses of these sectors, while the large number of enterprises in the population required a substantial share in the survey's resources. The decision to drop these sectors was supported by the fact that the concept of innovation turned out to be difficult to apply to these sectors, and by the lack of reporting requirements for CIS. It is important to note, however, that for panel purposes firms from these discarded sectors that had responded to the survey before 2005 remained in the panel sample after 2005 and were contacted in later survey waves. As a consequence, the sector composition of responding firms did not change substantially.

The sample is stratified by sector, size class and region. The number of cells varies by year owing to changes in the sector coverage (Table 6A.1) and sector classification schemes.[3] Currently, the MIP sample consists of 896 strata: 55 divisions and 1 group of NACE Rev. 2.0 (all divisions of sections B, C, D, E, H, J, K plus divisions 46, 69, 71, 72, 73, 74, 78, 79, 80, 81, 82 and group 70.2), 8 size classes (5 to 9, 10 to 19, 20 to 49, 50 to 99, 100 to 249, 250 to 499, 500 to 999, 1000 and more employees) and two regions (western and eastern Germany including Berlin). The sampling is disproportionally drawn; that is, the drawing probability varies by cell. Higher drawing probabilities are applied to cells from larger size classes, cells from eastern Germany and cells with a high variation of innovation activities. A minimum of ten enterprises per cell are drawn.

As mentioned, the original sample was drawn in 1993 from a firm database called the Mannheim Enterprise Panel (MEP).[4] As no information on the variation of innovation activities by cells was available at that time, variation in labour productivity (sales per employee) was used as a proxy instead. From the beginning, the survey was designed as a panel. In subsequent years, the original sample has been refreshed biennially to compensate for panel mortality and to account for the foundation of new firms. Panel mortality includes firms that ceased business as well as small and medium-sized firms (up to 499 employees) that did not respond in four consecutive survey waves. Large firms remain in the sample irrespective of their response behaviour. The same holds true for any firm that leaves the target population by either changing its main economic activity to a sector outside the core sectors or by shrinking below the five employee threshold.

Table 6A.2 reports the sector distribution of the MIP sample by survey years. About half of all firms are from manufacturing and almost a quarter belongs to business-related services. Firms from these sectors are clearly overrepresented compared to the total population, which is also true for mining, energy and water supply, sewage, transport, storage and communication, and financial intermediation.

In addition to the random sample, the MIP deliberately addresses an additional sample of firms that have received public funding for R&D and innovation activities. These firms were drawn from a database of recipients of public R&D grants provided by the BMBF. The main purpose of including publicly funded firms is to generate a database for evaluation purposes (see for empirical applications Aschhoff 2010; Czarnitzki et al. 2007; Hussinger 2008; Schmidt and Aerts 2008). These firms are not considered for weighting purposes, except when a publicly funded enterprise has entered the MIP through random sampling.

The original gross sample of the MIP in 1993 comprised 13 318 firms. After the extension to service sectors in 1995, the sample size increased to 22 201. In order to keep survey costs down, the sample has been confined to a subsample of firms every second year. When drawing this subsample the same stratification features apply, but drawing probabilities are reduced. At the same time, in each cell, firms that responded in the past receive priority in drawing over non-responding firms. This practice started in 1996 for service firms and in 1998 for all firms, and has been continued since. As a result, sample size varies by year in a biennial rhythm (see Table 6.1). Since response rates are clearly higher in years with a reduced sample thanks to the focus on previously responding firms as well as due to a shorter questionnaire (the following subsection on the questionnaire provides more details), the size of the net sample does not vary in the same way.

Over time, the sample size has been increased to compensate for a somewhat falling response rate, to allow for a more detailed sector breakdown of the sample and to increase the drawing quota (gross sample as a percentage of total population), which was 11.4 per cent in the 2011 wave. Depending on the survey year, for 5 to 18 per cent of the firms in the gross sample a neutral loss has been recorded because either the firm ceased operation or it could not be successfully contacted despite several attempts. The large variation in the share of neutral losses first and foremost represents different efforts of contacting non-responding firms and of identifying firms that ceased business. In 2011, particular efforts were undertaken both to clean the data by removing firms that were no longer operating and by contacting all firms that did not respond to the initial postal mail by telephone, including a manual check of all invalid telephone numbers. As a result, a large number of neutral losses have been identified. In other survey years, the share of neutral losses is likely to be underestimated.

Response rates in uneven years with a full sample was 26.6 per cent

Table 6.1   Sample size and response characteristics of the MIP, 1993–2011

Survey year	Gross sample	Responses	Non-response interviews	Drawing quota[a]	Share of neutral losses[b]	Net response rate[c]	Coverage rate[d]	Total sample rate[e]
1993	13318	2854	992	12.9	6.0	22.8	30.7	4.3
1994	12663	3064	0	12.6	3.8	25.1	25.1	3.7
1995	22201	5633	1097	5.8	4.6	26.6	31.8	1.9
1996	9944	2281	815	10.7	6.0	24.4	33.1	3.6
1997	21576	4789	1920	6.5	11.0	24.9	34.9	2.0
1998	10668	3704	1893	3.1	6.2	37.0	55.9	1.7
1999	22385	4786	3869	7.0	15.6	25.3	45.8	2.7
2000	12929	3993	1996	3.7	4.9	32.5	48.7	1.9
2001	24032	4845	4014	7.4	4.2	21.0	38.5	2.7
2002	14225	3877	3832	3.9	3.0	28.1	55.9	2.7
2003	26215	4538	3853	8.0	4.7	18.2	33.6	2.7
2004	20572	3892	3766	6.5	16.0	22.5	44.3	2.7
2005	33107	5207	4235	12.5	8.5	17.2	31.2	3.4
2006	21003	4728	3816	7.8	8.4	24.6	44.4	3.2
2007	30162	5215	4231	11.0	3.2	17.9	32.4	3.4
2008	21058	6110	4580	6.4	9.7	32.1	56.2	3.5
2009	35195	7061	4960	11.0	10.1	22.3	38.0	3.8
2010	24009	6226	5459	7.7	7.1	27.9	52.4	3.8
2011	35531	6851	8721	11.4	18.2	23.6	53.6	5.0

Notes:
a. Gross sample as a percentage of total population (only for that part of the gross sample that belongs to the current target population of the MIP; 1993–2003 excluding film and broadcasting; 1993–98 excluding energy and water supply); break in series in 2008 due to revised total population figures.
b. Closed firms and firms that could not be contacted for other reasons as a percentage of the gross sample.
c. Responses as a percentage of the gross sample adjusted for neutral losses.
d. Responses plus non-response interviews as a percentage of the gross sample adjusted for neutral losses.
e. Responses plus non-response interviews as a percentage of the total population.

Source: ZEW.

in 1995 and fell to 17.2 in 2005 but could be increased again to 23.6 per cent in 2011, mainly resulting from higher efforts in following up through telephone contact and by offering an online variant of the questionnaire from 2008 onwards. Compared to other CIS, the response rates are very low, owing to the non-mandatory status, a longer and more complex questionnaire than the standard CIS questionnaire (see next section) and the less official status of the organization that executes the survey (by contrast with statistical offices). In addition, there was a decision to deliberately refrain from urging firms unwilling to participate in the survey to respond. In one attempt to do so, the result was that the quality of responses in terms of accuracy, completeness and reliability fell significantly, including a substantial share of firms reporting no innovation activities despite clear evidence that such activities did exist (as revealed by corresponding statements on the Internet, in company reports or through press releases).

Since a low response rate may result in a biased net sample of responding firms in terms of the share of innovative firms, a non-response survey has been undertaken in each survey wave (except for 1994) among a stratified random sample of non-responding firms. In the non-response survey firms are asked on the telephone whether they have introduced product or process innovation, providing them the very same definition of both types of innovation as in the mail questionnaire. In addition, information on ongoing or abandoned innovation activities and in-house R&D activities is collected. In order to check the firm's stratification variable, firms are asked for the number of employees and a short description of the main good or service. The size of the non-response survey increased from a sample of about 1000 firms to more than 8700 firms in 2011. The results show that, in most years, the share of innovating firms (i.e. having introduced at least one product or process innovation during the previous three-year period) is significantly higher[5] among the non-responding than among the responding firms. Only in two survey years (1993 and 2005) is the opposite result found, and only in 2007 are differences not statistically significant (Table 6.2).

These results suggest that innovating firms are more likely to refuse to respond to the innovation survey. This would reflect a cost-minimizing behaviour of firms since the effort to respond to the survey is significantly higher for innovating than for non-innovating firms, as a large number of questions are only addressed to firms with product or process innovation activities. Interestingly, negative effects are found for the first year and for 2005 when the sample size has been significantly enlarged and a large number of not-yet-surveyed firms were added to the sample. This suggests that innovating firms are more willing to participate in the survey in the first year in which they are approached but become reluctant to participate in further years due to the high response burden imposed on them. In the next section the determinants of participating in the panel survey will be investigated more closely.

However, it may be argued that the results of a mail and a telephone survey cannot be compared as circumstances under which respondents answer are quite different. While respondents to a mail survey have

Table 6.2 Share of innovating firms among responding and non-responding firms, 1993–2011

	'93	'95	'96	'97	'98	'99	'00	'01	'02	'03	'04	'05	'06	'07	'08	'09	'10	'11
Responding	79.8	63.6	56.7	58.6	64.6	57.8	65.3	53.8	51.8	53.2	53.3	61.3	50.5	55.3	48.9	50.9	46.3	52.5
Non-responding	58.6	65.6	71.8	78.1	74.4	76.6	75.2	62.6	63.7	59.5	64.7	60.5	61.8	58.7	60.4	63.6	61.7	59.6
ME of NR survey	−16.4	11.8	22.2	21.5	10.3	17.6	9.3	8.9	14.7	8.5	13.4	−3.6	8.3	0.5	8.4	12.9	13.4	4.7
significant at 1% level	yes	yes	yes	yes	yes	yes	yes	yes	yes	yes	yes	yes	yes		yes	yes	yes	yes

Notes: ME: marginal effect (percentage points) of the effect of the non-response (NR) interview on the probability of being an innovator, estimated by probit models including log of no. of employees, industry and regional dummies.

Source: ZEW.

sufficient time to read and consider the definition, can see the questions that follow, and have a list of examples for product and process innovation at hand, respondents on the telephone have to react immediately and may be more likely to misunderstand the concept of innovation.

One simple test for a potential survey instrument bias is to analyse firms that responded in years $t - 1$ and $t + 1$ through the mail or online questionnaire and did not respond in year t, but provided information in year t through the non-response survey. If firms from this group were non-innovators in $t - 1$ and $t + 1$ (as collected from the mail survey), they should by definition also be a non-innovator at t (as collected by the non-response survey) since in each year the question on product and process innovation refers to the introduction of corresponding innovations in the previous three-year period. Reciprocally, firms that were innovators in $t - 1$ and $t + 1$ should also be innovators at t. A total of 737 firms fall in this group. For the large majority of firms, consistent answers are found. However, for 16.8 per cent the innovator status collected from the non-response survey was not consistent with that from the encircling mail surveys. A total of 20.9 per cent of firms that reported being non-innovators in the preceding and subsequent mail surveys stated that they were innovators in the non-response survey in between (Table 6.3). In contrast, 13.7 per cent of firms reporting innovator status in the mail surveys reported being non-innovators in the non-response survey. This result shows that there is inconsistency in firm responses on the introduction of product and process innovation over time, which can have various causes

Table 6.3   Consistency of innovator status of firms with three consecutive responses in the MIP by type of survey instrument

Type of survey instrument in $t - 1$ and $t + 1$	Status in $t - 1$ and $t + 1$	Type of survey in t	Status in t: non-innovator (%)	Status in t: innovator (%)	Share of inconsistent responses in t (%)*
Mail	non-innovator	NR	79.1	20.9	16.8
Mail	innovator	NR	13.7	86.3	
Mail	non-innovator	Mail	86.9	13.1	11.6
Mail	innovator	Mail	10.2	89.8	
NR	non-innovator	NR	76.3	23.7	12.0
NR	innovator	NR	8.5	91.5	

Note: * Inconsistent result given the assumption that information in $t - 1$ and $t + 1$ is correct.

Source: ZEW.

(see the section Innovation Indicators: A Longitudinal Perspective). However, inconsistencies also occur if the group of firms with three consecutive mail responses is examined (11.6 per cent with an innovator status at t not consistent with the status in $t - 1$ and $t + 1$) and with three consecutive non-response interviews (12.0 per cent). Inconsistencies are larger when firms were non-innovators in $t - 1$ and $t + 1$, but there is no clear bias to report an innovator status when being surveyed through a telephone interview.

Questionnaire

As the MIP is the German contribution to the CIS, the questionnaire is based on the harmonized CIS questionnaire for the respective survey year and applies the standard definitions as provided by the *Oslo Manual*. However, the MIP questionnaire goes beyond standard CIS question-naires in several respects. First, the MIP includes questions on financial data since data protection regulation in Germany does not allow for merging firm data from the MIP (or any other non-official source) with official enterprise statistics. Basic economic variables, however, that go beyond sales and employment figures are needed for many research ques-tions. Currently, financial information includes capital expenditure, fixed assets, labour costs, costs of material, energy and purchased services, expenditure for training, marketing expenditure, profit-to-sales ratio and exports. Some of this information (capital expenditure, exports) was gath-ered in early CIS questionnaires but was later dropped from the survey. Except for export figures, financial information is obtained in the MIP only in years when the full sample is surveyed. In order to establish annual time-series data, information is not only collected for the current year but also for the previous year. Since all firms are asked to provide financial information, these variables can be used to analyse effects of innova-tion on financial performance as well as interaction between innovation expenditure and other types of investment in tangibles and intangibles (e.g. Czarnitzki and Kraft 2010, 2012). In addition, the MIP obtains infor-mation on a firm's business environment on an irregular basis, includ-ing the number of competitors, market share, the significance of certain product market features and the role of different types of competition.

Second, the information collected on innovation activities is more detailed than in the standard CIS questionnaire. For example, the MIP captures the amount of cost savings due to process innovation in order to better quantify the likely economic impacts of process innovation. Since 2003, an additional output measure for product innovation, the sales share due to new products that have no predecessor product within the firm and which therefore broaden a firm's product range, is used to capture another dimension of product novelty that complements the new-to-the-market question (see Rammer et al. 2009 for a discussion of the two concepts of novelty). In the same year, a further output indicator for process innovations that aim at improving the quality of goods and services was introduced. This indicator measures the change in sales that can be attributed to such quality-improving process innovations. In addition, the MIP continues to survey the number of employees engaged in R&D activities as well as the share of graduate employees, information that the harmonized CIS questionnaire no longer collects. The MIP also collects data on planned innovation for the year of the survey and the following year in terms of both activities (product, process) and expenditure. Differences between planned and later actually realized innovation activities and expenditure can provide valuable information on the uncertainty of the environment for innovation or on changes in innovation strategy (e.g. Dobbelaere et al. 2009).

Third, questions on characteristics of the innovation process in the MIP go beyond the standard CIS questions on cooperation, information sources, objectives and consequences, public support, hampering factors and the use of IP protection methods. These additional questions are strongly driven by data needs of policy makers and of academic researchers both from the ZEW and from other institutions,[6] and vary over time. In recent years, additional innovation questions included, among others, the financing of innovation, innovation activities in foreign countries, sources of innovation (stimulated by the work of Mansfield 1998 on public research as a source of industrial innovation), the role of trademarks and marketing for innovation, innovation collaboration along value-added chains, infringement of IP and the role of IP in helping and restraining innovation, management of innovation projects, and the effects of economic crises on innovation activities.

An important issue when designing an innovation questionnaire is the degree to which questions attempt to take into account industry specificities. While innovation is a phenomenon relevant to all industries, how economic activities are being renewed differs considerably. Designing a questionnaire specific to a certain industry would clearly facilitate accurate response and would allow for addressing issues particularly relevant for one industry (and omitting those less relevant). However, cross-sector comparability would be greatly lost by this approach. Nevertheless, the MIP followed this approach in 1995 when a large number of service sectors were surveyed for the first time. Following extensive face-to-face interviews with service firms and cognitive testing, a survey design for service sectors was chosen that deviated substantially from the one introduced two years earlier in the production sector (which was in line with CIS 1). Innovations were defined by distinguishing three types, namely new or improved services for customers (product innovation), new or improved processes introduced within the firm (process innovation), and improvements in the organization of internal procedures. The last was not regarded as a process innovation but was introduced to avoid firms reporting what would now be called organizational innovation as process innovation.[7] For each type of innovation a list of typical examples was given on a separate page. Firms were asked to provide a short description of the most important innovation for each type, which allowed *ex post* analyses of how well the concept of innovation was understood. Another question obtained information on the link between the reported innovations and technologies. Innovation expenditures were surveyed as a total figure, followed by a qualitative assessment of the significance of certain components (roughly in line with the current list of innovation activities in the CIS) because interviews suggested that smaller firms in particular were not able to estimate figures for individual expenditure categories. On the contrary, other innovation-related questions on information sources, cooperation partners, R&D activities and hampering factors used the same design and wording as for the production sector. The service industry questionnaire contained additional questions on economic variables that were specifically designed for the service sector, for example the type of international activity or the type of service delivered, or IT investment.

In subsequent years, the questionnaires for both sectors gradually converged. Since 2003 a single questionnaire has been used. There were several reasons for this. First, the harmonized CIS 2 questionnaire (conducted in 1997) proposed a similar methodology for both the goods- and services-producing sectors based on the first revision of the *Oslo Manual* in 1997 (OECD/Eurostat 1997), including a uniform definition of innovation and innovation expenditure that made the main rationale for two versions obsolete. Second, interest in high comparability of survey results between goods and services producers, both from policy and from research (e.g. for analysing differences in determinants and outcomes of innovation), called for a unification of methodological approaches. Third, practical reasons in terms of simplifying the questionnaire, and its shipping and processing, as well as queries about what to do with firms that changed economic activity between the two sectors (sending the same version in order to maintain consistency over time, or sending the version that fitted the sector affiliation, with potential for confusing the firm and reducing comparability of firm data over time) played a role, too. Between 1997 and 2002, separate questionnaires were used to omit or add certain questions for the service sector (e.g. the question on sales share of new products was not used in the CIS 2 service sector version of the questionnaire) and to allow more space for presenting separate lists of innovation examples for goods- and services-producing sectors.

It is difficult to assess whether services would need a separate approach to survey innovation and whether the initial approach followed in the MIP would be more appropriate. A simple test reveals that the questionnaire used in 1995, specifically designed for the service sector, yielded a significantly higher innovator share in the services- than in the goods-producing sectors compared to the unified version used in 1997 for which no significant effect was found.[8] From this finding it cannot be established, however, which version better captures actual innovation activities in the service sector.

3.   PANEL PARTICIPATION

Although the MIP is a panel survey, the net sample of responses represents a highly unbalanced sample. The total number of firms that have been surveyed at least once during the 19 years from 1993 to 2011 (excluding firms that were identified as neutral losses in the first year they were surveyed) is 97 432; the total number of questionnaire responses received in the same period amounts to 89 654. Only 27 906 firms out of the total sample filled out the questionnaire at least once. The average number of responses per responding firm is 3.21.

The high number of firms with zero responses results from the strategy to remove firms from the sample (except for large firms) if they did not respond for four consecutive years. In addition, many firms have been first sampled in recent years and have only had a few occasions to participate. A further reason is high panel mortality, which steadily reduces the number of firms from a certain sampling year contained in the current panel sample. In 2011, only 12 per cent of firms initially sampled in 1993 were still part of the sample. As a consequence, the 2011 sample consists only of 5.3 per cent of firms that have been sampled from the first year on (see Table 6.4). After five years, less than a quarter of the original sample size remains. Panel mortality is the result of various events, including closures, mergers, demand by firms to be taken out of the sample and continuing refusal to respond to the questionnaire.

The unbalanced nature of the MIP is also due to regular refreshments of the sample in order to compensate for panel mortality. The 2011 sample, for example, consisted of one-third of firms that were first sampled in this year and another 36 per cent sampled in the previous six years. This

Table 6.4   Sample size of the MIP by sampling year, 1993–2011

Sampling year	Size in sampling year[a]		Survey year[a] (Sample size in sampling year = 100)											Sample size in 2011[b]	
	total	%	1993	1994	1995	1997	1999	2001	2003	2005	2007	2009	2011	total	%
1993	12642	13.0	100	86	47	35	29	29	26	19	17	16	12	1563	5.4
1994	1086	1.1		100	90	78	48	41	41	29	26	24	19	208	0.7
1995	14248	14.6			100	84	58	35	27	19	17	14	11	1552	5.4
1997	2119	2.2				100	76	60	39	25	22	18	13	285	1.0
1999	4632	4.8					100	92	51	34	30	25	19	893	3.1
2001	7880	8.1						100	76	48	38	30	23	1825	6.3
2003	7894	8.1							100	61	45	38	28	2234	7.7
2005	14479	14.9								100	39	31	25	3553	12.3
2007	10280	10.6									100	37	28	2926	10.1
2009	12325	12.6										100	35	4287	14.9
2011	9478	9.7											100	9478	32.8
others	369	0.4												51	0.2
Total	97432	100												28855	100

Notes:
a. Figures reported are for survey years in which panel refreshments have taken place.
b. Excluding neutral losses.

Source: ZEW.

147

implies that many firms have only had a few chances to participate in the panel so far.

A low average response rate of 24 per cent further lowers panel participation. Response rates do not decline, however, for firms staying in the panel for a long time, but rather increase, which results from the deliberate removal of firms with continuing non-response. In 2011, the response rate did not vary significantly by sampling year except for the newly sampled firms, which show lower response rates in every survey year (see Table 6A.3).

Despite decreasing sample participation, about 50 per cent of all responses received in the MIP up to 2011 were from firms that were sampled in the first three years of the panel (Table 6A.4), although only 14 per cent of all responses received in 2011 were from the first three sampling years.

Figure 6.1 illustrates the participation pattern of responding firms over time. Denoting year 0 as the first year a firm responded, the share of firms responding in the next year (year 1) is 52 per cent as an average across survey years 1994 to 2010. A total of 9 percentage points of the 48 per cent of non-responding firms in the consecutive year result from panel mortality, giving a 57 per cent response rate for those firms still surviving in year 1. While the mortality rate steadily increases (up to 70 per cent in year 18, which is for firms that responded the first time in the 1993 survey), the response rate of still surviving firms falls to 35 per cent for year 8 and remains at this level until year 15, afterwards slowly declining again. As a consequence of both developments, only 1.9 per cent of the initial sample (243 firms in absolute figures) also responded in the most recent survey year, 2011. However, most of these firms did not participate in every single year but show some gaps.

Figure 6.1 also shows that the maximum number of responses that can be obtained in subsequent panel years constantly decreases over time, which simply represents that only firms from the initial sampling year had the theoretical chance to respond in every following year, while firms with more recent sampling years naturally were able to participate only in a smaller number of years.

From the original sample drawn in 1993 (which consisted primarily of manufacturing firms), just 7.3 per cent of firms were part of the sample in every year up to 2011 (Table 6.5). Out of this small balanced sample, only a dozen (1.2 per cent) responded every single year, clearly indicating the difficulty of motivating firms to carry the burden of constant participation in a voluntary survey. The share of firms with continuous response in every year they were contacted increases only slightly with younger sampling years. For the 2001 sampling year, for example, only 2 per cent

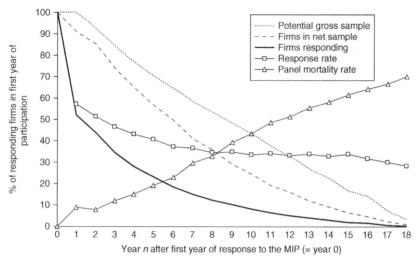

Notes:
Potential gross sample: share of firms that responded in year $t = 0$ (= first year the firm was part of the MIP sample) and could have been part of the sample in year $t + n$.
Firms in net sample: share of firms that responded in year $t = 0$ and were part of the sample in year $t + n$ and were not classified as neutral loss due to firm closure or continuous non-response.
Firms responding: share of firms that responded in year $t + 0$ and responded in year $t + n$.
Response rate: share of firms responding in year $t = 0$ and year $t + n$ in total net sample of firms in year $t + n$ that responded in year $t = 0$.
Panel mortality rate: share of firms responding in year $t = 0$ and that were not part in the net sample in year $t + n$ either due to firm closure or elimination from the sample due to continuous non-response.

Source: ZEW.

Figure 6.1 Participation in the MIP over time

of firms that were part of the sample in all 11 years from 2001 to 2011 also responded in all 11 years, although the sample size of this sampling year has been confined to only 13.3 per cent of its original size by 2011 due to firm closure and repeated non-response. This finding suggests that only a very small fraction of firms can be attracted to participate permanently in a survey as complex as the innovation survey, and most get lost very early from the group of firms that provide balanced panel observations.

A multivariate analysis of the probability of responding to the MIP reveals that the number of times a firm was previously part of the sample has a positive effect on survey participation, which simply reflects the strategy to take firms out of the sample if they refuse to respond for several consecutive years. Firm age has a positive though non-linear effect.

Table 6.5   Sampling and response behaviour in the MIP by sampling year

Sampling year	Firms that were part of the sample in every year from sampling year until 2011 (as a percentage of all firms in the sampling year)	Firms that responded in every year from sampling year until 2011 (as a percentage of all firms in the sampling year)	Average response rate from sampling year until 2011 (% of all sampled firms)
1993	7.3	1.2	28.4
1994	9.2	3.0	24.5
1995	6.4	2.8	27.5
1997	7.6	3.1	26.7
1999	9.5	2.0	21.2
2001	13.3	2.0	21.6
2003	19.0	3.0	20.1
2005	19.2	4.6	20.2
2007	25.7	6.6	21.0
2009	32.7	13.2	21.1
2011	100.0	16.0	16.0
Others	18.2	7.5	21.4
Total	24.7	10.3	23.9

Source: ZEW.

Firms older than 12 years at the time of the survey show higher response probability, as do very young firms. Firm size has a negative effect, again with some non-linearity. The highest response rates can be observed for firms with around 20 employees. Corporations are more likely to participate than partnerships, and firms from eastern Germany show a higher response probability than western ones.

4.   INNOVATION INDICATORS: A LONGITUDINAL PERSPECTIVE

Innovation surveys offer a variety of firm-based innovation indicators, ranging from expenditure on innovation activities to indicators on the occurrence of certain innovation activities (typically expressed as the share of firms showing a certain activity) and indicators of innovation results (such as the share of sales generated by new products). Up to now, these indicators have not been used very widely in studies on innovation performance, in contrast with R&D or patent indicators (see Smith 2005; Dodgson 2000). One reason is the concern about the reliability of these indicators, as they show high variation over time in certain countries. This variation is unlikely to represent real changes in innovation behaviour of firms, but may rather result from changes in sample composition (see Hollanders and van Cruysen, 2008 and Chapter 4 in this volume). For the German innovation survey, this limitation should be less severe thanks to the panel character of the sample. In addition, the annual survey allows the establishment of long annual time-series data for innovation indicators, which provides a sound base for analysing the reliability of indicators derived from innovation surveys.

The share of innovating firms is a key indicator of the spread of innovation-based competitive strategies within the firm population. The indicator is defined as the percentage of firms that have introduced at least one new or significantly improved product or new or significantly improved process in the three years before the end of the reference year. The level of this indicator is driven by the behaviour of small firms, as they make up the vast majority of all firms in the population. For the target sectors of the MIP, 86 per cent of all firms with five or more employees have fewer than 50 employees, and a further 13 per cent have between 50 and below 500. Over the past two decades, the share of innovators shows a downward trend in service sectors (Figure 6.2). Low-tech manufacturing reports a low innovator share for the early 1990s (note that the period 1992–94 was characterized by a significant recession in Germany), followed by a strong increase until 1999 and a declining trend until 2010. In high-tech manufacturing the share of innovating firms has been stable since the end of the 1990s, clearly exceeding the level of the three other sectors.[9]

For each of the sectors there is strong annual fluctuation, which is surprising when taking into account that the innovator share in each year refers to product and process innovations introduced in the previous three years. The unbalanced nature of the MIP may explain some of this fluctuation. Averaged across all survey years, the net sample of responding firms plus non-responding firms interviewed on their innovation activities through a non-response survey in year t consists of 52 per cent of firms that were also surveyed through one of the two instruments in year $t - 1$, which means that almost half of the sample on which weighted results for the share of innovators is based were not present in the net sample of the previous year. It may be that some firms do not properly refer to a three-year reference period but rather to innovations introduced in the reference year. This would explain some inconsistencies in the sequence of innovator and non-innovator status over time (see the section on the MIP above and the next section on the Persistence of Innovation). In some years the fluctuation of the share of innovating firms goes in the same direction in

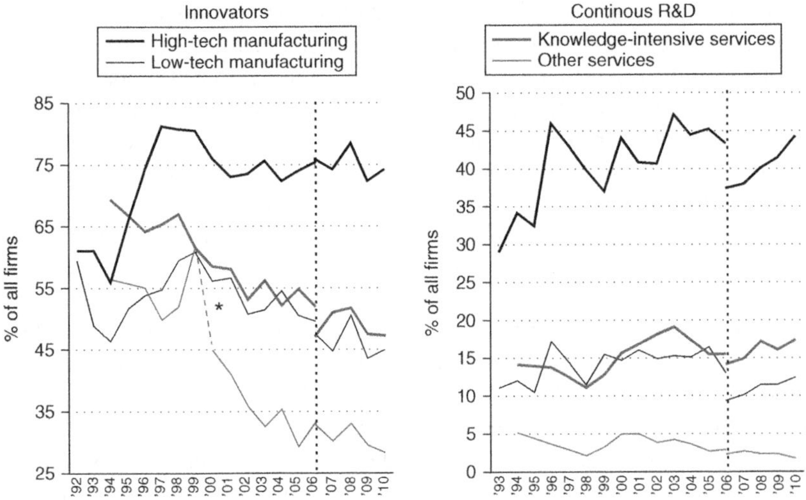

Notes:
Break in series in 2006 due to transit from NACE Rev. 1.2 to NACE Rev. 2.0 and a change
in the statistical base for population figures.
* Break in series for the share of product/process innovators for other services in 2000 due
to alterations in the survey question on product and process innovation.
All figures are extrapolated to the total population of firms with five or more employees.
Years are reference years of the surveys.

Source: ZEW.

Figure 6.2 *Share of product/process innovators and share of firms with*
continuous in-house R&D activity in Germany by sector,
1992–2010

all sectors (e.g. upwards in 2008 and downwards in 2009), which may be
associated with business cycle fluctuations. In reference year 2000, the
sharp fall in the share of innovators, particularly in other services (from 62
to 45 per cent), can be attributed to some extent to a change in the explanatory notes to the definition of product innovation in the trade business. In
contrast to previous surveys, firms in retail and wholesale were explicitly
advised from the 2001 survey onwards that reselling innovative goods
developed and introduced by other firms is not to be considered a product
innovation by retailers or wholesalers, which resulted in a significant drop
in the number of product innovations in the trade business.

Another CIS-based indicator on the diffusion of innovative activities in
the firm population is the share of firms with in-house R&D activities on a
continuous basis. In contrast to the innovator share, this indicator shows

an upward trend for most sectors, although the indicator is affected by a break in series in 2006 due to the new NACE classification and changes in the statistical base used for population figures. Again, significant annual fluctuation can be observed despite a three-year reference period for in-house R&D activities.

A key input indicator for innovation is the amount of money spent on innovation activities. The total amount of innovation expenditure in German manufacturing and service sectors doubled in nominal terms between 1995 and 2010, from €60.7 billion to €121.3 billion. This expenditure includes internal and external R&D, expenditure on the acquisition of machinery, equipment, software and other intangibles used for developing and introducing product or process innovation, and expenditure on training, marketing, design and other innovation-related activities. Across all sectors, innovation expenditure in Germany is about twice the amount of R&D expenditure. The growth rate of total innovation expenditure is higher than that for business enterprise intramural R&D expenditure. This does not necessarily imply that non-R&D innovation activities become more important over time. Since innovation expenditure includes costs of intramural and external innovation activities, double counting of innovation efforts by expenditure data may occur. For example, a firm purchasing and implementing a novel production technology will report these process innovation expenses as innovation expenditure. The firm that developed the new technology will most likely consider the development activities as own innovation effort, too, and report the associated costs as innovation expenditure. Similar cases can be made for a marketing campaign on a new product developed by an advertising firm, or for engineering and design activities for new products purchased from other firms. Since the CIS does not distinguish between intramural and external expenditure, the amount of double counting of innovation expenditure remains unclear.

Innovation expenditure as a percentage of sales shows an upward trend in high-tech manufacturing and in knowledge-intensive services (excluding financial intermediation) (Figure 6.3). In other services, this indicator is rather stable over time, while low-tech manufacturing and financial intermediation show a downward trend. Annual fluctuation is less articulated than for innovator shares. This may be attributed to the fact that the amount of innovation expenditure is largely driven by rather few very large firms, which are all represented in the weighted results in every year. Capital expenditure on innovations (i.e. acquisition of machinery, equipment, software and other intangibles) shows higher variations over time, which largely reflects investment cycles. The share of capital expenditure in total innovation expenditure tends to increase in other services, where

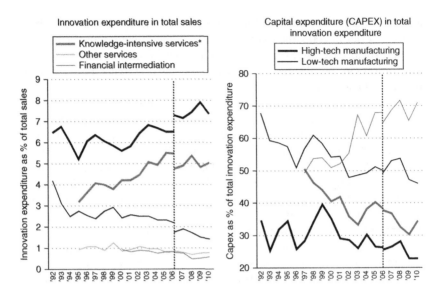

Notes:
Break in series in 2006 due to transit from NACE Rev. 1.2 to NACE Rev. 2.0 and a change
in the statistical base for population figures.
*Excluding financial intermediation for innovation expenditure as a share of sales.
All figures are extrapolated to the total population of firms with five or more employees.

Source: ZEW.

*Figure 6.3   Innovation expenditure in total sales and capital expenditure in
total innovation expenditure in Germany by sector, 1992–2010*

capital expenditure currently accounts for about two-thirds of total innovation expenditure. In knowledge-intensive services and low-tech manufacturing this share is decreasing while high-tech manufacturing shows
quite high fluctuations without a clear trend. When linking innovation-
related capital expenditure to total capital expenditure, a rather stable
share over time emerges. In high-tech manufacturing, about 50 per
cent of total capital expenditure in Germany is devoted to innovation
projects, while the other three sectors report an innovation share of capital
expenditure of below 25 per cent.

A key advantage of CIS as an empirical basis for innovation research
is the presence of an output indicator for product innovation. The share
of sales generated by new or significantly improved products introduced
during the past three years has been used by many researchers to analyse
the determinants of innovation success (see Kleinknecht et al. 2002;
Laursen and Salter 2006; Leiponen and Helfat 2010; Lööf and Heshmati

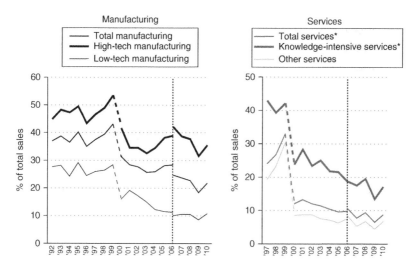

Notes:
Break in series in 2006 due to transit from NACE Rev. 1.2 to NACE Rev. 2.0 and a change in the statistical base for population figures.
* Excluding financial intermediation.
All figures are extrapolated to the total population of firms with five or more employees.

Source: ZEW.

Figure 6.4   Sales share of product innovations in Germany by sector, 1992–2010

2010; Cockburn et al. 2010; Rammer et al. 2009). In the MIP, this indicator has been used since the first survey wave for manufacturing and was introduced to the service sector in 1998. Until 2000, the indicator was split in two categories, share of sales from new products and share of sales from significantly improved products. From 2001 on, both categories were merged into one, following the policy of the harmonized CIS questionnaire. This led to a sharp fall in the sales share of new products (Figure 6.4). In manufacturing, the average share of sales in reference years 1992 to 1999 (i.e. based on the two categories question) was 38.4 per cent, while it was 28.0 per cent in 2000 to 2006 (with the merged categories). In services, the drop was even higher, from 27.9 per cent (1997 to 1999) to 11.2 per cent (2000 to 2006). This finding shows that rather small changes to the survey instrument may have significant consequences for innovation indicators.

Another indicator of product innovation success that is not affected by changes in the way the information is collected in the questionnaire is the

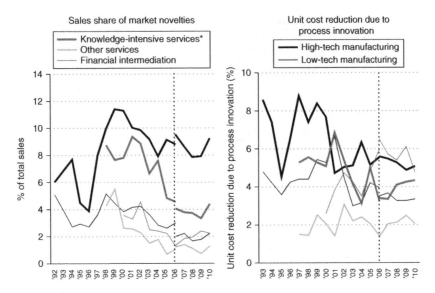

Notes:
Break in series in 2006 due to transit from NACE Rev. 1.2 to NACE Rev. 2.0 and a change in the statistical base for population figures.
* Excluding financial intermediation.
All figures are extrapolated to the total population of firms with five or more employees.

Source: ZEW.

Figure 6.5   Sales share of market novelties and unit cost reduction due to process innovation in Germany by sector, 1992–2010

sales share of market novelties. Market novelties are new products that have not been introduced into the market by any other firm before. The relevant market is defined by the innovating firm and need not refer to the world market but may relate to national or regional markets. This indicator shows rather high values both in manufacturing and services in the late 1990s and early 2000s (Figure 6.5). In this period, many firms exploited the new potential of IT applications to place new-to-the-market products. The indicator exhibits a downward trend until 2009 and rose again in 2010.

In contrast to the standard CIS questionnaire, the MIP also uses an indicator of process innovation success. Directly following the question on the introduction of process innovation, firms are asked whether any of these process innovations led to a reduction in the unit costs of production. Firm replying 'yes' are then asked to estimate the magnitude of unit cost reduction due to process innovation in the reference year of the survey. This indicator fluctuates quite strongly. High-tech manufacturing reports high unit costs reductions in the second half of the 1990s, followed by a rather stable development since 2001 at around 5 per cent. Low-tech manufacturing has the highest value in 2001, followed by a period of rather low unit cost reductions in recent years. Financial intermediation achieved high cost savings driven by process innovations in the past years (around 6 per cent), while other services were able to lower unit costs by about 2 per cent every year thanks to process innovation.

5. PERSISTENCE OF INNOVATION

One major virtue of innovation panel data is the fact that they illuminate the dynamics of firms' innovation behaviour. In a dynamic perspective, the question of whether firms persistently innovate, innovate discontinuously or whether they refrain from innovating over a long period of time and how this behaviour can be explained has gained importance in the last decade (see Flaig and Stadler 1994; Cefis and Orsenigo 2001; Cefis 2003; Peters 2009; Raymond et al. 2010). This is due to the fact that, for instance, endogenous growth models greatly differ in their underlying assumptions about the innovation frequency of firms (see, e.g., Romer 1990; Aghion and Howitt 1992). Permanent innovation activities are furthermore regarded as key to improving long-run firm performance and competitiveness. The empirical literature, however, has recently started to investigate performance effects of persistent innovation behaviour (Johansson and Lööf 2010). Since the dynamics of innovation behaviour are also likely to be related to the business cycle, the question of whether firms remain engaged in innovation projects has furthermore attracted greater attention in the current economic crisis.

The MIP data support the investigation of the dynamics of innovation over nearly 20 years, from 1992 to 2010 in manufacturing and from 1996 to 2010 in services. Persistence occurs when a firm that has innovated in one period innovates once again in the subsequent period. As already mentioned, innovation surveys collect data to measure innovation from an input and output perspective. Table 6.6 sheds light on the persistence of innovation input by depicting one-year transition probabilities of innovation activities. A firm is defined to have innovation activities if it spends a positive amount on innovation projects in a given year t. Since the MIP is an unbalanced panel, evidence is provided for three different samples: firms with at least four; at least seven, and at least ten (services) or 13 (manufacturing) consecutive observations. A first striking result is that there is a high and very similar degree of persistency in all three panels. Therefore the focus is on the sample with at least four consecutive

Table 6.6   Innovation activities: one-year transition probabilities (per cent), 1992–2010

Innovation status in t	Innovation status in $t + 1$ Panel with at least . . . consecutive observations								
	4			7			13 (M) / 10 (S)		
	Non-inno	Inno	Total	Non-inno	Inno	Total	Non-inno	Inno	Total
Manufacturing									
Non-inno	84.5	15.5	100.0	85.0	15.0	100.0	87.8	12.2	100.0
Inno	9.8	90.2	100.0	9.0	91.0	100.0	7.6	92.4	100.0
Total	38.1	61.9	100.0	36.9	63.1	100.0	38.6	61.4	100.0
Number of obs.			*37068*			*18775*			*4435*
Services									
Non-inno	85.3	14.7	100.0	85.8	14.2	100.0	86.4	13.6	100.0
Inno	20.5	79.5	100.0	20.3	79.7	100.0	21.5	78.5	100.0
Total	57.6	42.4	100.0	58.7	41.3	100.0	61.0	39.0	100.0
Number of obs.			*21942*			*8972*			*4139*

Notes: Inno and Non-inno are dummy variables indicating firms with and without innovation activities. A firm is defined to have innovation activities if it spends a positive amount on innovation projects in year t. M and S denote manufacturing and services. In services, the time period is from 1996 to 2010.

Source: ZEW.

observations. Around 90 per cent of manufacturing firms engaged in innovation activities in one year t remain innovative in the subsequent period. Innovation activities reveal themselves to be highly persistent in services as well, although service firms are less likely to continue innovation activities in the next year (79 per cent). The lower persistence might, for instance, reflect shorter average development times in services, fewer technological opportunities, less demand for innovation, or smaller sunk costs in R&D. The degree of persistence is likewise high for non-innovative firms. In both manufacturing and services, roughly 85 per cent of them also refrain from innovation in the following period, while 15 per cent entered into innovation activities. That also means that the probability of being innovative in period $t + 1$ was about 74.4 and 64.8 percentage points higher for innovators than for non-innovators in t in manufacturing and services, respectively, which can be interpreted as another measure of persistence.

As the decision to start with new innovation projects or to stop investing

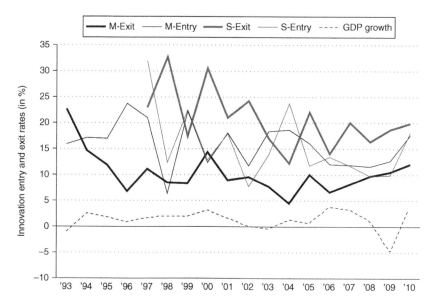

Notes: Sample: unbalanced panel with all firms with at least four consecutive observations. M and S denote manufacturing and services, respectively. The innovation entry rate in any given year *t* is defined as the share of non-innovative enterprises in year *t* − 1 which start innovation activities in year *t*. Similarly, the innovation exit rate in year *t* measures the share of innovative companies in year *t* − 1 which flow out of innovation activities in year *t*. GDP growth denotes the annual percentage change of real GDP.

Source: ZEW; real GDP growth; download from Eurostat server 22.06.2012.

Figure 6.6 Innovation entry and exit rates and business cycles, 1993–2010

in them might be related to the business cycle, Figure 6.6 contrasts the innovation entry and exit rates with the annual growth in GDP. Overall, it turns out that innovation exit rates in manufacturing have been rather stable from 1996 onwards. Interestingly, exit rates fluctuate more in services and all in all they seem to exhibit a decreasing trend over time.[10] In both manufacturing and services, entry rates move very similar over time. Furthermore, the figure reveals that the decision to start innovation projects is more volatile than the decision to stop them.[11] Despite fluctuations over time, no clear pattern of entry and exit rates over the business cycle can be observed. In manufacturing, the correlation coefficient between growth in GDP and entry is only slightly positive (0.009). The effect is stronger and negative between GDP growth and exit rates (−0.140). However, neither correlation is statistically significant. The same holds for services, where both correlations turn out to be positive. In contrast to manufacturing, the decision to exit from innovation is less

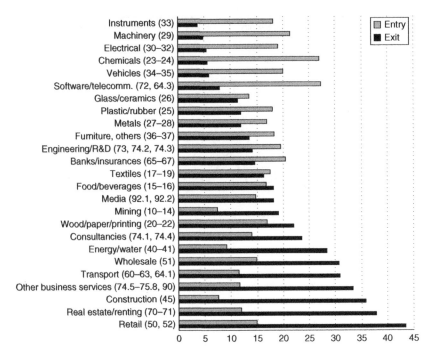

Notes: See Figure 6.6. Figures in parentheses give NACE Rev. 1.2 codes.

Source: ZEW.

Figure 6.7   Innovation entry and exit rates by industry, 1993–2010

correlated with the business cycle than the decision to start an innovation project (0.123 compared to 0.253).

Figure 6.7 and Table 6.7 illustrate innovation persistence by industry and size classes. Broadly speaking, three groups of industries emerge. The first group is characterized by very small exit rates and high entry rates. This group consists of high-tech industries such as precision instruments, electrical engineering, vehicles, machinery, chemicals and telecommunication. The figures imply that the firms steadily pursue innovation activities for a long period of time and even if they stop for a given year, they have a high likelihood of starting again in the next period. The second group of firms, which consists of glass/ceramics up to media, can be described as having similar entry and exit rates. All other manufacturing industries (except for wood/paper) as well as technical services and financial intermediation belong to this group. The third group, starting with mining (Figure 6.7) exhibits very high exit rates and small to moderate entry rates.

Table 6.7 Innovation activities: one-year transition probabilities by size classes, 1992–2010

Innovation status		Size class: number of employees in *t*							
Year *t*	Year *t* + 1	<10	10–19	20–49	50–99	100–249	250–499	500–999	1000+
Manufacturing									
Non-inno	Non-inno	90.8	87.8	84.0	82.3	80.7	75.0	79.6	76.8
	Inno	9.2	12.2	16.0	17.7	19.3	25.0	20.4	23.2
Inno	Non-inno	24.0	18.9	15.6	11.4	8.6	6.2	4.2	1.7
	Inno	76.0	81.1	84.4	88.6	91.4	93.8	95.8	98.3
Services									
Non-inno	Non-inno	87.9	85.2	85.6	83.5	85.0	80.3	78.3	80.6
	Inno	12.1	14.8	14.4	16.5	15.0	19.8	21.7	19.4
Inno	Non-inno	27.6	25.7	22.1	17.4	22.7	23.0	10.8	4.9
	Inno	72.4	74.3	77.9	82.6	77.3	77.0	89.2	95.1

Note: Sample: Unbalanced panel with all firms with at least four consecutive observations.

Source: ZEW.

This interplay of entry and exit describes a situation where many firms are not engaged in innovation projects and just innovate occasionally. If they start innovation projects, these are of a rather short time horizon, as 20 to 45 per cent of the innovating firms already cease to innovate in the subsequent year.

Table 6.7 highlights that innovation behaviour is more stable in larger firms, though also relatively enduring in small firms. In manufacturing, the probability of remaining innovative steadily increases from 76 per cent in firms below ten employees up to 98 per cent in firms with more than 1000 employees. In services, this linear increasing trend is not seen, as firms with between 20 and 499 employees are equally likely to stay on the innovation path in the next year. At the same time, the figures suggest that the propensity for non-innovators to take up such activities steadily rose as well. The entry rates increase with firm size, although firms with 250–499 employees in manufacturing and 500–999 employees in services show the highest propensity to start innovation projects.

Instead of using one-year transition probabilities, another way of looking at persistence of innovation activities is to examine survival rates. Figures 6.8 and 6.9 display survival rates of different innovator and non-innovator cohorts. The survival rate for the innovator cohort

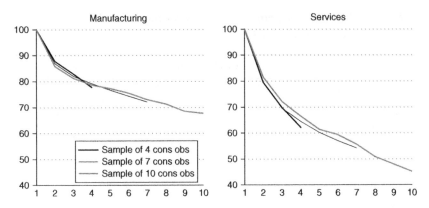

Source: ZEW.

Figure 6.8   Survival rates of initial innovator cohorts, manufacturing and services

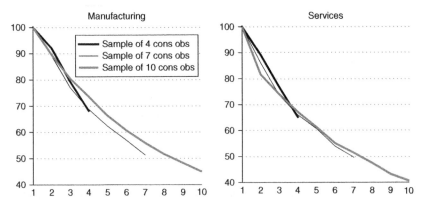

Source: ZEW.

Figure 6.9   Survival rates of initial non-innovator cohorts, manufacturing and services

in year s is the proportion of innovators in year $t = 1$ (the year in which the firms enters the panel) that is still innovating in year $t + s$, for $s = 1$, $2, \ldots S - 1$, with S being the number of consecutive observations of the panel. Similarly, the survival rate of the non-innovator cohort in year s is the proportion of non-innovators in year $t = 1$ that continuously refrain from innovating in year $t + s$. In order to investigate whether survival rates depend on the number of years an individual firm is observed in the data, survival rates are presented for different samples. In a nutshell, survival rates of different samples (for joint periods) differ only slightly. In particular, panels with a longer time dimension do not consist of firms with lower survival rates for non-innovators. And survival rates of initial innovators are only marginally higher in these panels. This suggests that, if at all, sample selection problems are of minor importance in this analysis.

In manufacturing, roughly four out of five initially innovating firms are still innovating after four years. After seven years a share of 73 per cent is still engaged in innovation projects. This proportion only decreases slightly to 68 per cent after ten years. That is, more than two out of three initial innovators incessantly innovate in the following ten years. In terms of persistence, survival rates reveal larger differences between manufacturing and services than one-year transition probabilities. With 66 per cent, the four-year survival rate for initial innovators is already lower than the proportion in manufacturing after ten years. Interestingly, the highest drop-out rates can be found as early as in the first two periods. That is why 56 per cent and 45 per cent of the initial innovators are still observed to be continuously engaged in innovation projects after seven and ten years.

In contrast to the innovator cohort, the survival rates of initial non-innovator cohorts are more similar in manufacturing and services. In services, 67 per cent, 51 per cent and 40 per cent of initial non-innovators still refrain from innovation activities after four, seven and ten years respectively. On the other hand, these figures imply that six out of ten firms that did not perform innovation activities in the first year of observation have started to do so in the next ten years. In manufacturing the corresponding figure is 45 per cent after ten and 40 per cent after 13 years. An analysis based on a balanced subsample has furthermore shown that those firms that experienced at least one change in their innovation behaviour exhibit a stronger tendency to return to the initial innovation status (Peters 2009).

Instead of persistence in innovation input, Table 6.8 considers persistence in innovation from an output perspective. Since innovation output indicators are defined for a three-year period, three-year transition probabilities are calculated in order to avoid the problem of overlapping periods. For all three output indicators (product innovation, process innovation and market novelties), the probability of remaining an innovator is very high, though somewhat smaller than from an input perspective. Furthermore, there is a clear pattern in both manufacturing and services: product innovators are more likely to remain product innovators in the subsequent period (around 83 per cent and 63 per cent) than process innovators (69 per cent and 57 per cent) and firms having introduced market novelties (68 per cent and 52 per cent). Compared to patent statistics, in particular the latter figures are unexpectedly high, meaning that

Table 6.8   Innovation output: three-year transition probabilities, 1992–2010

Innovation status in *t*	Innovation status in *t* + 3 Panel with at least . . . consecutive observations								
	4			7			13 (M) / 10 (S)		
	Non-X	X	Total	Non-X	X	Total	Non-X	X	Total
Manufacturing									
Non-PD	82.1	17.9	100.0	83.3	16.7	100.0	86.1	13.9	100.0
PD	17.0	83.0	100.0	15.8	84.2	100.0	12.1	87.9	100.0
Total	45.9	54.1	100.0	45.2	54.8	100.0	45.7	54.3	100.0
Non-PC	80.3	19.7	100.0	80.9	19.1	100.0	81.9	18.1	100.0
PC	30.8	69.2	100.0	29.5	70.5	100.0	28.8	71.2	100.0
Total	57. 5	42.5	100.0	56.8	43.2	100.0	57.7	42.3	100.0
Non-MN	88.5	11.5	100.0	88.7	11.3	100.0	90.1	9.9	100.0
MN	32.1	67.9	100.0	31.0	69.0	100.0	31.4	68.6	100.0
Total	69.7	30.3	100.0	68.9	31.1	100.0	71.0	29.0	100.0
Services									
Non-PD	87.1	12.9	100.0	89.2	10.8	100.0	89.8	10.2	100.0
PD	36.9	63.2	100.0	34.5	65.5	100.0	36.0	64.0	100.0
Total	68.8	31.2	100.0	70.1	29.9	100.0	68.7	31.3	100.0
Non-PC	85.3	14.7	100.0	86.8	13.2	100.0	87.2	12.8	100.0
PC	42.9	57.1	100.0	43.3	56.7	100.0	49.7	50.3	100.0
Total	72.8	27.3	100.0	74.5	25.5	100.0	74.8	25.2	100.0
Non-MN	94.9	5.1	100.0	94.9	5.1	100.0	95.3	4.7	100.0
MN	48.4	51.6	100.0	47.3	52.8	100.0	52.2	47.8	100.0
Total	86.8	13.3	100.0	87.0	13.0	100.0	89.7	10.3	100.0

Note: X denotes dummy variables indicating whether an enterprise introduced a product innovation (PD), process innovation (PC) or market novelty (MN), respectively.

Source: ZEW.

for instance two out of three manufacturing firms with market novelties in period *t* develop further market novelties in the subsequent period. In services it is every second firm.

In contrast to that, non-product innovators have a smaller likelihood of becoming innovators in the next period than process innovators. This also holds for both manufacturing and services. The smallest entry rates can be observed for firms without market novelties in period *t*. Just 11 per cent and 5 per cent of firms without such innovations in manufacturing and in services are able to subsequently develop and introduce a market novelty.

The previous tables and figures have shown that innovation behaviour is persistent to a large degree. However, these figures do not unveil the drivers of this phenomenon. In general, there are three sources of persistency: state dependence, and observed and unobserved firm heterogeneity. First, there might exist a causal behavioural effect in a sense that the decision to innovate in one period in itself increases the probability of innovating in the next period. This is called true state dependence. Sunk costs in setting up R&D facilities might be one explanation for state dependence as they act as a barrier to entry in innovation activities but also to exit from innovation activities (Sutton 1991). A second argument put forward in the literature is that innovations involve dynamic increasing returns (Nelson and Winter 1982; Malerba and Orsenigo 1993). Experience in innovation is associated with dynamic increasing returns in the form of learning-by-doing and learning-to-learn effects that enhance knowledge stocks and, as a consequence, the probability of future innovations. The fact that knowledge accumulates over time should therefore induce state dependence in innovation behaviour. The hypothesis that success breeds success might be a third explanation. Successful innovations might positively affect the condition for future innovations as successful innovators possess larger market power, more financial means and a larger set of technological opportunities (Phillips 1971; Mansfield 1968; Stoneman 1983; Nelson and Winter 1982).

But on the other hand, firms may also possess certain attributes that make them more likely to innovate. To the extent that these characteristics themselves are persistent over time, they will induce persistence in innovation behaviour as well. Such firm-specific attributes can be classified into observable characteristics, such as firm size, human capital or financial resources, and unobservable ones. For instance, technological opportunities, managerial abilities or risk attitudes are important for firms' decision to innovate, but are typically not observed (unobserved heterogeneity).

Disentangling sources of persistence is interesting from a policy point of view. If innovation behaviour is state dependent, public innovation subsidies are supposed to have a more sustained effect because they not only stimulate current innovation activities but are likely to induce a permanent change in favour of innovation. If, on the contrary, individual heterogeneity induces persistent behaviour, support programmes are unlikely to have long-lasting effects, and economic policy should concentrate more on measures that have the potential to improve innovation-relevant firm-specific factors and circumstances (Peters 2009).

In order to disentangle these three different sources, Peters (2009) and Raymond et al. (2010) have suggested estimating a dynamic random effects probit model. In addition to the lagged innovation status and observed explanatory variables, the model controls for unobserved heterogeneity.

In order to be able to estimate the model, Wooldridge (2005) has suggested explaining individual heterogeneity by the initial innovation status in the first observation period, the mean values of time-varying explanatory variables and additional time-constant explanatory variables.[12] Table 6.9 provides corresponding estimation results for manufacturing and services. The impact of variables that are controlled for in the estimation are firm size, credit rating, age, group status, training expenditure, share of high-skilled employees, export share, public subsidies, eastern Germany, foreign parent companies, public limited companies and private partnerships (for measurement details see notes to Table 6.9).[13]

The results by and large confirm the results found by Peters (2009) for the period 1994–2002. That is, all three sources are important drivers of innovation persistence, with lagged innovation activity being the most important one. The estimation results reveal that after conditioning on observed explanatory variables and unobserved individual heterogeneity, the probability to innovate in year t is still 31.5 and 33.4 percentage points higher for firms with innovation activities in year $t - 1$ than for prior non-innovators in manufacturing and services, respectively. This effect is highly significant in both samples and confirms the hypothesis that innovation behaviour is driven by true state dependence. In order to evaluate the quantitative importance, this effect is compared with the unconditional difference in the probability of innovating for prior innovators and non-innovators of 74.4 and 64.8 percentage points in manufacturing and services, respectively. As can be seen in Table 6.10, it turns out that in manufacturing roughly 42.5 per cent can be explained by true state dependence. In contrast to the results found by Peters (2009), the effect of state dependence is even higher for service firms at about 51 per cent. These estimates are based on the assumption that individual heterogeneity takes its average value (PEA: partial effect at the average value), which might reflect only a small proportion of firms. As an alternative, Wooldridge (2005) suggested calculating the average partial effect (APE) averaged across the distribution of the individual heterogeneity as well. Using the alternative measure, Table 6.10 shows that the state dependence effect is somewhat lower, but still ranging between 31 and 36 per cent in manufacturing and services, respectively.

Furthermore, it turns out that initial innovation status is also highly significant in both samples. This implies a substantial correlation between firms' initial innovation status and individual unobserved heterogeneity. Another important finding is that in addition to past innovation experience, knowledge provided by skilled employees has a crucial influence on generating innovations over time. In both industries, firms' effort to train their employees, and in services also the share of high-skilled employees,

Table 6.9   Dynamic random effects probit estimates

	Manufacturing		Services	
	Marg. effect	s.d.	Marg. effect	s.d.
Structural				
$Inno_{-1}$	0.315***	(0.013)	0.334***	(0.015)
Size	0.023	(0.015)	0.001	(0.021)
Rating	−0.010	(0.010)	−0.004	(0.024)
Age	0.003	(0.009)	0.012	(0.018)
Group	0.051***	(0.012)	0.054***	(0.018)
No training (1/0)	−0.124**	(0.005)	0.017	(0.066)
Training expenditure	0.009*	(0.052)	−0.009	(0.008)
High-skilled employees	0.067	(0.060)	−0.034	(0.056)
Export	0.325***	(0.074)	0.261	(0.161)
$Export^2$	−0.386***	(0.078)	−0.662***	(0.179)
Public	0.195***	(0.013)	0.237***	(0.035)
Foreign	−0.025	(0.019)	0.027	(0.036)
East	−0.055***	(0.012)	−0.036**	(0.014)
Public limited company	0.025	(0.025)	0.144***	(0.032)
Private partnership	−0.006	(0.015)	0.018	(0.017)
Time dummies (*p*-value)	0.000***		0.000***	
Individual heterogeneity				
$Inno_0$	0.286***	(0.015)	0.271***	(0.017)
M_Size	0.025	(0.015)	0.043**	(0.021)
M_Rating	0.001	(0.018)	−0.007	(0.029)
M_Age	−0.019*	(0.011)	−0.038*	(0.019)
M_Group	−0.018	(0.019)	0.020	(0.026)
M_No training	−0.351***	(0.066)	−0.518***	(0.085)
M_Training expenditure	0.042***	(0.008)	0.061***	(0.011)
M_High-skilled	0.108	(0.073)	0.139**	(0.065)
M_Export	0.184***	(0.051)	0.420***	(0.112)
M_Public	0.203***	(0.023)	0.315***	(0.043)
Industry dummies	0.000***		0.000***	
Sigma	0.611	(0.027)	0.502	(0.032)
Rho	0.272	(0.016)	0.201	(0.020)
LR: rho = 0	328.44 (1)***		127.52 (1)***	
LogLikelihood	−8882.5		−6892.4	
LR test	6921.4 (56)***		3883.86 (46)***	
McFadden R^2	0.280		0.220	
Correct predictions (in %)	87.67		83.53	
Correct predicted 1	90.97		77.04	
Correct predicted 0	82.33		88.32	
Number of observations	31 060		18 041	
Number of firms	5299		3518	

Table 6.9   (continued)

Notes: Firm size: log number of employees in year $t - 1$; rating: credit rating in year $t - 1$ (score between 100 and 600); age: log number of years; group: dummy variable indicating that a firm belongs to an enterprise group in year t; no training: dummy variable indicating that a firm did not invest in training in year $t - 1$; training expenditure: log training expenditure per employee if a firm invests in training in year $t - 1$; high-skilled: share of employees with a university or college degree in year $t - 1$; export: export to sales ratio in year $t - 1$; public: dummy variable indicating that the firm got public subsidies for innovation in year $t - 1$; foreign: dummy variable indicating that a firm has a foreign parent company; east: dummy variable indicating that a firm is located in eastern Germany; public limited company and private partnership: dummy variables indicating that a firm is a public limited company and private partnership, respectively (reference group: private limited liability companies. M_ denotes individual mean values of the corresponding variable. Sigma is the estimated standard deviation of the individual effect. Rho is the fraction of variance that is due to individual heterogeneity. Sample: unbalanced panel with at least four consecutive observations.

Source: ZEW.

Table 6.10   *Importance of state dependence effects in manufacturing and services*

	Observed (unconditional) probabilities			PEA			APE		
	$P(1\|1)$	$P(1\|0)$	Diff.	$\hat{P}(1\|1)$	$\hat{P}(1\|0)$	$\widehat{PEA}$		$\hat{P}(1\|1)$	$\hat{P}(1\|0)$	$\widehat{APE}$
						Abs.	In %			Abs. In %
Manuf.	0.902	0.155	0.744	0.871	0.555	0.316	*0.424*	0.770	0.539	0.230 *0.308*
Services	0.795	0.147	0.648	0.619	0.285	0.333	*0.514*	0.569	0.336	0.233 *0.360*

Notes: $\hat{P}(1\|1)$ and $\hat{P}(1\|0)$ denote estimates of the conditional probability of innovating in year t for an innovator and non-innovator in year $t - 1$ given the explanatory variables x, respectively. *PEA*: partial (marginal) effect at the average value of the individual heterogeneity. *APE*: average partial effect (averaged across the distribution of the individual heterogeneity).

Source: ZEW.

significantly explain individual heterogeneity across firms. Finally, even after accounting for many observed differences across firms, unobserved heterogeneity still matters for innovation persistence. The importance of unobserved heterogeneity in explaining the total variance can be gauged from the estimated rho. Unobserved heterogeneity still explains roughly 20 and 27 per cent of the variance in the innovation behaviour in services and manufacturing, respectively.

6. CONCLUSION

Panel data on innovation activities of firms offer a variety of opportunities for analysing innovation behaviour and its determinants and outcomes in more depth than is possible with cross-section data. This chapter presented one survey that provides such panel data for a large sample of firms from Germany, the so-called Mannheim Innovation Panel (MIP). The chapter was strongly focused on methodological issues, as these largely affect the analytical potential of the data. As the MIP is a voluntary survey that uses a complex questionnaire and collects a variety of firm information that goes beyond mere innovation data, which both put a serious burden on responding firms, panel participation is a data quality issue. While there were just 1.2 per cent of the original sample in the first year of the panel (1993) that participated in all 19 survey years, including 2011, decreasing panel participation is both a matter of panel mortality (firm closure and resistant non-response over many years) and of discontinuous response. Another important methodological issue is the potential selection bias of responding firms with respect to their innovation behaviour. In the MIP survey, a large non-response survey is conducted every year that shows that in most years responding firms are biased towards non-innovating firms, which may be attributed to the higher costs for innovating firms of replying to the questionnaire.

Innovation panel data can be used both for producing time-series data of innovation indicators and for analysing innovation behaviour over time. Innovation indicators based on panel data may be less susceptible to arbitrary movements due to changes in the sample of surveyed firms than cross-section surveys conducted only from time to time, particularly if panel firms become familiar with the underlying concepts of the questionnaire and respondents remain the same over some period. Innovation indicators produced from the MIP show indeed a rather stable development, although changes in survey methodology can result in break in series, and annual fluctuations reflecting the business cycle or other changes in the economic environment can be large for some indicators.

Analysing firms' innovation behaviour over time shows a high degree of persistence. Persistence of innovation is more prevalent in manufacturing than in services. It is also higher for larger firms and for firms in more R&D-intensive industries. When explaining persistence of innovation, state dependence, observed firm heterogeneity and unobserved heterogeneity do matter, although past innovation experience tends to be the most important driver. These findings reinforce the need of panel data and of accounting for dynamics in explaining innovation behaviour in empirical innovation research.

The analytical potential of panel data of course does not end with persistence analysis. Modelling the links between innovation input and output, and the underlying time lag between both, is another important study area. Peters (2008) used panel data to estimate productivity effects of innovation based on a model framework proposed by Crépon, Duguet and Mairesse (CDM) (1998). While most applications of the CDM model use cross-section data, employing panel data and carefully controlling for selectivity and endogeneity biases yields a lower estimated elasticity of innovation output (sales with new products) of about 4 per cent which is lower than the elasticity found by CDM (1998) and other studies (see Griffith et al. 2006; Parisi et al. 2006; Hall et al. 2008; Criscuolo and Haskel 2003; Janz et al. 2004; Polder et al. 2009; van Leeuwen and Klomp 2006 and the recent survey by Hall 2011) that are based on cross-section data.

This finding calls for more detailed analysis of the impacts of innovation on firm performance using firm panel data. Many national CIS provide few opportunities for such analysis since most have been conducted only every two or four years, and linking individual survey waves often results in a small and unrepresentative panel (with a strong focus on large firms). In addition, standard CIS data contain little information on firm performance and assets such as value added, profits or capital stock. When adding such data from other sources, the panel may become even smaller. The MIP was intended to respond to this need for firm panel data on innovation activities and firm performance that span a longer time period and cover both manufacturing and service sectors. While some econometric panel studies have been performed with this data (see Peters 2008, 2009; Schwiebacher 2012), a large potential for empirical analyses has yet to be exploited.

NOTES

1. For a recent description of the data, see Lachenmaier (2007). Recent empirical findings can be found in Becker and Egger (2009) or Lachenmaier and Rottmann (2011).
2. The survey is conducted by the ZEW in cooperation with the Institute for Applied Social Science (infas). From 1995 to 1998 and since 2005, the Fraunhofer Institute for Systems and Innovation Research (ISI) has been another partner in this undertaking.
3. The original sample was based on the sector classification scheme NACE Rev. 1. In 2009, sampling was adapted to the new industry classification NACE Rev. 2.0.
4. This panel is a joint effort of ZEW and Creditreform, Germany's largest credit-rating agency. The MEP includes literally all economically active enterprises in Germany, although some enter the database only several years after foundation. A comparison of the MEP with the Business Register of the Federal Statistical Office, established for the first time in 2006, shows a very high compliance both in terms of the number of enterprises and the size and sector distribution. ZEW constructs the MEP by merging twice a year a copy of the current state of Creditreform's enterprise data with previous copies of

this data, including data cleaning for multiple entries and identification of firm closures. The MEP contains, among others things, data on an enterprise's economic activity (NACE 5-digit), location and number of employees.

5. Statistical significance is analysed through a multivariate analysis (probit models) that takes into account industry, size and regional effects on the probability of being an innovator since the samples of responding and non-responding firms are not completely equally distributed in terms of sectors, size classes and regions.

6. The MIP is accompanied by a scientific advisory board consisting of academics, industry representatives and innovation policy makers, that provides, among other advice, crucial input to the questionnaire design.

7. Organizational innovation, along with market development, did not enter the *Oslo Manual* definition of innovation until the third edition (OECD/Eurostat 2005).

8. This was done by estimating a simple probit model on the probability of introducing a product or process innovation for the 1995 and 1997 samples separately with controls for size, sector, region and a few firm-specific characteristics while considering a dummy variable for firms that responded to the service sector variant of the questionnaire.

9. The sector classification is based on OECD (2007) and adjusted for NACE Rev. 2.0. For NACE Rev. 2.0, high-tech manufacturing includes divisions 20, 21 and 26 to 30, low-tech manufacturing includes divisions 5 to 19, 22 to 25 and 31 to 39. Knowledge-intensive services include divisions 58 to 66 and 69 to 73, while other services include divisions 46, 49 to 53, 74 and 78 to 82.

10. This is not related to the fact that a few less innovative industries such as retail and renting have been discarded from the sample. The figures look very similar over time if these industries are excluded in all time periods.

11. The standard deviation of entry and exit rates is 4.4 and 4.2 in manufacturing and 6.6 and 5.7 in services, respectively.

12. Wooldridge (2005) shows that under the additional assumptions of strict exogeneity of the explanatory variables and a normally distributed individual effect, the likelihood function turns out to be the same as in a standard probit model, with the initial innovation status and mean values of the explanatory variables as additional regressors.

13. The variables foreign, east, public limited company and private partnership can vary across individuals and time. However, due to the fact that hardly any variation showed up within a firm, the individual mean values are left out in order to avoid strong multicollinearity.

REFERENCES

Aghion, P. and P. Howitt (1992), 'A model of growth through creative destruction', *Econometrica*, **60**, 323–51.

Aschhoff, B. (2010), 'Who gets the money? The dynamics of R&D project subsidies in Germany', *Jahrbücher für Nationalökonomie und Statistik*, **230**, 522–46.

Becker, S.O. and P.H. Egger (2009), 'Endogenous product versus process innovation and a firm's propensity to export', *Empirical Economics*, online version: DOI: 10.1007/s00181-009-0322-6.

Cefis, E. (2003), 'Is there persistence in innovative activities?', *International Journal of Industrial Organization*, **21**, 489–515.

Cefis, E. and L. Orsenigo (2001), 'The persistence of innovative activities. A cross-countries and cross-sectors comparative analysis', *Research Policy*, **30**, 1139–58.

Cockburn, I.M., M.J. MacGarvie and E. Müller (2010), 'Patent thickets, licensing and innovative performance', *Industrial and Corporate Change*, **19**, 899–925.

Crépon, B., E. Duguet and J. Mairesse (1998), 'Research, innovation and productivity: an econometric analysis at the firm level', *Economics of Innovation and New Technology*, **7**, 115–58.

Criscuolo, C. and J. Haskel (2003), 'Innovations and productivity growth in the UK: evidence from CIS2 and CIS3', CeRiBA Discussion Paper EBPF03-3(10), London: Office of National Statistics.

Czarnitzki, D. and K. Kraft (2010), 'On the profitability of innovative assets', *Applied Economics*, **42**, 1941–53.

Czarnitzki, D. and K. Kraft (2012), 'Spillovers of innovation activities and their profitability', *Oxford Economic Papers*, **64**, 302–22.

Czarnitzki, D., B. Ebersberger and A. Fier (2007), 'The relationship between R&D collaboration, subsidies and R&D performance: empirical evidence from Finland and Germany', *Journal of Applied Econometrics*, **22**, 1347–66.

Dobbelaere, S., R.I. Luttens and B. Peters (2009), 'Starting an R&D project under uncertainty', Tinbergen Institute Discussion Paper 2009-044/3, Amsterdam and Rotterdam: Tinbergen Institute.

Dodgson, M. (2000), *The Management of Technological Innovation: An International and Strategic Approach*, New York: Oxford University Press.

Flaig, G. and M. Stadler (1994), 'Success breeds success: the dynamics of the innovation process', *Empirical Economics*, **19**, 55–68.

Griffith, R., E. Huergo, J. Mairesse and B. Peters (2006), 'Innovation and productivity across four European countries', *Oxford Review of Economic Policy*, **22**, 483–98.

Hall, B.H. (2011), 'Innovation and productivity', UNU-MERIT Working Paper Series 2011-028, Maastricht: UNU-MERIT.

Hall, B.H., F. Lotti and J. Mairesse (2008), 'Employment, innovation and productivity: evidence from Italian microdata', *Industrial and Corporate Change*, **17**, 813–39.

Hollanders, H. and A. van Cruysen (2008), 'Rethinking the European Innovation Scoreboard: a new methodology for 2008–2010', Maastricht: UNU-MERIT.

Hussinger, K. (2008), 'R&D and subsidies at the firm level: an application of parametric and semi-parametric two-step selection models', *Journal of Applied Econometrics*, **23**, 729–47.

Janz, N., H. Lööf and B. Peters (2004), 'Firm level innovation and productivity: is there a common story across countries?', *Problems and Perspectives in Management*, **2**, 184–204.

Johansson, B. and H. Lööf (2010), 'Innovation strategy and firm performance: what is the long-run impact of persistent R&D?', CESIS Working Paper 240, Stockholm Royal Institute of Technology.

Kleinknecht, A., K. van Montfort and E. Brouwer (2002), 'The non-trivial choice between innovation indicators', *Economics of Innovation and New Technology*, **11**, 109–21.

Lachenmaier, S. (2007), 'Effects of innovation on firm performance', Ifo Beiträge zur Wirtschaftsforschung 28, Munich: Ifo Institute for Economic Research and University of Munich.

Lachenmaier, S. and H. Rottmann (2011), 'Effects of innovation on employment: a dynamic panel analysis', *International Journal of Industrial Organization*, **29**, 210–20.

Laursen, K. and A. Salter (2006), 'Open for innovation: the role of openness in explaining innovation performance among UK manufacturing firms', *Strategic Management Journal*, **27**, 131–50.

Leiponen, A and C. Helfat (2010), 'Innovation objectives, knowledge sources, and the benefits of breadth', *Strategic Management Journal*, **31**, 224–36.

Lööf, H. and A. Heshmati (2010), 'Knowledge capital and heterogeneity in firm performance. A sensitivity analysis', *Economics of Innovation and New Technology*, **15**, 317–44.

Malerba, F. and L. Orsenigo (1993), 'Technological regimes and firm behaviour', *Industrial Corporate Change*, **2**, 45–71.

Mansfield, E. (1968), *Industrial Research and Technological Innovation: An Econometric Analysis*, New York: Norton.

Mansfield, E. (1998), 'Academic research and industrial innovation: an update of empirical findings', *Research Policy*, **26**, 773–6.

Nelson, R. and S. Winter (1982), *An Evolutionary Theory of Economic Change*, Cambridge, MA: Harvard University Press.

OECD (1992), *Proposed Guidelines for Collecting and Interpreting Technological Innovation Data – Oslo Manual*, OCDE/GD(92)26, Paris: OECD.

OECD (2007), *OECD Science, Technology and Industry Scoreboard 2007*, Paris: OECD.

OECD/Eurostat (1997), *Proposed Guidelines for Collecting and Interpreting Technological Innovation Data – Oslo Manual*, 2nd edition, Paris: OECD.

OECD/Eurostat (2005), *Oslo Manual: Guidelines for Collecting and Interpreting Innovation Data*, Paris: OECD.

Parisi, M., F. Schiantarelli and A. Sembenelli (2006), 'Productivity, innovation and R&D: micro evidence for Italy', *European Economic Review*, **50**, 2037–61.

Peters, B. (2008), *Innovation and Firm Performance. An Empirical Investigation for German Firms*, ZEW Economic Studies 38, Heidelberg and New York: Physica.

Peters, B. (2009), 'Persistence of innovation: stylized facts and panel data evidence', *Journal of Technology Transfer*, **34**, 226–43.

Phillips, A. (1971), *Technology and Market Structure: A Study of the Aircraft Industry*, Lexington, MA: Heath Lexington Books.

Polder, M., G. van Leeuwen, P. Mohnen and W. Raymond (2009), 'Productivity effects of innovation modes', Statistics Netherlands Discussion Paper No. 09033, The Hague: Statistics Netherlands.

Rammer, C., D. Czarnitzki and A. Spielkamp (2009), 'Innovation success of non-R&D-performers: substituting technology by management in SMEs', *Small Business Economics*, **33**, 35–58.

Raymond, W., P. Mohnen, F. Palm and S. Schim van der Loeff (2010), 'Persistence of innovation in Dutch manufacturing: is it spurious?', *The Review of Economics and Statistics*, **92**, 495–504.

Romer, P. (1990), 'Endogenous technological change', *Journal of Political Economy*, **98**, 71–102.

Schmidt, T. and K. Aerts (2008), 'Two for the price of one? Additionality effects of R&D subsidies: a comparison between Flanders and Germany', *Research Policy*, **37**, 806–22.

Schwiebacher, F. (2012), 'Complementary assets, patent thickets and hold-up threats – do transaction costs undermine investments in innovation?', ZEW Discussion Paper No. 12-015, Mannheim: ZEW.

Smith, K. (2005), 'Measuring innovation', in J. Fagerberg, D.C. Mowery and R.R. Nelson (eds), *The Oxford Handbook of Innovation*, New York: Oxford University Press, pp. 148–77.

Stoneman, P. (1983), *The Economic Analysis of Technological Change*, Oxford: Oxford University Press.

Sutton, J. (1991), *Sunk Costs and Market Structure*, Cambridge, MA: MIT Press.

Van Leeuwen, G. and L. Klomp (2006), 'On the contribution of innovation to multi-factor productivity growth', *Economics of Innovation and New Technology*, **15**, 367–90.

Wooldridge, J.M. (2005), 'Simple solutions to the initial conditions problem in dynamic non-linear panel data models with unobserved heterogeneity', *Journal of Applied Econometrics*, **20**, 39–54.

APPENDIX: ADDITIONAL INFORMATION ON THE MIP SURVEY

Table 6A.1   Sector coverage of the MIP, 1993–2012

NACE Rev. 1		NACE Rev. 2	
C (Mining and Quarrying)	1993–2007	B (Mining and Quarrying)	2007–12
D (Manufacturing)	1993–2007	C (Manufacturing)	2007–12
E (Electricity, Gas and Water Supply)	1993–2007	D (Energy Supply)	2007–12
F (Construction)	1993–2004	E (Water Supply, Sewage, Recycling)	2007–12
50 (Sale/Repair of Motor Vehicles)	1995–2004		
51 (Wholesale Trade)	1995–2007	46 (Wholesale Trade)	2007–12
52 (Retail Trade)	1995–2004	H (Transportation and Storage)	2007–12
I (Transport, Storage, Communication)	1995–2007	J (Information & Communication)	2007–12
J (Financial Intermediation)	1995–2007	K (Financial and Insurance Act.)	2007–12
70 (Real Estate)	1995–2004	69 (Legal and Accounting Act.)	2007–12
71 (Renting of Machinery etc.)	1995–2004	70.2 (Management Consulting)	2007–12
72 (Computer Activities)	1993–2007	71 (Architecture and Engineering)	2007–12
73 (Research and Development)[a]	1993–2007	72 (Research and Development)[a]	2007–12
74.1 (Legal Advice, Consulting etc.)	1995–2007	73 (Advertising, Market Research)	2007–12
74.2/74.3 (Architecture, Engineering, Technical Testing)	1993–2007	74 (Other Professional, Scientific and Technical Activities)	2007–12
74.4–74.8 (Advertising, Employment Act., Security Act., Services to Buildings, Other Business Support Act.)	1995–2007	78 (Employment Activities)	2007–12
		79 (Travel Agencies)	2007–12
		80 (Security Activities)	2007–12
90 (Sewage and Refuse Disposal)	1993–2007	81 (Services to Buildings)	2007–12
92.1/92.2 (Motion Picture, Radio and Television)	2002–2007	82 (Other Business Support Activities)	2007–12

Note: a.   Excluding public research organizations.

Source: ZEW.

Table 6A.2 Sector distribution of the MIP sample, 1993–2011

Survey year	NACE Rev. 1.1									Total
	C	D	E, 90	F	G	I	J	K, 92.1, 92.2	All other	
1993	1.5	79.9	3.9	5.9	1.8	0.1	0.0	6.9	0.1	100.0
1994	1.1	84.0	4.1	6.1	0.0	0.0	0.0	4.8	0.0	100.0
1995	0.7	45.5	4.0	5.3	12.1	6.1	6.0	20.3	0.1	100.0
1996	0.8	49.6	4.5	5.5	10.0	5.3	5.3	18.9	0.2	100.0
1997	0.6	43.7	3.7	3.7	14.0	7.1	6.6	20.3	0.2	100.0
1998	0.8	44.4	4.3	2.9	12.9	7.7	6.8	20.0	0.2	100.0
1999	0.9	43.0	2.9	2.4	13.5	8.5	6.2	22.1	0.5	100.0
2000	1.1	40.7	3.3	2.6	14.0	9.0	6.4	22.4	0.5	100.0
2001	1.2	42.1	3.6	3.0	11.5	9.0	4.7	24.5	0.5	100.0
2002	1.3	45.1	3.3	2.0	10.8	8.5	4.2	24.6	0.4	100.0
2003	1.2	45.6	4.6	2.5	7.8	8.1	4.3	25.3	0.4	100.0
2004	1.3	47.0	4.3	2.5	7.3	7.6	4.5	25.2	0.4	100.0
2005	1.6	50.4	5.7	1.9	5.7	7.8	4.7	21.8	0.5	100.0
2006	1.6	51.6	5.4	2.2	5.5	7.2	4.4	21.6	0.6	100.0
2007	1.4	51.3	5.5	1.7	5.3	7.4	3.8	23.2	0.5	100.0
2008	1.3	52.2	5.6	1.5	5.1	7.4	3.8	22.6	0.5	100.0
2009	1.3	51.7	5.6	1.5	4.9	7.6	3.5	23.4	0.5	100.0
2010	1.4	51.4	5.9	1.2	4.7	7.7	3.6	23.5	0.7	100.0
2011	1.2	51.8	5.5	1.4	4.6	7.5	3.6	23.6	0.8	100.0
Total	1.2	49.3	4.7	2.4	7.8	7.4	4.4	22.2	0.5	100.0
Total population, 2006[a]	0.2	17.7	0.9	13.0	20.4	5.4	1.0	15.5	25.9	100.0

Notes: a. Firms with five or more employees according to the Business Register of the Federal Statistical Office, excluding agriculture, hunting and fishing, and public administration.

Source: ZEW; Federal Statistical Office.

Table 6A.3 Response rates in the MIP by sampling year, 1993–2011

Sampling year	'93	'94	'95	'96	'97	'98	'99	'00	'01	'02	'03	'04	'05	'06	'07	'08	'09	'10	'11	Total
1993	23	25	35	29	33	36	33	37	25	32	26	27	29	29	24	36	29	30	28	29
1994		23	26	21	23	32	27	33	21	29	20	26	24	24	21	33	23	23	23	25
1995			23	19	22	41	25	36	27	37	24	27	29	32	26	38	31	34	31	28
1997					25	28	23	40	18	29	21	26	26	29	25	38	28	35	30	26
1999							21	20	15	20	18	24	24	24	21	34	24	27	26	21
2001									20	22	15	20	20	25	20	32	26	29	27	22
2003											14	18	18	24	19	28	22	27	25	20
2005													11	21	21	33	24	28	26	20
2007															11	29	25	31	28	21
2009																	17	24	27	21
2011																			16	16
Total	23	25	27	24	25	37	25	32	21	28	18	23	17	25	18	32	22	28	24	24

Notes: Response rate: share of responding firms as a percentage of the sample excluding neutral losses.
Note that from 1998 on, surveys in even years deliberately focus on firms with frequent response in prior years, resulting in higher response rates.

Source: ZEW.

Table 6A.4 Composition of responding firms by sampling year, 1993–2011

Sampling year	'93	'94	'95	'96	'97	'98	'99	'00	'01	'02	'03	'04	'05	'06	'07	'08	'09	'10	'11	No. of responses	
																				Total	%
	Share of firms from respective sampling year in total no. of responses (%)																				
1993	100	92	37	64	30	31	24	26	18	23	19	17	13	13	10	10	8	8	6	21226	23.7
1994		8	4	9	4	4	3	3	2	2	2	2	1	1	1	1	1	1	1	2088	2.3
1995			59	26	55	52	44	49	28	32	21	21	15	15	12	11	8	9	7	21321	23.8
1997					11	12	8	8	5	6	4	4	3	3	2	2	1	2	1	3302	3.7
1999							19	14	14	14	10	11	7	7	6	6	4	4	3	5692	6.3
2001									32	21	20	21	14	15	11	12	9	10	7	8525	9.5
2003											25	23	17	17	13	13	9	11	8	7013	7.8
2005													30	28	23	22	16	17	14	8603	9.6
2007															22	22	13	15	12	5206	5.8
2009																	30	23	18	4768	0.0
2011																			22	1515	1.7
others	0	0	0	1	0	1	1	1	0	1	1	1	0	0	0	0	0	0	0	395	0.4
Total	100	100	100	100	100	100	100	100	100	100	100	100	100	100	100	100	100	100	100	89654	0.0

Note: Response rate: share of responding firms as a percentage of the sample excluding neutral losses.
Note that from 1996 on, surveys in even years deliberately focus on firms with frequent response in prior years.

Source: ZEW.

7 Innovation and R&D surveys in Norway
Frank Foyn

1. INTRODUCTION

Norwegian surveys on innovation activity in the business enterprise sector have been undertaken by Statistics Norway in the form of representative sample surveys since the early 1990s. The surveys have been part of the Eurostat Community Innovation Survey (CIS), which has been developed gradually since the first innovation survey (CIS 1), undertaken for the year 1992. CIS 2 was carried through for the year 1997, CIS 3 for 2001, and since 2004 (CIS 4) the surveys have been performed every second year; the last one was CIS 2010.[1]

The Norwegian surveys have closely followed the Eurostat recommendations for CIS, both in content and methodology, given in the *Oslo Manual* (OECD/Eurostat 2005). Almost all themes/questions in CIS have been implemented in the Norwegian questionnaire. All core activity classes in CIS have been included in Norway, but with some additional ones. The Norwegian survey covers the entire manufacturing sector and large parts of the services sector. It also covers extraction of oil and gas, aquaculture and construction. In the CIS 2010 the tourism sector was also included. The lower size limit for enterprises to be included was ten employees up until 2004, and from 2006 onwards it was five employees.

In most European countries innovation surveys have been performed as separate surveys with a dedicated questionnaire, but some countries have experience with combining the innovation survey with the R&D survey. Norway is one of these countries. In Norway, coordination of the R&D and innovation surveys has developed from no coordination at all for CIS 1 for 1992 into full coordination with CIS 3 for 2001 and subsequent surveys.

This chapter describes the general procedures for the innovation surveys in Norway and the specific procedure for combined R&D and innovation surveys.

2. GENERAL METHODOLOGY

Statistical Unit

The recommended statistical unit in innovation surveys is the enterprise. An enterprise is defined as the smallest combination of legal units that is an organizational unit producing goods or services.[2] An enterprise may be a sole legal unit. An enterprise carries out one or more activities at one or more locations and may consist of one or more kind-of-activity units (KAU) or local kind-of-activity units (LKAU).

There are pro and cons in using the enterprise as the statistical unit. Strategic decisions will typically be taken at the enterprise level, although such decisions may also be made at the corporate level for enterprises that are linked together in groups. Since innovation activities are closely linked to strategy, the enterprise is assumed to be best suited to provide answers in the area.

Collection of data from companies linked to a group represents a special challenge. Here, decisions at the group level on innovation activities to be used in several of the group companies may be attributed to an enterprise that is responsible for development work.

A drawback with the enterprise as the statistical unit is that the enterprise is not delimited by economic activity or region. If an enterprise has innovation activity in several local units and/or in several industries, all this innovation is assigned to the main activity of the enterprise. Moreover, the innovation activity is placed geographically where the headquarters is located, even in cases where this activity is carried out by a unit located elsewhere. In other words, for multi-activity enterprises it may not be possible to classify all innovation activity correctly by region or activity class. In the Norwegian survey additional information is collected by asking all the LKAUs in the enterprises, listed in the questionnaire, if they have been involved in innovation activity or are performing R&D. This information has been used in the regional breakdown of innovation activity.

Population and Sampling

To run a statistical survey a target population has to be defined and there must be a representative register of units within the target population of enterprises – that is, a business register. The business register used for the Norwegian innovation survey is Statistics Norway's Central Register of Establishments and Enterprises. The register is continuously updated. For each enterprise, information on activity class, location, employment and turnover is available.

The CIS-like innovation surveys are dedicated to the business enterprise sector. In principle, innovation occurs throughout all types of businesses independent of size and activity, but in practice a delimitation of the population of enterprises to specific activity and size classes is necessary. Otherwise the response burden and the cost of running the survey will be too high. The first innovation survey covered only manufacturing industries, but the coverage has gradually been extended to service industries and other industries. The latest survey for 2010 in Norway covered the following activities in the European classification NACE 2007:[3] 03, 05–33, 35–39, 41–43, 46, 49–53, 58–66, 70–72, 74.9, 82.9.

Due to the large number of small enterprises, it is quite common to fix a lower size limit of the enterprises to be included. Normally the number of employees is used. In CIS the lower size limit has been ten employees. This has also been the case in Norway until the survey for 2006. Then the scope of the survey was expanded to include enterprises with five to nine employees. The main reason for this was to have more information on innovation activity among smaller enterprises and to allow for an expanded breakdown of results at detailed regional level. For enterprises with five to nine employees a somewhat reduced questionnaire is used.

Even though the target population for the survey is a subset of the population of all enterprises, the number of enterprises in the target population is normally too large to be included in the survey. A kind of representative sampling has to be done.

The Norwegian innovation survey is a census of all enterprises within the target population with at least 50 employees. Among enterprises with 5–49 employees a random sample is drawn within each stratum (NACE 2-digit and size class). The fraction rate is normally 35 per cent, but in some strata 5 and 10 per cent are used. The total sample of units is about 6800 (2010). The total number of enterprises in the target population was 18 600.

Capture and Treatment of Data

The data in the innovation survey have traditionally been collected by paper questionnaire. For 2005 an electronic questionnaire was introduced and electronic reporting has gradually increased. In the latest survey for 2010 an overwhelming majority of the enterprises used the electronic form.

All forms from the enterprises undergo different types of controls, checking whether all questions in the form have been filled in, if there are any obvious inconsistencies, if the data are consistent with data from the previous survey and with other information and so on. In the electronic questionnaire there are built-in controls for the enterprises to avoid severely inconsistent answers, and this has improved the quality of the received answers.

The electronic questionnaire has also reduced the item non-response. But there is still item non-response that varies across the questions. Most of the item non-responses are adjusted for during the data revision process, but automatic procedures for imputation can also be used.

The introduction of the electronic questionnaire has not caused any shift in the innovation rate in Norway, but this may happen. With a large paper questionnaire there could be a tendency for enterprises to neglect reporting of innovation activity to avoid having to answer many questions. In an electronic questionnaire the situation is different and there is less tendency to underreport on innovation.

The notion of innovation may, for some enterprises, be difficult to interpret and distinguish from related activities. There are indications that the data may to some extent be influenced by respondents' varying degree of understanding or attention to the concepts and activities covered by the survey.

The unit response rate for the survey in Norway is fairly high at 95 per cent due to mandatory surveys and use of fines for non-responding enterprises. The high response rate is valid for the different size classes and industries. Results should not, for that reason, be biased by non-respondents and a non-response survey is not necessary. In cases with low response rate the results could be biased and a non-response survey should be carried out. Norway has done some testing on the effects of high and low response rates in innovation surveys. A valid result seems to be that a voluntary survey with a low response rate shows stronger innovation performance than a mandatory survey with a high response rate.

Estimating National Totals

Normally innovation surveys are performed as sample surveys, often as a census of enterprises above a certain threshold of employees and a representative sampling of smaller enterprises. In the Norwegian survey, enterprises with 5–49 employees are based on a sample of units. For this part of the survey population it is then necessary to scale the results to provide representative figures for the total population of enterprises based on the sample units. The scaling is performed in strata defined by industry and size groups, that is, the same groups that were used during the sample selection. These are based on the 2-digit industry codes (NACE 2007) crossed with enterprise size.

For each firm in the net sample a weight proportional to its representation of the total enterprise in the relevant stratum is calculated. Different weights can be used depending on the variable to be grossed up. For binary variables (i.e. whether a company is innovative or not, and the importance of hampering factors), the weights are based on the number of units. This means that all the enterprises in the same stratum have the same weight. For quantitative variables (i.e. the cost of innovation), the ratio used is based on the number of employees, giving larger weights for large enterprises.

Since stratification and weights are based on NACE (2-digit) and number of employees, incomplete updating of these variables in the business register as well as the entry and exit of enterprises from the sample may cause errors in the results.

Since the Norwegian survey is a census of all enterprises with 50 employees or more, no weighting is necessary for this group (weight = 1). However, in principle correction for non-response should be made, specifically if the response rate is low. One method is to calculate weights also for this group based on the net sample or to estimate figures for non-responding enterprise using other sources, such as figures from the last survey.

3. COMBINED SURVEYS COMPARED WITH SEPARATE SURVEYS

Benefits of Integration

Statistics Norway is responsible both for R&D surveys and innovation surveys for the business enterprise sector. R&D surveys were performed by Statistics Norway every second year until 2001 (uneven years). From 2001 onwards the R&D survey has been performed on an annual basis. The frequency of innovation surveys has followed the CIS, with some deviation (1992, 1997, 2001). From 2004 innovation surveys have been performed every second year (2004, 2006, 2008, 2010).

The first innovation survey for 1992 was done separately with no coordination at all with the R&D survey. CIS 2 for 1997 was partly coordinated with the R&D survey. Two different questionnaires were used, but were sent out together. The target population for the surveys was mainly the same (NACE groups and size classes). The selection/sampling of units in the survey was partly coordinated, but not completely; all enterprises participating in the innovation survey were also included in the R&D survey, but there were enterprises in the R&D survey that did not take part in the innovation survey.

The innovation survey for 2001 (CIS 3) was fully integrated with the

R&D survey and the coordination of the surveys has continued until now. These surveys are closely related and the main reason for the coordinated approach was to have a more consistent and efficient system for reporting of R&D and innovation activity from the enterprises.

- Enterprises reacted negatively to the number of surveys and surveys/ questions that partly overlapped. For the enterprises involved an integrated survey would imply a lower response burden than two separate surveys.
- Administration costs for the statistical office are also lower for one large survey compared with two surveys.
- Integrated surveys would also eliminate the discrepancy in results, on both the micro and the macro level, that happened with separate surveys. This was specifically the case for R&D expenditure.
- Integrated surveys may allow for a more flexible questionnaire with a core set of questions on R&D and innovation each time, and a rotating set of other questions. One year the questionnaire may be dominated by innovation-related questions, but the next survey may put more focus on R&D questions and other possible topics, with a reduced number of innovation questions compared to the 'core questions'.

How are the Surveys Integrated?

First of all, a completely integrated questionnaire is used. The first integrated questionnaire was organized in three parts:

- Part A: Background information on the enterprise;
- Part B: R&D; and,
- Part C: Innovation.

R&D expenditure was asked about in both Part B and Part C (part of innovation expenditure), but the link between these questions was highlighted and instructions given that these amounts should be the same. The R&D part of the questionnaire was slightly reduced compared with the R&D questionnaire in the former surveys to avoid too large a questionnaire.

The structure of the integrated questionnaire in the latest survey is more or less the same, but the part dealing with background information of the enterprise has been reduced (using administrative information) and removed to the end. In the electronic questionnaire in use now there is also an automatic link between the R&D expenditure in the R&D part and in the innovation part.

The statistical unit in the R&D survey was previously kind-of-activity unit (KAU). With the coordinated survey the statistical unit is now common to R&D and innovation: the enterprise. But to have the best distribution of R&D by sector and region the enterprises are asked also to specify their total R&D expenditure and R&D personnel at a more detailed level, by local kind-of-activity unit (LKAU) (establishment) listed in the questionnaire. The enterprises are also asked to specify which establishments are involved in innovation activity. This is done to give regional breakdown of innovation activity.

The target population is identical for the R&D and innovation part with respect to NACE groups and size classes.

The sampling of survey units is also fully integrated with the following structure:

1. Enterprises with 50 employees or more: census of all enterprises
2. Enterprises with 5–49 employees:
    (a) enterprises with reported R&D above a certain size from the last survey are included (either at least NOK 1 million of intramural R&D or at least NOK 5 million of extramural R&D);
    (b) random sample of other enterprises with 5–49 employees, stratified by NACE (2-digit) and size class. The fraction rate was normally 35 per cent, but in some strata 5 and 10 per cent were used. However, the minimum number of enterprises in each stratum was set to 15, unless the total number in the population was lower.

The reason for having group 2(a) is to ensure that large R&D performers, but small in terms of employment, are included in the R&D statistics. A separate innovation survey would not have included such a group. The results for enterprises with 5–49 employees are grossed up within each stratum using weighting factors. Enterprises in group 2(a) have the weight 1.

For more information see Statistics Norway (2004).

R&D and Innovation Activity in Norway

Norway is a small open economy with 5 million inhabitants that relies heavily on exploitation of several natural resources, specifically oil and gas. The Norwegian GDP per person is among the highest in the world; Norway also has a good performance on economic indicators related to

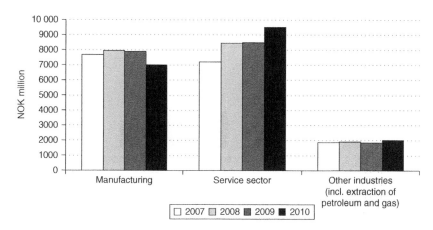

Source: Statistics Norway.

Figure 7.1   *Intramural R&D expenditure in business enterprises in Norway, by main industry, 2007–10, NOK million at current prices*

standard of living. However, in international comparison on R&D and innovation activity Norway ranks relatively low compared to other countries. One explanation for this has been the industry structure in Norway with a large oil and gas sector and low activity in the most R&D-intensive sectors. Total R&D expenditure as percentage of GDP is around 1.8 per cent, below the average of both the EU and the OECD. Compared to other countries the share for the business sector is low, around 0.9 per cent of GDP.

In the Norwegian business enterprise sector there has been a steady growth in R&D activity. This is mainly due to service industries. In manufacturing and other industries (including oil and gas) activity has been more stable (see Figure 7.1).

The large enterprises dominate in R&D activity in Norway. Enterprises with more than 500 employees have close to 40 per cent of total R&D expenditures (see Figure 7.2). The concentration can also be illustrated by the fact that 10 per cent of R&D performers, the largest, account for 72 per cent of total R&D and 20 per cent account for 84 per cent.

The innovation rate is also low in Norway. The share of product and process innovators is 30 per cent on average, compared to 33 per cent for the EU-27. As in other countries the share of innovators increases with size of the enterprises, from 27 per cent for the smallest to 59 for the largest (see Figure 7.3).

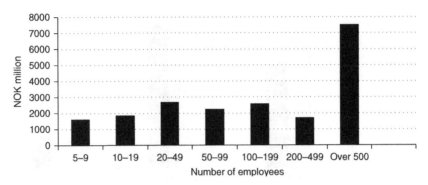

Source: Statistics Norway.

Figure 7.2   *Intramural R&D expenditure in business enterprises in Norway, by size group, 2010, NOK million*

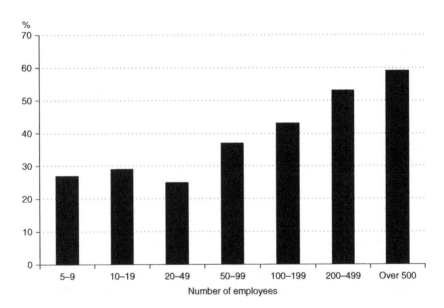

Source: Statistics Norway.

Figure 7.3   *Share of innovative enterprises in Norway, by size group, 2008–10*

4. EXPERIENCE WITH THE COORDINATED APPROACH

Questionnaire

There have been no negative reactions from the enterprises on the integration of these topics. Even though the questionnaire is quite comprehensive, and longer than separate questionnaires for R&D and innovation, neither have there been many negative reactions to the length of the questionnaire. A separate innovation questionnaire would also have been quite long. The response rate of 95 per cent is also very satisfactory, even for a mandatory survey.

Methodology

The methodology used is fully acceptable both for the R&D and innovation statistics. It is important that the sample of enterprises is representative also for the innovation part; this means specifically that the sample not only includes R&D performers, but, as explained above, it is still possible to have separate subsamples of R&D performers if they are treated correctly.

Potential Effects

One important aspect is the effect on the reported figures from the enterprises. Does the combined questionnaire influence the answers from the enterprises in a negative or non-intended way that could give biased results? Possible problems could be:

- The questionnaire could prevent innovators from reporting on their innovation activity since it starts with the R&D questions and innovators find the questionnaire focused on R&D. This could be the case specifically for enterprises with no R&D activity.
- Innovators that normally would report no R&D activity in a standard R&D survey could now classify (part of) their innovation activity as R&D.
- The effect on the R&D and innovation expenditures and the distribution of types of cost could be different.

The effect on innovation rates
Evidence from time-series results and the results of an additional survey are considered.

Table 7.1   Share of enterprises with innovation activity: manufacturing industry, 1992–2010 (%)

1992	1997	2001	2004	2006	2008	2010
38	39	36	37	35	33	32

Table 7.2   Share of enterprises with innovation activity: service industries, 1997–2010 (%)

1992	1997	2001	2004	2006	2008	2010
:	22	30	28	28	28	25

Time-series results   The potential effect of fewer enterprises reporting innovation activity was not observed when the structure of the survey was changed. The surveys are not directly comparable throughout the whole period from 1992, but the share of innovating enterprises in manufacturing industry does not seem to be affected in a significant way by this change (see Table 7.1).

For service industries, included in the survey from 1992, there was an upward shift from 1997 to 2001, opposite of what might be expected. From 2001 the share of innovation enterprises in services has stayed rather stable with a downward trend in the latest year (see Table 7.2).

Looking at innovating enterprises not engaged in R&D, this share has been quite stable throughout the period, also from 1997 to 2001. However, the situation is different for manufacturing and service industries. Among innovating enterprises in services the share of enterprises not engaged in R&D is in fact higher in the 2001 survey than in the 1997 survey (respectively 49 and 34 per cent). The distribution by size class gives the same picture. But, as already mentioned, the share of innovating enterprise in total services increased by around 8 percentage points from 1997.

The situation for manufacturing is different. Among innovating enterprises the share of enterprises not engaged in R&D activities was reduced from 37 to 31 per cent from 1997 to 2001. This decline occurred mostly for the small enterprises, but there was also a decline for the medium-sized.

From this partial analysis of aggregated time series it is difficult to draw robust conclusions. On the basis of the evidence, it cannot be said that the combined questionnaire has prevented innovators with no R&D activity from reporting on their innovation activity.

However, the innovation rate in Norwegian businesses has been generally rather low compared to other countries since the start of the innovation surveys. Users of the statistics, like policy makers and others, are partly worried, partly astonished by this, and several types of explanations have been given. In addition to the Norwegian industry structure, the effect of the mandatory combined R&D and innovation survey (with high response rate) has often been used as an argument for the low rate for Norway compared to countries with separate innovation surveys with considerable lower response rates.

For this reason Statistics Norway tested these hypotheses by performing an additional separate innovation survey in 2010 among small enterprises – mandatory for one group of enterprises and voluntary for another group. For full documentation see Wilhelmsen (2012).

Results from additional survey 2010   The general research design chosen for testing was to implement a version of the questionnaire without the R&D module and to send this to two different samples. One of these samples would be mandatory – with a goal of maintaining the response rate of the standard survey – while the other would be voluntary, and thus likely to achieve a substantially lower response rate. The questionnaire for the special surveys was based directly on the original questionnaire for the combined R&D and innovation survey, adding as few alterations as possible for it to work as a stand-alone survey. The most important and obvious difference was the R&D module preceding the innovation questions being completely cut.

The two special studies were developed and implemented after the regular survey was put in the field. Overlap in samples for the different surveys was avoided. Since the regular survey is a census for all enterprises with more than 50 employees in most industries, it was decided to limit the extra samples for this project to enterprises with fewer than 50 employees. It was also decided to limit the response burden of the smallest enterprises, and therefore no enterprises in the five to nine employee size group were chosen.

Rather than spreading the additional samples over more industries, a collection of strata was chosen from ten industries. The gross population of enterprises was 4506 in these industries. The gross sample of enterprises was 819 in the additional mandatory survey, and 1020 in the ordinary combined survey. The mandatory extra sample reached a response rate of 95 per cent – just 1 per cent point lower than for the ordinary survey.

The results showed that there was a significantly higher share of enterprises with innovation activity (product/process) in the additional survey than in the ordinary survey: 36 and 24 per cent respectively. This indicated that a combined survey compared with a separate innovation survey had an impact on the results (see Figure 7.4). Looking at the industry

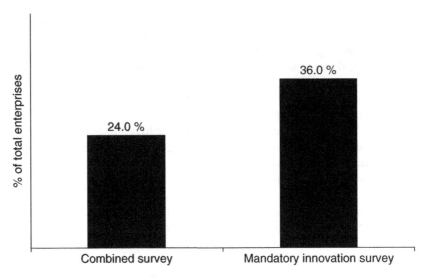

Source: Statistics Norway.

Figure 7.4   *Product and/or process innovation: share of all enterprises in specific NACE classes (combined survey compared with the mandatory innovation survey, 2008–10)*

breakdowns, it seems that the change from a combined survey to a separate innovation survey will have the biggest impact on the industries with low R&D intensity as well as industries that previously reported a low incidence of innovators (see Figure 7.5).

When it comes to organizational innovation, the rate is slightly higher in the mandatory extra sample. The difference is not major – from 15 to 20 per cent – but it is significant. Most of the additional organizational innovators came from the increased share of enterprises with innovation activity in general.

The same trend, although slightly weaker and only of borderline significance for the samples as a whole, is also present with regard to marketing innovations, where there is a slightly higher rate reported for enterprises in the mandatory sample than in the regular sample – a change from 16 to 20 per cent.

The results show that there are clear and significant differences in the results based on whether the innovation survey is carried out separately or integrated with the business enterprise R&D survey. However, the results do not show clearly which of the two sets of data is technically most accurate. Neither is it obvious that the most accurate set of results is also the

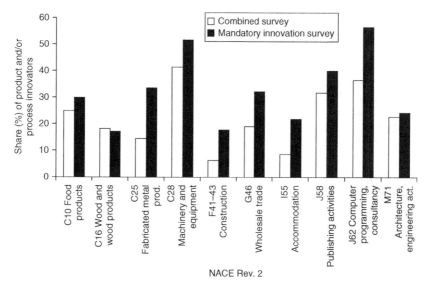

Source: Statistics Norway.

Figure 7.5 *Product and/or process innovation, by NACE: share of all enterprises (combined survey versus mandatory innovation survey, 2008–10)*

most useful for any particular purpose, as long as the less valid set is also reliable and has other advantageous properties that the other may lack.

The effect on number of R&D performers

When introducing combined surveys it was not expected that this would influence the reporting of R&D. But one option could be that innovators that would normally report no R&D activity in a standard R&D survey could classify (part of) their innovation activity as R&D in the combined survey. One method to evaluate this could be to check whether there were many new small R&D performers compared with the separate R&D survey. This was not found.

Results from the additional survey in 2010 showed, however, that the number of R&D performers in the separate innovation survey was higher than in the combined survey. Among innovators, the share of R&D performers was 66 per cent in the separate survey and 59 per cent in the combined survey. This trend was even more significant for enterprises having external R&D – 31 and 16 per cent respectively.

The results are perhaps surprising. One would expect that any increase in the observed innovation rate caused by eliminating the detailed

R&D module from the questionnaire would primarily come from lower-threshold non-R&D-performing innovators. Thus we would expect the number of R&D performers to stay more or less unchanged between the samples while the share of innovation active enterprises involved in R&D would be seen to decrease.

One possible explanation could be the much simpler formulation of the R&D questions in the CIS. The presence of more detailed questions on R&D in the full R&D survey could limit the overall level of reporting R&D. The threshold for defining an activity as R&D seems to be lower in a sole innovation survey. If this is the case, the question arises as to whether the threshold for defining an activity as innovation in the innovation survey is too low, or if the threshold in the combined survey is too high.

The effect on R&D and innovation expenditures

Switching from combined to separate surveys, one might expect some effects on the R&D and innovation expenditures and the distribution of types of cost. One hypothesis would be that innovation expenditures other than R&D are underreported in a combined survey.

One positive effect of combined surveys is first of all that the official R&D figures for Norway are consistent with the R&D expenditure as part of the total innovation expenditure. This does not mean that these figures were consistent in the two different parts of the paper questionnaire for all the enterprise reports that were received. For a majority of reports this was the case, but in several cases inconsistencies had to be corrected, in agreement with the enterprises. In the electronic version of the questionnaire consistency is *per se* obtained by logical control.

What was experienced was that the distribution by type of innovation expenditures differed in the 1997 and 2001 surveys. In the 2001 survey the share of R&D is considerably higher than in the 1997 survey. In CIS 2 for 1997 the R&D share was around 30 per cent in both the manufacturing and the service sector. These shares were considerably lower than the average for the EU countries (around 50 per cent). The R&D expenditure in CIS 2 was also lower than the figure in the Norwegian R&D survey for the same year. If we had substituted the CIS 2 figures with the figures from the R&D survey, the R&D shares would have been respectively 37 and 33 per cent in manufacturing and services, of the increased total innovation expenditure.

In CIS 3 for 2001 the R&D share for Norway was as high as 63 per cent in manufacturing and 51 per cent in the service sector. It should be mentioned that there has been a high increase in R&D expenditure in this period. And this trend with high R&D dominance in costs has continued

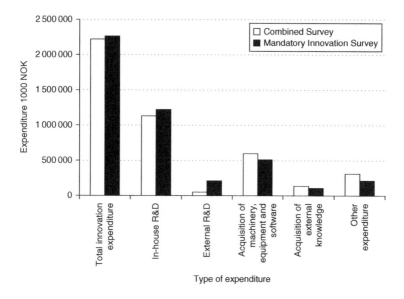

Source: Statistics Norway.

Figure 7.6 *Innovation expenditure, by type in specific NACE classes (combined survey compared with the mandatory innovation survey, 2008–10)*

in later surveys, escalating to 66 and 72 per cent for 2008 (manufacturing and services respectively). In the ordinary 2010 combined survey, extra resources were used to improve the quality of the data on innovation expenditure. But even for 2010 the R&D dominance is quite high.

Results from the additional innovation survey in 2010 are quite interesting. Total innovation expenditure is estimated to be more or less the same in the separate innovation survey and in the combined survey for the same population of enterprises. And the distribution by type of cost shows also more or less same pattern across the two surveys (see Figure 7.6). In-house R&D is the dominating type – 51 per cent in the ordinary combined survey (subsample) and 54 in the separate extra survey. Notable for external R&D, the shares are even relatively higher in the separate innovation survey, 9 and 2 per cent respectively. These results are in line with the share of the number of R&D performers in the two surveys. In general the average cost per enterprise is lower in the separate survey than in the combined survey.

It is difficult to draw strong conclusions from the effect of innovation expenditure in the separate questionnaire compared with the combined questionnaire. It seems that there are more reliable figures on R&D expenditure in a combined survey than in a separate innovation survey. But it is also known that measuring the other types of innovation expenditure is difficult. The hypothesis that the underreporting of other costs is more dominating in combined surveys than in separate surveys seems hard to prove.

5.   CONCLUSION

There are positive and negative aspects both with integrated R&D and innovation surveys and separate surveys. There is no obvious recommendation on which alternative to choose. The choice will depend on users' priorities at national level, available resources for surveys, respondents' motivation, if surveys are being used for the first time or have a history, and so on.

The main positive aspects with integrated surveys are as follows:

- Combined surveys are cost-effective compared to two separate surveys for the statistical agencies.
  Only one questionnaire has to be worked out, with only one procedure for sending out questionnaires and reminders and receiving data, and control and check of received data.
- Integrated surveys are the best tool for obtaining consistent results on related items, in particular R&D expenditure.
  Two separate surveys will quite often result in inconsistencies in answers from the same enterprise. The same enterprise can report on R&D activity, but no innovation activity, or no R&D activity, but innovation activity including R&D activity. These inconsistencies may be reduced by common control of the reports, but this means additional costs for the statistical agency.
  Inconsistencies at the micro-level are a distorting factor in micro-data analyses, but will also result in some inconsistencies at the macro-level. Different sampling will also result in inconsistencies at the macro-level.
- The integrated approach will normally imply a reduced response burden on the enterprises compared with separate surveys.
  Small and medium-sized enterprises participating in both surveys in the same year will normally find this an extra resource burden and may also be confused since the difference in concepts is not always clear. For large enterprises the situation may be different.

The main positive effects with separate surveys are as follows:

- The concepts of R&D and innovation are different.
  Combined surveys may give different results compared to separate innovation surveys. Starting with the R&D questions may put too much focus on R&D and be answered by persons from R&D or accounting departments. The reporting on innovation may be negatively biased and result in underreporting of innovation activity.
- Sampling and coverage of activity classes may be different.
  Splitting the surveys may reduce the number of enterprises answering both surveys, but is unlikely to balance the increased total response burden.

NOTES

1. The Community Innovation Surveys are discussed in more detail in Chapter 3.
2. See Council Regulation on Statistical Units (EEC) no. 696/93.
3. Nomenclature général des activités economiques dans les Communautés Européenes. See Council Regulation no. 1893/2006. NACE is based upon the UN's International Standard Industrial Classification (ISIC).

REFERENCES

OECD/Eurostat (2005), *Oslo Manual: Guidelines for Collecting and Interpreting Innovation Data*, Paris: OECD.

Statistics Norway (2004), *Innovation Statistics in the Business Enterprise Sector 2001*, NOS D304.

Wilhelmsen, Lars (2012), 'A question of context. Assessing the impact of a separate innovation survey and of response rate on the measurement of innovation activity in Norway', Documents 2012/51, Statistics Norway.

8 Innovation surveys: experience from Japan
Tomohiro Ijichi[1]

1. INTRODUCTION

This chapter describes the Japanese experience of innovation surveys. Innovation is recognized as essential for sustainable growth and economic development. Innovation policy requires evidence to support it. The measurement and analysis of innovation activities and the innovation system provide the fundamental evidence required.

Economic activities are globalized. In these circumstances, innovation policy needs to take this into account when dealing with the national innovation system. This can be done by undertaking internationally harmonized measurement of innovation. Japan, as an OECD member country, has contributed to this harmonization. Also, it has adapted it to the Japanese environment in order to exploit rich and useful information from the results. Some of what makes Japan different is now described.

First, Japan is a non-EU country. Innovation surveys have been conducted as repetitions of the Community Innovation Survey (CIS) in European countries. In other non-EU OECD countries, including Japan, Korea and China, innovation surveys have been conducted that are comparable with the CIS. In the case of the European Economic Area (EEA) countries, each country has to transmit the determined statistics to Eurostat according to an EU decision[2] and regulation.[3] These provide the justification for each country to conduct an innovation survey and to provide the results to Eurostat, the statistical office of the EU. However, Japan has no framework for regulating an innovation survey. For this reason, enormous effort is needed to reach understanding on the necessity of conducting an innovation survey with wider stakeholders as well as with direct users and to receive official approval to do so.

Second, Japan has a different cultural and social background from other countries, especially European countries. For example, Japanese is quite different from languages used in Europe and America and is expressed by different types of characters. Concepts represented held by the Japanese may differ considerably from those used in the European and American countries. Hence, in statistical surveys, the understanding of respondents may deviate from that of those in other countries if the questionnaire is not translated carefully. In particular, innovation is a topic that has been unfamiliar and has come to be known only recently. This different background may influence the design and implementation of statistical surveys.

Third, in Japan, the innovation survey has been conducted as an official statistical survey by an institute that was originally established to conduct policy research. This is also the case for some other countries, such as Germany (Chapter 6) and Korea. National statistical offices retain statistical competences, in general. On the other hand, when policy research institutes conduct statistical surveys, they are able to design a questionnaire that directly reflects policy relevance and takes account of the analytical perspective. The Japanese experience, to be described further below, may provide suggestions for the linkages between the statistical implementation function and the research function.

This chapter describes the Japanese experience in conducting innovation surveys by demonstrating similarities and differences between Japan and other countries, especially EU member states. It also tries to address challenges in order to contribute to developing a framework for making the measurement of innovation more effective and more useful for the production of internationally comparable indicators and data. Then it describes the framework and background for conducting innovation surveys in Japan. It deals with how innovation is recognized, what has been the policy background, and what are the characteristics of the statistical system. After that, it shows the outlines of innovation surveys, including questionnaires and methodologies. Also, it presents how data and indicators from the Japanese innovation surveys have been used and have made an impact. Finally it shows what has been learned in Japan and provides some suggestions for ensuring internationally comparable statistics.

2. FRAMEWORK AND BACKGROUND FOR CONDUCTING INNOVATION SURVEYS

Understanding of 'Innovation' in Japan

In terms of language, understanding of 'innovation' in Japan has been slightly different from that in other countries using alphabets because Japanese uses two types of characters, ideograms and phonograms. Formerly, words borrowed from foreign languages were translated into ideograms using Chinese characters. At present, however, more and more words are borrowed from English, such as computer and Internet, and these have been expressed in phonograms due to the difficulties in finding suitable and common ideograms. Innovation is now expressed as *inobeshon* in phonograms in Japanese.

In academia, the concept of innovation, that is new combinations of existing constituents, was introduced early on. The English translation of Schumpeter (1911), written in Germany, was published in 1934. The Japanese version, translated by the scholars who studied under him, was also published in 1937.

In policy, the innovation was first mentioned in the *Annual Report on the Japanese Economy* in FY1956 (EPA 1956). In this document, the word *inobeshon* was first used in a policy document and was accompanied by the Japanese equivalent in an ideogram, *gijutsu-kakushin*, which meant 'technologically radical change' in a literal translation. After that initial introduction, the word 'innovation' was not used for a long time in Japanese business and society, and innovations were recognized as technologically radical changes, which are limited in comparison with what innovation should mean.

Development of Innovation Policy and Needs for the Measurement of Innovation Activities to ensure Policy Making

The current assessment is that the promotion of innovation has not been well treated as a prioritized policy issue by the Japanese government. Innovation policy is now treated as an extension of science and technology policy. While the importance of innovation has been recognized in small and medium enterprise policies since the 1980s, the word 'innovation' has not been used. In the current policy framework, stipulated by the Science and Technology Basic Act, the government decides the Science and Technology Basic Plan (STBP), which is a five-year policy guideline for the promotion of science and technology with a decadal perspective. The third STBP for FY2006–FY2010 was the first to use the word 'innovation', but it had not developed innovation policies. In the Abe Administration of 2006–07, the first Minister of State for Innovation was appointed. Then the long-term strategic guidelines, 'Innovation 25', was adopted by the Cabinet. But it was hardly referred to or developed after that because it merely collected existing recommendations. In addition, the prime minister changed, and that removed a driver of the issue. In 2008, the so-called Act for Enhancing Research and Development Competences was enacted. It was the first to use the word *inobeshon* in the text of Japanese laws. Also, it states that the creation of innovation, as well as the increased level of science and technology, shall be the purposes of enhancing R&D capacities as a nation. The fourth STBP for FY2011–FY2015 adopted by the Cabinet in August 2011 stated that the innovation policy shall be included in the scope of the policy framework, and promoted and integrated with science and technology policy.

However, in the fourth STBP, the necessity of a fundamental statistical survey with a view to underpinning innovation policy was not present. Also, the results of innovation surveys have not, as yet, been utilized as evidence for policy making.

The Innovation Survey in the Statistical System of Japan

The framework of official statistics in Japan is regulated by the Statistics Act, which was enacted in 2007 and replaced the previous Statistics Act of 1947 and the Statistical Reporting Co-ordination Act of 1952.

The Japanese statistical framework is characterized by a mixture of centralized and decentralized systems. Some official statistical surveys have been conducted by many mission-oriented administrative offices, including ministries; other official statistical surveys related to the nation, people's lives and business activities in general, such as the Population Census, the Labour Force Survey and the Economic Census for Business Activity, are conducted by the Statistics Bureau of the Ministry of Internal Affairs and Communications, the national central statistics office.

All the official statistical surveys are required to receive approval by the Minister for Internal Affairs and Communications, who is responsible for official statistics, and the Directorate General for Policy Planning (Statistical Standards) was established within the Ministry of Internal Affairs and Communications (MIC) to review statistical surveys and to establish statistical standards. Also, in the current statistical system, the Statistics Commission is established within the Cabinet Office to deliberate on the basic plans of developing national official statistics, the guidelines for building the system of national accounts, and core statistical surveys.

Under this administrative and statistical system, the National Institute of Science and Technology Policy (NISTEP) is deemed to be the most appropriate institute for conducting innovation surveys. NISTEP is a research institute on science and technology policy within the Ministry of Education, Culture, Sports, Science and Technology (MEXT).

In Japan, innovation policy is implemented as an extension of science and technology policy. In the administrative system, each ministry is required to coordinate with the others, including the Cabinet Office, to discharge the administrative function as a whole in the government in order to execute its own duties. The mandate of MEXT, stipulated in the Act of Establishing the MEXT, includes the planning, formation and promotion of basic policies related to science and technology and the assessment of impacts of R&D on economy, society and people's lives. The Council for Science and Technology Policy (CSTP) of the Cabinet Office is the highest coordination and advisory body on science and technology policy in the government. It is chaired by the prime minister, and is composed of six ministers and eight learned members. It has the role of reviewing and deliberating upon basic policies and guidelines for allocation of resources, including budget and human resources, that are necessary for promoting science and technology as well as giving opinions on basic policies and critical issues. CSTP has the responsibility for design, planning and general coordination of policies, but has a limited implementation function. For this reason, statistical surveys that may contribute to the duties of the CSTP have to be conducted by other administrative institutes.

Official statistical surveys can be classified into the following two types:[4] 'core statistical surveys' and 'general statistical surveys'. 'Core statistical surveys' include the Population Census, the Economic Census for Business Activity and other statistical surveys that were introduced much earlier, just after 1945. 'Core statistical surveys' can be mandatory surveys. On the other hand, many recently established surveys have remained as 'general statistical surveys' and must be voluntary surveys. Under these conditions, the innovation survey, which started recently, has been treated as a 'general statistical survey' and it is impossible to impose a mandatory response.

Also, while the 'Basic Plan of Developing National Official Statistics' was adopted by the Cabinet in 2009 on the basis of the deliberation by the Statistics Commission, it mentioned neither R&D nor innovation. Then, at the stage where science, technology and innovation policies were envisaged to be developed in the framework of the fourth STBP, the Statistics Commission showed an interest in innovation statistics, and held a meeting with statistical users. In Japan, the discussion on the measurement of innovation at the governmental level has just started. This contrasts with the EU, where the implementation of innovation statistics has been reported to the European Parliament and the Council of the European Union,[5] and the development of innovation indicators at different levels has been undertaken,[6] and with the USA, where the measurement of innovation has been discussed by the National Research Council[7] and the Department of Commerce.[8]

Secondary use of statistical data has to be balanced between the effective exploitation of statistical data and the protected confidentiality of respondents. Under the previous Statistics Act, secondary use of statistical data was prevented in principle. Mandatory surveys could be used for secondary purposes, but only if the secondary purposes were specified and especially approved. Voluntary surveys could be used for secondary purposes but only if the data were anonymized. Under the current Statistics Act, secondary use can take place, which makes it possible to compile other statistics and to conduct statistical research in general. However, the secondary use of filled-in questionnaires is still strictly limited.

The secondary use of data from the innovation surveys has been permitted under certain conditions and through the prescribed procedures. Yet the proposed secondary purposes are sometimes not compatible with confidentiality. Also, the secondary use has often had negative effects due to the incomplete understanding of the survey itself and the inappropriate interpretation of analytical results.

NISTEP as a Statistical Office

NISTEP is one of the survey implementation institutes as it conducts the innovation survey as an official statistical survey. In general, the design of statistical surveys requires making proactive responses to policy issues and assuming that analytical research will make use of the results. Also, the design and implementation of the survey requires the knowledge, competence and skills of statistical surveying. As a policy research institute, it must anticipate policy makers' inquiries and capture probable policy needs and issues. NISTEP is located close to the offices of policy makers in MEXT and CSTP. But, as the policy makers tend to tackle short-term issues, the fundamental research institute is a suitable place for designing surveys with mid- or long-term perspectives.

The innovation survey was the first official statistical survey for NISTEP.[9] As a result, the competences needed to produce official statistics had to be acquired.

3.   OUTLINES OF INNOVATION SURVEYS

This section describes the Japanese National Innovation Survey 2003 (J-NIS 2003), which was conducted by NISTEP as the first round of official statistical surveying in Japan as well as the CMU-NISTEP survey that had been conducted by NISTEP before the J-NIS 2003.

CMU-NISTEP Survey

Motivation
Levin et al. (1987) did an empirical study on innovation activities in firms using a questionnaire survey called the 'Yale Survey' because

of the researchers' affiliation. It had a considerable impact on the innovation studies that followed. Among them, one survey was conducted as an internationally comparative study based on the Yale Survey, and was called afterwards the 'Yale II Survey' or the 'CMU-NISTEP Survey'. The Japanese side of the survey was conducted by NISTEP. The US side was conducted by Carnegie Mellon University. The motivation of the survey was to clarify the mechanism of innovation, especially in terms of technological opportunity and appropriability. Although attempts had been made to cooperate with the EU, the survey was eventually conducted as a joint survey between Japan and the USA. Later, the EU conducted the second Community Innovation Survey (CIS 2).

Questionnaire
The questionnaire of the 'CMU-NISTEP Survey' was well coordinated and designed in advance by the researchers in both countries. As for the survey, it is important to deal with the effects due to the differences in language in order to have internationally comparable results. As a first step the English version was designed. Then the Japanese version was prepared based on the English version. In addition, the Japanese version was translated into English by a third party, and both versions were compared in order to ensure that they were identical.

Survey methodology
The population of the Japanese side of the CMU-NISTEP survey was 1219 R&D-performing large-sized firms with ¥1 billion or more of paid-in capital in manufacturing, which had been identified by the Science and Technology Agency (STA), one of the predecessors of MEXT. All of them were selected as the sample for the survey. The survey questionnaire was sent by post on September 1994. Of the firms surveyed, 643 firms responded, giving a response rate of 52.7 per cent. This relatively high rate was helped by sending out a reminder.

Key results
From this survey, Cohen et al. (2002) clarified the similarities and differences in knowledge flows and spillovers in terms of technological opportunity and the role of patents in terms of appropriability. Before this, Goto and Nagata (1997) showed the preliminary survey results in Japanese.

Important experience
Throughout, deliberations were made in the preparation and completion of the survey for both sides to ensure international comparability of the

results. Also, in terms of language, great care was taken in the translation of the questionnaire.

Attention was paid to the correspondence of industrial classifications and to the currency exchange rate between the countries. The survey results in international comparison were represented by using weights by industrial classification in consideration of difference in industrial structure, or distribution of firms among economic activities. In other words, this suggests that simple representation of the results from innovation surveys would include the difference in industrial structure in each country.

Furthermore, the population for the CMU-NISTEP survey differed substantially from that for the CIS and the J-NIS 2003. The sample size was much smaller than that of those innovation surveys.

J-NIS 2003 as the First Official Statistical Survey on Innovation in Japan

Background

When the J-NIS 2003 was initiated, few policy makers had paid attention to innovation policies, but policy researchers and some policy makers had recognized that an understanding was needed of innovation systems and how to make them function better in areas such as industry–academia linkages.

In the latter half of the 1990s, researchers in NISTEP had observed that, in the EU, innovation policies attracted more and more interest and resulted in the exploitation of the data from the CIS. As policy analysts, they acknowledged the importance for Japan of expanding policy interests to include innovation policy, going beyond science and technology policy. They also anticipated that national data of selected indicators from innovation surveys, based on the *Oslo Manual*, would be collected by international organizations, such as the OECD, and shared internationally in future in the same way that data from R&D surveys, based on the *Frascati Manual* (OECD 2002), had been compiled. As some time had passed since the CMU-NISTEP survey, there was an expectation that there would be another innovation survey in Japan.

At that moment, the OECD (Muzart 1999) examined international comparability on the basis of the survey results from the CIS 1 and the CIS 2. Considering the findings, OECD and Eurostat jointly developed the core questionnaire and the recommended survey methodology for the CIS 3, while starting discussions towards revision of the *Oslo Manual*. The researchers in NISTEP understood the issues of innovation surveys through these activities, and started to consider both the survey questions and the survey methodology that could be implemented in Japan. In parallel, thanks to discussions with the experts in the OECD Secretariat, Eurostat, and institutes conducting CIS and those publishing statistical reports, they learned from their experience.

In addition, in 2001, under the second STBP (FY2001–FY2005) that aimed at reforms of the science and technology system, it became possible to ensure the resources for conducting a new round of innovation surveys that would contribute to a better understanding and improvement of the innovation system, including industry–academia linkages.

In Japan, when institutes conduct official statistical surveys, they have to receive the approval from MIC. After starting this survey project, NISTEP enhanced coordination within the institute, including the involvement of the researchers in charge of the Japanese side of the CMU-NISTEP survey, in order to receive approval smoothly and to implement the survey appropriately. In the process of receiving approval, the draft questionnaire and the draft survey methodology were scrutinized by the Directorate General for Policy Planning (Statistical Standards), which further requested the Japan Business Federation to have them examined by its member companies.

Questionnaire
As for the questionnaire of the J-NIS 2003, it was decided to utilize the core questionnaire and the recommended survey methodology for the CIS 3. This provided a basis for non-EU countries to develop international comparability.

The questionnaire was prepared not only in Japanese but also in English. The English version followed the text used in the core questionnaire for the CIS 3 as closely as possible.

At the time, most of the firms in Japan were not familiar with the term and concept of 'innovation'. The researchers in NISTEP distinguished between 'innovation' and '*gijutsu-kakushin*', or technologically radical changes. For this reason, NISTEP was urged to prepare the English version as well as the Japanese version when MIC approved implementation of the J-NIS 2003. The condition was based on the comments from some firms that participated in the pre-test of the questionnaire requested by the Directorate General for Policy Planning (Statistical Standards).

Also, to ensure consistency between the versions, the draft Japanese version questionnaire was translated into English by an independent expert translator, and the translated document was compared with the English version.

In addition, some specific questions were added to collect useful information for Japan, and some questions were modified to fit in the Japanese setting, while not jeopardizing international comparability.

First, questions on non-technological innovation that had already been included in the core questionnaire of the CIS 3, such as organizational changes, strategy, marketing and aesthetic changes, were subdivided so as to present the changes in more detail. It had been discussed in NESTI that non-technological innovation as well as technological innovation should be observed. Freeman (1987), who produced the first publication which referred to the national innovation system (Edquist 2005), mentioned that the Japanese innovation system in the 1980s was characterized by organizational and marketing innovation. Accordingly, it was interesting to see whether these characteristics would be still observed at the beginning of the 2000s.

Second, some questions related to the appropriability in the CMU-NISTEP survey were added to the J-NIS 2003 so as to observe the changes between the two surveys. In general, as indicated in data of patent applications and registrations to the main patent offices in the world, many large Japanese firms in manufacturing have emphasized intellectual property as well as R&D activities.

Third, alternatives in some questions related to geographical issues, such as areas of activities, locations of partners of innovation activities and information sources, were subdivided for the Asian economies with which the firms in Japan had close relations in economic and trade activities so as to obtain more detailed information.

Survey methodology
Outlines of the survey methodology for the J-NIS 2003, including the quality, are described in the appendix.

In particular, industrial classifications and enterprise size classes were carefully designed. The results of statistical surveys should be easily connected to other national statistics and be internationally comparable. To satisfy these requirements, the strata were established so as to correspond with both the Standard Industrial Classification of Japan (SICJ) and the International Standard Industrial Classification of All Economic Activities (ISIC) as much as possible by using lower levels of the SICJ. The strata in enterprise size classes were established on the basis of the *Oslo Manual*, in spite of Japanese conventional classifications.

Non-response analysis
As the J-NIS 2003 was a voluntary survey according to the regulations of the Japanese statistical system, the response rate was 21 per cent, which was lower than that in other countries conducting the CIS 3.

The results of the non-response analysis showed that many firms declined to reply to the survey because it was the first round, although they clearly understood which divisions should take charge of the reply. They also implied that more innovating firms and more innovation-active firms might exist among non-responding firms than among responding firms. As 10 per cent of firms declined to participate even in the non-response analysis, the survey results were not adjusted.

Succeeding Surveys

The Japanese National Innovation Survey 2009 (J-NIS 2009), the second round of the innovation survey in Japan, was conducted by NISTEP in 2009. The questions of the J-NIS 2009 differed from those of the CIS 2008, although the J-NIS 2009 was intended to follow the *Oslo Manual*.

It was expected that the questions would be better understood and more easily filled in by the firms in Japan. Some alternatives were simplified and integrated. Also, instead of filling in figures, respondents were asked to reply within specified numeric intervals. As a result, the J-NIS 2009 became less comparable with the CIS. Also, questions on the recognition of market structure by firms were added besides the core questions of the CIS 2008.

As mentioned above, the J-NIS 2009 was different from the J-NIS 2003 as well as from the CIS. For this reason, the J-NIS 2009 is subject to restriction in data availability, especially for internationally comparable innovation indicators that are newly developed.

Now, the Japanese National Innovation Survey 2013 (J-NIS 2013), the third round of the innovation survey in Japan, has been launched. The reference period of the J-NIS 2013 is the years 2009 to 2011. In light of the experience of the J-NIS 2009, the J-NIS 2013 is designed to be comparable with the CIS 2010 again as much as possible, given the limited resources.

4.   IMPACTS OF THE SURVEY

The statistical report of the J-NIS 2003 (Ijichi et al. 2004) was published. Also, for data on manufacture of pharmaceuticals that were not tabulated in this report due to a subdivision in a stratum, Ijichi and Odagiri (2006) tabulated the results of the industry and clarified the characteristics in comparison with those of all the economic activities and with manufacturing.

The data from the J-NIS 2003 have been utilized as the Japanese data on innovation activities based on innovation surveys in several OECD reports (OECD 2007, 2008, 2010a). Also, OECD undertook the Innovation Strategy, in which the development of new internationally comparable indicators and analyses was also proposed (OECD 2009, 2010b, 2010c,

2010d). For this work, the national data were utilized. In addition, researchers and businesses were interested in the survey and referred to the data in their works or publications. Some of them contacted NISTEP to make further enquiries.

The experiences of the J-NIS 2003 were utilized in the revision of the *Oslo Manual*, especially for the deliberations on non-technological innovation. They were also shared through seminars (Ijichi 2008).

On the other hand, the survey results were also misused. For example, in the OECD *Economic Survey*, although the data from the J-NIS 2003 were mentioned within the reports (OECD 2006; Jones and Yokoyama 2006), neither the survey nor the statistical report was referred to accurately, with the note that '[t]here is a need for caution in evaluating such surveys because of the low response rate in Japan'. They were concerned about the quality of the J-NIS 2003 only because of the lower response rate, without considering the survey methodology and the result of non-response analysis. The J-NIS 2003 was also partially utilized and mentioned by the Annual Economic and Fiscal Report of FY2005 (Cabinet Office 2005), a yearly macroeconomic report by the Minister of State for Economic and Fiscal Policy, and its related staff discussion paper (Nakano 2005). The data from the J-NIS 2003 were complemented by a small-sample non-official survey that was commissioned to a private research firm by the Cabinet Office.

At this writing, the results of the J-NIS 2003 have not been used well in policy making. This might raise questions, such as whether the J-NIS 2003 was conducted too early and whether policy making requires such evidence in Japan. However, the results of the J-NIS 2003 indicate that the Japanese innovation system can be characterized as large firm dominated, non-technological oriented and less internationally active in comparison with the systems of other countries. The results suggest that innovation policy should focus on innovation-active firms, especially small- and medium-sized innovation-active firms, to promote new-to-the-world product innovation as well as on improving linkages between different actors and framework conditions. Now that, in the light of the fourth STBP, the government intends to promote evidence-based policy making for science, technology and innovation, it is envisaged that innovation statistics will be utilized more appropriately and effectively by policy makers and will also be emphasized in the near future.

5. CONCLUSION

This chapter described how innovation statistics have been developed and what has been learned so far in Japan.

On the user side, there has been insufficient recognition of innovation policies and inappropriate recognition of measurement and statistics for ensuring policy making and analysis. In these circumstances, the producer side needs to anticipate user needs in advance and to implement the necessary surveys. In this regard, Gault (2011; Chapter 1 in this volume) discusses how manuals, surveys and indicators of innovation statistics have been developed and used in terms of the social impact.

The development of innovation statistics has been linked, stimulated and supported by the activities of the OECD (Chapter 12), and the various efforts of the EU and of many countries.

The J-NIS can provide information on various characteristics of the Japanese innovation system. For example, the data from the previous surveys show lower ratios of product- and process-innovative firms and of innovation-active firms in Japan rather than in other countries. Also, the information on sample errors, especially for the large-sized firms that were collected by census, became available.[10] Nevertheless, some concerns about the quality of the statistical surveys were raised because those findings were different from the stylized image that Japanese industry was eager to promote.

It is important to anticipate long-term and irreversible trends of policy issues. In general, statistical surveys require a long time to be conducted and to produce results and suggestions, while policy needs for the quantitative information sometimes arise.

What is Needed to Conduct a Statistical Survey Outside the Framework of the EU?

A research institute

In Japan, as a non-EU country, it was necessary for NISTEP to ensure that relevant stakeholders understood the necessity to conduct innovation surveys before the survey was started. On the other hand, in the EEA countries, it is now stipulated by an EU decision and a Commission regulation that the member states shall complete and transmit the innovation statistics to the European Commission (Eurostat). To do so, as a consequence, the member states are obliged to conduct innovation surveys. In addition, the data obtained by the innovation surveys have been continuously utilized as various indicators, and in reports and publications by the European Commission as well as the member states themselves so as to monitor the situation.

As for innovation statistics, the data exploitation and provision through international organizations have contributed to obtaining better understanding of the measurement of innovation from wider stakeholders. The same applies to R&D statistics, which are obtained through R&D surveys conducted by many countries on the basis of the *Frascati Manual* and which result in various kinds of publications both by each country and by international organizations such as the OECD.

Furthermore, in the current Japanese statistical system, it would have been difficult for the central statistical institute to conduct the statistical surveys that require expertise in novel subjects, such as innovation, and to improve in each round. It was necessary that a research institute that was addressing policy needs, and had the research capability, took on the role.

In any case, to allow an international comparison for statistical surveys, it is important for cooperation between countries, through international organizations, to undergo continuous improvement and internationally harmonized implementation, while being satisfied with or reconciling specific requirements in each country.

What has been learned and some implications for further work

The experience gained suggests that the institutes should be well grounded in the four types of competences, knowledge and skills.

First, in terms of statistical interests, as data producers, it is indispensable for the institutes to have specialized knowledge and skills in designing and implementing statistical surveys.

Second, in terms of policy and administrative interests, they must ensure relevance to policy issues and needs in designing statistical surveys. Also, official statistical surveys need to perform various administrative procedures. For this reason, it is desirable for them to cope with those processes appropriately.

Third, in terms of research and knowledge creation interests, the institutes should have the perspective of the data users in order to design more meaningful questions and to better exploit the survey results. It is valuable for them to anticipate future or potential policy issues besides current policy topics.

Also, it is appropriate for them to understand innovation studies in order to better understand innovation systems. For example, as for the economic approach to innovation, it should be taken into account which variables should be utilized and combined, and how those variables would be used for analysis.

In addition, it is important for them to have broad knowledge related to innovation. This includes management and accounting for innovation-active firms. To reduce the respondents' burden, it is desirable that the survey questionnaire be designed to reduce the gap between what should be observed and what has been practised in the firms as much as possible. FAQs should be also prepared to bridge the gap.

Furthermore, it is essential for them to know how the respondents in the firms comprehend innovation and the innovation survey questionnaire. It is crucial for them to accumulate knowledge on many cases of varied innovations.

Finally, in terms of international interests, the institutes should take an active role in international collaboration in order to ensure international comparability. As it might be an inherent characteristic in Japan, where the country is not regulated by any international framework for innovation statistics, unlike the EU member states, it is exhausting to argue the necessity for international collaboration with other organizations, including the statistical regulation office not interested in innovation policies.

In this regard, the existence of the *Oslo Manual* is critical in the process of receiving approval for conducting innovation surveys. In Japan, not only ensuring but also improving international comparability of statistical standards and surveys coincide with the stipulations of the current Statistics Act and the guidelines indicated in the current 'Basic Plan of Developing National Official Statistics'. The *Oslo Manual* is indispensable to gain more shared understanding about the international relevance of innovation statistics within the country. For this purpose, it is beneficial to provide the experience and to contribute to the revision and improvement of the *Oslo Manual*.

The institutes have often been requested to provide information on the current situations of innovation surveys and statistics in other countries as well as on the latest data resulting from innovation statistics. Now that the promotion of innovation is one of the main policies in many countries in the world, it is also desirable for international organizations to provide continuously internationally comparable data and metadata by collecting those from each country.

NOTES

1. The views expressed in this chapter are solely those of the author, and do not necessarily represent the view of any organization.
2. Decision No. 1608/2003/EC of the European Parliament and of the Council of 22 July 2003 concerning the production and development of Community statistics on science and technology, *Official Journal of the European Union*, L 230, pp. 1–3, 16.9.2003.
3. Commission Regulation (EC) No. 1450/2004 of 13 August 2004 implementing Decision No. 1608/2003/EC of the European Parliament and of the Council concerning the production and development of Community statistics on innovation, *Official Journal of the European Union*, L 267, pp. 32–5, 14.8.2004.
4. Under the previous Statistics Act before 2007, the official statistics were composed of 'statistical surveys' and 'collections of statistical reporting' which required approvals by the Minister for Internal Affairs and Communications on the basis of the Statistical Reporting Co-ordination Act.

5. Commission of the European Communities, 'Report from the Commission to the Council and the European Parliament on the implementation of Decision No 1608/2003/EC of the European Parliament and of the Council', Brussels, 14.12.2007, COM(2007) 801 final; European Commission, 'Report from the Commission to the European Parliament and the Council on the implementation of Decision No 1608/2003/EC of the European Parliament and of the Council on science and technology statistics', Brussels, 11.4.2011, COM(2011) 184 final.
6. For example, the High-Level Panel on the Measurement of Innovation in the Directorate General of Research and Innovation published a report recommending key elements for the headline indicator of innovation for the Europe 2020 strategy as well as other thematic reports.
7. The US National Research Council has repeatedly set up panels to conduct studies on the measurement, statistics and indicators of innovation under the sponsorship of the National Science Foundation (NSF). The report *Measuring Research and Development Expenditures in the US Economy* was published in 2005. A panel has been conducting the project 'Developing Science, Technology, and Innovation Indicators for the Future' since 2011, and has published an interim report (National Research Council of the National Academies 2012).
8. The Advisory Committee on Measuring Innovation in the 21st Century Economy established in the US Department of Commerce published the report 'Innovation Measurement: Tracking the State of Innovation in the American Economy' in 2008.
9. The Technology Foresight Surveys used to be conducted as official statistical surveys. They, however, were not typical.
10. For example, the percentage of large-sized product and process innovating enterprises in manufacturing and mining was 56 ± 3% (95% confidence intervals).

REFERENCES

Cabinet Office (2005), *Annual Report on the Japanese Economy and Public Finance: FY2005 (Report from the Minister of State for Economic and Finance Policy) – No Gains Without Reforms V*, Tokyo: Cabinet Office (in Japanese).

Cohen, W.M., A. Goto, A. Nagata, R.R. Nelson and J.P. Walsh (2002), 'R&D spillovers, patents and the incentives to innovate in Japan and the United States', *Research Policy*, **31**, 1349–67.

Economic Planning Agency (EPA) (1956), *Annual Report on the Japanese Economy: FY1956*, Tokyo: Economic Planning Agency (in Japanese).

Edquist, C. (2005), 'Systems of innovation: perspectives and challenges', in J. Fagerberg, D.C. Mowery and R.R. Nelson (eds), *The Oxford Handbook of Innovation*, Oxford: Oxford University Press, pp. 181–208.

Freeman, C. (1987), *Technological Policy and Economic Performance: Lessons from Japan*, London: Pinter.

Gault, Fred (2011), 'Social impacts of the development of science, technology and innovation indicators', UNU-MERIT Working Paper Series, 2011-008, Maastricht: UNU-MERIT.

Goto, A. and A. Nagata (1997), 'Technological opportunities and appropriating from innovation: comparison of survey results from Japan and the U.S.', NISTEP Report, No. 48, Tokyo: National Institute of Science and Technology Policy (in Japanese).

Ijichi, T. (2008), 'Measuring non-technological innovation: experience from the Japanese Innovation Survey', in Eurostat (2008), *32nd CEIES Seminar: Innovation indicators – More than technology?*, Århus, Denmark, 5–6 February 2007, Luxembourg: Office for Official Publications of the European Communities.

Ijichi, T. and H. Odagiri (2006), 'A comparative study of the Japanese pharmaceutical industry with the national innovation survey data', Discussion Paper No. 43, Tokyo: National Institute of Science and Technology Policy (in Japanese).

Ijichi, T., T. Iwasa, H. Odagiri, H. Keira, T. Koga, A. Goto, Y. Tawara, A. Nagata and Y. Hirano (2004), *Statistics on Innovation in Japan – Report on the Japanese National Innovation Survey 2003 (J-NIS 2003)*, Tokyo: National Institute of Science and Technology Policy (in Japanese).

Jones, R.S. and T. Yokoyama (2006), 'Upgrading Japan's innovation system to sustain economic growth', OECD Economics Department Working Papers No. 527, ECO/WKP(2006)55, Paris: OECD.

Levin, R.C., A.K. Klevorick, R.R. Nelson and S.G. Winter (1987), 'Appropriating the returns from industrial R&D', *Brookings Papers on Economic Activity*, No. 3, Special Issue on Microeconomics, Washington, DC: Brookings Institution, pp. 783–820.

Muzart, G. (1999), 'Description of national innovation surveys carried out, or foreseen, in 1997–99 in OECD non-CIS 2 participants and NESTI observer countries', STI Working Papers, 1999/1, DSTI/DOC(99)1, Paris: OECD.

Nakano, T. (2005), 'An analysis of innovation activities in the Japanese firms: an empirical analysis using micro data', Economic and Financial Analysis Discussion Paper Series, DP/05-3, Tokyo: Office of the Director General for Policy Planning (Economic and Financial Analysis), The Cabinet Office (in Japanese).

National Research Council of the National Academies (2005), *Measuring Research and Development Expenditures in the US Economy*, Panel on Research and Development Statistics at the National Science Foundation, eds Lawrence D. Brown, Thomas J. Plewes and Marisa A. Gertstein, Committee on National Statistics, Division of Behavioral and Social Sciences and Education Washington, DC: National Academies Press.

National Research Council (2012), *Improving Measures of Science, Technology and Innovation: Interim Report*, Panel on Developing Science, Technology and Innovation Indicators for the Future, eds R.E. Litan, A.W. Wyckoff and K.H. Fealing, Committee on National Statistics, Division of Behavioral and Social Sciences and Education, Washington, DC: National Academies Press.

OECD (2002), *Frascati Manual: Proposed Standard Practice for Surveys for Research and Experimental Development*, Paris: OECD.

OECD (2006), *OECD Economic Surveys: Japan*, Paris: OECD.

OECD (2007), OECD *Science, Technology and Industry Scoreboard 2007*, Paris: OECD.

OECD (2008), OECD *Science, Technology and Industry Outlook 2008*, Paris: OECD.

OECD (2009), *Innovation in Firms: A Microeconomic Perspective*, Paris: OECD.

OECD (2010a), *OECD Science, Technology and Industry Outlook 2010*, Paris: OECD.

OECD (2010b), *Ministerial Report on the OECD Innovation Strategy: Innovation to Strengthen Growth and Address Global and Social Challenges – Key Findings*, Paris: OECD.

OECD (2010c), *The OECD Innovation Strategy: Getting a Head Start on Tomorrow*, Paris: OECD.

OECD (2010d), *Measuring Innovation: A New Perspective*, Paris: OECD.

OECD/Eurostat (2005), *Oslo Manual: Guidelines for Collecting and Interpreting Innovation Data*, Paris: OECD.

Schumpeter, J.A. (1911), *Theorie der wirtschaftlichen Entwicklung: eine Untersuchung über Unternehmergewinn, Kapital, Kredit, Zins und den Konjunkturzyklus*, Leipzig: Duncker & Humblot.

APPENDIX: OUTLINE OF THE SURVEY METHODOLOGY FOR THE J-NIS 2003

The survey methodology for the J-NIS 2003 basically followed that for the CIS 3.

The target population was all the enterprises in the economic activities in the SICJ Rev. 10 that corresponded to agriculture, hunting and forestry (ISIC Rev. 3, Section A), fishing (B), mining and quarrying (C), manufacturing (D), electricity, gas, heat supply and water (E), wholesale trade and commission trade, except of motor vehicles and motorcycles (Division 51 in G), transport, storage and communications (I), financial intermediation (J), computer and related activities (72), research and development (73), and architectural, engineering and other technical activities (Group 742). Sections A and B were also covered beyond the frame for the CIS 3 because those industries were covered by the R&D survey in Japan. The frame population was all the enterprises with ten or more 'persons engaged' in those industries. In the Japanese statistical framework, 'persons engaged' means all people who belong to and work for the enterprise, including permanent employees and paid executives. The observation period was between 1 January 1999 and 31 December 2001. The reference year was 2001.

The survey participation was voluntary. The survey type was a combination of census and sampling where large-sized firms, that is, enterprises with 250 or more persons engaged, were covered by census.

The variables used for the stratification of the sample were both the economic activity of the enterprise (64 classes) and the number of persons engaged in the enterprise (three classes: 10–49, 50–249 and 250+). A stratified random sampling was applied for the sampled enterprises. The results of the Establishment and Enterprise Census 2001 were used as sampling frame. The size of the frame population was 216 585. The sample size was 43 174 (i.e. the sample rate was 20 per cent). The number of realized samples was 9257 (i.e. the unweighted response rate was 21 per cent). Weighting factors were calculated as the inverse of the sampling fraction.

The survey was conducted from January to March 2003. The questionnaire was sent by post, and the filled-in questionnaire was collected by post. The electronic questionnaire (PDF file) was sent upon request. The Japanese version questionnaire was mainly used, and the English version questionnaire was used upon request. Reminders were sent twice by post. Reminder calls were also made to the enterprises in the strata where the response rates would be lower without any further contact.

Quality checks were applied. Concerning measurement errors, some firms reported the data inconsistently, especially for numeric variables, which were edited manually as much as possible on the basis of reliable variables.

All the realized samples reported key variables for identifying innovating firms and innovation-active firms. When firms omitted to respond for those variables, they were contacted by telephone to complete.

Coverage errors were not observed.

A non-response survey was conducted for 339 firms. Only 294 responded and imputation was not used. Due to the low rate of response, the results were not used to adjust the survey weights.

The statistical report was published in December 2004.

In terms of coherence with R&D and business statistics, the data of the J-NIS 2003 were compared with those of the R&D survey of 2002 and the Basic Survey of Japanese Business Structure and Activities of 2002. For example, the reporting on R&D performing and patent holding was more or less consistent. The exercise also suggested that non-response and inconsistent reporting between different surveys should be further reduced for better microdata analysis and additional statistics by combining them, although there were still challenges regarding differences in frame population and sampling method.

PART IV

DEVELOPING AND USING INDICATORS

9   The OECD measurement agenda for innovation

Fernando Galindo-Rueda[1]

1.   INTRODUCTION

This chapter seeks to explain how the Organisation for Economic Co-operation and Development (OECD) develops indicators to help member countries and other economies build an environment conducive to translating science, technology and knowledge into innovation to enhance economic performance and improve social welfare. It highlights some illustrative examples from recent OECD experience in implementing its innovation measurement agenda and reviewing the innovation measurement framework, from which it draws some implications for the development and revision of measurement guidelines and the future of indicator development at the OECD.

The mission of the OECD[2] is to promote policies that will improve the economic and social well-being of people around the world. In support of this mission, indicators play a key role in presenting an accurate and comparable picture of the state of play of innovation and innovation policies across countries.[3] Measurement matters as the 'first essential step in the direction of learning any subject', as famously noted by Lord Kelvin (1883), who went on to add that 'when you can measure what you are speaking about, and express it in numbers, you know something about it; but when you cannot measure it, when you cannot express it in numbers, your knowledge is of a meagre and unsatisfactory kind.' This argument in support of the relevance of measurement has a clear resonance for those who work on a regular basis with policy makers in the domain of science, technology and innovation (STI). STI indicators are, to a large extent, the most tangible and user-friendly statistical output for policy makers in this area. Indicators provide a 'ready-to-use' source of performance benchmarking information which can be used to confirm or refute widely held views about the reality of specific aspects of the innovation system, assess changes over time and drive the policy debate. Indicators are at their most useful when they help set out a core set of relevant facts that policy makers and the public can agree and build upon towards a more sophisticated debate.

In order to present the OECD work on STI indicators in context, Section 2 discusses the entire chain of indicator production and use that spans the process of standards development through to the use of indicators in policy publications and analytical outputs, paying particular attention to recent publications focused on communicating an enhanced portfolio of key innovation indicators. Section 3 follows by providing a summary description of the emerging findings of OECD work to review the measurement framework for innovation. Section 4 concludes.

2. THE PRODUCTION AND USE OF STI STATISTICS AT THE OECD

The design, production, publication and use of STI indicators at the OECD are part of a broader effort to produce policy-relevant evidence which is clearly defined by the objective of achieving international comparability. This is an effort that spans different OECD committees,[4] their subsidiary bodies with their membership of designated national experts,[5] and the OECD secretariat, which supports the day-to-day implementation of the committees' work agenda. While responsibility within the OECD for leading the statistical and quantitative analysis work on STI work sits primarily within the Economic Analysis and Statistics (EAS) division[6] at the Directorate for Science, Technology and Industry, the 'whole-of-government' nature of innovation policy predicated by the OECD Innovation Strategy (see OECD 2010a; Chapter 12 in this volume) clearly signals the importance of indicators developed within other OECD divisions and directorates.

Figure 9.1 provides a summary flow representation of the broad range of STI measurement and analytical activities carried out by the OECD and their interdependence, illustrating links with data providers and users.

Standards and Guidelines

The challenging objective of achieving a sufficient degree of international comparability underpins the STI measurement standard-setting activity in the OECD. This entails the review and update of existing guidelines as well as the examination of new areas sufficiently mature for harmonization and codification. OECD standards guide primary data collection activities in OECD members and observer economies across a number of STI domains, most notably statistics on the resources devoted to R&D as set out in the *Frascati Manual* (OECD 2002) and business innovation – the *Oslo Manual* (OECD/Eurostat 2005). The *Frascati* 'family' of manuals also comprises guidelines on patent statistics (OECD 2009a), technol-

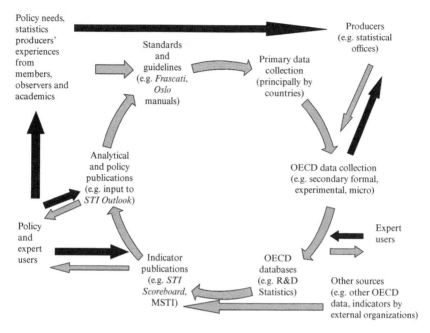

Note: Grey arrows signal flows of data, reports and information; black arrows depict feedback flows.

Source: OECD.

Figure 9.1   OECD activities relating to STI measurement

ogy balance of payments (OECD 1990), human resources for science and technology (HRST) – the *Canberra Manual* (OECD/Eurostat 1995) – and biotechnology statistics (OECD 2009b, 2012a). Other relevant methodological frameworks for STI measurement, indicators and interpretation outside the *Frascati* 'family' include the *OECD Guide to Measuring the Information Society* (OECD 2011a) and the *OECD Handbook for Internationally Comparative Education Statistics* (OECD 2004a).[7]

The existence, scope and content of OECD manuals and guidelines on STI measurement relate to the nature of user needs, the feasibility of implementing recommendations and the specific added value of OECD engagement. The last largely rests in its institutional ability to effectively interact with experts and official organizations with responsibility for data collection and reporting at the national level, promoting the adoption of best practices that render indicators and analyses both relevant and internationally comparable. For example, the OECD promotes the harmonization of methodologies on patent statistics (OECD and

European Patent Office 2008), addressing the complexity of patent data and providing statisticians and analysts with guidelines for constructing and analysing patent-related indicators, building on its partnership with the European Patent Office (EPO), which gathers standardized data from patent offices worldwide through the Worldwide Patent Statistics Database (PATSTAT). The *Frascati* and *Oslo* manuals build on the experience of pioneering research and statistical institutes in developing principally survey-based statistical tools to gather information about R&D and innovation activities on a consistent and comparable basis. The direct involvement, and in many cases, leadership of national STI statisticians – that is, those in charge of producing, collecting and interpreting statistics at the national level – in the design and construction of statistics and methodological manuals sets the OECD apart from related organizations, research institutes and think tanks. This approach enables the organization to rapidly gauge which approaches are most likely to be feasible and help secure buy-in for their implementation once approved in its consensus-based environment.

Data Collection

As in many other statistical domains, the collection of primary data on STI is not directly carried out by the OECD itself but by national agencies with direct access to major statistical infrastructure and resources, which decide for themselves on the best approach for implementing OECD guidelines.[8] The OECD collects secondary data from statistics producers within participating countries, encompassing regular data collections such as the one carried out jointly with Eurostat on R&D resources, and experimental data collections the objective of which is to provide a more tentative picture on an issue of interest in order to identify the feasibility of carrying out meaningful international comparisons, support analytical and policy projects, and potentially incorporate the findings into the existing body of measurement guidelines.

Databases

When the STI data collected by the OECD meet quality and relevance requirements, these are processed and released in the form of databases mainly for use by experts outside the OECD. This is the case of the R&D Statistics database,[9] which can be downloaded from the main OECD statistics portal, and the accompanying 'Sources and Methods' metadata tool, which provides detailed information on how R&D statistics are collected on a country and topic basis.[10] Due to their size, detailed OECD patent databases are intended for research and analytical work only and can be downloaded from a secure – password-protected – server.[11] At present, there is no standard OECD database that covers *Oslo Manual*-based innovation statistics. This decision reflects difficulties experienced to date in comparing results based on different survey methodologies, particularly between countries that follow the Eurostat CIS model questionnaire[12] and other non-EU countries that implement the same concepts and definitions in different ways, as will be discussed in the next section.

Indicator Publications

Indicators are probably the most easily recognizable STI measurement outputs of the OECD. In designing, selecting and publishing a given set of indicators, the OECD goes beyond the mere role of data aggregator and provider, serving users with a portfolio of key issue-oriented evidence on the state of innovation across countries. Indicators are identified on the basis of their policy relevance, analytical soundness, statistical quality and reliability for international and time-series comparisons. By publishing any given STI indicator, the OECD endorses its quality, robustness and international comparability. STI indicators feature within a diverse range of publications.

The *OECD Main Science and Technology Indicators* (MSTI) is published biannually, providing the core set of STI indicators based on the latest available OECD data on R&D expenditures and personnel, patents, technology balance of payments and international trade in R&D-intensive industries.

The OECD also releases compendia on specific topics on an *ad hoc* basis, as for example in the case of the *Patent Statistics Manual* (OECD 2009a), the *OECD Biotechnology Indicators* (OECD 2009b) and the *Science and Technology Statistical Compendium 2004* (OECD 2004b), which was prepared for the January 2004 meeting of the Committee for Scientific and Technological Policy (CSTP) at ministerial level.

Measuring innovation: a new perspective
The 2010 OECD monograph dedicated to *Measuring Innovation* (OECD 2010b) was produced as part of the OECD Innovation Strategy (OECD 2010a), closely mirroring its broad, horizontal focus. *Measuring Innovation* (OECD 2010b) presented new measures and new ways of looking at traditional indicators. Building on the OECD's half-century of indicator development, it sought to reflect adequately and as comprehensively as possible the diversity of innovation actors and processes and the linkages among them. *Measuring Innovation* (OECD 2010b) moved forward the OECD Blue Sky measurement agenda (OECD 2007) – described in a

section below – on STI indicators and drew on measures of education, entrepreneurship, economic, environmental and social outcomes, and the framework conditions that support or inhibit innovation.

Measuring Innovation set out a number of 'positioning indicators' for which there is broad international coverage over time and which helps countries to compare themselves to other countries and monitor their progress towards a desired national or supranational policy goal. It also attempted to illustrate the link between the positioning indicator and a policy measure, proxying a policy mix or instrument that can be used to progress towards an outcome or target; for example, if a country sets a target in terms of business R&D intensity (R&D/GDP), a policy mix indicator can provide a picture of the extent of direct or indirect public support to business R&D. Some of these indicators were more experimental in nature, had less country coverage or were even first-time indicators. Some have already or might eventually become part of the regularly produced OECD indicators repertoire.

The Science, Technology and Industry Scoreboard
A varying selection of more established indicators are typically reported in the *Science, Technology and Industry Scoreboard*,[13] an OECD flagship publication that is produced every two years by the EAS division and formally produced under the aegis of the OECD Committee for Industry, Innovation and Entrepreneurship, setting out the latest international evidence on the state of science, technology and industry.[14] The 2011 *Scoreboard* (OECD 2011b) drew in particular on the latest internationally comparable data to explore the challenges faced by member countries of the OECD and other leading economies as the repercussions from the recent financial and economic crises that started in 2007/8 continued to be felt, and data, often available with a lag, began to become available. Over 180 indicators illustrated and analysed trends in science, technology, innovation and industrial performance in OECD and major non-OECD countries (notably Brazil, the Russian Federation, India, Indonesia, the People's Republic of China and South Africa), presenting indicators traditionally used to monitor developments in science, technology, innovation and industry, and complementing them with experimental indicators that provide new insights into areas of policy interest.

As in most OECD publications, the *Scoreboard* contents are driven by the need to allow policy makers and analysts to compare their economies with others of a similar size or with similar structure, and monitor their progress towards desired national or supranational policy goals. It therefore avoids the explicit 'ranking' of countries on a single dimension and the synthesis of its indicators into a single composite indicator. The main audience of the OECD *Scoreboard* is the policy analyst with a good level of understanding of the use of indicators and all those engaged in producing indicators for policy making. A few paragraphs introduce each of the indicators and offer interpretations, accompanied by a 'Definitions' box for those less familiar with the methods used. A 'Measurability' box summarizes measurement challenges, gaps and recent initiatives, hinting at the direction of the OECD measurement agenda. To facilitate access and practical usage, all charts and underlying data can be downloaded using *Statlinks*, that is, hyperlinks to a web page.

A number of examples in the 2011 *Scoreboard* illustrate the direction of the OECD measurement agenda on indicators. For example, experimental patent quality indicators developed under the aegis of the Working Party of Industry Analysis were first presented in 2011 aiming to capture the technological and the economic value of inventions. The indicators, based on patent citations, claims, patent renewals and patent family size, draw on the findings in the academic literature and present plausible and meaningful measures of research productivity correlated with the social and private value of the patented inventions.

The *Scoreboard* also shows that when comparing countries it is important to take into account differences in their industrial structure (see Figure 9.2). For example, when comparing total business research and

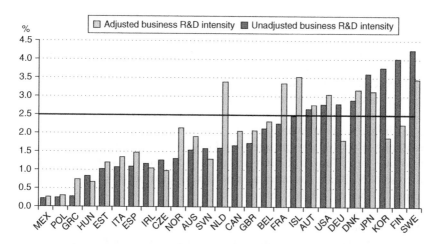

Source: OECD (2011b). Based on the Structural Analysis (STAN) and ANBERD databases, July 2011; OECD, Main Science and Technology Indicators databases, June 2011.

Figure 9.2   Business R&D intensity (% industry value added) adjusted for industrial structure, 2008

development (R&D) intensity (R&D expenditure relative to value added or GDP), while there is significant variation in R&D intensity within sectors, some sector-specific patterns make it very difficult for a country to raise its R&D intensity significantly without fundamentally changing its industrial structure. An understanding of the extent to which structural differences can account for observed differences in overall business R&D intensity can be achieved by constructing an indicator that shows what a country's total R&D intensity would be if it had the same industrial structure as the average for OECD countries. Work is being currently carried out to produce similar indicators focused on broader measures of business innovation.

Indicators produced and used at the OECD are underpinned by data that are principally but not necessarily collected in line with OECD standards and obtained directly through members. The OECD role as a clearing house for the exchange of information and experience on methods of collection, compilation, analysis and presentation of science and technology indicators implies a duty to stay closely engaged in external developments, bringing those to the attention of experts and policy makers from member and observer countries who aim to access an evidence base on STI as comprehensive as possible. The OECD approach towards indicators, based on 'external sources' is that of leading user, with an interest in sharing of best usage practice for informing policy, as is the case with bibliometric indicators.[15]

Beyond Indicators – Analysis and Policy Publications

STI indicators publications by the OECD typically remind users that the appropriateness of a given set of indicators ultimately depends on its use. One pitfall of indicators is the ease with which particular combinations of aggregate indicators may end up misinterpreted as evidence of causal relations. For this reason, the OECD places considerable emphasis on informing users about the limitations of indicators as well as promoting the use of STI data for more advanced analytical purposes and inclusion in policy-focused publications.

Analytical publications
This approach is exemplified in analytical publications such as the *Innovation in Firms* monograph (OECD 2009c), which is the main output of the first phase of the Innovation Microdata Project launched in 2006. The project was designed to examine a range of issues relating to innovation and business performance using a common methodology, making the most of innovation survey data collected by OECD countries and

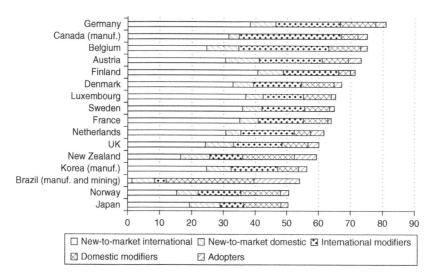

Notes: For New Zealand: 2004–2005; for Japan: 1999–2001; for Brazil: 2003–2005.

Source: OECD (2009c), based on OECD innovation Microdata Project, 2008.

Figure 9.3 Output-based modes of innovation, all firms, 2002–2004

observer economies. The project demonstrated the potential for better understanding the diversity of innovation performance at the micro level, making use of information typically neglected when compiling traditional aggregate indicators.[16] Relatively simple cross-tabulations of indicators, as in the example reproduced in Figure 9.3, which effectively combines information on whether the innovation was new to the international or domestic market and whether the company developed the innovation itself (as opposed to adopting it), give rise to five different modes of innovation.

Furthermore, it enabled the detailed exploration of the link between innovation and productivity and the role of intellectual property rights in a consistent way, for example using a common set of control variables and an econometric behavioural model with which to test hypotheses. This in turn further highlighted the importance of promoting the development of a microdata infrastructure that reduces the burden on statistical offices and respondents, supports data linking and empirical analysis, including policy evaluation.

Indicators within policy publications

Another key outlet for OECD STI indicators is the *OECD Science, Technology and Industry Outlook*, which is produced under the aegis of the

Committee for Science and Technological Policy by the Country Studies and Outlook Division at DSTI in alternate years to the *Scoreboard*. The main focus of the *Outlook* is to inform policy makers responsible for STI policies about recent and possible future changes in the global patterns of science, technology and innovation, and their possible implications for national science and innovation policies. It allows countries to benchmark themselves against each other in the field of innovation and provides comparative analysis of new policies and instruments being used in OECD countries and beyond. A dedicated chapter within the *Outlook* presents, in a series of country profiles, the main features, strengths and weaknesses of national STI systems and major recent changes in national STI policy. In the *OECD Science, Technology and Industry Outlook* (OECD 2012b) 2012 edition, the country profiles have been expanded to cover from 20 to over 300 key indicators in selected STI areas, with particular focus on innovation performance, structural features of the innovation systems and the policy mix. An important novelty in this latest edition is the combined presentation of quantitative indicator data with qualitative information collected through a dedicated policy questionnaire from which government officials from 43 countries have provided information on national STI priorities and recent policy developments in their own countries.

The integration of indicators and policy-related information is also a key feature of a new product currently in development by the OECD. The OECD Innovation Policy Platform[17] is an experimental web-based tool aimed at providing policy makers and 'shapers' (stakeholders, analysts etc.) with a navigable knowledge management system that guides them in identifying the problems that characterize their system of innovation and in designing appropriate policy solutions. Indicators will be part of its base layer information repository also comprising briefs, country profiles and case studies that are intended to inform analyses and associated interpretation processes. A consultation process is under way regarding, among other things, the appropriate contents (e.g. country coverage, types of indicators) and functionalities for indicators to be ultimately provided by the Platform.

Finally, policy briefs and thematically focused policy publications make intensive usage of STI indicators developed at the OECD, as is customary in OECD reports across most subjects. The use of indicators plays not only a vital role in contextualizing the policy discussion,[18] but is also a key driver of development work towards producing actual policy indicators, as exemplified in the brief that contained the OECD testimony to the US Senate Committee on Finance on the international experience with R&D tax incentives.[19]

3. THE MEASUREMENT AGENDA: REVIEWING AND DEVELOPING CONCEPTS, DEFINITIONS AND MEASUREMENT PRACTICES

The 'Blue Sky Indicators Project' and its Follow-up

In the mid-1990s, OECD science ministers requested that the organization launch a 'New S&T Indicators' project. This 'Blue Sky indicators' project set out to think creatively about developing new indicators to meet policy needs, proposing new indicators that would shed light on the broad system of innovation. The first Blue Sky Forum took place in Paris in 1996, followed ten years later by the Blue Sky Forum II held in Ottawa (Canada). In the interim period, the scope of OECD work on STI indicators had significantly broadened in terms of the number of areas covered, resulting for example in new measures of human resources devoted to science and technology (HRST), patent, ICT[20] and biotechnology indicators. Another substantial development over this period was, as described in Chapter 2, the third revision of the *Oslo Manual* (OECD/Eurostat 2005). This revision consolidated the move – already initiated in its second revision – towards enhancing the existing conceptual framework to better capture non-technological forms of innovation and innovation practices in the service sector, codifying new concepts and approaches that had already been tested in several OECD countries with promising results.

Notwithstanding these important developments, changes in the nature of science, technology and innovation have continued to add on new questions and proposals to an already long list of policy questions for which existing indicators could provide only a partial picture. The Blue Sky II appraisal of the supply of innovation indicators was a critical one, highlighting the challenge posed by the fact that the available range of STI indicators was almost entirely limited to inputs, in particular R&D resources, innovative activities and intermediate indicators that measure invention, or the disclosure component of the innovation process, such as patents and bibliometrics (OECD 2007). Blue Sky II thus triggered a significant broadening of the types of measurement approaches used, with a marked increase in microdata, analytical work more directly linked to research on the economic impacts of innovation and their policy implications, with the launch of Innovation Microdata Project in that same year.

The *Measuring Innovation* monograph (OECD 2010b) reflected OECD progress towards meeting some of the objectives highlighted in Blue Sky II – for example on micro-based estimates of innovation, within and outside R&D-performing firms, indicators of science–technology linkages, career and mobility of doctorate holders and policy-related indicators of support for R&D through the tax system.[21] Furthermore, it also highlighted outstanding measurement gaps and proposed international action for advancing the measurement agenda in five broad areas:

- develop innovation indicators that can be linked to aggregate measures of economic performance;
- invest in a high-quality and comprehensive statistical infrastructure to analyse innovation at the firm level;
- promote measures of innovation in the public sector and for public policy evaluation;
- find new and interdisciplinary approaches to capture knowledge creation and flows; and
- promote the measurement of innovation for social goals and of social impacts of innovation.

These key action areas have provided the basis for the OECD proposed forward-looking, longer-term, international measurement agenda for innovation. The roadmap 'tool' used within OECD expert groups such as NESTI has proved to be useful to build a consensus and a 'momentum' around setting and implementing priorities, requiring a continued communication effort with regard to external stakeholders. The strategic priorities expressed by policy committees and the engagement of countries in the development of the roadmap have enabled OECD to prioritize its work among a wide range of possible activities in the framework of the Innovation Strategy Measurement Agenda.

Understanding Why and How Innovation Happens in Firms

'Innovation surveys' were primarily developed to increase knowledge about innovation in firms, with the dual purpose of improving the understanding of the processes and outcomes of innovation and developing effective innovation policies. As part of its review of the measurement framework for innovation, the OECD set up in 2010 a task force to review current business R&D and innovation surveys, and to provide suggestions for future improvements with a view to identifying issues to be addressed in forthcoming revisions of the *Frascati* and *Oslo* manuals. A key component of this work is the review and assessment of the quality and comparability of innovation surveys in order to monitor how the revisions adopted in the 2005 *Oslo Manual* are being implemented. Surveys comprising questions on innovation based on the *Oslo Manual* framework have been carried out in nearly 80 countries over more than 20 years, with the USA and China being among the most recent adopters. There is an important virtuous circle at work in this agenda. Better understanding of why and how inno-vation happens in firms leads to improved measurements, which in turn leads to a better understanding of innovation and its policy implications.

This justifies the strong methodological focus of the work, in which the use of qualitative research methods becomes critical given the complex nature of innovation concepts. Although it is a resource-intensive initiative, the inclusion of open-ended questions in surveys prompting for examples of innovation has proved a useful source of information for STI researchers and statisticians.[22] In this vein, Francoz and Corbel (2005) contributed to the latest review of the *Oslo Manual* review process by making an innovative use of techniques aimed at evaluating the robust-ness of responses to qualitative questions open to subjective interpretation, as is the case of many *Oslo* concepts. The 'vignette' technique presented summary descriptions of a number of hypothetical business change sce-narios so that respondents could indicate whether these conform to a given definition of innovation. The technique, which was applied to the group of NESTI experts as well as companies in a number of participat-ing countries, provided a useful mechanism for identifying differences in perceptions and difficulties in implementing the existing concepts. This evi-dence supported a move away from a purely technological interpretation of product and process innovation towards a framework more focused on identifying the degree of novelty of the innovation. Other elements tested included the respondents' view of organizational and marketing innovations – and their relationship to product and process innovation in the services sector – and the role of R&D, including in the social sci-ences and humanities. The vignette approach has been recently applied by experts at the National Institute of Science and Technology (NISTEP) in Japan (Yonetani 2012), comparing responses from the USA, Germany and Japan. Based on nearly 3000 replies from individuals, the preliminary results indicate a considerable degree of national difference in the appre-ciation of what is meant by innovation, with highest reluctance to define a given vignette as an innovation found for Japan, followed by Germany, relative to the USA. The potential for further use of vignette methods in the measurement of business innovation is high; they will probably play a helpful role in a future revision of the *Oslo Manual* and in promoting inter-national comparability, both as a testing tool and as an instrument within innovation surveys.

A form of cognitive interviewing widely applied in other disciplines and also by the US National Center for Science and Engineering Statistics (NCSES) is now being used by the OECD with a similar objective. Early scoping cognitive interviews have been taking place across a number of participating countries for the first time to shed light on how companies

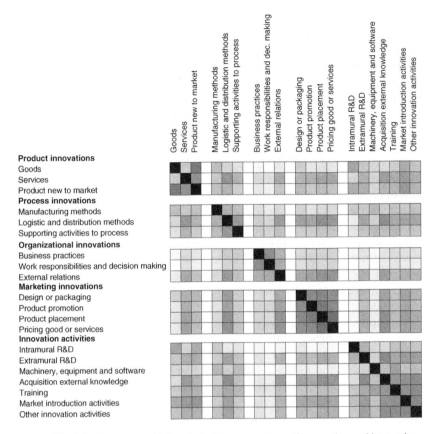

Note: Shaded cells represent higher similarities across types of innovation and innovation activities.

Source: OECD, based on pooled CIS 2008 microdata for 16 EU countries deposited at Eurostat's Safe Data Centre.

Figure 9.4   Similarities in types of innovation and innovation activities across European firms, 2006–2008

with different profiles manage and think about innovation as part of the broad strategy and approach to change, and their ability to relate their own experiences to the framework of the *Oslo Manual*. In addition to helping assess the continued relevance of concepts and definitions, scoping interviews are a key step towards developing model questions for detailed testing in a coordinated fashion in an international context.

Analysis of innovation microdata can help improve our understanding of how firms innovate. Figure 9.4 displays a 'heatmap' of the similarities across the different types of innovation recognized in the *Oslo Manual* third edition and the innovation activities in firms that made their CIS 2008 anonymized microdata available for analysis by the OECD at the Eurostat Safe Data Centre.[23] The heatmap provides a visualization of how similar the different 'modes' are by portraying frequently co-occurring innovations and activities in shaded cells of the interaction matrix. This provides, for example, a fairly simple way to inspect the relevance of including organizational and marketing innovation. Comparing goods and service innovation, for example, it is possible to see that the former is only visibly close to manufacturing methods innovation, R&D and market introduction methods. In contrast, service innovation displays substantial proximity to nearly all variables, with the exceptions of R&D and investment in plant and machinery. In addition to service innovation, both organizational and marketing innovations are very weakly related to R&D. This central positioning of service innovation in the broad innovation mode landscape appears to confirm the importance of the decision to extend the broad definition of innovation in order to better capture the nature of innovation in services. This display also suggests that some generic types of innovation are quite cohesive, as is the case of marketing innovations, while within organizational innovations those oriented towards external relations appear to be more similar to marketing innovations.

As demonstrated by the OECD Innovation Microdata Project (OECD 2009c), microdata analysis allows for a detailed examination of the interdependence of various facets of innovations and business characteristics, providing a means for assessing potential anomalies in the data themselves from which indicators are constructed; understanding whether it is structural conditions that underpin – to any significant extent – observed innovation rates; assessing the external validity of innovation indicators by exploring their association with economic outcomes of interest; and facilitating the construction of indicators based on the association between variables to reflect different 'modes' of innovation. Since the publication of the results of phase one, the OECD work on innovation microdata analysis has continued through the development of typologies of innovation modes or strategies for groups of firms (Frenz and Lambert 2012), measures of sectoral innovation intensity, the innovation and productivity link and the role of product market competition and more recent analytical assessments of the impact of service innovation and innovation in the service sector, in the framework of the EU FP7-funded KNOWINNO-INNOSERV project.[24]

Innovation Indicators and Aggregate Measures of Economic Performance

There is a pressing user need to reflect new patterns of R&D and innovation in existing and new innovation indicators, which can in turn be linked to aggregate measures of economic performance. The challenges identified in the Blue Sky II Forum, such as a globalization and the adoption of open and collaborative innovation strategies and the use of social science research methods in business, particularly within services, are increasingly important phenomena that call for new indicators and revised measurement frameworks.

Such trends also affect the ability of reporting units to provide reliable information from which to construct and interpret existing indicators. For instance, the ongoing adoption of new corporate reporting rules and practices in firms, which also take into account the tax advantages conferred upon certain innovation activities, will shape the type of information companies will be able to report via statistical surveys in future years. Some evidence suggests that a non-trivial number of firms responding to business enterprise expenditure on R&D (BERD) surveys may be facing serious challenges when attempting to identify intra/extramural expenditure, as well as when trying to distinguish R&D expenditure (own funds) from R&D income (e.g. from grants, contracts). Firms may also be facing problems when reporting subcontracted R&D carried out for others, or when accounting for payments as part of collaborative R&D projects.[25] This implies both a challenge and an opportunity for STI statistics, in that the widespread use by firms of internal measures such as R&D expense or R&D eligible for tax incentives might be used as a starting point for surveys upon which to retrieve *Frascati*-like data and indicators. Furthermore, for some types of firms, such data may be used to reduce survey burdens if they can provide a reasonably good statistical approximation to the magnitude of interest.[26]

The recognition of R&D as an asset-creating activity in the 2008 *System of National Accounts* (EC et al. 2009) and its adoption of the OECD *Frascati* definition provide a unique opportunity to make a more explicit link between an important indicator of innovative activity and macro-economic performance. This is relevant not only for STI policy makers in the traditional sense, but also for those in central economic policy roles for whom it is vital to understand the role of intellectual capital in measures of spare capacity or trade imbalances. Subject to 'bridging' adjustments laid out in the OECD *Handbook on Deriving Capital Measures of Intellectual Property Products* (OECD 2010c), *Frascati* R&D data will be the main input into the construction of new investment and capital stock series which can feed into traditional measures of productive potential as well as growth-accounting exercises.

While satellite R&D accounts can be reasonably approximated with existing *Frascati* sources, building measures that fit into the mainstream national accounts will require in the medium term more detailed information than is currently available. National accountants and STI statisticians worldwide are currently debating how *Frascati* sources can be best adapted to meet SNA needs, as the latter focus on the nature of the economic – not necessarily financial – transactions between different parties. National accountants have benefited from the expertise of STI statisticians to implement new questions aimed at drawing a distinction between R&D expenditures on a performance, funding and ownership basis, or aiming to identify the expected useful life of R&D investments.[27] The experience so far has shown that such questions can be asked but some of these concepts should be substantially adapted in order to work in practice, rather than asking directly about them. Traditional R&D-based indicators have also much to gain from this process in which the OECD is playing a leading role. When R&D becomes capitalized it will increase the value of the headline measure of GDP. Since GDP is used to normalize gross domestic expenditures on R&D (GERD), this will lead to apparently lower R&D intensity rates than would otherwise be reported. With some exceptions, the accounting impact on the level of GDP is expected to be for most countries of a similar order of magnitude to the current measure of R&D intensity.[28]

Over the last decade, there has been an explosion of interest in the role of a broader range of intangible assets other than R&D, encompassing investments such as software, training, brands and organizational capital as sources of innovation and growth at the micro and macro levels.[29] Measures of intangible asset investment, also known as knowledge-based capital, have joined the set of instruments used to measure and assess the performance of knowledge-based economies. The neoclassical macroeconomic framework developed by Corrado et al. (2005) has been particularly influential through its focus on capturing the cost of activities that give rise in principle to intangible assets, all within an expanded national-accounts-like capitalization framework.

However, it is important to recall that the capitalization of R&D or other intangibles will not by itself provide estimates of the broad impact of R&D in the way that most policy users tend to think, including spillovers, because in the SNA the attribution of benefits to R&D or any other asset is based on the principle of economic ownership. Spillovers are by construction excluded although they can implicitly show up as unexplained changes in multifactor productivity. Nonetheless, the enhanced availability of indicators on intangibles should facilitate the study of externalities and other market failures in the production and use of knowledge-based capital, complementing existing and new measures of intellectual property rights. The intangibles framework has been welcomed and adopted by many innovation researchers and experimental exercises in constructing internationally comparable indicators.[30]

The analogies between the notion of intangibles and expenditures on innovation activities are considerable.[31]Investment in knowledge refers to the accumulation of knowledge-based assets that are expected to deliver benefits to their owner beyond the current period, while innovation activities are, broadly speaking, knowledge-intensive activities or 'steps which intend to lead to the implementation of innovations', as defined in the *Oslo Manual*, which highlights the potential use of innovation expenditures to calculate returns to innovation activities. In a recent survey of NESTI members, this was identified as the most problematic question for companies responding to innovation surveys. The OECD has provided a forum for discussing experiences from pilot surveys dedicated to measuring expenditures on intangibles by firms. Such an exercise has already been carried out twice in the UK and once in Italy for large R&D performers, while similar questions are intended for inclusion in the 2013 Japanese National Innovation Survey alongside standard innovation questions. The relationship between micro-based measures of intangibles and measures of expenditures on innovation activities is of particular interest given the (untested) potential for the intangible 'accounting'-type measures to provide a basis upon which to elicit a meaningful answer to the *Oslo* concepts. This could in principle help overcome the current lack of systematic alignment between OECD innovation definitions and business accounting practices.

The review of the innovation measurement framework is equally concerned with the use of innovation survey indicators for international benchmarking purposes. The adoption of different types of survey instruments for collecting information on the innovation activities of firms has long been suspected of reducing the scope for international comparisons. The OECD has recently carried out a comprehensive collection of metadata on innovation surveys across members and observer countries, adopting a model based on Eurostat quality reviews for European countries, with the objective of investigating for the first time the impact of survey design methodologies for implementing *Oslo*-based questions.[32] This has helped document differences in the design of innovation surveys, covering elements such as (a) the use of stand-alone innovation surveys versus combination with R&D or more generic business surveys, (b) differences in sector coverage, (c) the extent to which response by business is compulsory and enforceable, and (d) the nature of the unit in charge of implementing the survey and the extent to which it can draw upon the authority of a national statistical office. Preliminary results exploring the correlation between these design and implementation features and survey results appear to indicate that there may be systematic impacts. While this could have an impact on cross-country and time-series benchmarking, work is ongoing to fully assess the implications and draw better recommendations that serve the intended uses of innovation data.

Capturing Knowledge Interactions

In order to implement a measurement agenda linking inputs, outputs and outcomes, it is critical for indicators to be integrated within an analytical system that captures the essential structure of the actual innovation system it seeks to portray. The term 'national innovation system' was coined to represent the interplay of institutions and the interactive processes at work in the creation of knowledge and in its diffusion and application. Introduced by Freeman (1987) and subsequently adopted in OECD work – for example OECD (1997) – the concept stresses that the flow of technology and information among people, enterprises and institutions plays a key role in the innovative process. The study of innovation systems directs attention to the linkages or web of interaction within the overall innovation system (OECD 1997). The production of new knowledge is often a collective process involving a significant number of individuals and organizations and requiring communication and coordination. Knowledge produced in such a complex but structured way may have public-good aspects. Such interactions or 'networks' may be usefully tracked and embedded into the innovation measurement framework.

However, linkages are not obvious objects of statistical measurement. Their potential diversity in numbers, partners and intensity levels does not easily fit within surveys, while administrative sources cover only specific aspects such as citations, co-inventorship or co-authorship, and very rarely financial transactions. As science and innovation activities increasingly rely on dispersed networks of actors, they sometimes tend to cluster in certain places or around certain institutions (e.g. a leading university or a research laboratory of a multinational corporation). To analyse the changing landscape of science, technology and innovation, it is likely that new units of analysis will be required with different geographical scope, as well as novel sources that have yet to demonstrate the necessary statistical robustness.

One area of particular policy interest is the measurement of technology transfer between universities and industries. While some countries and associations carry out specific surveys that apply, for example, to the activities of their technology transfer offices, so far only a few countries, such as Canada, Australia and Israel, have carried out dedicated official surveys and no specific international measurement framework is in place. A key challenge in this area is to go beyond pure measures of commercialization (such as licensing revenue or spin-offs) to measures that provide indicators of the return to public funding provided to those organizations, given the fact that universities carry out a wider range of third-mission activities, from collaborative R&D through to consultancy, infrastructure services and other types of community support.[33]

The OECD has been constructing a broad research agenda for developing a new generation of indicators on knowledge flows. The relationship between the science base and the research system is being addressed by the OECD by taking forward an ambitious data linking agenda matching scientific and patent literature through bibliographic references included in the latter. Initial results point, for example, to the importance of fundamental disciplines in providing the knowledge base for supporting inventions in the green technology domain (OECD 2010b, 2011b). Rapidly developing enabling technologies such as information and communication technologies (ICT), biotechnologies and nanotechnologies draw on interdisciplinary research and tend to be 'general purpose technologies' that can be used across a broad range of industries (see Chapter 15 in this volume). An OECD project has been looking at the feasibility of producing a consistent measurement framework across technologies that might not only facilitate a better integration with existing statistical sources but also help make it possible to compare their impacts. The work has so far highlighted the diversity of efforts to measure technology development and usage, which could be better integrated into the existing measurement framework, and the importance of adopting new statistical methods and interdisciplinary approaches to data collection.

The training of an educated workforce is probably the largest contribution of universities to the innovation system and, in all likelihood, the largest knowledge market is that for skilled labour. Indicators of how graduates and individuals with postgraduate qualifications in different subjects are deployed across the economy, in different sectors and occupations, are in significant demand but the supply is still very limited. The mobility of the highly skilled implies knowledge flows across disciplines, sectors and borders. Survey data, including from recent data collections as part of the project on the Career of Doctorate Holders,[34] have provided some key new insights and the OECD is carrying out further work to ensure a wider country coverage and better analysis of existing data at the micro and macro levels. A more sophisticated and linked use of bibliometric, patent and other administrative data may also help reveal how these multidisciplinary, transnational networks are evolving.

The *Oslo Manual* highlights how the study of linkages can make a valuable contribution to understanding the innovation system and the role of policies. One question that has been successfully tested in the past concerns whether third parties have been involved in developing product or process innovations implemented by the firm, although results appear to indicate that a very low proportion of implementers are only adopters. This may signal some bias in the understanding of the generic innovation question, which may lead to the exclusion of some adopters (see Chapter 5 in this volume). This question is rarely asked of organizational or marketing innovations. A second type of questions concerns the nature of innovation activities. Some, like extramural R&D and the acquisition of existing IPRs, directly identify knowledge inflows. Others are ambiguous, as software can be developed in house or acquired, as is the case of training for innovation, marketing, organizational or general design costs. In practice, most innovation survey users relate the concept of linkages to questions on sources of information for innovation (some of which may be paid for as services and included in the previous category), and types of innovation collaboration, which requires active cooperation with other firms or public research institutions on innovation activities (and may also include purchases of knowledge and technology).

The survey implementation of the *Oslo* concepts on linkages is still to be fully subject to cognitive testing in most countries. There is a clear trade-off between designing a comprehensive taxonomy of knowledge flows and having a set of questions that companies can easily respond to. One particular dimension that is currently missing in most official innovation surveys is the outward dimension of open innovation, that is, the innovation activity of companies whose knowledge 'products' are implemented or adopted by other companies. The OECD has been following recent developments principally led by academics to measure such outward flows.[35]

Understanding the Role of Government and the Economic and Social Impact of Innovation Policies

While universities and firms are covered by conventional indicators, current measures do not fully take account of the roles of individuals (in multiple roles, e.g. as consumers, employees etc.) and government in the innovation process. There are several compelling reasons for developing indicators and definitions for innovation in the public sector and measures of policy efforts to foster innovation. There is a need to account for the use of public funds for innovation, improve learning outcomes and the quality of the provision of education, health or other public services, particularly at a time when most governments worldwide are looking for efficiency savings while maintaining or enhancing current service provision levels.

Public sector innovation

Internationally agreed concepts and comparable indicators for studying innovation in the public sector do not yet exist. In addition to this, through a review of the business innovation measurement framework, the OECD has begun to explore how to extend the scope of the innovation measurement framework to reflect the role played by a broader range of actors, including assessing the feasibility of producing guidelines for the measurement of public sector innovation. Work on this topic, covered in detail in Chapter 17 of this handbook, has highlighted some of the limitations of the framework as currently implemented in the business sector, primarily across industry and a subset of service sectors. For example, the subject-based approach adopted in the *Oslo Manual* might be better suited to units with well-defined performance measures such as firms, for which output and productivity measures can be estimated based on market prices. The challenge of measuring productivity in many services and in the public sector in particular requires a fundamental rethink not just of what is an innovation in this context, but also of what is the purpose of measurement and its potential uses. One further contribution the OECD is expected to make in the near future in this domain is to consolidate the very diverse set of definitions often used interchangeably to describe innovation by economic activities typically associated with public services (i.e. public administration, but also health and education in many countries), innovation carried out by units in the government or the non-profit sector, as opposed to those operating in the market sector (which comprises both private and public enterprises); and innovation understood in a broad sense with public or social goals. This may require a concept of 'policy-driven' innovation that can also respond to social challenges or address social needs. Some innovations that generate income for firms may, of course, reduce environmental impacts and improve social well-being.

Existing classification systems, concepts and definitions from various frameworks can be fruitfully deployed to facilitate discussions on which are the most promising measurement approaches. The increasing number of pilot experiences is expected to provide a wealth of information that could be complemented by the use of methodological approaches such as those described in the context of business sector innovation. The OECD is ready to play a coordination role as initiatives are developed and users begin to demand indicators for a number of possible uses, leveraging on the input of its various policy committees with an interest in this topic.[36]

Measuring the economic and social impacts of science and innovation policy
The effort towards developing indicators of innovation in the public and
private sectors raises the question of how to produce better output and
outcome indicators for innovation to measure its impacts, while, as the
public debate begins to recognize that innovation is more than just R&D, it
becomes apparent that much needs to be done to achieve high-quality and
internationally comparable measures of innovation inputs. While this may
suggest that there is a hard choice to be made between focusing on inputs or
outputs and outcomes as priorities for indicator development, the OECD
experience is that these two objectives are in reality highly complementary,
particularly when a robust infrastructure is in place that supports linking
those measures at the micro, meso and macro levels. The analysis of impacts,
the evaluation literature shows, is not particularly well served by attempts
to design 'impact' indicators as directly drawn from answers to questions.
In a survey context, direct questions on impacts can be interpreted in very
different ways if there is no clear counterfactual. The process of indicator
design applied in *Measuring Innovation* and the *STI Scoreboard* highlights
the scope for using already-available indicators of economic and social outcomes of interest and, from there, working to identify which are the relevant
innovation input and throughput data and indicators worth collecting. The
analysis of impacts requires being able to link hard-to-find measures of
inputs and outputs in a meaningful research design context. In the case of
policy evaluation, a number of approaches can be adopted to ensure that
impacts can be identified using econometric and other statistical methods.[37]

As innovation policies become more widely applied and nuanced, a
new generation of indicators and guidelines for measuring public support
for R&D and innovation is in high demand by policy users. *Measuring
Innovation* included as one of its priority actions the development of
indicators to capture the nature, direction and intensity of public support
for innovation, at national and sub-national levels. This is one of the
areas of the highest policy interest and one in which OECD has provided
quantitative evidence on the balance across different mechanisms used to
support R&D and innovation (OECD 2010b, 2011b). In recent years, the
OECD has successfully introduced regular data collections on the design
and financial cost to governments of providing tax incentives for R&D.
Based on this experience, it may soon be possible to codify these concepts
and definitions so that they can be integrated into the R&D measurement
framework, potentially alongside existing guidelines on measuring government budget appropriations or outlays on R&D (GBAORD) given the
similar administrative/budgetary nature of these data.

In parallel to this work on improving the comparability of data on the cost
of R&D tax incentives, an OECD project has been assessing the feasibility

of producing policy-relevant breakdowns of available GBAORD estimates beyond the traditional socioeconomic objectives, identifying among other things what prioritization mechanisms governments use when allocating funds in support for R&D, for example by entrusting arm's-length institutions and third parties with decisions on which projects to fund, or allocating funds directly through programmes (van Steen 2012). The review and future implementation of *Frascati* guidelines on measuring public funds for R&D to fully encompass R&D tax incentives and identify the contributions of specific policy instruments (such as procurement and subsidies) provide a key opportunity to strengthen the policy user input into the design of STI indicators and guidelines.

A more experimental line of work currently being pursued at the OECD concerns the measurement of public support for innovation in its broader sense. National experts participating in OECD discussions are being increasingly compelled to report how much governments spend on promoting innovation and how these funds are allocated. The difficulties experienced in measuring business expenditure on innovation activities and the fact that most subsidy-based support for innovation occurs through R&D grants appear to have prevented experimentation with approaches to estimating funding breakdowns by sector, as done for R&D. On the funder side, currently available budget-based measures are difficult to compare internationally, although some experimental innovation budget indicators might be feasible for a reduced set of countries with comparable sources. Such difficulties call for a detailed examination of which approaches are most likely to meet key user priorities. For example, the Europe 2020 flagship initiative 'Innovation Union' stipulates that 'from 2011, Member States and regions should set aside dedicated budgets for pre-commercial procurements and public procurements of innovative products and services'. Some countries are in the process of adopting policy targets (e.g. as a proportion of total procurement budgets) that will require an underlying measurement framework in order to be monitored effectively. Given the sheer size of general procurement budgets and their potential impact in driving demand for new goods and services and the link to the issue of public sector innovation, the measurement of public procurement is being subject to research by OECD as part of its innovation measurement agenda.

4.   CONCLUSION

The OECD Blue Sky Forum meeting held in 2006 pointed to the need to address the state of fragmentation of research in innovation, particularly in the domain of data infrastructure and collection activities, highlighting the need for a general framework of analysis and greater coordination of research efforts. The goal to this day continues to be the improved understanding of the entire story of innovation, from inputs to economic and social impacts, embedded into a coherent system framework.

This chapter has shown how the OECD constructs, publishes and uses indicators as part of its complete range of STI statistical and analytical activities. The OECD central role in setting standards for the collection and interpretation of STI statistics enables the use of such indicators for meaningful international comparisons and dissemination of best measurement practices. This, as highlighted in the second part of this chapter, requires a continued and dynamic review of what works and what does not within the existing measurement framework, creating new concepts and definitions, refining existing ones and, in some cases, abandoning approaches that proved impossible to implement, were less effective or became unnecessary. The ongoing review of the innovation measurement framework will shape and inform the next revisions of OECD manuals in the *Frascati* family of measurement guidelines.

As part of this review process, the NESTI Advisory Board held a special workshop in June 2012 in partnership with the US National Academies Panel on the subject of 'Developing Science, Technology and Innovation Indicators for the Future'. The workshop contributed to link the work of the Panel to that of the OECD, the first STI Blue Sky Forum held in 1996 in Paris and its follow-up in 2006 in Ottawa, which looked at new STI indicators, the use of existing indicators for STI purposes, and the better use of existing STI indicators, providing a first step towards building the agenda of the next Blue Sky Forum anticipated for 2016. The main recurring themes in the workshop echoed the priorities set out in the OECD measurement agenda – to improve the comprehensiveness and timeliness of the currently available set of indicators while driving indicator and related econometric research to move forward from innovation inputs and activities to include the outputs and impacts of innovation. Mapping the innovation system, understanding it, and explaining it to policy makers – all themes in the workshop – require a strategic approach that goes beyond the specific notion of indicator design but greatly benefit from it.

A clear lesson from past and recent work is that meeting user needs for STI statistics requires adopting a sufficiently long-term perspective, particularly if the objective is to achieve indicators and analytical results that can be meaningfully compared across countries. Setting realistic expectations for new developments is of paramount importance in the current financial environment, in which the development of new indicators and their underlying sources has to take place within increasingly narrow resource constraints. Several data collection initiatives have been discontinued or reorganized in recent years. In this context, the OECD also attempts to be a vehicle for communicating experiences on how this process of consolidation can be supported by a high-quality and flexible data infrastructure, backed by reliable registers that enable the linking of different sources and administrative records to help reduce both collection and respondent burdens. Access to data by the research community in a privacy and confidentiality-preserving environment is critical so that research questions can be formulated and addressed through data analysis and assist the indicator prioritization process. The OECD is doing its part through the development of its own microdata lab. This resource is intended to support the analytical work required by OECD committees, including supporting the regular flow of indicators based on data linking across scientific publications, patents and other IPRs, and business data, to cite some examples. A key feature of the STI lab at the OECD is its openness to the expertise of external researchers wishing to visit the OECD to collaborate in projects of common interest.

To conclude, the next revision of the *Frascati* family of guidelines is likely to prove a substantial undertaking not only for the OECD but for the broader STI analytical community. There is considerable wealth of experiences accumulated across OECD members, and other economies, particularly in developing countries, from which new recommendations and guidelines will be drawn over the next few years. Following the Blue Sky II objective of achieving a marked improvement in the policy relevance of innovation research, users will be asked to play an active role in this review process. Through this effort and the new and ongoing projects discussed above, the OECD will continue to serve the needs of its national experts as well as its rapidly expanding user community.

NOTES

1. The views expressed here are solely those of the author and do not reflect those of the OECD, its Council or its member countries. The author would like to acknowledge the useful comments provided by OECD colleagues.
2. The OECD is a Paris-based international organization that provides a forum for policy makers from 34 member countries and observer economies to meet in specialized committees to advance ideas and review progress in specific areas pertaining to economic cooperation and development. The Council, which comprises permanent representatives from countries and in which decisions are taken by consensus, sets the mandate and programme of work of the OECD committees, which are supported in their day-to-day work by the OECD Secretariat, led by the Secretary General and structured and organized into thematically focused directorates. See www.oecd.org/about.
3. A recent example of the increasing user interest in the role of indicators for the purpose of policy monitoring is the declaration by the G8 group of countries at the Deauville Summit in May 2011, where G8 members noted: 'we also invite the OECD to develop

in a fully inclusive, open and accountable way in co-operation with relevant international organizations, measurements of innovation performance, focussing on concrete impacts on growth and jobs rather than inputs and investigating the systemic relationship between indicators' (accessed from http://www.g20-g8.com/g8-g20/g8/english/live/news/renewed-commitment-for-freedom-and-democracy.1314.html).

4. The key committees at the OECD with responsibility for science, technology and innovation issues are the Committee on Industry, Innovation and Entrepreneurship, the Committee for Information, Computer and Communications Policy, and the Committee for Science and Technological Policy.

5. The measurement of STI within the OECD has its roots in the formal creation of the Working Party of National Experts on Science and Technology Indicators (NESTI) in 1962, pre-dated by an informal group in 1957 within the OECD's predecessor – the Organisation for European Economic Co-operation – leading to an international agreement on a standard for carrying out surveys on research and experimental development (R&D), the *Frascati Manual* (OECD 1963).

6. EAS supports three statistically and analytically focused OECD working parties, namely the Working Party of Industry Analysis (WPIA), the Working Party on Indicators for the Information Society (WPIIS) and the Working Party of National Experts on Science and Technology Indicators (NESTI). The remit of these working parties concerns, respectively, the analysis of industrial competitiveness as it relates to innovation, indicators for the information society, and generic science, technology and innovation statistics and analysis, reporting to different committees supported by DSTI although often engaging in joint activities.

7. Further relevant frameworks concern the classification of high technology sectors (Hatzichronoglou 1997) and bibliometric indicators (Okubo 1997).

8. Countries thus have a considerable degree of flexibility on what specific data to collect and how to do so. Such an approach stands in contrast, for example, with projects such as the OECD Programme for International Student Assessment (PISA), where a central team directly coordinates primary data collection from schools, their students and staff. Common guidelines, requests for clearly defined data and metadata (as in the case of the joint OECD/Eurostat R&D data collection) are sometimes complemented by the use of model questionnaires to promote a basic degree of uniformity. International comparability may sometimes be reduced in order to allow countries to implement potentially more cost-effective solutions within their own specific context.

9. See www.oecd.org/sti/rds. A related database, linked to the STAN family of industry structural databases, provides information on R&D resources devoted by business at the industry sector level: www.oecd.org/sti/anberd.

10. See http://webnet.oecd.org/rd_gbaord_metadata/default.aspx.

11. See http://www.oecd.org/sti/innovationinsciencetechnologyandindustry/oecdpatent databases.htm.

12. Eurostat publishes results from the Community Innovation Survey for the EU and associated member states in its statistics portal. See http://epp.eurostat.ec.europa.eu/portal/page/portal/science_technology_innovation/data/database.

13. There are other sets of indicators regularly published by OECD, such as the OECD key biotechnology indicators, bringing together the latest available economic and activity data on biotechnology and innovation. See http://www.oecd.org/sti/keybiotechnologyindicators.htm.

14. Led by the CIIE, it benefits from contributions by the CSTP and ICCP committees.

15. Bibliometric data are gathered by commercial organizations that compete in their offer to provide access to a more comprehensively indexed scientific literature. The OECD carries out its work on bibliometric indicators by means of partnerships with leading research institutes with demonstrated expertise and access to 'cleaner' sources and, in some instances, carrying out analysis on data directly licensed from data compilers. See Okubo (1997).

16. In other words, traditional indicators based simply on the frequency of responses to a given question.

17. For further information, see http://www.oecd.org/innovation/policyplatform/.
18. For example, see the policy brief on open innovation in global networks: http://www.oecd.org/science/innovationinsciencetechnologyandindustry/41721342.pdf.
19. See http://www.finance.senate.gov/imo/media/doc/OECD%20SFC%20Hearing%20testimony%209%2020%2011.pdf.
20. See, for example, http://www.oecd.org/sti/interneteconomy/oecdkeyictindicators.htm. The first edition of the *OECD Guide to Measuring the Information Society* was first issued in 2005.
21. Some examples are illustrated in Chapter 12 of this handbook.
22. See for example Arundel et al. (2010).
23. See http://epp.eurostat.ec.europa.eu/portal/page/portal/microdata/cis.
24. www.oecd.org/sti/innoserv.
25. Finne (2011) has documented different drivers of potential over- and under-reporting in Norwegian firms. See also Hough et al. (2012) on the experience of redesigning the US business R&D and innovation survey and Howells (2009) on specific challenges for services.
26. For example, Statistics Canada stopped surveying the small performers and funders of R&D in Canada to reduce the reporting burden on companies; it replaced the data previously gathered by the survey by administrative data from the Canada Revenue Agency.
27. Survey-based approaches to estimate R&D asset lives have been already tested in a number of countries, including the USA, Germany, Israel and the UK. The R&D capitalization process also requires producing estimates of R&D deflators, nowcasting estimates of R&D to feed into quarterly national accounts, and, in many countries, constructing regional measures to feed into regional accounts.
28. The likely impact of R&D capitalization on GDP growth rates has been estimated only in a minority of countries. This figure tends to be quite small because R&D is relatively stable compared to overall GDP. Unlike the capitalization of software, the capitalization of R&D will not signal a dramatic change in estimates of past changes in GDP.
29. See OECD (2006, 2008).
30. See Corrado et al. (2012) for a set of estimates of intangible investment and net stocks for European countries and the USA. These estimates are the authors' own elaboration of work they previously conducted under three projects: two funded by the European Commission 7th Framework Programme (COINVEST http://www.coinvest.org.uk/bin/view/CoInvest and INNODRIVE http://innodrive.org/) and an ongoing effort of The Conference Board (http://www.conference-board.org/data/intangibles).
31. Organizations such as Nesta portray the measured contribution of TFP and intangibles accumulation to economic growth as that of innovation. See, for example, http://www.nesta.org.uk/home1/assets/features/innovation_index_2012.
32. The UNESCO Institute of Statistics has been carrying out a project to collect relevant information on innovation surveys carried out in developing countries. See http://www.uis.unesco.org/ScienceTechnology/Pages/innovation-statistics.aspx.
33. The European Commission recently published a report by an expert group on knowledge transfer metrics that provides an overview of activities carried out to date (EC 2011). Abreu et al. (2011) provide comprehensive evidence of the wide range of university interactions with the rest of the economy.
34. See www.oecd.org/sti/cdh for key indicators and further publications and information on this joint OECD–Eurostat–UNESCO project.
35. See, for example, Cosh and Zhang (2011).
36. For example, an Observatory of Public Sector Innovation is being developed under the aegis of the Public Governance Committee to systematically collect, categorize, analyse and share innovative practices from across the public sector. See http://www.oecd.org/governance/oecdobservatoryofpublicsectorinnovation.htm.
37. See Jaffe (2002).

REFERENCES

Abreu, Maria, Vadim Grinevich, Alan Hughes and Michael Kitson (2011), *Knowledge Exchange between Academics and the Business, Public and Third Sectors*, UK Innovation Research Centre: University of Cambridge and Imperial College London, http://www.cbr.cam.ac.uk/pdf/AcademicSurveyReport.pdf.

Arundel, Anthony, Kieran O'Brian and Ann Torugsa (2010), 'Errors in the interpretation of "innovation": preliminary results from a 2007 innovation survey in Australia', Presentation to the Eurostat Working Group Meeting on Science, Technology and Innovation, Luxembourg, 22–23 November. See also Chapter 4 in this volume.

Corrado, C.A., C.R. Hulten and D.E. Sichel (2005), 'Measuring capital and technology: an expanded framework', in Carol Corrado, John Haltiwanger and Daniel Sichel (eds), *Measuring Capital in the New Economy, Studies in Income and Wealth*, Vol. 65, Chicago, IL: The University of Chicago Press, pp. 11–45.

Corrado, C., J. Haskel, C. Jona-Lasinio and M. Iommi (2012), 'Intangible capital and growth in advanced economies: measurement methods and comparative results', Working Paper, available at http://www.intan-invest.net.

Cosh, Andy and Joanne Zhang (2011), 'Open innovation choices – what is British enterprise doing?', University of Cambridge, Cambridge: UK Innovation Research Centre, http://www.cbr.cam.ac.uk/pdf/OI_Report.pdf.

EC (2011), 'Metrics for knowledge transfer from public research organizations in Europe', Report from the European Commission's Expert Group on Knowledge Transfer Metrics, Brussels: DG Research and Innovation.

EC, IMF, OECD, UN and the World Bank (2009), *System of National Accounts 2008*.

Finne, Hakan (2011), 'Is R&D in the business enterprise sector in Norway under-reported?', SINTEF Report A20772, October, Oslo: SINTEF.

Francoz, Dominique and Patrick Corbel (2005), 'L'utilisation des vignettes dans les enquêtes "entreprise" dans le cadre de la mise en œuvre d'une nouvelle définition internationale de l'innovation', *Actes des Journées de Méthodologie Statistique 2005*, Paris: INSEE, accessed from http://jms.insee.fr/files/documents/2005/438_1-jms2005_session15_corbel-francoz_actes.pdf.

Freeman, Christopher (1987), *Technology and Economic Performance: Lessons from Japan*, London: Pinter.

Frenz, Marion and Ray Lambert (2012), 'Mixed modes of innovation: an empiric approach to capturing firms' innovation', OECD Science, Technology and Industry Working Papers, DSTI/DOC (2012) 6, Paris: OECD.

Hatzichronoglou, Thomas (1997), 'Revision of the high-technology sector and product classification', OECD Science, Technology and Industry Working Papers, 1997/02, Paris: OECD.

Hough, R.S., B. Shackelford, John Jankowski and Ray Wolfe (2012), 'The Business R&D and Innovation Survey: lessons learned from the redesign of the Survey of Industrial Research and Development', paper for the US Federal Committee on Statistical Methodology Research Conference, January.

Howells, Jeremy (2009), 'Services R&D', IPTS Working Paper on Corporate R&D and Innovation No. 05/2009, JRC/IPTS, Brussels: European Commission.

Jaffe, Adam (2002), 'Building programme evaluation into the design of public research support programmes', *Oxford Review of Economic Policy*, **18**(1), 22–34.

Kelvin, Lord (Sir William Thompson) (1883), *Popular Lectures and Addresses*, vol. 1, 'Electrical Units of Measurement', 1883-05-03 (quote accessed from http://zapatopi.net/kelvin/quotes/).

OECD (1963), *The Measurement of Scientific and Technical Activities: Proposed Standard Practice for Surveys of Research and Experimental Development, DAS/PD/62.47*, Paris: OECD.

OECD (1990), *Proposed Standard Method of Compiling and Interpreting Technology Balance of Payments Data – TBP Manual 1990*, The Measurement of Scientific and Technological Activities Series, Paris: OECD.

OECD (1997), *National Innovation Systems*, Paris: OECD.
OECD (2002), *Frascati Manual, Proposed Standard Practice for Surveys on Research and Experimental Development*, 6th edn, Paris: OECD, www.oecd.org/sti/frascatimanual.
OECD (2003), *Turning Science into Business: Patenting and Licensing at Public Research Organizations*, Paris: OECD.
OECD (2004a), *OECD Handbook for Internationally Comparative Education Statistics: Concepts, Standards, Definitions and Classifications*, Paris: OECD.
OECD (2004b), *Science and Technology Statistical Compendium 2004*, Paris: OECD, http://www oecd.org/science/innovationinsciencetechnologyandindustry/23652608.pdf.
OECD (2006), *Creating Value from Intellectual Assets, Meeting of the OECD Council at Ministerial Level 2006*, Paris: OECD.
OECD (2007), *Science, Technology and Innovation Indicators in a Changing World: Responding to Policy Needs*, Paris: OECD.
OECD (2008), *Intangible Assets and Value Creation. Synthesis Report.* Paris: OECD, http://www.oecd.org/dataoecd/36/35/40637101.pdf.
OECD (2009a), *OECD Patent Statistics Manual*, Paris: OECD.
OECD (2009b), *OECD Biotechnology Indicators*, Paris: OECD.
OECD (2009c), *Innovation in Firms: A Microeconomic Perspective*, Paris: OECD.
OECD (2010a), *The OECD Innovation Strategy: Getting a Head Start on Tomorrow*, Paris: OECD.
OECD (2010b), *Measuring Innovation: A New Perspective*, Paris: OECD, www.oecd.org/innovation/strategy/measuring.
OECD (2010c), *Handbook on Deriving Capital Measures of Intellectual Property Products*, Paris: OECD.
OECD (2011a), *OECD Guide to Measuring the Information Society*, Paris: OECD.
OECD (2011b), *OECD Science, Technology and Industry Scoreboard 2011*, Paris: OECD, www.oecd.org/sti/scoreboard.
OECD (2012a), *OECD Key Biotechnology Indicators*, Paris: OECD, http://www.oecd.org/innovation/innovationinsciencetechnologyandindustry/keybiotechnologyindicators.htm.
OECD (2012b), *OECD Science, Technology and Industry Outlook 2012*, Paris: OECD, www.oecd.org/sti/outlook.
OECD/European Patent Office (2008), *Compendium of Patent Statistics*, Paris: OECD.
OECD/Eurostat (1995), *The Measurement of Scientific and Technological Activities. Manual of the Measurement of Human Resources Devoted to S&T 'Canberra' Manual*, OCDE/GD(95)77, Paris: OECD.
OECD/Eurostat (2005), *Oslo Manual: Guidelines for Collecting and Interpreting Innovation Data*, Paris: OECD, www.oecd.org/sti/oslomanual.
Okubo, Y. (1997), 'Bibliometric indicators and analysis of research systems, methods and examples', OECD Science, Technology and Industry Working Papers, 1997/01, Paris: OECD.
van Steen, Jan (2012), 'Public funding of R&D: towards internationally comparable indicators', OECD Science, Technology and Industry Working Papers, 2012/04, Paris: OECD.
Yonetani, Yutaka (2012), 'A report on the comparative survey regarding the perception of "innovation" in Japan, USA and Germany', Research Material No. 208, Tokyo: National Institute of Science and Technology Policy (NISTEP), March.

10 Developing harmonized measures of the dynamics of organizations and work

Nathalie Greenan and Edward Lorenz

1. INTRODUCTION

This chapter presents an overview of a set of guidelines for collecting and interpreting harmonized information on organizations and on processes of organizational change and innovation. The guidelines are the result of an EU Coordination Action Project, MEADOW (Measuring the Dynamics of Organisations and Work), which involved 14 teams covering nine European countries.[1] The guidelines have been designed to provide a framework within which existing European surveys could evolve towards comparability, as well as providing norms for the construction of new survey instruments in the field (MEADOW Consortium 2010). The starting point of the project was that reliable harmonized statistics on organizations and organizational change could make a significant contribution both to research and to policy initiatives at the EU and national levels.

There are a number of reasons why a deeper understanding of organizations and processes of organizational change is of research and policy relevance. First, as the discussion in the third edition of the *Oslo Manual* (OECD/Eurostat 2005) points out (Chapter 2 in this volume), the full range of changes that affect firm performance and the accumulation of knowledge requires a broader framework than technological product and process innovation and in particular should include organizational changes and innovations. In part, this widening of the concept of innovation to include organizational innovations reflects an appreciation that in many service sectors innovation is less technological in nature and takes the form of changes in the organization of interactions between service providers and their clients.

Second, as developed in the literature on organizational design and performance, the capacity of firms to develop new products and processes is affected by their internal structure, including the way work is organized. Forms of work organization that stimulate interaction among agents with a diverse set of experiences and competences could be more creative, leading to the development of original ideas for new products and processes. Work organization forms that delegate responsibility for problem solving to a wide range of employees could be more successful, both in upgrading the competences of workers and in transforming ideas into new products and processes.[2]

Third, organizational structure and change have an impact on employee outcomes. Job stress is directly affected by the design of tasks and the way teamwork is structured. Job satisfaction depends in part on intrinsic rewards associated with the potential for work activity to offer opportunities for the creative use and further development of skills and knowledge. Thus policies focusing on improving the quality of working life can benefit from better information on how work is organized and how employees experience organizational change and innovation.

These different areas of research and policy relevance are reflected in two central features of the guidelines developed in the MEADOW project. The first, which concerns the scope of measurement, is that the guidelines develop definitions and concepts suitable for measuring both organizational change and prevailing organizational structures or states. Knowledge-based theories emphasize the way changes in the economic and institutional context require firms to be more adaptable and innovative than in the past. Dynamic or adaptive capabilities at the levels of technology, product development and markets often require complementary changes in organizational practices and methods, and for this reason there is great theoretical interest in the extent and nature of organizational changes and their relation to economic fluctuation.

Capturing organizational states is of paramount importance for policy makers, and measures of organizational change that are not linked to measures of initial states can lead to mistaken policy evaluations by giving the impression of stagnation or inertia when in fact the relevant changes were implemented before the survey reference period. In the EU context many areas of policy making, including employment, innovation and information and communication technology (ICT) policy, rely on the 'open method of coordination' in which harmonized surveys are used to identify best practice or sets of best practices as a basis for setting targets and for judging the progress of nations and regions in achieving them. Such targets can be quite general and can serve as a basis for national or regional specific policies that take into account particular features of the local context. Adopting the kinds of organizational structures that promote greater flexibility in enterprises and employees is a general target of this nature and a harmonized survey measuring organizational structure and change could contribute to developing relevant indicators for benchmarking in this area.

The second central feature, which concerns the general survey framework, is that the proposed guidelines consider a survey that links the interview of an employer with the interviews of his or her employees as the richest survey setting for measuring organizational change and its economic and social impacts. From the research perspective, a linked survey can enrich information derived from one level with information from the other. For example, employer-level information provides useful contextualization to the description of work provided by employees, while employee-level information can be used to compute indicators on topics that cannot be easily observed by an employer, such as the nature of intrinsic rewards or work-related stress. Developing a linked survey also allows choosing the most informed and relevant respondent for each topic of the survey. For example, an employer will be better informed about the organization's strategy and overall structure, while an employee can more easily describe his or her job characteristics, such as whether colleagues can provide assistance in carrying out a job. Developing both employer-level and employee-level measures can therefore bring about an improvement in the measurement strategy for each level, which can also feed back into conceptual considerations.

From the policy perspective, linked surveys could provide useful indicators for policy making that cannot be constructed with single-level survey instruments. For example, adding an employee questionnaire to an employer-level survey providing measures of innovation performance would allow scoring the share of employees with innovative behaviour or specific further training and computing this score in the population of innovative employers and non-innovative employers across European countries. Linked surveys could also be used in monitoring the impact of labour market or industrial government intervention. An example is active ageing, which is moving up the policy agenda. Analysis based on linked surveys of organizations could contribute to identifying the flexible working arrangements, the types of further training or the job design characteristics that are best suited to maintain older workers in employment. The effect of employer incentives to keep older workers in employment could also be assessed using the temporal and spatial variation in policies across European countries.

A linked employer–employee survey adds complexity to the practical side of data collection. It may increase costs if it requires adding a new survey to an already-existing employer or employee survey. It also requires that the two survey levels be coordinated. In terms of the choice of primary sampling unit (PSU), the most common strategy in existing linked surveys is to take the employer as the PSU. However, it is also possible first to sample and interview the employees and to then derive the interviewed sample of employers in a second stage. These two different ways of linking are not equivalent, and in Section 3 the advantages and disadvantages of each linking method are considered. Section 3 also examines the advantages and disadvantages of a panel and retrospective questions for capturing processes of change. Before discussing these aspects of the survey design, Section 2 presents the measurement framework developed in the MEADOW project for characterizing organizational change and its economic and social impacts. The framework draws on the major theories of organizational structure and change, and identifies key organizational elements, their determinants, and the relations between the elements in order to provide guidance on the choice of indicators of organizational change. Section 4 provides more detail on the choice of indicators and discusses the employer- and employee-level questionnaires that were developed in order to measure organizations, their evolution and their impacts. As there is insufficient space here to present the entire questionnaires, the emphasis in Section 4 is on the complementary nature of the employer and employee survey questions designed to measure organizational design and its change.

The MEADOW project included a phase of cognitive testing of the employer and employee survey questionnaires in order to ensure that the questions were understood in the same way by respondents from different linguistic and cultural areas, working in different sectors, and employed by firms or organizations of vastly different sizes.[3] The project did not involve full-scale tests of the survey instruments. A first large-scale test of the employer-level survey instrument was undertaken independently by Statistics Sweden in 2010.[4] Key results of the Swedish employer-level survey are presented in Section 5.

2.   THE ORGANIZATIONAL MEASUREMENT FRAMEWORK

Figure 10.1 presents the basic measurement framework adopted in the MEADOW guidelines. The measurement framework draws inspiration from an overview of the major theories of organizational structure and change (Nielsen et al. 2008a),[5] as well as a background report on the state of the art in surveys of organizational change (Nielsen et al. 2008b).

The framework does not reflect a particular theory of organizational structure and change. Rather, its purpose is to recognize the key elements and relations between elements that are identified in the major theories in order to provide guidance for the choice of indicators. Ideally the results of a survey measuring the different indicators would allow researchers to test propositions associated with different and possibly competing theories of organizational structure and change. An important proviso is that it is recognized that there are clear limitations to what can be reliably meas-

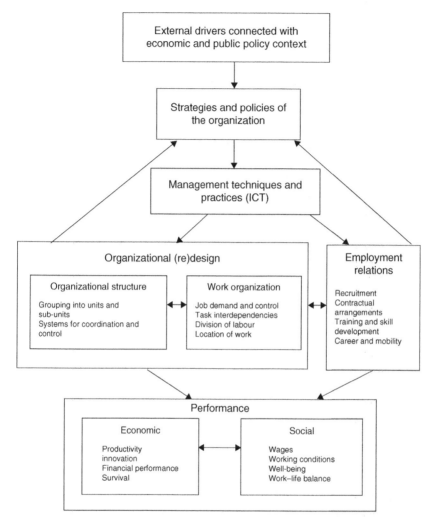

Figure 10.1   Basic measurement framework

ured with surveys. It is very difficult to measure unplanned incremental changes in work and interactions that often even go unrecognized by the actors directly involved. Thus, for the purposes of the measurement framework, organizational change is defined only to include intended changes in the organizational structure and the organization of work.

The framework draws attention to the driving forces behind organizational change. Key aspects of the external environment that affect the internal policies of enterprises include those connected to global competition and technology as well as changes in public policies, notably in the areas of labour markets, systems of education and training, health and safety, and the environment. Organizational change surveys can provide some information on these contextual factors but it will necessarily be limited to the perceptions of respondents concerning how these external economic or institutional factors are experienced.

The strategies and policies of the organization affect the specific management practices and techniques adopted. One area that is especially important to the objectives of EU employment policy is the adoption of practices designed to increase organizational flexibility and adaptability. Flexibility has external and internal dimensions. Organizational practices and techniques that increase internal flexibility include job rotation, multi-skilling and the set of 'lean' production methods designed to minimize inventories and allow the customer to pull value from the producer (Womack and Jones 2003). ICT tools such as performance-tracking software and client relationship software may contribute to increased flexibility and performance. Another policy-relevant area is practices and techniques designed to improve product quality. Total quality management (TQM) refers to a set of techniques for monitoring and improving product quality, including the use of quality circles and delegating responsibility for quality control to the individual employee. A third area is knowledge management practices, including the use of databases documenting good working practices or the monitoring of external ideas and technical developments (OECD 2003).

In Figure 10.1, downward-pointing arrows indicate that the practices and techniques adopted affect the design of the organization and its employment relations. Organizational design is seen as being composed of the organizational structure and the organization of work. Organizational structure refers to the grouping of people, tasks and objects (e.g. equipment or buildings) into sub-units and divisions and the systems to ensure coordination and control both horizontally and vertically within the boundaries of the organization and outside these boundaries, with suppliers, customers and other business partners. The coordination mechanisms, including relations of authority and control, are central to how the management governs and changes the organization, and to how employees experience their working conditions and possibilities for personal development.

Work organization refers to how work is actually divided into tasks, the bundling of tasks into jobs and assignments, the interdependencies of workers in performing the job, the job demands, and the degree of control over the work done. As the arrow linking the organizational structure and the organization of work suggests, these two components of the organizational design are closely related. In organizations relying on relatively decentralized control mechanisms employees will tend to exercise greater control over their work activity and job descriptions will tend to be broader, incorporating multiple tasks.

The research literature shows that key elements of the organization can be combined in various ways, leading to different types of organizational designs and related outcomes. A common theme in the contemporary literature is the move from bureaucratic and/or authoritarian types to more organic and flexible organizations. An example is the concept of an 'adhocracy' (Mintzberg 1979). This type is characterized by specialists deployed in project teams, much training, little formalization and coordination by mutual adjustment. While the MEADOW project placed emphasis on developing indicators for organic or flexible organizations, it was also recognized that many organizations are characterized by bureaucratic dimensions and that it is common to combine both bureaucratic and non-bureaucratic structural features in the same organization.

The measurement framework includes an arrow connecting the organizational design to employment relations. While employment relations are not defined as components of the organization's structure *per se*, a vast literature shows that both economic and social performances are affected not only by the organizational design but also by the system of employment relations. Employment relations include such elements as recruitment practices, contractual arrangements, training and competence development, and career paths and internal mobility. The literature on human resource management (HRM) argues that employment relations are highly complementary to the organization of work and that they have an impact on job quality and hence on work-related stress and job satisfaction. A recent strand of literature has focused on identifying the positive performance effects of combining specific sets of HRM practices with managerial practices designed to enhance employee discretion and more fully involve employees in problem-solving activities. In the organizational behaviour literature, this issue is conceptualized as one of HRM complementarities (Ichniowski et al. 1997; Laursen and Mahnke 2001; Lorenz et al. 2004; Michie and Sheehan 1999).

The measurement framework shows that the organizational design in combination with various elements of the employment relations affect both economic and social performance. The framework includes an arrow connecting economic performance to social performance. The reasons for this are to some extent implicit in the literature on HRM complementarities, which points to the way worker well-being including intrinsic rewards, impact on employee morale and commitment to the organization's goals with further effects on productivity. The stability of employment tenures and career prospects within the organization will affect an employee's interest in investing in firm-specific skills, which in turn will affect the ability of the employee to contribute to making improvements to the quality of products and processes.

There is a growing focus on how to reform public sector organizations so that they become more market oriented, assuming that this leads to more efficiency in terms of serving the needs of citizens, customers and clients at low costs. This is related to the modernization agenda in the public sector, influenced by new public management (NPM), which advocates performance measures for the efficient use of resources and personnel in public sector organizations comparable to those in the private sector and by the implementation of e-government schemes. The common objectives of many management practices mean that many of the core elements and interrelations identified in the measurement framework apply to both private and public sector organizations and are relevant for constructing common indicators for the entire economy; this is the approach taken in the MEADOW project.

At the same time, organizations in the public sector are exposed to transformation pressures emanating from the political system, as well as to pressures from the changing demands of citizens around such issues as access to education and training and work–life balance. Further, while reforms based on the NPM model have seen the introduction of private sector type performance measures into the public sector, there are dimensions of performance with no obvious private sector counterparts. These include the scientific output of public research organizations, the level and quality of education and training, and the quality and level of coverage of health care. Public administration may also be evaluated on the criteria of transparency and justice as related to democratic principles. Transparency laws are thus seen as means of increasing public trust in government, and the optimistic view is that they will produce a culture of openness in public organizations. The MEADOW survey does not develop measures for these features of public sector organizations and they could be the focus of specialized modules.

3.   ELEMENTS OF A GENERAL SURVEY FRAMEWORK

Linked Employer–Employee Surveys

Although the MEADOW employer and employee surveys were designed so that they could be administered independently, as discussed above there are a number of reasons for preferring a linked survey for measuring the different elements and interrelations summarized in the measurement framework. There are two possible methods for administering such surveys that are not equivalent in terms of advantages and drawbacks. The employer can be sampled first, while the employee is sampled later in a second stage (linked employer–employee survey). Or, the opposite procedure may be adopted, with the employee sampled and interviewed first, and the interviewed sample of employers being derived from this employee sample (linked employee–employer survey).

Among existing linked survey instruments, the most common practice is for the employer to be designated as the primary sampling unit. One reason for doing this is that it seems obvious to explore the employer level first in a survey focusing on organizational change, as it can be assumed that changes are more often initiated at the employer level than at the employee level. Further, it is reasonable to begin by interviewing persons in a position both to have an understanding of the organization as a whole and to impart this information. There are also a number of more practical advantages to this approach. First, taking the employer as the primary sampling unit (PSU) makes it easier to survey the various employees who are linked to it. A clustered sample is obtained, which is both simpler and cheaper to administer than a simple random sample, as fewer contacts are needed overall. Second, in the absence of linked employer–employee registers, the unit that is sampled first will be easier to follow up in the case of a longitudinal survey. Consequently, if employees are the PSU it will be more difficult to obtain a panel of employer units. Third, the representativeness of the sample of employers should be easier to guarantee in a setting where the employer is the PSU since the dispersion of sampling rates is always higher within the sample for the second stage.

Taking the employer as the PSU may, however, result in several practical difficulties. One problem is that it may result in a bias in the employee sample towards employees who are more satisfied with their employer or their work (social climate bias) if they are selected from a list given by the employer. Thus, even if employees are randomly selected from this list, it will be practically much more difficult to obtain a random sample of employees because the employers provide the sampling frame for the employee survey within their units.

From the EU perspective, a main difficulty with the employer-first approach is the absence of a harmonized employer register. At the European level, no exhaustive and up-to-date database is available that includes: addresses of employer units (headquarters, subsidiaries etc.); a classification of industries such as the NACE; and more generally the information that is required to stratify and optimize sampling rates. In practice, existing harmonized employer surveys cope with this constraint in two quite different ways. One approach is centrally coordinated with a single organization developing and translating a questionnaire, prescribing the survey methodology, and contracting out the fieldwork to a network of contractors. The European Foundation for the Improvement of Living and Working Conditions (EFILWC) plays this role in the case of the European Company Survey (ECS).[6]

The Community Innovation Survey (CIS) and the European Structure of Earnings Survey (ESES) illustrate a decentralized mode. These surveys are covered by European regulations that require each member state to participate. Eurostat is responsible for coordination and quality issues and, in close cooperation with EU member states, develops a standard core questionnaire in English and an accompanying set of definitions and methodological recommendations. The responsibility for implementing the survey at the national level lies in most cases with the national statistical office.

With respect to the MEADOW framework, the ESES is of particular interest as it is the only harmonized European linked employer–employee survey. This survey was carried out in 1995, 2002, 2006 and 2010 and has been progressively extended to all 27 member states of the EU. A central feature of ESES is flexibility: information can be obtained from 'tailor-made' questionnaires, existing surveys, administrative data, or from a combination of these sources. In some countries, participating organizations provide general information about their wage policy and then assemble information from their own files about the individual earnings of a sample of employees or, in some cases, their whole workforce. In other countries, employer-provided information about wage policies is enriched by administrative data on the earnings of all employees working for the participating employer units. Some countries, such as France, survey a random sample of establishments and a random sample of employees within these establishments using a linked employer–employee register.

While the cross-national experience of carrying out several waves of the ESES provides an important knowledge base for implementing a MEADOW-style organizational survey, its flexible approach has some drawbacks as it creates certain barriers to comparability (Desai 2008). At the most basic level, the definition of the survey unit can be variable. Thus European-wide results obtained from the data sometimes fall below the standards applied at a national level due to differences in the units of observation, sampling frames and classifications. The consequences of these differences are difficult to assess, since much of the knowledge about them remains tacit, and is related to the routines and practices of national statistical offices in each country. However, Eurostat's coordination of the survey promotes further convergence in these practices and progressively improves the documentation of cross-country differences through a series of quality reports (Eurostat 2006, 2009).

An advantage of taking the employee as the PSU is that in contrast to the situation in respect of employer databases, good-quality household databases can be obtained in most European countries through the national statistical offices or other national institutions.[7] Moreover, taking the employee as the PSU allows one to cover a very large field of employers (all kind of establishments, in all sectors, as well as the self-employed) in a way that does not depend upon the availability of a business register and the extent to which it is up to date. The sample of employers derived from a random sample of employees will be automatically proportionate to the size of employer units. The sample will reflect the employer unit's share in total employment and can be easily weighted to make it representative of the population of organizations (Leombruni 2003).

When consideration is given to using the MEADOW framework for surveys conducted outside the EU in developing or emerging market economies, a further factor that may favour an employee-first approach is the existence of a large informal sector. Even where there are up-to-date business registers they are unlikely to include units in the informal sector. This limitation of business registers explains the trend in recent years to survey the informal sector through mixed-household enterprise surveys in which a survey of households is used in a first phase to identify owners and then in a second phase a sample of enterprise owners is interviewed to gain information on their operations.[8]

The employee-first option may lead, however, to some specific difficulties. There is the risk of attrition and bias because of the refusal or inability of some employees to provide good contact information about their employer. There is also the fact that the distribution of businesses in terms of size is skewed and thus it is difficult to reach very large employer units for which a census is generally conducted in employer-level surveys such as CIS. Other drawbacks are simply the counterparts of the advantages of an employer-first approach, namely: the representativeness of the employer sample; difficulties in following up employers over time; and budget optimization.

Although both linking options face limitations, either could provide linked data of good quality. Besides the methodological issues emphasized above, practical issues such as sampling database availability, and legal constraints regarding the access rights for individual data will necessarily play a role in the choice of survey design. While the ability of employers to provide relevant information on the overall structure and strategy of the organization constitutes a strong argument in favour of an employer-first approach for a survey focusing on organizational change, problems related to the lack of availability or poor quality of registers of employers make it nonetheless worth considering the alternative of a linked employee–employer survey.

The Longitudinal Aspect: A Combination of Retrospective Questions and a Panel

The first section of this chapter discussed the importance of measuring organizational states and their relation to knowledge development and performance. Measuring changes without measuring states can result in pooling together employer units that remain inert and units that have undergone major changes in previous periods. But changes in the organization also need to be identified. Measuring the dynamics of change at the employer level is central in order to make some assessment of organizational flexibility and adaptation. It is also important in order to identify the adjustment costs of change, including training needs, renewal of the labour force, accidents, and perception of work intensification and stress. To understand barriers to the diffusion of organizational forms that appear to be virtuous in terms of performance requires collecting information on how firms are adopting and absorbing changes.

Retrospective questions and a panel considered as alternative methods for capturing the dynamics of organizations have advantages and drawbacks. Whereas a panel by definition consists of measurements at two or more points in time (e.g. over a time period of several years), the immediate availability of retrospective data is an argument in favour of their use. Moreover, a sole reliance on retrospective questions removes the requirement for repeated surveys and is therefore cheaper. Another factor favouring the use of retrospective questions is the possibility of focusing on the most recent organizational innovations in a manner that cannot be done with a panel. With retrospective questions, after having described features of the organization and its use of managerial practices at two dates, it is possible to ask the respondent to focus on the major change that occurred during that period and to describe the difficulties encountered. This cannot be done in a panel design, which seeks only to measure states, at least when organizational innovation takes place between panel measurements.

Another advantage – albeit one that concerns only the employer level – is that retrospective questions can provide more consistent and comparable information on activities carried out by organizations and workers, because an individual provides all the information at a single point in time. Thus there is no bias linked to a change of respondent between two different waves, as can occur in an employer-focused panel survey, and changes in the general context in which the organization operates are not likely to influence the interpretation of a given question.

Counterbalancing these advantages are certain drawbacks of using retrospective questions. One is that if organizational changes lead to mobility and turnover among management, the respondent may not have experienced the change and may have only limited or no knowledge of it. Thus, if retrospective questions may serve to limit some biases in the measurement of change, the *quid pro quo* is that information may be missing or incomplete. Another principal drawback is the risk of 'recall error': memories may be short, leading to omission, or unauthentic, leading to a 'telescoping effect', in which respondents report things in the current period that actually took place in a prior period (especially when people are dealing with daily problems and plan for the future).[9]

In this respect, one obvious advantage of a panel design is that it does not rely upon memories. However, panels can only measure changes that can be consistently defined over time, and there is then a significant emphasis on fixing the content of the questionnaire at wave 1. This poses a problem for a survey on organizational change, as it is likely that a fraction of the survey will have to evolve over time. For example, management practices follow fads (Abrahamson and Fairchild 1999), and from one wave to the next some practices may become obsolete while others may evolve during their diffusion process. Using two waves of the workplace employment relations survey (WERS), Freitas (2008) investigated employers' use of 'quality circles' and 'business process reengineering' through measures based on questions that were identically formulated in 1990 and 1998. She finds that the patterns of use of these practices have changed over time. An explanation is that these practices refer to management concepts that are soft rather than precisely defined, and that are constantly recycled as they diffuse in relation to changes in the social and competitive environment. Thus a longitudinal survey of these practices calls for a renewal of some questions from one survey to the other, even if they relate to the same management concept. This points to the need for qualitative investigation in preparing survey questionnaires, along with an analysis of management publications, in order to monitor the evolution and renewal of management concepts.

Another argument in favour of panel surveys is the possibility of analysing changes not only within the organization, but also between them (and especially between the older ones and those more recently established). Of course, this implies that employers from previous waves are followed up while the panel is refreshed with new enterprises, some of these being newly created organizations. Indeed, such data should enable one to observe the demographics of organizations and thus to estimate the effects of the structural transformation of the economy on the dynamics of organizations and work. Here again there is a drawback as it is expensive and time-consuming to trace employers, employees or both.[10] Even with adequate resources and appropriate procedures, there will be some attrition, which means that a part of the initial sample is lost in each of the following waves since some particular companies, workplaces or employees prefer to stop participating in the panel after a while.[11] Another point is that the initial sample has to be large enough to cope with any attrition, both in aggregate and within each stratum. So the initial sampling is more complex in a panel. The refreshment strategy, taking into account birth, death and attrition, is another important issue, and attention must be given to the computation of dynamic weights (Forth 2008).

A strategy to derive benefits from the advantages of each option and to limit the associated disadvantages is to combine the use of retrospective questions and a panel design. An advantage of using a combined approach is that data from the first wave are available quickly to support the analysis of the dynamics of organizations and of work in the recent past. Then, repetition of the survey in a second wave makes it possible to monitor trends in change and to undertake longitudinal analyses that can investigate the causality of relationships. Asking retrospective questions in a subsequent wave fills the gaps in the longer timeline and provides useful additional information.

Figure 10.2 represents a combined approach consisting of a four-year follow-up period between the employer survey waves combined with the use of retrospective questions, which have a (maximum) recall period of two years.[12] This would be adequate for measuring the organization of work, which may change quickly but also needs time to show its effects. With a four-year cycle, two waves of the survey provide four distinct time points, each separated by a two-year period.

In this survey design, information on changes over periods of two years might not be fully comparable from one period to the other. For example, changes between 2012 and 2014 are assessed through retrospective questions addressed to a unique respondent, while changes between 2014 and 2016 are based on the comparison between a state variable given by one respondent describing the situation at the date of the survey in wave 1 and a state variable given by another respondent in wave 2 and deriving from a retrospective question. The comparability of these two different measures of change over a time period of two years would need further assessment. Figure 10.2 indicates that a one-year follow-up for the employee survey could be considered, leading to a two-wave employee panel. This design makes it possible to analyse short-term effects at the employee level using the panel dimension of the data.

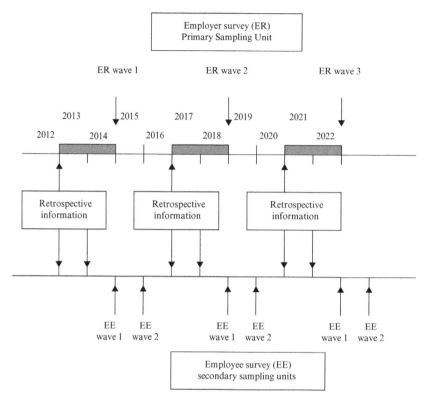

Figure 10.2 A proposed survey design

4. INDICATORS FOR MEASURING ORGANIZATIONAL DESIGN AND ITS CHANGE

A central theme in this chapter has been the advantage of a linked survey framework for measuring organizations and their dynamics. This relates to the fact that information gathered at one level can be enriched by information at another. Employers, for example, are better placed than employees to answer questions about the overall structure of the organization, while employees are better placed to describe the characteristics of their daily work activity and how they interact with other employees. In order to illustrate the complementary nature of the information that can be collected at the employer and employee levels, this section presents selected questions from the MEADOW employer and employee surveys designed to measure organizational design and its change.[13]

Box 10.1 lists questions from the employer-level questionnaire. As discussed in Section 2 above, there is an important literature looking at the relation between performance outcomes and the design of the organization, including the types of coordination mechanism used. An important theme in this literature has been the move from bureaucratic or hierarchical organizational structures to more decentralized ones in which elements of decision-making authority are delegated to employees at lower levels of the organizational hierarchy. Such decentralized organization structures are seen as being more flexible or adaptable and hence better able to compete in global markets often characterized by rapid technological change.

While it is difficult to measure directly at the employer level the use of different coordinating mechanisms, much can be learned by asking questions about the divisional structure of the organization, the use of teamwork and by identifying the category of personnel responsible for different types of decision making and activities.

As the literature on 'learning organizations' has argued, an objective in delegating decision-making authority and increasing the control employees exercise over their jobs is to foster employee learning and creativity. Much of this literature argues that in hierarchical structures crucial elements of the organization's knowledge base that could contribute to improved performance, including innovative performance, remain untapped (Senge 1990; Garvin 2003; Jensen et al. 2007; Greenan and Lorenz 2010). Employers are poorly placed to provide detailed information on what employees do and learn at work; Box 10.2 presents questions from the employee questionnaire designed to capture such aspects as how much learning and problem solving takes place on the job and the extent to which employees are able to choose or change the way they undertake their jobs. Employee-level questions can also be used to provide direct measures of the types of coordinating mechanism exercised in the organization. In particular it is possible to ask employees about the factors that determine their pace of work: one's boss or supervisor; the automatic movement of equipment, or the requirement to respect quantitative production targets. Questions about the forms of assistance employees receive or give at work can be used to measure the importance of more informal methods of coordination, or what Mintzberg (1979) calls 'mutual adjustment'.

5. RESULTS FROM THE SWEDISH EMPLOYER SURVEY

The first full-scale test of the MEADOW employer survey was conducted by Statistics Sweden under the coordination of Hans-Olof Hagén in 2010.

BOX 10.1   EMPLOYER-LEVEL QUESTIONS FOR ORGANIZATIONAL STRUCTURE AND INTERNAL COORDINATION

B1HIE How many organizational levels are there in your establishment, including the highest level (for example, senior management) and the lowest level (for example, production staff)?
Number _____

B1HIE2007 How many organizational levels were there two years ago?
Number _____

B1DIVTYPE Does this establishment have each of the following types of divisions or departments?
[Provide separate 'yes or no' response options to each of questions a to c]
a.   Separate divisions or departments by function: sales, production, administration, research etc.
b.   Separate divisions or departments by type of product or service
c.   Separate divisions or departments by geographical area: sales regions etc.

1.   Yes
2.   No

B1NDIV How many separate departments or divisions report directly to the head of this establishment?
Number: _____

B1STRUCT Who normally decides on the planning and execution of the daily work tasks of your non-managerial employees?
1.   The employee undertaking the tasks
2.   Managers or work supervisors
3.   Both employees and managers or supervisors

B1DLGQLT Are each of the following responsible for quality control?
[Provide separate 'yes or no' response options to each of questions a to e]
a. The employee undertaking the tasks
b. Managers or work supervisors
c. Specialist group or division within the enterprise or organisation
d. External groups – customers, external evaluation experts etc.
e. [only ask if responses to a to d all 'no'] Quality control not relevant to this establishment

1. Yes
2. No

B1TEAM Are any of the employees at this establishment currently working in a team, where the members jointly decide how work is done?
1. Yes
2. No

B1TEAMPER What percentage of the employees at this establishment currently works in such teams?
1. Up to 24%
2. 25% to 49%
3. 50% to 74%
4. 75% or more

B1TEAM2007 Did any of your employees work in such a team two years ago?
1. Yes
2. No

B1TEAMCHG Compared with two years ago, has the percentage of employees currently working in such teams:
1. Increased?
2. Decreased?
3. Remained approximately the same?

B1DLGSCHD Can any of the non-managerial employees at this establishment choose when they begin or finish their daily work, according to their personal requirements?
1. Yes
2. No

B1DLGSCHDPER What percentage of the <u>non-managerial</u> employees at this establishment can currently choose when they begin or finish their daily work?
1. Up to 24%
2. 25% to 49%
3. 50% to 74%
4. 75% or more

B1DLGSCHD2007 Could any of the non-managerial employees at this establishment choose when to begin or finish their daily work two years ago?
1. Yes
2. No

The Swedish MEADOW survey was administered at the company rather than at the establishment level, with no employee-level counterpart, which is one of the possible implementation options of the guidelines. As a matter of fact, this survey is inscribed in the prolongation of a previous company-level survey, the Flex survey, conducted in 1995 and 1997, which focused on measuring work organization and learning. In 1997, the flex survey was matched with a linked employer–employee register that produced some additional information for the purpose of secondary analysis. This linking option was retained for the Swedish MEADOW survey and it could be used in future waves for developing a linked employer–employee survey. However, in the 2009 edition, another option was explored: that of a positive coordination with the sampling frames of the Community Innovation Survey (CIS) and the Information and Communication Technology use survey (ICT use), two harmonized surveys coordinated by Eurostat. The MEADOW employer questionnaire was thus sent to the 1400 firms with over 15 employees that participated in both of these surveys in 2009.

Even though the MEADOW survey was voluntary in Sweden, it achieved more than the 60 per cent target response rate recommended in the MEADOW Guidelines: 64 per cent. Some possible reasons for this

BOX 10.2 EMPLOYEE-LEVEL QUESTIONS FOR COORDINATION AND WORK ORGANIZATION

Work organization and task description

BWRKGROUP In performing your tasks, do you ever work together in a permanent or temporary team? *(Interviewer note: People could be from your firm [organization] or from another firm [organization])*
1. Yes
2. No
8. Don't know
9. Refused

BWRKGROUPb Does this team have a team leader?
1. Yes
2. No
8. Don't know
9. Refused

BWRKGROUPe Excluding the team leader, can the others in this team influence what tasks you do yourself?
1. Yes
2. No
8. Don't know
9. Refused

CAUTC In your job, what proportion of the time can you choose or change the content of your work tasks?
1. Less than 25% of the time
2. 25% up to 50% of the time
3. 50% up to 75% of the time
4. 75% or more of the time
8. Don't know
9. Refused

CAUTH What proportion of the time can you choose or change how you undertake tasks?
1. Less than 25% of the time
2. 25% up to 50% of the time

3. 50% up to 75% of the time
4. 75% or more of the time
8. Don't know
9. Refused

DLRNNEW How often does your job involve learning new things?
1. Every day
2. At least once a week
3. At least once a month
4. Less often than once a month/never
8. Don't know
9. Refused

DPROBSOLVE In your work, are you ever confronted with new or complex problems that take at least 30 minutes to find a good solution? Only consider the time needed to THINK of a solution, not the time needed to carry it out.
1. Yes
2. No
8. Don't know
9. Refused

Internal coordination

BWORKPRES Are any of the following important in determining the pace of your work:
[Rotate order of questions randomly]
a. Clients or customers
b. Supervisor or manager
c. Your co-workers
d. Your own discretion
e. Pay incentives
f. A computer or computer system
g. A machine or assembly line
h. Targets you have been set

1. Yes
2. No
7. Not applicable
8. Don't know
9. Refused

BQUALMON Thinking of your job as a whole, who usually monitors the quality of your work? You may answer yes to one or more of the following:

a. You yourself
b. Your supervisor or manager
c. The team you work with most often [Ask if BWRKGROUP=1]
d. A person from a separate department
e. Customers or clients

1. Yes
2. No
8. Don't know
9. Refused

BWRKASSIS Sometimes people want to get assistance with a work overload or difficult situation. Do you ever feel the need for assistance?

1. Yes
2. No
8. Don't know
9. Refused

BWRKASSISa In these situations, how often do you receive assistance from your supervisor or manager?

1. Always
2. Sometimes
3. Never
7. Not applicable
8. Don't Know
9. Refused

BWRKASSISb In these situations, do you receive assistance from other co-workers?

1. Always
2. Sometimes
3. Never
8. Don't know
9. Refused

relatively high response rate in a voluntary survey are the use of register data and the piggy-backing on the CIS and ICT survey, which limited the time of the interviews to 15–20 minutes. The availability of additional information from these databases allowed an in-depth analysis of the non-response, showing that there are no large differences in productivity, innovation and ICT use for the non-responding group of firms compared to the responding group, which confirms the quality of the data.

The main results of the survey were published in a collective volume entitled *Learning Organisations Matter* (Statistics Sweden 2011). Here, selected results are summarized to show how the information from a MEADOW employer survey can be used to characterize learning forms of organization. Learning organizations are those that are able to adapt and compete through learning. Most of the research sees the learning organization as a multi-level concept and defines learning organizations in terms of the interrelations of managerial practices, team organization and individual behaviour. Three composite indices were constructed from the survey results in order to capture key characteristics of learning organizations: decentralization, individual learning and structural learning. They are based on questions about the way the firm operates at the date of the survey, in 2009. Each index sums a varying number of questions with different item responses in a standardized way so that it takes values between 0 and 1.

The decentralization index is based on five of the questions on organizational structure and coordination displayed in Box 10.1: B1HIE on the number of hierarchical layers, B1STRUCT on the planning of daily tasks, B1DLGQLT on quality monitoring, B1TEAMPER on the proportion of employees working in autonomous teams and B1DLGSCHDPER on the flexibility of hours worked per day. An index close to 1 indicates a high level of decentralization for operational decisions, structured around autonomous teams.

Box 10.3 presents the questions related to individual learning. This index tries to capture the importance of continuous learning at the individual level. It includes both formal and informal learning activities. Two questions in this list are specific to the Swedish MEADOW survey: the one on competence development and the one on non-paid time off the job for training purposes.

The index of structural learning measures activities that aim to develop knowledge in a systematically organized way (Box 10.4). Employee participation in continuous improvement (B1CIRCLE) as well as regular meetings between the line managers and the workers they are responsible for (CBRFANY) contribute to a learning culture where all employees play a part in knowledge development around daily activities. Technological

BOX 10.3   EMPLOYER-LEVEL QUESTIONS FOR INDIVIDUAL LEARNING

Is competence development part of the normal everyday work?
1. Yes
2. No

CTRNONPC What proportion of employees have received on the job training over the past 12 months?
1. Up to 24%
2. 25% to 49%
3. 50% to 74%
4. 75% or more

CAPPPC Approximately what proportion of your employees have a performance appraisal or evaluation interview at least once a year?
1. None
2. 1 % to 24%
3. 25% to 49%
4. 50% or more

CTRNOFFPC What proportion of employees have been given paid time off from their work to undertake training in the past 12 months?
1. Up to 24%
2. 25% to 49%
3. 50% to 74%
4. 75% or more

What proportion of employees have been given non-paid time off from their work to undertake training in the past 12 months?
1. Up to 24%
2. 25% to 49%
3. 50% to 74%
4. 75% or more

BOX 10.4 EMPLOYER-LEVEL QUESTIONS FOR STRUCTURAL LEARNING

B1CIRCLE What percentage of employees at this firm currently participates in groups who meet regularly to think about improvements that could be made within this workplace?
1. Up to 24%
2. 25% to 49%
3. 50% to 74%
4. 75% or more

CBRFANY How often do you have meetings between line managers or supervisors and all the workers for whom they are responsible?
1. Every day
2. At least once a week
3. At least once a month
4. At least once a year
5. Never

B2QUAL Does this firm monitor the quality of its production processes or service delivery?
1. Yes, on a continuous basis
2. Yes, on an intermittent basis
3. No
4. Not relevant

B2KMBASE Do employees in this firm regularly update databases that document good work practices of lessons learned?
1. Yes
2. No
3. Not relevant

B2KMEX Does this firm monitor external ideas or technological developments for new or improved products, processes or services?
1. Yes, using staff assigned specifically to this task
2. Yes, as part of the responsibilities of general staff
3. No

B2CUSAT Does this firm monitor customer satisfaction through questionnaires, focus groups, analysis of complaints, or other methods?
1. Yes, on a regular basis
2. Yes, but infrequently
3. No

intelligence through quality monitoring (B2QUAL), internal and external knowledge management practices (B2KMBASE, B2KMEX), as well as customer orientation (B2CUSAT) contribute to strengthening the knowledge base of the firm.

Decentralization, individual and structural learning are positively correlated with one another, suggesting that they represent complementary dimensions of a model of learning organization.

The three learning organization indices are then correlated with measures of innovation from the CIS survey, with the classic distinctions between product, process, organizational and marketing innovations (Table 10.1). All coefficients are positive, and the highest correlations relate the different types of innovation with the individual learning index.

These results are still tentative and need more in-depth analysis, but they are promising and show that a MEADOW survey allows capturing some important organizational features that are conducive to more innovativeness. These characteristics combine work organization practices,

Table 10.1   *Learning organization indexes and innovation: Pearson correlation coefficients*

	Mean (std)	Product innovation	Process innovation	Organizational innovation	Marketing innovation
Decentralization	0.43 (0.23)	0.13	0.13	0.13	0.09
Individual learning	0.64 (0.33)	0.18	0.16	0.22	0.11
Structural learning	0.73 (0.17)	0.11	0.17	0.10	ns

Note: All correlation coefficients are significant at the 1% level; ns means not significant at the 10% level.

Source: Statistics Sweden (2011).

human resource management and supportive technologies. Moreover, the structure of the survey that links information collected at the employer and employee levels creates new opportunities for investigating economic performance as well as quality of working life issues that are key to achieving the EU 2020 objectives of smart, sustainable and inclusive growth in ageing economies. It is hoped that the MEADOW linked employer–employee surveys that have been administered in Norway in 2011 and in Denmark and Finland in 2012 will contribute to demonstrate the usefulness of such a survey instrument to guide evidence-based policies for firms as well as for administrations and governments.

NOTES

1. The MEADOW Guidelines are a collective effort. In addition to the core consortium members responsible for the drafting of the Guidelines, the project benefited from the assistance of a large number of external contributors. A complete list of the consortium team members and external contributors is provided in the Appendix.
2. For an overview of the literature on the relation between organizational structure and innovation, see Lam (2004).
3. The cognitive testing was coordinated by Anthony Arundel and Adriana van Cruysen from UNU-MERIT in the Netherlands. For a detailed presentation of the cognitive tests, see the synthesis report in the Annex to the MEADOW Guidelines (MEADOW Consortium 2010).
4. The Swedish employer-level survey was undertaken at the initiative of Hans-Olof Hagén, Statistics Sweden. See Statistics Sweden (2011).
5. Work on the measurement framework, including the overview of major theories, was coordinated by the team from the University of Aalborg, Denmark, under the leadership of Peter Nielsen.
6. This survey could provide the primary sampling units for a linked employer–employee survey at the European level.
7. For a discussion of the availability of registers of employers and employees in EU member countries that might serve as sampling frames for surveys in which either the employer or employee comprises the primary sampling unit, see the Guidelines (MEADOW Consortium 2010, ch. 7). Work on survey methodologies, including sampling, was coordinated by John Forth from the National Institute of Economic and Social Research in the UK.
8. For a discussion of mixed-household enterprise surveys, see OECD (2002) and Asian Development Bank (2011).
9. Moser and Kalton (1971) refer to these dual problems. They noted that 'recall loss' or 'omission' is likely to be greater if the recall period is longer, while the telescoping effect can be greater for shorter recall periods. They identify diary methods as an approach that has been used in surveys of individuals to address the problem of recall loss. Another approach is bounded recall, where the respondent is reminded of some information concerning the previous period, but in this case additional panel information is needed.
10. Statistics Canada implemented an ambitious linked employer–employee frame, the Workplace and Employee Survey (WES), where establishments were followed in a panel and employees were followed for two years. Three waves were carried out, in 1999, 2001 and 2005 respectively (see Statistics Canada 2008).
11. However, attrition does not necessarily imply a bias. It depends on who falls out and whether their characteristics are correlated with the behaviour one wants to observe.

For example, in its long labour supply and demand panels in the Netherlands, the Institute for Labour Studies (OSA) has not found that attrition has been concentrated in specific size groups or sectors.

12. Regarding the follow-up period between the waves, it is important to find a balance. It should not be too short (e.g. one or two years) since such regular observations are not required to measure organizational changes. Moreover, such an option would be costly and lead to practical difficulties and an extra burden for companies. However, a low frequency (e.g. six or eight years) is not practical either since it would probably lead to important attrition biases (one might encounter major difficulties in tracing employers, and even more so in tracing employees). It would also leave part of the timeline unobserved and the data would suffer from the obsolescence of a large fraction of the questions.

13. The drafting of the employer questionnaire was coordinated by Amelia Román of the Institute for Labour Studies (OSA), The Netherlands. The drafting of the employee questionnaire was coordinated by Francis Green of the University of Kent in the UK. For downloadable versions of the core English questionnaires and translations into the seven other languages represented by the MEADOW Consortium, see http://www.meadow-project.eu/index.php?option=com_content&task=view&id=25&Itemid=41.

REFERENCES

Abrahamson, E. and G. Fairchild (1999), 'Management fashion: lifecycles, triggers, and collective learning processes', *Administrative Science Quarterly*, **44**(4), 708–40.

Asian Development Bank (2011), *A Handbook on Using the Mixed Survey for Measuring Informal Employment and the Informal Sector*, Manila, Philippines: Asian Development Bank.

Desai, T. (2008), 'Development of linked and panel datasets for European labour market and social policy analysis', in D. Marsden (co-ord.), (2008), *Study and Conference on European Labour Market Analysis using Firm-level Panel Data and Linked Employer–Employee Data*, Final Report, March, Project for the European Commission DG Employment, Contract N. VT/2006/0046, Brussels: European Commission.

Eurostat (2006), *Structure of Earnings Survey 2002*, Unit F2 Quality Report, May, Luxembourg: Eurostat.

Eurostat (2009), *Structure of Earnings Survey (SES) 2006 – Synthesis of Quality Reports*, Unit F2, Luxembourg: Eurostat.

Forth, J. (2008), 'Methods for longitudinal panel surveys', in *Methodological Review of Research with Large Businesses*, Paper 6, Prepared for HM Revenue and Customs, London: HM Revenue and Customs.

Freitas, I.M.B. (2008), 'Sources of differences in the pattern of adoption of organisational and managerial innovations from early to late 1990s in the UK', *Research Policy*, **37**, 131–48.

Garvin, D.A. (2003), *Learning in Action. A Guide to Putting the Learning Organization to Work*, Boston, MA: Harvard Business School Press.

Greenan, N. and N. Lorenz (2010), *Innovative Workplaces. Making better use of skills within organizations*, Paris: OECD. http://dx.doi.org/9789264095687-en.

Ichniowski, C., K. Shaw and G. Prennushi (1997), 'The effects of human resource management policies on productivity: a study of steel finishing lines', *American Economic Review*, **87**(3), 291–313.

Jensen, M., B. Johnson, E. Lorenz and B.-Å. Lundvall (2007), 'Forms of knowledge and modes of innovation', *Research Policy*, **36**, 680–93.

Lam, A. (2004), 'Organisational innovation', in J. Fagerberg, D. Mowery and R. Nelson (eds), *The Oxford Handbook of Innovation*, Oxford: Oxford University Press, pp. 115–47.

Laursen, K. and V. Mahnke (2001), 'Knowledge strategies, firm types, and complementarity in human-resource practices', *Journal of Management and Governance*, **5**(1), 1–27.

Leombruni, R. (2003), *Firm Data Analysis in Linked Employer–Employees Datasets*, available at SSRN: http://ssrn.com/abstract=886683 or http://dx.doi.org/10.2139/ssrn.886683.

Lorenz, E., J. Michie and F. Wilkinson (2004), 'HRM complementarities and innovative performance in British and French industry', in J.L. Christensen and B.-Å. Lundvall (eds), *Product Innovation, Interactive Learning and Economic Performance*, Amsterdam: Elsevier, pp. 181–210.

MEADOW Consortium (2010), *The MEADOW Guidelines*, Project funded within the 6th Framework Programme of the European Commission's DG Research, Grigny: France, http://www.meadow-project.eu/index.php?/Article-du-site/Guidelines.html.

Michie, J. and M. Sheehan (1999), 'HRM practices, R&D expenditure and innovative investment: evidence from the UK's 1990 Workplace Industrial Relations Survey', *Industrial and Corporate Change*, **8**(2), 211–34.

Mintzberg, H. (1979), *The Structuring of Organisations*, Englewood Cliffs, NJ: Prentice-Hall.

Moser, C. and G. Kalton (1971), *Survey Methods in Social Investigation*, 2nd edn, London: Heinemann.

Nielsen, P., R. Lund, B.-Å. Lundvall, A.N. Gjerding, R.N. Nielsen, J.G. Rasmussen, A.D. Hesselholdt, C. Makó, M. Illéssy, P. Csizmadia, A. Härenstam, E. Bejerot, O. Som, E. Kirner, R. Huys, N. Lazaric and A. Coutts (2008a), 'Multi-level theoretical framework, theoretical key elements and interactions reflected in data collection on organisational change, innovation and work conditions', MEADOW background document, No. 1, http://www.meadow-project.eu/images/docmeadow/backdocument_mtf.pdf.

Nielsen, P., R.N. Nielsen, R. Lund, B.-Å. Lundvall, J.G. Rasmussen, A.N. Gjerding and A. Hesselholdt (2008b), 'Grid report, state of the art in surveys on organisational change', MEADOW background document, No. 2. http://www.meadow-project.eu/images/doc meadow/back_gridreport.pdf.

OECD (2002), *Measuring the Non-Observed Economy, A Handbook*, Paris: OECD.

OECD (2003), *Measuring Knowledge Management in the Business Sector: First Steps*, Paris: OECD.

OECD/Eurostat (2005), *Oslo Manual: Guidelines for Collecting and Interpreting Innovation Data*, Paris: OECD.

Senge, P. (1990), *The Fifth Discipline: The Art and Practice of the Learning Organization*, New York: Doubleday Currency.

Statistics Canada (2008*)*, *Workplace and Employee Survey Compendium 2005*, September, Ottawa: Statistics Canada, http://publications.gc.ca/Collection/Statcan/71-585-X/71-585-XIE.html.

Statistics Sweden (2011), *Learning Organisations Matter*, Stockholm: Statistics Sweden, http://www.scb.se/statistik/_publikationer/NR9999_2011A01_BR_NRFT1101.pdf.

Womack, J. P. and D.T. Jones (2003), *Lean Thinking. Banish Waste and Create Wealth in Your Corporation*, New York: Free Press.

APPENDIX: MEADOW CONSORTIUM AND EXTERNAL CONTRIBUTORS

MEADOW Consortium

Centre d'Etudes de l'Emploi (CEE), France
Research Unit: Dynamics of Organisations and Work
EU Project coordinator and team leader: Nathalie Greenan

Thomas Amossé
Sophie Bressé
Danièle Guillemot
Sylvie Hamon-Cholet
Jenny Koutsomarkou
Samira Ouchhi

Université de Nice Sophia Antipolis (UNSA), France
Project coordinator and team leader: Edward Lorenz

Adam Coutts (University of Cambridge)
Nathalie Lazaric
Fabrice Le Guel
Rakhi Rashmi

Aalborg Universitet (AAU), Denmark
Department of Economics, Politics and Public Administration
Team leader: Peter Nielsen

Bengt-Åke Lundvall
Anders Hesselholdt
Jørgen Gulddahl Rasmussen
Allan Naes Gjerding

Katholieke Universiteit Leuven (KU LEUVEN), Belgium
Team leader: Monique Ramioul

Rik Huys

Bundesagentur für Arbeit, Institut für Arbeitsmarkt- und Berufsforschung (IAB), Germany
Team leader: Lutz Bellmann

André Pahnke

Fraunhofer Institute for Systems and Innovation Research (ISI), Germany
Industrial and Service Innovations
Team leader: Eva Kirner

Oliver Som

Szociologiai Kutatointézete/Institute of Sociology of the Hungarian Academy of Sciences (ISB), Department: Research Group of Organization and Work, Hungary

Italian National Research Council (CNR), Italy
Institute on Population and Social Policy (IRPPS)
Team leader: Daniele Archiburgi

Team leader: Prof. Csaba Mako

Miklos Illéssy
Peter Csizmadia

Giorgio Sirilli
Stefano Sirilli

Maastricht Universiteit (UNU-MERIT), The Netherlands
Team leader: Anthony Arundel

Adriana van Cruysen

Institute for Labour Studies (OSA), The Netherlands
Labour market research department
Team leader: Amelia Román

Nederlandse organisatie voor toegepast natuurwetenschappelijk onderzoek (TNO) TNO Quality of life: Work and Employment, The Netherlands
Team leader: Karolus Kraan

Irene Houtman
Ernest de Vroome

University of Gothenburg (UGOT)- Sweden
Department of Work Science
Team leader: Annika Härenstam

Eva Bejerot

National Institute of Economic and Social Research (NIESR), UK
Team leader: John Forth

University of Kent (UKENT), UK
Economics Department
Team leader: Prof. Francis Green

Stephen Allan

External contributors

Eurostat
Bernard Felix
Veijo-Ismo Ritola

Organisation for Economic Cooperation and Development (OECD)
Alessandra Colecchia

NORC, University of Chicago and National Science Foundation (USA)
Julia Lane

Adviser European Affairs
Johan van Rens

University of Warwick (UK)
Peter Elias

European Foundation for the Improvement of Living and Working Conditions (EFILWC)
Agnès Parent-Thirion
Greet Vermeylen

DG Employment, Social Affairs and Equal Opportunities, European Commission
Radek Maly
Joao Medeiros

Statistics Sweden (SCB), Sweden
Hans-Olof Hagén

The Swedish Hotel and Restaurant Association (SHR), Sweden
Anette Nylund

Italian National Statistical Office (ISTAT), Italy
Giulio Perani

French Ministry of Employment – DARES, France
Elisabeth Algava
Thomas Coutrot

Institute of Labour and Social Studies, Poland
Lukasz Sienkiewicz

Faculty of Management, Comenius University, Slovak Republic
Lubica Bajzikova

S&T Statistics Department, National Research Center for Science and Technology for Development, China
Gao Changlin

European Agency for Safety and Health at work (OSHA), Spain
William Cockburn

Hungarian Central Statistical Office (HCSO), Hungary
Judith Lakatos

11 Scoreboards and indicator reports
Hugo Hollanders and Norbert Janz

1. INTRODUCTION

Innovation scoreboards are an attempt to summarize innovation indicators and to compare innovation performance of countries, regions or sectors. Although they are becoming more and more popular and relevant for policy making, there still seems to be no standard definition of a scoreboard. Do scoreboards include rankings by several and/or single (composite) indicators? Do they include profiles of countries or regions? Do they include benchmarking against the average, best practice and/or others?

In this chapter the term scoreboard is used in a very broad sense and includes international comparative reports that do not use the term. Similar to the review of innovation scoreboards by Arundel and Hollanders (2008), we do not restrict the comparison to innovation scoreboards and reports, but include more general international reports, especially competitiveness reports, if they include an important innovation dimension. This survey partly updates the information collected in Arundel and Hollanders (2008) as well as in Weissenberger-Eibl et al. (2011), but using the perspective of innovation surveys and illustrating how innovation surveys are used (or not used) in selected reports.

This chapter is structured as follows. In Section 2 the most prominent innovation scoreboards and international innovation indicator reports are presented: the *Innovation Union Scoreboard* (formerly *European Innovation Scoreboard*), the *OECD Science, Technology and Industry Scoreboard* as well as the *OECD Science, Technology and Industry Outlook* and INSEAD's *Global Innovation Index*. To these is added a recently modified German attempt, *Innovationsindikator*, because of its methodological approach.

Section 3 follows with more general reports including an important innovation dimension: the *Innovation Union Competitiveness Report*, the *European Competitiveness Report*, the World Economic Forum's *Global Competitiveness Report* as well as *Europe 2020 Competitiveness Report* and the *Atlantic Century* by ITIF in the USA and the European–American Business Council (Atkinson and Andes 2009, 2011).

For each scoreboard or report summarized in Table 11.1, there is a brief presentation of the approach, indicators and data sources. Comments

Table 11.1   Overview and summary of innovation scoreboards

Name	Short	Editing institution	Preparing institution	First edition	Latest edition	Frequency
Innovation Union Scoreboard (European Innovation Scoreboard)	IUS (EIS)	European Union	MERIT	2001	2011	Annual
OECD Science, Technology and Industry Scoreboard	STI Scoreboard	OECD	OECD	1991	2011	Biennial
OECD Science, Technology and Industry Outlook	STI Outlook	OECD	OECD	1998	2010	Biennial
Global Innovation Index	GII	INSEAD, WIPO	INSEAD, WIPO	2007	2012	Annual
Innovationsindikator	II	Telekom Stiftung, BDI	Fraunhofer ISI, ZEW, MERIT	2005	2011	Annual
Innovation Union Competitiveness Report	IUC	European Union	European Commission	2011	2011	Biennial
European Competitiveness Report	ECR	European Union	European Commission	1997	2011	Annual
Global Competitiveness Report	GCR	World Economic Forum	Centre for Global Competitiveness and Performance	1979	2011	Annual
Europe 2020 Competitiveness Report	E2020-CR	World Economic Forum	Global Competitive Network	2012	2012	Annual
Atlantic Century	ITIF-AC	ITIF, EABC	ITIF	2009	2011	Biennial
Knowledge Assessment Methodology	KAM	World Bank	World Bank	2001	2012	Regularly updated

Notes:
a. Country profiles.
b. Country fiches ECR 2009.

Source: Summary of the authors based on respective reports (see references).

Standard structure	Target countries	Number of indicators	thereof based on innovation surveys	Selection criteria	Composite indicator	Sensitivity analysis	Special feature
Yes	EU member states	25	6	Reasoning, correlation analysis	Yes	Yes (EIS)	Innovation growth performance interactive visualization tool
No	OECD member countries	~180	34	Reasoning	No		
No	OECD member countries	13[a]	3[a]	Not available	No		
Yes	World	84	None		Yes	Yes	Innovation efficiency index
Yes	Germany and selected European countries	38	None	Model, regression analysis	Yes	Yes	Regression model based
Unknown	EU member states	51	None		No		
No	EU member states	25[b]	2[b]	Depending on focus	No		
Yes	World	117	None		Yes		
Yes	EU member states	65	None		Yes		
Yes	USA	16	None	Reasoning	Yes		
Yes	World	148	None		Yes		Interactive visualization tool

follow on the usage of innovation surveys as well as on special features, strengths and weaknesses with respect to reports on innovation. Recent attempts to improve scoreboards by providing interactive tools are presented in Section 4. A general comparison as well as a general outlook is given in the final section.

2.   INNOVATION SCOREBOARDS AND INTERNATIONAL INNOVATION REPORTS

Innovation Union Scoreboard/European Innovation Scoreboard

The vision of an innovation union as part of the EU was announced and communicated by the European Commission in 2010 as a strategic approach to tackle the challenges of the rapidly changing global economy (EC 2010a). *The Innovation Union Scoreboard* (*IUS*) as a performance scoreboard for research and innovation is part of the monitoring system of the European Commission included in the resulting agenda and task list.

Results of the first IUS were published in 2011 (EC 2011a). The annual *IUS* is based on and closely related to the previous *European Innovation Scoreboard* (*EIS*) dating back to 2000 (EC 2001). The *EIS* started with a set of 17 indicators covering at that time 15 member states of the EU. From the very beginning, benchmarking EU member countries against major global competitors such as the USA and Japan was an integral part of the EIS concept.

Thus the most recent second edition of the *IUS* (EC 2012) is in fact the eleventh edition. If the first outline (EC 2000) is included, twelfth. Using a set of 25 indicators predefined in the EC communication announcing the Innovation Union (EC 2010b), the *IUS* defines three main groups of indicators divided into a total of eight innovation dimensions: Enablers (with dimensions Human resources, Research systems and Finance & support), Firm activities (Firm investments, Linkages & entrepreneurship, Intellectual assets) and Outputs (Innovators, Economic effects).

Four of these dimensions make use of six indicators based on innovation surveys (EC 2012: figure 1 and annex C). These indicators mainly refer to small and medium-sized enterprises (SMEs) as the target population (see Table 11.2) and provide a better picture of the innovative status of SMEs than business R&D. Separate data for SMEs are worthwhile because they form the majority of firms in most countries and can play a vital role in innovation, for example as developers of new ideas and as adopters of new technologies. Innovation-survey-based indicators are accompanied by indicators based on R&D surveys, patent statistics, publication statistics,

Table 11.2   Use of innovation-survey-based indicators in a selected number of innovation scoreboards

	IUS	STI Score	STI Outlook
Recent edition	2011	2011	2010
Innovation-survey-based indicators			
Technological innovation	Yes	Yes	Yes
Non-technological innovation	Yes	Yes	Yes
In-house innovation	Yes		
Innovation expenditure	Yes		
Sales with product innovation	Yes		
R&D in innovation		Yes	
Training for innovation		Yes	
Public support for innovation		Yes	
Collaboration for innovation	Yes	Yes	Yes
Sources of knowledge for innovation		Yes	
Main reference groups			
All firms			Yes
Innovative firms		Yes	
All SMEs	Yes		

Source: Authors.

population statistics and export data, among others. Eurostat provides the main data source, supplemented by sources of the OECD, of UN institutions and of a few others (EC 2012: annex C).

Focusing on a set of well-defined 24 indicators, the IUS provides a ranking of countries using composite indicators at differing levels of aggregation (see Table 11.3). The results are used to identify four groups of countries: Innovation leaders (ranks 1 to 4 in Table 11.3), Innovation followers (ranks 5 to 14), Moderate innovators (ranks 15 to 23) and Modest innovators (ranks 24 to 27) among the EU-27 (EC 2012: ch. 3). These countries as well as the EU average are compared to and benchmarked against global competitors (EC 2012: ch. 4).

Performance rankings and benchmarks are supplemented by country profiles highlighting their relative strengths and weaknesses in innovation performance (EC 2012: ch. 5). As a special feature, the use of a limited set of indicators, relatively stable over time, allows the calculation of innovation growth performance. Adding this dynamic dimension of innovation performance leads to another category grouping countries into Growth leaders, Moderate growers and Slow growers (EC 2012: ch. 3 and technical annex).

Table 11.3 Ranking of EU-27 member countries in innovation scoreboards

	IUS 2011	GII 2011–12	GCR 2011–12	E2020CR 2012	II 2011	ITIF-AC 2011	KAM 2012
Sweden	1	1	1	1	1	2	1
Denmark	2	5	5	3	7	4	3
Germany	3	8	3	6	2	9	5
Finland	4	2	2	2	3	1	2
Belgium	5	11	7	9	6	6	8
UK	6	3	6	7	9	3	7
Netherlands	7	4	4	4	4	5	4
Austria	8	12	9	5	5	10	9
Luxembourg	9	7	10	8	–	–	11
Ireland	10	6	11	12	10	8	6
France	11	13	8	10	8	7	13
Slovenia	12	14	22	13	–	15	16
Cyprus	13	16	19	17	–	20	22
Estonia	14	10	12	11	–	12	10
Italy	15	21	16	21	12	18	17
Portugal	16	20	18	14	–	15	21
Czech Republic	17	15	14	16	–	11	14
Spain	18	17	13	15	11	14	12
Hungary	19	19	20	24	–	13	15
Greece	20	27	27	25	–	22	23
Malta	21	9	21	18	–	–	18
Slovakia	22	23	24	22	–	16	20
Poland	23	25	15	23	–	21	25
Romania	24	26	26	26	–	–	26
Lithuania	25	22	17	20	–	19	19
Bulgaria	26	24	25	27	–	–	27
Latvia	27	18	23	19	–	17	24

Source: Authors.

The set of indicators used in the *IUS* is a reduced set of the indicators used in the latest EIS based on 'rational reasoning' (Hollanders and Tarantola 2011). The selection of indicators for the EIS is based on various statistical correlation analyses (EC 2003). Composite indicators are calculated as the unweighted average of rescaled scores of all indicators contained in the composite indicator. Rescaling includes normalization as well as transformation of skewed data (EC 2011a: technical annex). Sensitivity analyses of differing weighting schemes have been produced for the preceding *EIS* (EC 2003). Growth performance is calculated as the geometric average of outlier-adjusted indicator growth rates (EC 2012: technical annex).

The relatively stable and clearly arranged set of indicators avoiding redundancies is the main advantage of the IUS. Moreover, the IUS relies on high-quality established data sets including innovation surveys following the *Oslo Manual* (OECD/Eurostat 2005). Relatively reliable analysis, comparisons and benchmarks including dynamic dimensions are the result. Because of demanding data requirements, possibilities of comparisons with countries outside EU and OECD are limited.

OECD *STI Scoreboard* and OECD *STI Outlook*

On a biennial basis the OECD publishes its broad *Science, Technology and Industry (STI) Scoreboard* alternating with its *Science, Technology and Industry (STI) Outlook*. The most recent, eleventh, *STI Scoreboard* (2011) makes use of some 180 indicators to illustrate and analyse trends in innovation performance of countries (OECD 2011: executive summary).

In contrast to the *Innovation Union Scoreboard (IUS)*, the *STI Scoreboard* does not rank or benchmark country performance using composite indicators. Nevertheless, using graphical presentation, the *STI Scoreboard* ranks countries with respect to several innovation dimensions relevant for policy decision making. Analyses in the *STI Scoreboard 2011* are summarized in five thematic chapters: Building knowledge, Connecting to knowledge, Targeting new growth areas, Unleashing innovation in firms and Competing in the global economy (OECD 2011: executive summary). Four of the five thematic chapters make use of a total of 34 indicators based on innovation surveys. They are most prominently used in 'Connecting to knowledge' and 'Unleashing innovation in firms' (OECD 2011: chs 3 and 5). Compared to the *IUS*, these indicators have a different target population: mostly innovative firms, including large firms and SMEs. They have a strong focus on interactions within the innovation system and less on innovation output and outcome (see Table 11.2). Thus there is only very limited overlap with the *IUS*.

Other indicators used in the *STI Scoreboard* are based on R&D, education, occupation, employment and trade data as well as on specialized information, for example biotechnology, health innovation or broadband data. In addition to OECD and Eurostat, sources from, among others, the International Monetary Fund (IMF), the World Bank, different patent offices and the International Labour Organization (ILO) are used (OECD 2011: data sources). The very broad set of indicators is used to compare the 20 founding and thereafter 14 joining OECD member countries with each other and with invited (Russia) and cooperating countries, especially South East Asian countries, resulting in up to 59 countries (OECD 2011: reader's guide). The selection of indicators is based on reasoning, with policy relevance as a factor (OECD 2011, foreword).

Published in years when the *STI Scoreboard* is not, the *STI Outlook* supplements the *STI Scoreboard*, especially with country profiles of the OECD member countries. The most recent eighth edition, *STI Outlook 2010*, applies a set of 13 indicators to benchmark them against the OECD average. Three of these indicators are based on innovation surveys (OECD 2010: table 3.A1.3). Again the target population is different: all firms (see Table 11.2). Thus these indicators show little overlap with the *IUS* or even with the *STI Scoreboard*.

In most parts of the *STI Outlook* aggregates of countries, for example eurozone countries, EU-27 or OECD countries, are compared to Japan and the USA. If possible, developments over time are presented. Time series of indicators based on innovation surveys are rarely available. In consequence, only a few of these indicators are used and mostly for illustrative purposes. Referring to indicators, the *STI Outlook* has a less stringent approach than the *STI Scoreboard* and is more focused on the comparison of innovation policies.

The strength of OECD's *STI Scoreboard* is the combination of a complete coverage of developed economies with the use of a broad set of high-quality data stemming mainly from statistical institutions in charge of the official statistics for the topic under consideration. Among existing scoreboards it uses the largest number of indicators based on innovation surveys. However, reports on single indicators are only loosely connected, hampering the development of a comprehensive view. This is partly overcome by the accompanying *STI Outlook*, which, however, is not very closely connected to the indicators presented in the *STI Scoreboard*.

Global Innovation Index

The annual *Global Innovation Index* published by INSEAD and WIPO started with a pilot study in 2007 (Dutta and Caulkin 2007) before its regular introduction with its second edition in 2009 (INSEAD 2009). The most recent fifth edition, *Global Innovation Index 2012*, is a joint report of INSEAD and the World Intellectual Property Organization (Dutta 2012).

The *Global Innovation Index* (*GII*) covers the largest number of countries of all existing innovation scoreboards. The recent *GII 2012* has accomplished an innovation ranking of 141 countries, from Switzerland and Sweden as the top-ranked to Niger and Sudan as the bottom-ranked countries (see Table 11.3 for ranking of EU members). The *GII 2012* ranking is based on a hierarchy of two sub-indexes, seven pillars and 21 sub-pillars utilizing a total number of 84 indicators (Benavente et al. 2012). Rankings for the two sub-indexes, the Innovation Input Sub-Index and the Innovation Output Sub-Index, are provided, too.

The two sub-indexes have the same weight in the creation of the *GII*, although the Innovation Output Sub-Index is based on only two pillars (Knowledge and Technology Outputs and Creative Outputs) with six sub-pillars and 25 indicators. The Innovation Input Sub-Index is based on five pillars (Institutions, Human Capital and Research, Infrastructure, Market Sophistication, Business Sophistication). Scores for sub-indexes, pillars and sub-pillars are calculated as weighted averages of the score of the next lower level (Dutta 2012: appendix IV).

In addition to the *GII*, an Innovation Efficiency Index as a ratio of the Innovation Output Sub-Index to the Innovation Input Sub-Index is created. This is a unique feature compared to other innovation scoreboards. Rankings are provided by pillars, sub-pillars and each single index. Indicators used for the *GII* change over time (Benavente et al. 2012). Rankings are accompanied by country profiles (Dutta 2012: appendix I). Using statistical methods, the impact of weighting schemes as well as modelling assumptions referring to, for example, missing values on index scores and the resulting ranking are extensively analysed (Saisana and Philippas 2012).

A large variety of indicators and data sources is used: from the World Bank's Political Stability and Absence of Violence/Terrorism Index to electricity consumption provided by the International Energy Agency to the number of videos uploaded on YouTube provided by Google. The majority of indicators are collected from publications of international institutions such as UNESCO, the OECD, the World Bank or the IMF.

None of the 84 indicators used is actually based on innovations surveys. Indicators close to the innovation-survey-based indicators mentioned above, such as R&D collaboration between universities and industry as part of the pillar Business Sophistication, are based on the Executive Opinion Survey of the World Economic Forum (Dutta 2012, appendix III). Thus there is little overlap of the *GII* with the IUS or OECD's STI

Scoreboard and Outlook, but more with the *Global Competiveness Report* (see Section 3, subsection on the *Global Competitiveness Report* and the *Europe 2020 Competitiveness Report*).

Using OECD and Eurostat sources, selected information from innovation surveys is used for additional illustration and the investigation of special aspects of the *GII*, such as indicators on collaboration for innovation (Wunsch-Vincent 2012) or on innovation expenditure (Gokhberg and Roud 2012).

The large number of countries covered by the *GII* is both its strength and weakness. Availability of reliable data on innovation activities and innovative performance is limited. Thus the *GII* has to rely on opinion survey data where cross-country comparability is questionable and answers reflect perception and satisfaction more than expectation. Comparison of opinion survey with innovation survey data for those countries where both are available would be helpful for decision makers.

Innovationsindikator (Innovation Indicator)

The project Innovationsindikator (German for innovation indicator, but combined into one word) started in 2005 as a joint attempt of Deutsche Telekom Stiftung (a German corporate foundation dealing with telecommunication services) and BDI (the Federation of German Industries representing mainly manufacturing firms). In 2011, the project was fundamentally restructured and prepared in an international collaboration of three research institutes: Fraunhofer ISI, UNU-MERIT and ZEW Centre for European Economic Research (Schubert et al. 2011).

The Innovationsindikator 2011 uses a set of 38 indicators to benchmark Germany against 11 other EU member countries and another 14 international competitors of advanced and emerging economies. The selection of indicators is based on the socioeconomic model of Systems of Innovation where the specific variables used were selected by using econometric regression models. The composite indicator was created as the unweighted mean of standardized indicators. Simulation analyses using random weights are used to analyse the sensitivity of the composite indicator and the resulting ranking (Schubert et al. 2011).

Following the innovation system approach, the indicators are grouped into five subsystems: Education (consisting of nine indicators), Society (four indicators), State (eight indicators), Enterprises (16 indicators) and Public research (eight indicators). Some of the indicators are also used in differing subsystems. None of these indicators is based on innovation surveys. In fact, none of the indicators is close to information collected in innovation surveys.

Table 11.4   *Rank correlations of EU-27 member countries' ranking in innovation scoreboards*

	IUS 2011	GII 2011–12	GCR 2011–12	E2020CR 2012	II 2011	ITIF-AC 2011	KAM 2012
IUS 2011	1	0.84	0.87	0.91	0.78	0.84	0.90
GII 2011–12	0.84	1	0.84	0.91	0.63	0.92	0.90
GCI 2011–12	0.87	0.84	1	0.91	0.89	0.87	0.91
ECI2020 2012	0.91	0.91	0.91	1	0.85	0.89	0.91
II 2011	0.78	0.63	0.89	0.85	1	0.55	0.73
ITIF-AC 2011	0.84	0.92	0.87	0.89	0.55	1	0.93
KAM 2012	0.90	0.90	0.91	0.91	0.73	0.93	1.00

Source: Authors.

Most of the indicators are based on statistics published by international institutions such as the OECD, the World Bank, the European Patent Office or United Nations institutions. Seven of the 38 indicators are, like the Global Innovation Index, based on the World Economic Forum's Executive Opinion Survey (see previous section) and are thus open to criticism with respect to international comparability.

The main strength of the Innovationsindikator is its model-based and econometrically tested selection of variables. But the selection of variables is, like the Global Innovation Index, closer to competitiveness than to innovation. Because of this, Innovationsindikator shows the highest rank correlation with the Global Competitiveness Index (see Table 11.4). Moreover, innovation-survey-based variables on linkages within the innovation system are missing.

3. INNOVATION INDICATORS IN COMPETITIVE REPORTS

Innovation Union Competitiveness Report

The very first of the prospectively biennial *Innovation Union Competitiveness (IUC)* reports was published in 2011 by the European Commission under the guidance of the Directorate-General for Research and Innovation (EC 2011b). In contrast to the established *European Competitiveness Report* (see next subsection), the term competitiveness refers more to the competitiveness of the research and innovation system of a country than to that of the economy as a whole. The *IUC* report is meant to be an analytical strategic report building partly on the *Innovation Union Scoreboard* (*IUS*) and trying to identify causes for possibly insufficient performance (EC 2011b: executive summary).

The *IUC* report is a strongly indicator-based report. Each step of analysis is based upon an accurate investigation of relevant available indicators. The *IUC* report lists 51 indicators used to produce extended profiles of member and associated countries and to benchmark these countries and the total EU against its international competitors: the USA, Japan, China and South Korea. None of these indicators used for benchmarking is based on innovation surveys (EC 2011b: section II and annex).

But the introducing statement of the performance of the European research and innovation system directly refers to the results of the *IUS*, which intensively uses innovation-survey-based indicators (EC 2011b: overall picture). Subsequent detailed analysis uses only few innovation-survey-based indicators, such as extent and structure of innovation expenditure (EC 2011b: analysis part III). However, the overwhelming majority of indicators build on traditional indicators from R&D statistics, statistics on human resources devoted to science and technology, patent statistics accompanied by specialized information on, for example, university rankings and participation in EU framework programmes.

European Competitiveness Report

The *European Competitiveness Report* (*ECR*) is not an indicator-based report or scoreboard and follows an approach different to the *IUC* report (previous subsection). It is composed under the Directorate General for Enterprise and Industry of the European Commission. As an annual report starting in 1997, the *ECR* analyses the competitiveness of European industries with respect to recent economic trends and developments (EC 2011c: foreword).

The report does not follow a standardized structure every year. Utilization of innovation-survey-based indicators depends heavily on the main focuses of the particular report.

The *ECR 2010* in its section on Foreign Corporate R&D and Innovation in the European Union draws heavily on the results of the Community Innovation Survey, especially its German version the Mannheim Innovation Panel (EC 2010a: ch. 3; see Chapter 6 of this volume). The *ECR 2009* benchmarks member country performance to the EU average in its 'Microeconomic Data – Country Fiche'. From the 25 indicators used, two are based either directly or indirectly, through the IUS, on innovation surveys (EC 2009: ch. 6).

Other editions occasionally make use of innovation survey data. The most recent *ECR 2011* draws attention to eco-innovation using special questions of the European Community Innovation Survey 2008 (EC 2011c: ch. 5).

Global Competitiveness Report and *Europe 2020 Competitiveness Report*

In 1979 the World Economic Forum managed to establish the first acknowledged attempt of a worldwide comparison and benchmarking of countries' competiveness: the *Global Competitiveness Report* (*GCR*). The most recent *GCR 2011–12* (Schwab 2011) covers and ranks 142 countries.

Ranking in the *GCR 2011–12* is based on 117 indicators divided into 12 sections called 'pillars' (Schwab 2011: ch. 2.2). The twelfth pillar is called 'Innovation', but covers mainly aspects of R&D and patenting. Information that could be collected by innovation surveys is contained in the ninth pillar, 'Technological readiness' and the eleventh pillar, 'Business sophistication'. Actually, none of the indicators is based on innovation surveys.

Half of the 78 indicators are based on the World Economic Forum's 'Executive Opinion Survey' (Browne and Geiger 2011), especially nearly all variables on aspects of innovation. In the *GCR 2011–12*, indicators at the country level are calculated as a weighted average of the referring opinion surveys of 2010 and 2011 where the annual value of the variable is a sector-weighted average of individual responses assuming a four-sector economy.

Rankings are provided by the *GCI*, sub-indexes, pillars and indicators. Each composite indicator is calculated as a weighted average of the lower level indexes or indicators (Sala-i-Martin et al. 2011). Country profiles complete the *GCR*.

In 2012, the *GCR* was for the first time supplemented by the *Europe 2020 Competitiveness Report* (World Economic Forum 2012), a reduced version using 65 indicators and focusing on the EU member states, candidate countries and a few international competitors. The vast majority of 41 indicators are based on the above-mentioned opinion survey, especially the innovation-related indicators. None of the indicators is based on innovation surveys, although they would be available for the countries analysed. Based on the set of indicators grouped into seven pillars, a composite competitiveness index is calculated. Each pillar has the same weight in the composite competitiveness index although the number of variables contained differs. Additionally, three sub-indexes are produced (World Economic Forum 2012: appendix A). Rankings in the *Europe 2020 Competitiveness Report* are relatively highly correlated to all country rankings covered in this chapter (see Table 11.4), which complicates the identification of the value added.

The main weakness of both reports is the predominant reliance on opinion surveys where cross-country comparability is questionable (see Section 2, subsection on the Global Innovation Index).

The Atlantic Century

The Atlantic Century, published by the Information Technology and Innovation Foundation (ITIF) in cooperation with the European–American Business Council (EABC), claims to be an assessment of global innovation-based competitiveness and especially a benchmarking of the USA against its major global competitors. *The Atlantic Century II*, published in 2011, is the second edition of this relatively new approach (Atkinson and Andes 2011).

Competitiveness of the USA is benchmarked against 23 of the 27 EU member states, omitting the small member states Luxembourg and Malta as well as new member states Bulgaria and Romania (see Table 11.3). This is completed by benchmarks against EU aggregates EU-10, EU-15 and EU-25, as well as East Asian and Latin American competitors.

Analyses and benchmarks within the *Atlantic Century* are based on 16 indicators, which is the smallest number of indicators in the reports under consideration. The selection of indicators is based on 'rational reasoning' (Atkinson and Andes 2009, 2011). Scores of single indicators are standardized. The composite indicator is a weighted average of single indicators where weights depend on 'rational reasoning' (Atkinson and Andes 2009, 2011). Rankings are provided by both the composite indicator and each of the single indicators. The composite indicator is relatively highly correlated with the Global Competitiveness Index (see Table 11.4).

The main data sources are official statistics from international organizations such as the OECD, UNESCO and the World Bank. None of the 16 indicators is based on innovation surveys. Moreover, non-R&D innovation activities are only summarily covered.

4.   INTERACTIVE SOFTWARE TOOLS

Access to and use of innovation data can be improved by providing interactive benchmarking tools. The purpose of interactive tools is to allow users to explore data in further detail than possible in a written report or static Excel files. Such tools should be intuitive and easy to use. Two such interactive tools are the Knowledge Assessment Methodology (KAM) developed by the World Bank and the Innovation Union Scoreboard (IUS) Dashboard.

The Knowledge Assessment Methodology (KAM) measures the performance of countries in four Knowledge Economy pillars: 'Economic Incentive and Institutional Regime', 'Education', 'Innovation', and 'Information and Communications Technologies'. KAM uses data for 148 indicators for 146 countries and provides two summary indexes: the Knowledge Economy Index (KEI) and the Knowledge Index (KI). None of the 29 indicators used for measuring the innovation system uses innovation survey data; indicators used include R&D expenditures and researchers, royalty and licence fees, scientific publication, patents and exports. KAM does not provide a report, as do the scoreboards described in Sections 2 and 3, but it does provide users with a wide range of scorecards and other data visualization tools on its website.[1] The KAM interactive tool gives users the flexibility to construct their own personal country-to-country benchmarks and thereby greatly contributes to improving the accessibility to and use of innovation-related data. 'Basic scorecards' can be used to compare up to three countries on their performance on 12 key variables for 1995, 2000 and the most recent available year. 'Custom scorecards' can be used to compare up to three countries on any combination of the 148 indicators for 2000 and the most recent available year. 'Cross-country comparisons' provide bar-chart comparisons of KEI and KI indexes for up to 20 countries.

The Innovation Union Scoreboard (IUS) is supported by a visualization tool, the 'IUS Dashboard', providing an interactive user interface with four modules allowing customer-made comparisons of the data used in the *IUS 2011* report.[2] Yearly historical data back to 2007 are also included to study innovation performance over time.

The 'Overview module' provides a comparison of the performance on each of the IUS innovation dimensions and indicators, showing current performance, performance over a five-year time period and a direct comparison of any pair of European countries. The tool encourages interactive exploration and provides different options for the user to change the content of the display. The 'Country profile module' provides detailed information for each country and shows the performance relative to EU-27 performance for each of the indicators and their time trends. The 'Compare profiles module' provides a direct comparison using spider diagrams between any two European countries on their current and growth performance. The 'Scatter plots module' provides direct comparisons between each pair of indicators showing the correlation between these indicators.

5.   COMPARISON AND GENERAL OUTLOOK

Selection of Indicators

Arundel and Hollanders (2008: 33) identified four criteria for the selection of indicators: '1) the indicators should be of similar importance as measures of the drivers of innovative activity; 2) the indicators should be based on reliable statistics; 3) the indicators should hold their value over time; and 4) the indicators should be of relevance to medium and long-term policy issues'.

An innovation scoreboard should capture different types of indicators using both so-called hard statistical data and softer survey data, but hardly any indicator will meet all four criteria. Indicators that are relevant for policy issues require recent data, whereas reliable statistics using non-survey data usually become available with at least a two- to three-year lag. Opinion-survey-based data can be less reliable due to differences in perceptions between respondents in different countries and industries. Innovation survey data are more reliable than opinion survey data and should be included for two reasons (Arundel and Hollanders 2008): they can signal relevant areas for innovation and as such trigger policy support for future improvements in data quality; and, due to a lack of hard data for many aspects of innovation, it might be better to include data perceived to be of lesser quality than no data at all, in particular for measuring the outputs of innovation.

Innovation Output Indicators

One of the main purposes of an innovation scoreboard is to measure the innovation performance of countries, regions or sectors. Performance is directly related to measuring outputs or the results of innovation. Indicators measuring inputs such as R&D expenditure or throughputs such as patents are relevant but not sufficient for measuring innovation performance. In addition, scoreboards need to include indicators capturing the success of innovation. Edquist and Zabala (2009: box 1) identify possible output indicators using innovation survey data from the CIS. Their list can be revised taking into account changes in more recent versions of the CIS (see Table 11.5) capturing shares of enterprises with different types of innovation distinguishing between more incremental (product innovations new to the innovating firm) and radical innovations (product innovations new to the innovating firm's market) and sales due to incremental and radical product innovations. Innovation output indicators are not included in the competitiveness reports including an

Table 11.5   Innovation output indicators using innovation survey data

---

Enterprises with product innovation (% relative to all enterprises)
Enterprises with process innovation (% relative to all enterprises)
Enterprises with marketing innovations (% relative to all enterprises)
Enterprises with organizational innovations (% relative to all enterprises)
Share of firms that have introduced new to the firm products
    (% of enterprises with innovation activities)
Share of firms that have introduced new to the market products
    (% of enterprises with innovation activities)
Turnover of new or significantly improved products new to the firm
    (% of total turnover)
Turnover of new or significantly improved products new to the market
    (% of total turnover)

Source: Revised from Edquist and Zabala (2009).

innovation dimension and as such these reports do not properly capture innovation performance. The innovation scoreboards using innovation survey data do capture output indicators, in particular the IUS and STI Scoreboards (see Table 11.2).

6.   CONCLUSION

The discussion of innovation scoreboards and competitiveness reports has shown that there is a wide variety in the number of indicators, type of data and coverage of countries. Scoreboards differ depending on their objectives, for example where the *IUS* focuses on European countries, the *GII* takes a global perspective. But despite these differences, innovation scoreboards should try to capture all the relevant dimensions of innovation for which data are available.

NOTES

1.   The Knowledge Assessment Methodology interactive tool is available at http://web.
worldbank.org/WBSITE/EXTERNAL/WBI/WBIPROGRAMS/KFDLP/EXTUNIK
AM/0,,menuPK:1414738~pagePK:64168427~piPK:64168435~theSitePK:1414721,00.
html.
2.   The IUS Dashboard is available at http://ec.europa.eu/enterprise/archives/IUS2011/
IUS2011.html.

REFERENCES

Arundel, A. and H. Hollanders (2008), 'Innovation scoreboards: indicators and policy use', in C. Nauwelaers and R. Wintjes (eds), *Innovation Policy in Europe: Measurement and Strategy*, Cheltenham, UK and Northampton, MA, USA: Edward Elgar, pp. 29–52.

Atkinson, R. and S. Andes (2009), *The Atlantic Century: Benchmarking EU & US Innovation and Competitiveness*, Washington, DC: The Information Technology & Innovation Foundation.

Atkinson, R. and S. Andes (2011), *The Atlantic Century II: Benchmarking EU & US Innovation and Competitiveness*, Washington, DC: The Information Technology & Innovation Foundation.

Benavente, D., S. Dutta and S. Wunsch-Vincent (2012), 'The Global Innovation Index 2012: stronger innovation linkages for global growth', in S. Dutta (ed.), *The Global Innovation Index 2012: Stronger Innovation Linkages for Global Growth*, Fontainebleau: INSEAD, ch. 1, pp. 3–41.

Browne, C. and T. Geiger (2011), 'The Executive Opinion Survey: an indispensable tool in the assessment of national competitiveness', in K. Schwab (ed.), *The Global Competitiveness Report 2011–12*, Geneva: The World Economic Forum, chapter 1.3, pp. 75–83.

Dutta, S. (ed.) (2012), *The Global Innovation Index 2012: Stronger Innovation Linkages for Global Growth*, Fontainebleau: INSEAD.

Dutta, S. and S. Caulkin (2007), 'The world's top innovators: globalization has pushed innovation to the top of the agenda, but which countries respond best to the new challenges', *World Business*, January–February, 26–37.

EC (2000), 'Innovation in a knowledge driven economy', Communication from the Commission to the Council and the Parliament, COM (2000) 567, Brussels: European Commission.

EC (2001), *European Innovation Scoreboard 2001*, Cordis Focus Supplement 18, Brussels: European Commission.

EC (2003), *2003 Innovation Scoreboard, Technical paper no. 6, Methodology report*, European Trend Chart on Innovation, Luxembourg: European Union.

EC (2009), *European Competitiveness Report 2009*, Commission Staff Working Document SEC (2009), 1657, Luxembourg: European Commission.

EC (2010a), *European Competitiveness Report 2010*, Commission Staff Working Document SEC (2010) 1276, Luxembourg: European Commission.

EC (2010b), 'Europe 2020 Flagship Initiative Innovation Union', Communication from the Commission to the European Parliament, the Council, the European Economic and Social Committee and the Committee of Regions, COM (2010) 546, Brussels: European Commission.

EC (2011a), *Innovation Union Scoreboard 2010: The Innovation Union's Performance Scoreboard for Research and Innovation*, Brussels: European Commission.

EC (2011b), *Innovation Union Competitiveness Report 2011*, Brussels: European Commission.

EC (2011c), *European Competitiveness Report 2011*, Luxembourg: European Union.

EC (2012), *Innovation Union Scoreboard 2011: Research and Innovation Union Scoreboard*, Brussels: European Commission.

Edquist, C. and J.M. Zabala (2009), 'Outputs of innovation systems: a European perspective', Lund: CIRCLE Electronic Working Paper 2009/14.

Gokhberg, L. and V. Roud (2012), 'The Russian Federation: a new innovation policy for sustainable growth', in S. Dutta (ed.), *The Global Innovation Index 2012: Stronger Innovation Linkages for Global Growth*, Fontainebleau: INSEAD/WIPO, ch. 6, pp. 121–30.

Hollanders, H. and S. Tarantola (2011), 'Innovation Union Scoreboard 2010, methodology report', ProInno Europe, Innometrics, mimeo.

INSEAD (2009), *Global Innovation Index 2008–2009*, Fontainebleau: INSEAD.

OECD (2010), *OECD Science, Technology and Industry Outlook 2010*, Paris: OECD.

OECD (2011), *OECD Science, Technology and Industry Scoreboard 2011*, Paris: OECD.

OECD/Eurostat (2005), *Oslo Manual: Guidelines for Collecting and Interpreting Innovation Data*, Paris: OECD.

Saisana, M. and D. Philippas (2012), 'Statistical tests on the Global Innovation Index', in S. Dutta (ed.), *The Global Innovation Index 2012: Stronger Innovation Linkages for Global Growth*, Fontainebleau: INSEAD, annex 3, pp. 71–80.

Sala-i-Martin, X., B. Bilbao-Osorio, J. Blanke, M. Drzeniek Hanouz and T. Geiger (2011), 'The Global Competitiveness Index 2011–2021: setting the foundations for strong productivity', in K. Schwab (ed.), *The Global Competitiveness Report 2011–12*, Geneva: The World Economic Forum, ch. 1.1, pp. 3–49.

Schubert, T., P. Neuhäusler, R. Frietsch, C. Rammer and H. Hollanders (2011), 'Innovation Indicator, Methodology Report 2011', mimeo.

Schwab, K. (ed.) (2011), *The Global Competitiveness Report 2011–12*, Geneva: The World Economic Forum.

Weissenberger-Eibl, M., R. Frietsch, H. Hollanders, P. Neuhäusler, C. Rammer and T. Schubert (2011), *Innovationsindikator 2011*, Bonn: Deutsche Telekom Stiftung and Bundesverband der Deutschen Industrie.

World Economic Forum (2012), *The Europe 2020 Competitiveness Report: Building a More Competitive Europe, 2020*, Geneva: The World Economic Forum.

Wunsch-Vincent, S. (2012), 'Accounting for science–industry collaboration in innovation: existing metrics and related changes', in S. Dutta (ed.), *The Global Innovation Index 2012: Stronger Innovation Linkages for Global Growth*, Fontainebleau: INSEAD/WIPO, ch. 4, pp. 97–107.

PART V

INNOVATION STRATEGY

12 The OECD Innovation Strategy: science, technology and innovation indicators and innovation policy
Andrew W. Wyckoff[1]

1. INTRODUCTION

Motivation

> OECD countries are at a critical economic and social juncture. Most of the fiscal and monetary levers available to revive the economy have been exhausted, and the scars of the crisis – starting with unemployment and inequalities – are still deep and fresh. In this context, governments have no choice but to swiftly implement far-reaching structural reforms to support growth . . . This imperative makes the case for a more intelligent type of growth, one that is welfare enhancing, inclusive and sustainable, driven by new ideas, new technologies, new entrepreneurs, new business models and new social organisations. The world economy needs traditional 'Schumpeterian' innovation, as well as social innovation.
>
> (Gurria 2012)

A Historical Snapshot of Measuring STI at the OECD

Fifty years after the creation of the OECD, Angel Gurria, its Secretary General, echoes a theme that has prevailed throughout the life of the organization: science, technology and innovation (STI) are essential elements for sustainable growth. A constant companion on this journey has been the role of indicators and the interplay of indicators and policy. In its founding year (1961), the Secretary General of the OECD formed an *ad hoc* group under the direction of Pierre Piganiol that was mandated to produce a report, *Science and the Policy of Governments* (Piganiol 1961), which analysed the importance of 'harnessing science and technology to the broad economic objectives of the OECD' (King 1974: 35). Later this report would be credited with 'providing a starting point for the consideration of science policy as we now know it' (ibid.). The Piganiol Report led to the first Ministerial Meeting on Science in 1963, which recognized science as a 'national investment and as an element of growth', and invited the OECD to start work on comparable indicators of national expenditures on R&D (ibid.: 41). The first edition of a proposed standard practice for surveys of R&D, better known as the *Frascati Manual* (OECD 1963), was produced in 1963 and is now in its sixth edition (OECD 2002). At the second Meeting of Science Ministers at the OECD in 1966, a commissioned report by Professor Christopher Freeman and Alison Young, which contained indicators of the relative position of national efforts on R&D, sparked a debate between the USA versus Europe that fuelled demand for the OECD to intensify its work in measuring R&D. By the third Meeting of Science Ministers at the OECD in 1968, a *'Gaps in Technology'* (OECD 1970) report was delivered to Ministers which was a *tour de force* that covered educational attainment and expenditures, a discussion of the 'brain drain', R&D performance by sector and by size of firm, as well as a section devoted to technological innovation both in terms of diffusion (e.g. significant innovations since 1945, receipts and payments for licences of patents) and the use of specific technologies (e.g. plastics, computers, man-made fibres). Writing in 1971, Harvey Brooks in *Science, Growth and Society: A New Perspective* (Brooks 1971) notes that this Ministerial marked a turning point in science policy where the focus shifted from a preoccupation with science and the pursuit of the endless frontier to a systemic view of STI. Ministers recognized the fact that R&D efforts could not by themselves explain differences in economic performance. Rather, many other factors were involved, 'including capital availability, fiscal policy, management competence and attitudes, entrepreneurship, marketing skills, labour relations, general levels of education and even culture and national psychology' (Brooks 1971: 42).

While the policy dialogue recognized this broader system, the analytical focus remained primarily upon science, technology and technological innovation because the primary methodology and associated data series of the day were based on the *Frascati Manual*. In 1988, the OECD's Technology Economy Programme (TEP) was launched to better understand the interactions of technology, the economy and society (OECD 1992a). While it recognized the endogeneity of technological change and the need to characterize innovation as an interactive, as opposed to linear, process, it still relied heavily on R&D indicators and country snap-shots of scientists and engineers. This report gave a political impetus to the need for improved measures of innovation and its diffusion, and for intangible investment and its components.

This led to a sustained statistical effort to measure innovation that resulted in a new statistical manual, the *Oslo Manual*, dedicated to the measurement of 'technological product and process innovation in manufacturing'. First appearing in 1992 (OECD 1992b), the *Oslo Manual* was revised collaboratively with Eurostat in 1997 (OECD/Eurostat 1997) to cover services and thereby provide a close-to-total economy perspective.

The third edition in 2005 (OECD/Eurostat 2005) significantly broadened the view of innovation to include non-technological innovations such as organizational change, business practices and market development, thereby better reflecting the nature of innovation in services.

These advances were enabled by a series of forums on new indicators for science, technology and innovation dubbed the 'Blue Sky' forums because they offered a place where participants could come to discuss new approaches, unimpeded by the lack of a developed methodology or data series. The first was held in 1996 (OECD 2001) and provided a first stocktaking of the systematic efforts to measure innovation through the Community Innovation Surveys (CIS). This, in turn, contributed to the first revision of the *Oslo Manual* (OECD/Eurostat 1997).

The second Blue Sky Forum in 2006 went further by showcasing new work that measures innovation, especially those innovations that do not directly depend on the performance of R&D. It also highlighted the heightened pace and complexity of change caused by globalization, information and communication technologies and the trend towards 'open' innovation (OECD 2007a). Importantly, John Marburger, the US Presidential Science Advisor, reaffirmed in his keynote address the need for models that can act as a 'pedagogical device' in the formation of science and innovation policy. Pointing to an era of 'dynamic change' that has eroded the utility of old taxonomies and the predictive value of old correlations, he gave support to the concept of 'science of science and innovation policy' (SciSIP) and the development of models that simulate social behaviours and can be used 'to make intelligent guesses at what we might expect the future to bring and how we should prepare for it' (OECD 2007a: 31).

These early developments to better understand and measure innovation, extending back to TEP in the early 1990s, finally began to generate a knowledge base built by a wide range of researchers that enabled an in-depth analysis of innovation and policies for innovation, setting the foundation for the OECD Innovation Strategy.

2. THE OECD INNOVATION STRATEGY

Observing that many countries (e.g. Australia, Finland) were in the process of developing innovation strategies, Ministers meeting at the OECD in 2007 concluded 'that in order to strengthen innovation performance and its contribution to growth, a strategic and comprehensive cross-government policy approach is required' (OECD 2007b), and launched the OECD Innovation Strategy (IS). Developed over a three-year period, the IS marked the arrival of a broader view of innovation policies that included S&T at its core, but which encompassed a broader systems perspective including education, health, entrepreneurship, consumer, general-purpose technologies such as information and communication technologies (ICT), biotechnology and nanotechnology policies as well as 'framework conditions' such as taxation, competition, finance, product and labour markets (OECD 2010a). It marked the adoption and application of the statistical concepts, and the systems approach, launched at TEP and developed in the revisions of the *Oslo Manual* into a high-level policy analysis. For the OECD, the IS marked the first of a new generation of OECD 'horizontal' projects that engaged a large number of OECD committees and different parts of the OECD Secretariat.

The OECD Innovation Strategy: What It Is, and Is Not

The IS sought to take a whole-of-government view of innovation policy, recognizing that while S&T and, more narrowly, R&D policies are essential, they are only one element in a broader system. In fact, much of the earlier focus on R&D and human resources for science, technology, engineering and mathematics (STEM) and infrastructure was a supply-side view and as such represented only half of the system. The IS broadened the perspective to include the demand side, which encompasses entrepreneurship, government regulation and procurement, as well as the need for STI policies to address grand challenges such as climate change, ageing societies and development. Policy makers from a wide range of policy fields – consumer, competition, regional, taxation, environment, education, ICT, trade and development, many of whom never considered themselves players in innovation policy – participated in this project.

The objective of the IS was not to develop a new theoretical paradigm such as national systems of innovation (OECD 1997) or to generate breakthrough empirical results such as international comparisons of e-commerce activity (OECD 2000). Rather, the main new contribution of the IS was on a political level as it helped governments view policies for innovation more broadly and repositioned innovation policy as a core element of the economic policy toolbox, akin to labour, trade or financial policies. This disappointed some observers, especially the core group of S&T policy advisers or those academics involved in developing the concept of innovation who wanted an analysis that pushed the envelope, replete with new findings and new policies. Some critics suggested that the IS was simply 'old wine in a new bottle'. This characterization is not completely wrong, but this narrow, academic focus missed the political value of extending the interest in innovation policy from the converted to a wider audience, and in doing so effectively advancing the mainstreaming of innovation policy and recognizing that other policies – finance, labour, competition – need to be part of the mix of policies for innovation.

Changes in the Economic and Social Environment of Innovation

In the midst of the IS, the worst economic crisis in 70 years hit, and with it a deterioration of the economic environment for innovation characterized by a dramatic drop in finance, especially risk finance; a general decline in consumption and a heightened level of risk adversity. Many governments responded with stimulus packages that had significant pro-innovation elements – indicative of the importance of innovation as a mainstream economic factor (OECD 2009a). To take one prominent example, the USA allocated more than US$100 billion to innovation (about 12 per cent of the total US stimulus package) – or about half of the present-day cost of the Apollo Program of US$180 billion (US Executive Office of the President 2010). This included US$30 billion for renewable energy and energy efficiency; US$20 billion for health information IT; and a US$10 billion increase for the National Institute of Health (NIH) from US$30 to US$40 billion.

As the crisis of 2008 and 2009 extended into 2012, with unemployment remaining stubbornly high, and as attention began to focus on the growing inequality of incomes that afflicts many OECD countries, the focus on how to nurture new sources of growth – new products, new firms, new sectors and especially new jobs – becomes more intense. This is further fuelled by the recognition that while the crisis has severely affected most OECD countries, the period has been one of strong growth for emerging economies such as Brazil, India, Russia and especially China. With their rise, global value chains have become prevalent and with this the global arbitrage of wages and capital (Freeland 2012). To remain competitive, OECD countries look to new sources of growth that provide high-value-added jobs and profits. While many factors can help stimulate new growth – for example investment in human and physical capital – many are reaching diminishing returns or demographic limits. Innovation, as reflected in multifactor productivity growth and as embodied in products or processes, is increasingly sought to improve competitiveness and drive growth that can simultaneously generate employment, tax revenue and provide profits for continuing the cycle of innovation that drives productivity growth and, with it, improvements in standards of living.

As is frequently the case, the crisis was a catalyst for changes that were already under way: the rise of Asia, especially China, as an economic power and a growing source for STI; cost pressures that force firms to adopt new business models including more collaborative STI practices ('open' innovation); and the increased diffusion and application of ICT tools as the digital economy became less of a buzz-word and more the norm. At the same time, grand challenges such as climate change, rapid demographic changes and the rise of neglected infectious diseases, as well as issues such as the growing scarcity of clean water and the security of food, have quickly risen up the policy agenda. While market mechanisms alone, such as removing subsidies or internalizing externalities through taxes on 'bads' such as carbon, might help solve the problem, it is clear – as work by Philipe Aghion and others has illustrated – that this will take a long time at a high price that could limit growth (Aghion et al. 2009). Innovation, combined with market mechanisms, is clearly needed to address these challenges and can create a double dividend of improving social welfare while generating jobs and growth.

3. THE ROLE OF INDICATORS IN FRAMING POLICY DIALOGUES

An essential pillar within the IS was a stream of work to develop new indicators that better reflect the nature of modern-day innovation and the impact of various policies. The crisis, the ascendency of the grand challenges and the search for new sources of growth have added impetus to many of the streams of work that had been launched by the 2006 Blue Sky indicators conference, including developing indicators on health, sustainable development and business/university linkages, and indicators that sought to measure the effect of STI policies. *Measuring Innovation: A New Perspective* (OECD 2010b) went beyond previous work by juxtaposing traditional 'positioning indicators' based on official methodologies and statistics with new, experimental indicators, many of which were based on new data collections or the matching of microdata files to generate new indicators. This work provided an empirical narrative for the key policy messages that framed the study and was instrumental in helping communicate these messages to a wide audience of policy makers and advisers.

This story-line was delivered through roundtables in more than 20 countries as well as to an equal number of high-level events in Europe, Asia, North America and Latin America. These events reached a number of high-level policy makers (e.g. ministers and vice ministers) who would not normally attend official OECD meetings at headquarters, visit the OECD website, or read OECD reports. Many countries used these roundtables as a mechanism for drawing together different ministries to discuss policies for innovation from a whole-of-government perspective, launching efforts to generate a strategy for innovation, or reorienting existing strategies.

A compelling feature of these events was the indicators that provided an evidence base for the key elements of the IS and which sparked a dialogue in capitals as policy makers sought to better understand why their country appeared where it did in various cross-country comparisons.

Because no one indicator or composite is deemed sufficient to capture the multidimensional nature of innovation, *Measuring Innovation* contains over 100 indicators covering human capital, innovation by firms, government investments in support of innovation, collaboration and efforts to address global challenges. The report is part of a larger package of deliverables prepared as part of the IS as well as a stand-alone resource for those interested in quantitative measures of STI and international comparisons of performance. In practice, it became the source for presentations at the roundtables and conferences, which typically contained 20 slides of indicators. Seven stand out as having had an important impact on policy and were instrumental in providing the empirical story-line to the presentation of the key findings and the policy implications. These seven indicators provide a basis for demonstrating the linkage between indicators and the impact on policy development.[2]

R&D Funding: Direct and Indirect

As much as OECD IS illustrated that innovation was a broader activity that extended beyond scientific and technological activity, it also reaffirmed the importance of R&D as critical, especially for the realization of radical, break-through innovations such as the invention of the transistor or a vaccine for polio. Because of the well-recognized 'market failure' associated with business investment in R&D where firms have difficulty capturing all the benefits as they 'spill over' to other entities, the bulk of government policy, particularly when it comes to expenditures, is devoted to R&D.

In support of the IS, a measurement initiative was undertaken to better understand the types of government support to business enterprise R&D, comparing for the first time government funding of business R&D through contracts, grants and awards (direct expenditures) with expenditures (foregone tax revenue) associated with R&D tax credits (indirect expenditures) across a wide cross-section of countries.

For the first time, policy makers were able to compare the cost of the two measures, effectively getting a sense of the policy mix and how their country compared with other developed countries. Figure 12.1 started a discussion in several countries, including Germany, Finland, Sweden and Switzerland, about whether or not they needed to add indirect policies to support business R&D both to adjust the policy mix and create a defence against those countries that had introduced generous measures.

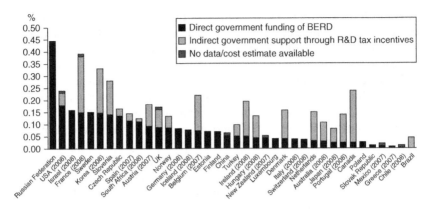

Source: OECD, based on OECD R&D tax incentives questionnaires, January 2010 and June 2011; and OECD, Main Science and Technology Indicators database, June 2011.

Figure 12.1   Direct government funding of business R&D and tax incentives for R&D, 2009, as a percentage of GDP

In Canada, where the policy mix was heavily orientated towards tax measures, the discussion focused on whether the mix between direct and indirect measures was still appropriate (Expert Panel 2011).[3] In testimony to the US Senate Finance Committee, policy makers looking at the figure questioned whether or not US tax incentives were sufficiently generous (US Senate Committee 2011).[4]

More generally, Figure 12.1 has sparked a renewed interest in indirect measures of support for R&D, which, while philosophically appealing because they provide a 'neutral' policy that all qualifying firms can take advantage of, may be more expensive and hence less cost-efficient than many realized. For example, a review panel of Canadian R&D conducted 'a first of its kind' compilation of federal government support to business R&D that covered 60 programmes, delivered by 17 federal entities, totalling C$4.96 billion. They discovered that that 70 per cent (C$3.47 billion) of the total spending could be attributed to the SR&ED tax credit (Expert Panel 2011) and questioned whether they were getting sufficient return on their relatively expensive investment. The 2012–13 Canadian Budget seeks to rebalance the mix by providing more funding for direct support programmes (Canadian Budget 2012).[5]

Innovation is More than R&D

While it has been recognized for decades that innovation could occur without directly conducting R&D, international comparisons that pro-

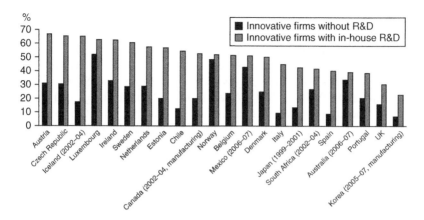

Source: OECD, Innovation microdata project based on CIS 2006, June 2009 and national data sources.

Figure 12.2   *New-to-market product innovators, 2004–06, as a percentage of innovative firms by R&D status*

vided evidence of this phenomena had been lacking because it required access to innovation microdata and the creation of a consortium of researchers with access to these microdata who could collectively construct such an indicator using common techniques and methodologies. This exercise – the Innovation Microdata Project – was launched in 2006 and concluded in 2009 with the publication of *Innovation in Firms* (OECD 2009b), which was one of more than a dozen reports that supported the IS. This indicator provided a much-needed balance to the ubiquitous R&D indicators and made the point that innovation can occur without performing R&D (Figure 12.2). Rather, innovators can benefit from R&D done elsewhere, underscoring the need for linkages and adaptive capacity, or from activities other than R&D such as organizational change, design or marketing. This type of innovation is especially important for service sector innovations that, due to measurement challenges, have failed to garner much attention from either the research or the policy community even though services constitute 70 per cent of most OECD economies. Long overdue, this indicator established the need for a broader view of investments that support innovation, going beyond R&D.

Recasting Innovation Activities as Investments that Drive Growth

Extending this observation that innovation and innovation policy involve more than just conducting or supporting R&D was work on 'intangibles' that sought to develop an investment series for a range of knowledge-based assets including R&D but also software, designs, firm-specific human capital and organizational know-how. Initial work on 'investments in knowledge' was developed by the OECD (Khan 2001) in the late 1990s, but the work by Corrado, Hulten and Sichel in 2005 (Corrado et al. 2005) for the USA was more systematic and gained greater visibility, leading to complementary efforts in many OECD countries (COINVEST,[6] INNODRIVE[7] and the Conference Board[8]). The OECD worked to compile this work and incorporate it into the IS.

The international comparisons compiled by the OECD showed that, when aggregated, these investments in 'intangibles' matched or exceeded investment in tangibles such as structures, equipment and machinery. When used in growth accounting models, intangibles contributed as substantially to labour productivity growth in a wide range of countries (e.g. Austria, Denmark, Finland, France, Sweden, the USA) (Corrado et al. 2009) (Figure 12.3).

This provided an important economy-wide extension to the finding that innovation could occur in non-R&D-performing firms – rather a range of innovation-related activities, such as the development of new business models based on an innovative organizational structure (e.g. Easy Jet) or

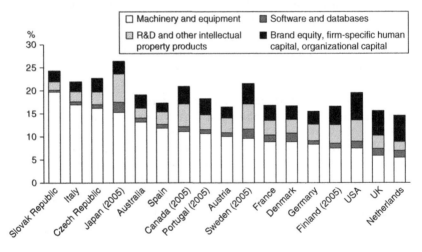

Source: OECD Science, Technology and Industry Scoreboard 2011. Data on intangible investment are based on COINVEST (www.coinvest.org.uk) and national estimates by researchers. Data for fixed investment are OECD calculations based on OECD, Annual National Accounts and EU KLEMS databases, March 2010.

Figure 12.3   Investment in fixed and intangible assets as a percentage of GDP, 2006

the exploitation of mobile phone geo-location data to better optimize bus routes should be considered as innovation investments that are linked to growth. By analysing these investments as a group, as opposed to discrete activities, they can be viewed as a bundle of complementary, interacting investments. Lastly, this work has given added weight to the argument that 'hard' investments in science are not sufficient by themselves to produce innovative outcomes; rather they need to be complemented with 'soft' investments such as marketing and new business models to gain commercial success. This broader perspective echoed the thinking behind the 2005 revision of the *Oslo Manual*.

By adopting concepts used in the system of national accounts, using the growth accounting model and productivity analysis, this analysis and the resulting figures provided a bridge between S&T or industry ministries and ministries of finance and central banks. The macroeconomists could now see, using tools and concepts that they were familiar with, that collectively these intangible investments were on a par with the traditional concept of investment – and that they were the source of badly needed growth. For the S&T and industry ministries, it forced them to recast their work in an economic framework. The intangibles work provided a composite index that many had been searching for that avoided issues of mixing units and assigning proper weights while providing a clear link to a policy objective: growth and labour productivity.

These developments were a twist on the outcome of the 2006 Blue Sky indicators conference, where the focus had been on equipping ministries involved directly in developing innovation policy with useful 'pedagogical' tools similar to those enjoyed by finance ministries. Rather, the intangibles work borrowed these existing tools and in doing so helped to mainstream the concept of innovation and innovation policy as a broader endeavour.

Innovation is Multidisciplinary

The importance of multidisciplinary approaches to science and innovation and their implications for policy have been recognized for some time. Alexander King, the first director of the Directorate for Scientific Affairs at the OECD, devotes a chapter to this subject in his autobiography where he asserts that 'many attempts to solve complex problems failed because one or more facets of the difficulty were undetected or ignored as insignificant' (King 2006: 199). The relevance of this perspective has grown as many innovation strategies have been oriented towards large socio-economic objectives, the so-called 'grand challenges' like climate change mitigation or adaption, addressing demographic challenges or developing new sources of energy.

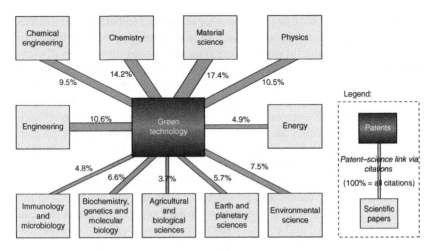

Source: OECD calculations, based on Scopus Custom Data, Elsevier, July 2009; OECD, Patent Database, January 2010; and EPO, Worldwide Patent Statistical database, September 2009.

Figure 12.4   The innovation–science link in 'green' technologies, 2000–2007

Both from a political and from a policy perspective, this linkage to broader objectives is sound, but in many cases the rhetoric did not acknowledge that this shift would require a reorientation of innovation policies away from the traditional focus on specific ministries, scientific fields or technologies to a multidisciplinary, transversal view which required coordination, cooperation and collaboration across areas. This point was underscored by an experimental indicator for 'green' technology patents that used the fields of scientific literature cited in the patent application to quantify the multidisciplinary nature of 'green tech' and found that energy and environmental sciences only accounted for about 12 per cent of all the cited literature. Rather, a wide range of science extending from material sciences to immunology, microbiology and biochemistry is drawn upon to develop green technologies (Figure 12.4).

In the course of the IS roundtables, the implications of 'multidisciplinarity', endemic to addressing grand challenges, were identified. The implications for funding mean less emphasis on specific fields, disciplines and technology and more emphasis on proposals directed to an outcome related to the grand challenge (e.g. carbon-free transportation) as well as the need to develop other policies that 'pulled' innovation through demand-side measures such as standards, performance-based regulations

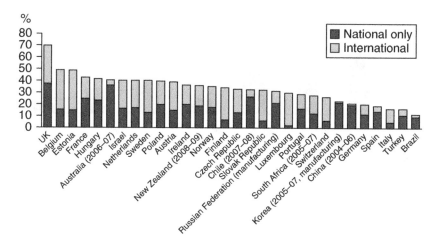

Source: OECD, based on Eurostat (CIS 2008) and national data sources, June 2011.

Figure 12.5 National and international collaboration on innovation by firms, 2006–08, as a percentage of innovative firms

or performance awards achieved through prizes. It also led to discussions on the proper governance structure for organizations that sought to foster multidiscipinary research.

Reflecting the Shift towards 'Open Innovation'

Measuring Innovation uses a series of indicators to show the growth in collaboration between firms (i.e. international and national), between scientists (i.e. scientific co-authorship trends), between organizations (i.e. co-patenting between firms and universities or public research organizations) and especially across borders (i.e. co-patenting where inventors are from different countries, scientific publications where authors are from different countries etc.) Collectively, these indicators illustrated that collaboration was rising, especially across borders. Across a range of countries considered to be innovative – such as Finland, Australia, Sweden, Israel, Estonia and the UK – a third or more of innovative firms were engaged in collaboration with international partners (Figure 12.5). This raises important policy questions about the utility of trying to restrict access to government programmes to domestic firms, the need to facilitate linkages across organizations, especially universities, industries and public research organizations and mechanisms that encourage the mobility of researchers.

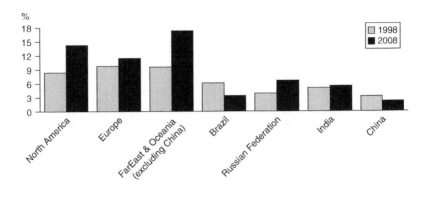

Source: OECD calculations, based on Scopus Custom Data, Elsevier, December 2009.

Figure 12.6 Scientific collaboration with BRIC countries, 1998 and 2008, as a percentage of total international co-authored articles

The Changing Topography of Innovation

Key to this notion of collaboration was its changing location, as a number of indicators revealed the shift in innovative activity away from the most developed, G7 countries to a broader array of players, especially in the emerging economies of Brazil, Russia, India, China and South Africa (BRICS). While the rise of China as an emerging force had been documented in terms of R&D spending for some time (OECD 2008), *Measuring Innovation* provides insights into the emergence of a new cluster of scientific collaboration that appears to be forming between the BRICS and the 'Far East and Oceania' (excluding China). In the past, much of the innovative activity in the BRICS countries had been attributed to foreign direct investment or collaboration with leading Western universities, but the identification of a growing network of scientists from the BRICS countries working together with other Asian countries is suggestive of a third pole of scientific expertise rising in Asia. OECD policy makers have interpreted this shift in different ways, ranging from a threat to their dominance to a more enlightened recognition that the size of the global science commons is growing, and with it the need to reorient policies towards gaining access to this research and assimilating the results (Figure 12.6).

Targeting Young, Innovative Firms

The IS devoted significant attention to the 'framework conditions' needed to create an environment conducive to innovation-driven entrepreneurial activity. The role of new firms that are willing to embrace unproven, radical technologies or champion a new business model like Amazon, Skype or Easy Jet are known to be important for establishing new sources of growth and leading to productivity gains through structural change. To date, much of the evidence tends to be anecdotal. In terms of policy making, new firms tend to be subsumed under the much broader category of small and medium enterprise policies. But analysis shows that the vast bulk of SMEs are not particularly innovative and tend to generate jobs only in the early years after their birth. The linking of company information and patents at the firm level provides an opportunity to look at young, innovative firms and focus on the role they play as technology developers, job generators and agents of productivity gains.

Measuring Innovation included an experimental indicator of patenting activity by firms younger than five years – both as a measure of the percentage of all patenting firms these young firms constituted and as a share of all patents filed (Figure 12.7). This figure helped support a debate that was already occurring in many capitals about the relative role of large, small and new firms and their role in the system of innovation. It also generated interest in this subset of SMEs as well as the policies needed to nurture

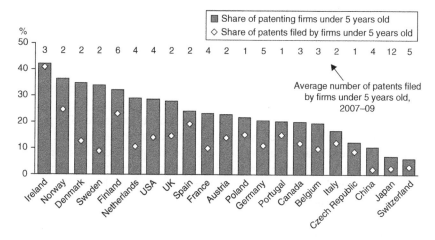

Source: *OECD Science, Technology and Industry Scoreboard 2011* based on the Worldwide Patent Statistical database, EPO, April 2011; and ORBIS© database, Bureau van Dijk Electronic Publishing, December 2010; matched using algorithms in the Imalinker system developed for the OECD by IDENER, Seville, 2011.

Figure 12.7   *Patenting activity of young firms, 2007–09: share of young patenting firms and share of patents filed by young patenting firms, EPO and USPTO*

this cadre of firms whose innovativeness and fast growth require special financing, skills and linkages to S&T organizations. The EU is exploring the feasibility of developing an indicator that proxies the 'high-growth innovative firms' as one of its 'Innovation Union Headline' indicators and a US National Research Council of the US National Academy panel on future STI indicators has made a recommendation that NSF develop a similar indicator as it revamps its indicator portfolio (NRC 2012). Much work remains to make this experimental indicator more robust since the firm-level economic data available internationally (ORBIS[9]) are not well suited to this type of analysis.

4.   CONCLUSION: THE 'MAINSTREAMING' OF INNOVATION POLICY

The OECD IS is part of a longer trend to mainstream STI policy as an element of broader economic and social policies that have their origins in World War II and extend far beyond the work undertaken by the OECD itself. Within the OECD as an organization, the IS is the latest manifestation of this phenomenon, which moves in fits and starts, but because of a confluence of factors including economic pressures to find new sources of growth, the desire to climb up the value chain and the growing importance of grand challenges such as climate change, the discourse surrounding policies for innovation have entered the main-stream policy dialogue of nearly all countries – developed, emerging and developing. Indicators, as described above, have been instrumental in this repositioning.

This is a significant change since, for most of its existence, STI policy has been considered a 'sectoral policy' and failed to achieve the same attention or legitimacy that was devoted to labour, fiscal or monetary policy. But that is changing, providing a large opportunity for the STI research and policy community that needs to be seized. To do this, a statistical system needs to be established that is of the quality of the sta-tistical systems that support other major economic policy fields where, for example, labour policy have data on populations, schooling, training, occupation, wages, unemployment and stocks of labour force. Given the current budgetary pressures, a different path will need to be followed that utilizes non-survey data sources such as administrative records and web sources such as the Conference Board's help-wanted online database, which can provide a source of demand for STEM jobs (Conference Board 2011).

Associated with this is the need to improve the ability to engage in the evaluation of STI policies and codify what works and what does not, and share this information broadly. This field of policy analysis, for many good reasons, not the least of which is the serendipitous nature of innovation and the time lags associated with the process of innovation, makes evaluation difficult. As Brooks (1971: 63) noted, 'Innovation is not, and cannot be, an entirely planned process, because it includes the revelation of the not yet known or understood.' Nevertheless, too much STI policy is based on anecdotes, intuition and the ideas of a few. The usual factors that constitute the political economy around policy limit the ability to learn from policy failures: few countries are willing to discuss their mistakes at the OECD table. As a consequence, STI policies, like many public policies, are susceptible to fads – the proliferation of biotech, nanotech and ICT clusters of excellence or the widespread targeting of R&D to GDP intensities are a testament to this phenomenon. As innovation policy becomes mainstream, more analytical rigour is needed and improved statistics and indicators are instrumental in meeting this challenge. Efforts in many countries to develop a 'science for science and innovation policy' are an important step towards achieving this goal. The OECD itself needs to do more in this area, as a developer of indicators, as an evaluator of policies and as a forum where policies are discussed.

As policy making recognizes the importance of STI policy, it is important that practitioners, advocates and students of the area retain humility about its limits – it is not a silver bullet for all policy problems; rather, innovation can often be worthless or even harmful, as witnessed by financial innovation that has badly damaged many parts of the economy and society. Policy makers need to be reminded that the end goal is not innovation, but the economic performance and social welfare that innovation can generate.

NOTES

1. Alessandra Colecchia, Ken Guy, Yuko Harayama and Dirk Pilat provided useful comments and new insights for which I am thankful. Alessandra Colecchia and her team, especially Elif Koksal-Oudot, worked diligently to produce the indicators used in this chapter. All errors and the views expressed are those of the author and do not reflect those of the OECD, its Council or its member countries. The author would like to acknowledge the guidance and support of the editor of this volume.
2. Many of the indicators described challenge or provide new insights into many of the conventional wisdoms on innovation, and therefore question standard policies. But rarely can indicators by themselves be used as a basis for new policy; rather a more complete statistical analysis is needed to better understand the determinants.
3. See http://rd-review.ca/eic/site/033.nsf/eng/home.
4. See http://finance.senate.gov/hearings/hearing/?id=ef6a4c10-5056-a032-5212-fbf59e314035.
5. See http://www.budget.gc.ca/2012/plan/chap3-1-eng.html.

6.   See http://ec.europa.eu/research/social-sciences/projects/359_en.html.
7.   http://www.innodrive.org/.
8.   http://www.conference-board.org/data/intangibles/.
9.   ORBIS© Database, Bureau van Dijk Electronic Publishing.

REFERENCES

Aghion, Philippe, David Hemous and Reinhilde Veugelers (2009), 'No green growth without innovation', Bruegel Policy Brief, No.7, November, Brussels: Bruegel, http://www. bruegel.org/publications/publication-detail/publication/353-no-green-growth-without-innovation/.

Brooks, D. Harvey (1971), *Science, Growth and Society: A New Perspective*, Paris: OECD.

Canadian Budget (2012), *Chapter 3.1: Supporting Entrepreneurs, Innovators and World-class Research*, Ottawa: Government of Canada, www.budget.gc.ca/2012/plan/chap3-1-eng. html.

Conference Board (2011), *The Conference Board Help Wanted Online™ Data Series Technical Notes*, Washington, DC: Conference Board, www.conference-board.org/ pdf_free/HWOLJan11_TN.pdf.

Corrado, C.A., C.R. Hulten and D.E. Sichel (2005), 'Measuring capital and technology: an expanded framework', in C. Corrado, J. Haltiwanger and D. Sichel (eds), *Measuring Capital in the New Economy: Studies in Income and Wealth*, Vol. 65, Chicago, IL: The University of Chicago Press, pp. 11–45.

Corrado, C.A., C.R. Hulten and D.E. Sichel (2009), 'Intangible capital and U.S. economic growth', *Review of Income and Wealth*, International Association for Research in Income and Wealth, **55**(3), 661–85.

Freeland, Chrystia (2012), 'Some see two new gilded ages, raising global tensions', in *New York Times*, 22 January, http://www.nytimes.com/2012/01/23/business/global/wrenching-the-globe-into-a-new-economic-orbit.html?pagewanted=all.

Expert Panel (2011), *Innovation Canada: A Call to Action*, Ottawa: Industry Canada, http:// rd-review.ca/eic/site/033.nsf/eng/home.

Gurria, Angel (2012), 'Fostering growth through innovation', presentation at G8: Route 2012 – the Road to Recovery, Munk School of Global Affairs, May, Toronto: University of Toronto, http://www.g8.utoronto.ca/newsdesk/campdavid/.

Khan, Mosahid (2001), 'Investment in knowledge' in OECD, *Science, Technology and Industry Review, Special Issue on New Science and Technology Indicators*, No.27, Paris: OECD, pp. 19–47.

King, Alexander (1974), *Science and Policy: The International Stimulus*, Oxford: Oxford University Press.

King, Alexander (2006), *Let the Cat Turn Round*, London: CPTM.

National Research Council (2012), *Improving Measures of Science, Technology and Innovation: Interim Report*, Washington, DC: The National Academies Press.

OECD (1963), *Proposed Standard Practice for Surveys of Research and Development: The Measurement of Scientific and Technical Activities*, Directorate for Scientific Affairs, DAS/ PD/62.47, Paris: OECD.

OECD (1970), *Gaps in Technology*, Paris: OECD.

OECD (1992a), *Technology and the Economy: The Key Relationships*, Paris: OECD.

OECD (1992b), *OECD Proposed Guidelines for Collecting and Interpreting Technological Innovation Data – The Oslo Manual*, Paris: OECD.

OECD (1997), *National Innovation Systems*, Paris: OECD.

OECD (2000), *Measuring Electronic Commerce*, Paris: OECD.

OECD (2001), *Science, Technology and Industry Review, Special Issue on New Science and Technology Indicators*, No.27, Paris: OECD.

OECD (2002), *Frascati Manual: Proposed Standard Practice for Surveys on Research and Experimental Development*, Paris: OECD.

OECD (2007a), *Science, Technology and Innovation Indicators in a Changing World*, Paris: OECD.

OECD (2007b), *OECD Meeting of Council at Ministerial Level: Chairman's Summary*, Paris: OECD, www.oecd.org/mcm2007.

OECD (2008), *OECD Science, Technology and Industry Outlook*, Paris: OECD.

OECD (2009a), *Policy Responses to the Economic Crisis: Investing in Innovation for Long-Term Growth*, Paris: OECD, http://www.oecd.org/dataoecd/59/45/42983414.pdf.

OECD (2009b), *Innovation in Firms: A Microeconomic Perspective*, Paris: OECD.

OECD (2010a), *The OECD Innovation Strategy: Getting a Head Start on Tomorrow*, Paris: OECD.

OECD (2010b), *Measuring Innovation: A New Perspective*, Paris: OECD.

OECD/Eurostat (1997), *Proposed Guidelines for Collecting and Interpreting Technological Innovation Data – Oslo Manual*, Paris: OECD.

OECD/Eurostat (2005), *Oslo Manual: Guidelines for Collective and Interpreting Innovation Data*, Paris: OECD.

Piganiol, Pierre (1961), *Science and the Policy of Governments: The Implication of Science and Technology for National and International Affairs*, Paris: OECD.

US Executive Office of the President (2010), 'The recovery act: transforming the American economy through innovation', Washington, DC: US Executive Office of the President, http://www.whitehouse.gov/sites/default/files/uploads/Recovery_Act_Innovation.pdf.

US Senate Committee on Finance (2011), 'Tax reform options: incentives for innovation', 20 September, Washington, DC: US Senate, http://finance.senate.gov/hearings/hearing/?id=ef6a4c10-5056-a032-5212-fbf59e314035.

13 The Finnish approach to innovation strategy and indicators
Esko Aho, Mikko Alkio and Ilkka Lakaniemi

INTRODUCTION

Finland has been a high performer in international comparisons on innovation capability. The high performance of the Finnish innovation system can be said to rely on policies and conditions that closely reflect the Washington Consensus, such as a strong rule of law, stable macroeconomic policy, domestic competition, a healthy financial sector and openness to outside ideas, and free trade (Williamson 2004).

The Finnish innovation strategy has greatly benefited from national characteristics ranging from a national affinity for technology and the speed of technology diffusion in the country, to the quality of higher education and the central role that engineers, both Finns and non-Finns, have played in Finnish industrialization. Of these characteristics, long-term investments in education, a positive attitude towards technology and Finnish engineering skills are key determinants of Finnish success in innovation.

In recent international comparisons, Finland has been ranked among the top performers by the *OECD STI Scoreboard* (OECD 2011), the EU *Innovation Union Scoreboard* (EC 2012), the World Economic Forum *Competitiveness Report* (World Economic Forum 2012a) and the *Global Information Technology Report* (World Economic Forum 2012b), and reports of various academic institutions such as the INSEAD/WIPO *Global Innovation Index* (INSEAD 2012). These indicators support the Finnish brand as a leading technological economy.

This chapter on the Finnish approach to innovation strategy and indicators describes how Finnish investments in research and development (R&D) and innovation, and measuring these investments, have evolved, what has changed, and what has worked at different times.

The chapter also introduces future issues, such as how Finland is looking anew at its national innovation potential and adapting its innovation system to better meet domestic and international challenges. As in other European economies, Finland is searching for a new model to reflect the evolving nature of innovation and to respond to the global influence on the division of capital, labour and innovation.

HISTORY OF STRATEGY IN FINLAND

This section examines the reaction of Finland to the economically turbulent 1970s, the economically and politically turbulent 1980s and the transformation of the Finnish economy in the 1990s, driven by information and communication technologies (ICTs).

The Classic Finnish Industrial Strategy until the Late 1970s

Industrialization of Finland took place in two different stages. The first started in the latter part of the nineteenth century when Finland was still a part of the Russian Empire. The second phase began after the Second World War, when Finland was still primarily an agrarian society with approximately 60 per cent of the workforce employed in the agriculture and forestry sectors.

Early Finnish industrial history is mostly about entrepreneurship, knowledge and technology transfers in an open environment. Many inventions and innovative ideas arrived in Finland to find new markets. The nature of Finnish geography and natural resources led to rapid technology diffusion, primarily in the forestry-related technologies and secondly in the communications and transport technologies.

This early Finnish industrial model led to an investment-driven economy. This meant developing a national policy framework to support export-oriented industrial assets of the country, leading to (Rouvinen 2002):

- a low level of both general and sector-specific R&D investments;
- the majority of R&D serving the traditional industrial sectors; and
- the absence of a national technology policy.

Forestry-related investments in education and in R&D and initiatives in trade policy served the needs of the traditional exporting industry. Electronics research, the cradle of the Finnish ICT industry, was largely on the margin of the classic resource-based Finnish innovation map.

The main focus of the classic Finnish innovation model was on the supply side, based on the following goals for spurring innovation in Finland up to the late 1970s (Rouvinen 2002). They were:

- the raising of national educational levels;
- the provision for more R&D investments;
- the investment in national infrastructure and production facilities;

- the creation of stability and predictability in the business environment; and
- the maintenance of social cohesion.

The steady investments in production, infrastructure and the maintenance of a supportive business environment contributed to a positive economic development in Finland coupled with rapid job creation. Thanks to these investments, Finland industrialized faster than any other European country and quickly strengthened its role as a rising industrial economy.

The positive domestic development was greatly supported by extensive barter trade with the Soviet Union and the contemporary international trends favouring trade liberalization, high-technology diffusion and the relative global stability of the cold war world.

The classic Finnish approach in science, technology and innovation supported the development of Finland from an agrarian economy to an industrial one while enabling social transformation and generating the required engineering skills.

At the time, due to the export-oriented growth patterns, statistics on international trade in goods, tangible investments, incremental product innovations, currency exchange rates and access to capital were the key indicators for Finnish policy makers right up to the 1970s.

This rather stable situation started to change in the middle of the 1970s, when the Finnish economy was hit by a substantial economic downturn and, in the aftermath of the oil crisis, the period of fast industrialization and the industrial strategy in Finland came to an end.

Emerging Role of National Technology Policy Planning – the 1980s

The rapid industrialization of Finland started to reach its peak just before the oil crisis hit the world economy. This prompted new thinking within the Finnish business and policy circles, aiming to find potential opportunities provided by rapid developments in new technologies. The central and crucial role of science and technology in future economic development was becoming widely acknowledged, and significant increases in R&D were regarded as an essential tool to overcome any emerging challenges to economic growth.

A key result of this transformation in thinking was the new Finnish national technology strategy designed by the Parliamentary Technology Committee in 1980. This strategy included an ambitious target for R&D spending in Finland. In 1980 Finnish R&D investments amounted to roughly 1 per cent of Finnish GDP, below the OECD average. The new investment target was to double Finnish R&D investments to the level of 2 per cent of GDP by 1990.

The new R&D-centric strategy was further complemented by significant institutional reforms. By the early 1980s, the only special institution to foster applied research was the Finnish Innovation Fund – SITRA, which was established in 1967 as a unit linked to the Bank of Finland. Since its beginning, SITRA had become an agent for change for new ideas or new approaches to remodel existing Finnish processes such as healthcare and other public services. In 1991, SITRA was transformed into an independent organization reporting to the Finnish Parliament.

SITRA's funding comes from an original, separate fund and not from government funding. In recent evaluations of the Finnish innovation system (SITRA 2011), the role of SITRA remains distinct as an agent for innovative pilots and for searching for diversity in ideas for public–private sector partnerships. As an example, SITRA is said to have introduced the venture capital investment model to Finland.

Today, SITRA focuses on wider social development issues such as sustainable lifestyles, smart use of natural resources and generating new efficiencies in the public administration by holistic policy initiatives (SITRA 2011).

Another key institution for the Finnish innovation system was created in 1983 to maximize the benefits of increasing R&D spending, the Finnish Funding Agency for Technology and Innovation, TEKES. It first aimed to align Finnish industrial policy approaches to better serve future-oriented technology needs. TEKES's first programme reflected the sign of the times by focusing on semiconductors.

Throughout the 1980s and the 1990s, TEKES assumed a leading role in coordinating national R&D efforts. Since then, it has supported large enterprises as well as small and medium-sized firms (SMEs) with targeted public funding, especially in terms of incremental innovation. Its funding has helped companies to enhance their productivity and young companies to cross the 'valley of death' (Ministry of Employment and the Economy 2012).

In 2012, an evaluation of TEKES indicated that as an instrument for innovation in Finland, it had participated in the funding of more than 60 per cent of the well-known Finnish innovations and in 94 per cent of the innovations based on scientific breakthroughs created in the time period of 1985–2007 (TEKES 2012).

Among the TEKES-supported large enterprises, Nokia received approximately €210 million of TEKES funding in 1995–2011. During the same time period, Nokia is estimated to have contributed directly and indirectly close to €20 billion to the Finnish economy (Ali-Yrkkö et al. 2012).

In addition to SITRA and TEKES, the creation of the Finnish Science and Technology Council in 1987 further fostered the integration of government, business and academic resources. The council organized the successful implementation of the national technology strategy and its coordination between various actors. In 2008, the Council changed its name to the Research and Innovation Council.

The 1990s Onwards – 'the Great Transformation' towards an ICT-driven Innovation Economy

The Finnish technology strategy and policy framework came to a critical point in the early 1990s when Finland was hit by a dramatic economic shock.

There were several simultaneous factors behind this deep economic shock. Financial sector deregulation had created a financial bubble that burst in the early 1990s. Diminishing international competitiveness of Finnish traditional industries led to chronic current account deficits. The Finnish economy also suffered from the collapse of the Soviet Union and simultaneous slower economic growth in Europe.

Finland entered the deepest economic recession of any OECD country since the Second World War. In 1990, Finnish GDP dropped by 7 per cent. The economic crisis led to high unemployment, a growing fiscal deficit and urgent need for reforms.

The economic crisis of 1990–93 forced Finland to design a new strategy for future growth. In this strategy both R&D and innovation played key roles. Innovation activities gained status as a source for new competitiveness, growth and job creation. The key questions were now how to regain the competitiveness of traditional industrial sectors and simultaneously reap maximum benefits from investment in new science and technology.

Despite the doom and gloom of the overall prospects for the Finnish economy, one crucial element of the Finnish approach was maintained and even strengthened at the height of the crisis. In spite of substantial cuts in all major governmental expenditure areas, radical increases in R&D expenditure were continued. As an example, funding for TEKES was doubled during the first part of the 1990s, when all Finnish economic indicators were in free fall.

STRATEGY AND TECHNOLOGY: REAPING THE BENEFITS

This section discusses the role of innovation strategy in transforming the economy over the last 20 years and the indicators used to track the transformation.

The Finnish Success Story of the 1990s

Thanks to the radical changes in Finnish economic policy, the Finnish economy returned to growth in 1993. The main driver for the new growth was technology-driven export industry. Its strength was supported by the expansion of the Finnish ICT sector led by Nokia.

In 1993, the Finnish Ministry of Trade and Industry issued a National Industrial Strategy White Paper setting objectives for the creation of a new national innovation system based on redesigned industrial clusters. The report highlighted ICT as the industrial cluster for future economic development in Finland. This cluster was envisioned to spur innovation and eventually lead to new economic growth and job creation.

The above assumption about the role of ICT was firmly based on the realization that information technology had become pervasive in all OECD countries. Beside this major trend, Finland had also developed domestic assets in ICT by making long-term investments in radio communications technology and electronics.

Long-term, smaller-scale ICT R&D efforts and close links between the private sector and the public sector, such as with the military, had existed even before the Second World War. Now, in the early 1990s, tangible examples of domestic inventions and a new kind of technical-driven innovation capability started to emerge. Data and mobile communications were growing and Finland possessed competitive knowledge and global competitive advantage in the field.

At the same time, Finland's full membership in the EU provided the country with new opportunities for market access and easier access to EU programmes. Europe was also able to tap into a highly competitive ecosystem in mobile communications led by opening competition in the markets and the successful development of the GSM (Global System for Mobile communications) standard adopted in Copenhagen in 1987.

Thus, in the 1990s, Finland rose in status from an unremarkable industrialized European country to becoming a global, high performer in such essential areas as:

- global competitiveness;
- human development;
- regulatory quality and openness;
- number of ICT researchers;
- level of collaboration between universities and firms;
- number of patent applications;
- number of Internet connections; and
- computers per 1000 people.

At the time, there was a growing understanding that the more these activities grew, the more the country could gain from ICT-enabled growth. Of course, indicators played a role in showing how these activities were changing.

While investing heavily in ICT and funding ICT-related R&D, Finland also improved its global competitiveness in the other economic sectors by acquiring the best global technologies available. Through this process, initiated by the economic crisis, Finland transformed itself from an investment-driven economy to an innovation-driven economy (Rouvinen 2002).

Traditionally, Finland had benefited from improving on imported knowledge and technologies. Now, thanks to new innovative companies, universities and supporting policies, Finland became more and more an indigenous innovator especially in the field of mobile communication technologies.

National Strategies Supporting the Nokia Growth Story

Nokia, founded in 1865, and partly active in the forestry industry, was originally engaged in paper production, later expanding to rubber and cable products, and in the 1980s to consumer electronics. Before 1992, Nokia was among the beneficiaries of the classic Finnish industrial system.

In the midst of the national economic crisis, Nokia faced a radical transformation as well. Being close to bankruptcy in the early 1990s, Nokia adopted a new strategy concentrating completely on telecommunications technology and mobile products, transforming the company from an old-fashioned conglomerate into a nimble and focused company.

For that purpose, the 1990s Finnish national technology strategy was a perfect tool to support Nokia. It provided Nokia with access to R&D funding and other assets to build the company's global competiveness and innovation capacity. Besides the R&D funding, the national university system supported Nokia's long-term growth.

Through coordinated dialogue and converging strategies between Nokia and the Finnish national strategy implementation, the company was able to become a globally relevant actor. Newly created and rapidly expanding markets for Nokia-made mobile phones drove the growth of the company, and also Finland, to worldwide recognition as a leader in the ICT-enabled world. The Finnish innovation system and Nokia became a success story to be monitored, followed and copied (Dahlman et al. 2006).

Internet, Technology Convergence and the Changing Role of Globalization

The Finnish transformation to a role model in innovation was reflected in a host of international studies explaining the Finnish success story and looking for common lessons to be learned by other countries.

While the old strategy was still being efficiently applied with fairly good results, there started to emerge real weaknesses in the Finnish innovation system (Ministry of Trade and Industry 2003). These signs of national weaknesses were also reflected in the relative decline in Nokia's innovation capacity from the middle of the first decade of the 2000s.

In 2004 a Finnish government report proposed initiatives to maintain innovation capacity. These initiatives included further increases to public R&D resources by at least 7 per cent per annum up to the end of the decade, focus on growth entrepreneurship, strengthening the attractiveness of the Finnish universities and enhancing the international mobility of the Finnish workforce (Prime Minister's Office 2004).

The Ministry of Employment and the Economy (2008) put forward a proposal for a new Finnish national innovation strategy focusing primarily on innovation ecosystem issues rather than on industrial clusters. The proposal reflected the changing times and the wider role of technology in societies. The new innovation strategy proposed a renewal based on four main principles.

1. Innovation activity in a world without borders: In order to join, and position itself within, global competence and value networks, Finland must actively participate and exert influence and be internationally mobile and attractive.
2. Demand and user orientation: Innovation steered by demand, paying attention to the needs of customers, consumers and citizens in the operations of the public and private sector alike, requires a market with incentives and shared innovation processes between users and developers.
3. Innovative individuals and communities: Individuals and close innovation communities play a key role in innovation processes. The ability of individuals and entrepreneurs to innovate, and the presence of incentives, are critical success factors of the future.
4. Systemic approach: Exploitation of the results of innovation activities also require broad-based development activities aiming at structural renewal, and determined management of change.

The references to the global flow of innovation and the requirements for systemic changes were the essential elements of the 2008 innovation strategy. Statistics Finland, through the Finnish Community Innovation Survey, is producing innovation indicators to monitor changes in the system.

At the same time, the Federation of Finnish Technology Industries (2008) produced an economic study emphasizing the wider socioeconomic impact of the ICT sector in the Finnish economy. It also stated the importance of cross-sectoral utilization of ICT for increased future competitiveness. This economic analysis indicated that without increased ICT usage, in both the private and public sectors at all levels, future Finnish economic growth potential would be gravely jeopardized.

Finland is facing dramatic changes in demographics, especially in declining labour supply. This situation foresees future economic growth almost entirely dependent on ICT-enabled productivity improvements. These basic facts are driving changes and improvements in the Finnish innovation system.

The changing position of Finland in the global industrial value chain, outsourcing of production, the stronger role of emerging markets in the global economy and the growing role of the Internet in the ICT industry require Finland to make a leap from an ICT manufacturing and producing country to being a service-led innovator – an active user of the Internet and other ICT-enabled services.

The changing situation of Finland was also described in a 2012 Ministry of Communications and Transport study on the economic impact of the Internet in Finland. The study made it clear that measuring the economic impact of ICT on the Finnish economy with old indicators, such as number of ICT equipment investments, was creating a false sense of satisfaction about the true state of the Finnish information society and the Finnish ICT cluster. The study also highlighted that the high ranking of Finland in the contribution of the Internet to GDP was almost entirely dependent on foreign trade surpluses in ICT equipment and ICT services. Finland still appears a better ICT provider than an innovative ICT user (Ministry of Communications and Transport 2012).

THE FUTURE

Based on experience gained in the recent past, Finland must build ecosystems and platforms on which future innovations can be based. Given the growing healthcare demands of an ageing population, this is an obvious and urgent opportunity to demonstrate that the ecosystems and platform approach can work.

Healthcare

During recent decades, Finland has invested heavily in education, research and innovation activities in the health sector. Finland has some first-class individuals in the field of healthcare, and the quality of science is high. Investments made in health are also considerable in terms of the healthcare system as a whole. However, while Finland has fared well in creating this strong basis of knowledge, it has done poorly in commercializing inventions in the health sector.

From a business perspective, the countries that will prevail in the competition are those that are able to produce a strong basis of knowledge and high-quality, world-class science, as well as to build partnerships with operators in the private sector. Finland's Nordic neighbours Denmark and Sweden seem to have a clear strategy for growth, investment and commercialization of their strong competence base in healthcare.

Despite its present success, Denmark is aiming to further improve its competitive position with a new and ambitious healthcare development plan. The development plan includes 23 concrete initiatives divided into five different sections (clinical research, new hospital centres, increase in the use of innovative welfare solutions, export of health and welfare solutions, as well as marketing and foreign investments).

In Denmark, for instance, the country's most extensive construction project to date is currently under way: more than €5.5 billion have been invested in the construction of five new hospital complexes. A total of 11 existing hospitals are being expanded and renovated. The largest hospital, Skejby Sygehus, with an area of 400 000 square metres, is due to be completed in 2019. A new medical faculty will further be established to Odense hospital to enhance, in particular, the cooperation of companies in the field of clinical pharmaceutical research. Even while under construction, the new hospital complexes are portrayed as global examples of healthcare and welfare solutions as well as test laboratories. New hospitals offer companies a possibility to test new and innovative products and solutions as well as to demonstrate to doctors and patients how the new solutions can be put into use. Denmark is also aiming to market itself more as a potential target of future health sector investments.

Sweden is another good example. It is currently undergoing what is possibly the largest European public contract ever for a new hospital, Karolinska Solna, which is being constructed in the Stockholm area. The hospital is due to be completed in 2017. The overall value of the investment is over €5 billion. After its completion, the hospital is also planned to support research and education. Sweden also has a significant four-year plan to sustain the high investments in the field of clinical research.

Regardless of the accepted strategies and policy alignments, Finland has had difficulties in rising to the challenge of internationalization of research and innovation activities. Finland has fared quite poorly when measured by international standards relating to investments, foreign R&D personnel and foreign entrepreneurship. In terms of both cooperation in the field of international inventions relating to patents as well as foreign research development funding, Finland is lagging behind the OECD average.

At the moment, Finland does not have a comprehensive strategy regarding the development of the healthcare sector and, in particular, a strategy for the competition of international research investments. However, the present government of Prime Minister Jyrki Katainen has clearly increased focus on foreign direct investments. The Ministry of Labour and the Economy has also initiated, in close cooperation with the Ministry of Social Affairs and Health, an in-depth evaluation of the growth and commercialization opportunities of the pharmaceutical and health technology sector.

The grand challenge in the healthcare sector in Finland is to create a national ecosystem that attracts significant, international pioneers of health research. Furthermore, instead of focusing only on start-up businesses, more importance should be given to the commercialization of Finnish research activities in connection with global-research-oriented companies. These global value chains of health innovation are creating opportunities – as in Sweden – for the future. New structures that provide universities and research institutes with sufficient resources to carry out globally competitive research in the long term need to be developed. Regulatory development also plays a major role. Here Sweden is also a model for putting the newest inventions to use in the healthcare system (Alkio 2011; TEKES 2009).

CONCLUSION

Since the beginning of the 1980s, the main strength of the Finnish innovation system has been in creating comprehensive, long-term strategies. These strategies have been efficiently implemented by a well-orchestrated collaboration between the public and private sector actors, universities and other key stakeholders (Ornston and Rehn 2006). Finland has also given high priority to R&D and education as key elements of the national strategy and the innovation system.

As seen in the evolutionary story of the Finnish innovation system, the multi-stakeholder dialogue between policy makers, industries, industry associations, economic research institutes, employee organizations and universities has led to several reassessments and cross-checks – for example, in measuring the impact of policies and institutions central to innovation.

This open national dialogue has not only been a positive agent for change, but has also put pressure on the Finnish innovation system to deliver changes when the country has faced grave challenges such as the economic crisis of the early 1990s (Dahlman et al. 2006).

As stated in the National Innovation Strategy adopted in 2008, there are new global requirements that are challenging Finland's innovation capacity. The most critical components to tackle these requirements are Finland's improved integration into the global innovation flows and an improved capacity for systemic changes.

Finland's main weaknesses in the application of modern technologies have been slowness of reforms and low risk taking. Unfortunately, Finland is already seeing unwanted changes in its global competitiveness due to these weaknesses.

Finland has a huge potential for economic growth and greater social welfare. It is an open and small economy with high dependence on exports, making it vulnerable to global economic shocks, but it has good assets such as high R&D performance, a strong education system and ICT cluster to support international competitiveness. Of late, it has not performed as well as in the recent past, and this presents another challenge to be resolved by Finland's collective and inclusive approach to problem solving.

REFERENCES

Ali-Yrkkö, J., P. Rouvinen and P. Ylä-Anttila (2012), *Nokia Shrinks – ICT Services Grow*, Helsinki: ETLA.

Alkio, M. (2011), *Terveyden kustannuksella (At the Expense of Health)*, Helsinki: WSOY.

Dahlman, C.J., J. Routti and P. Ylä-Anttila (eds) (2006), *Finland as a Knowledge Economy: Elements of Success and Lessons Learned*, Washington, DC: World Bank Institute.

EC (2012), *Innovation Union Scoreboard 2011*, Brussels: European Commission.

Federation of Finnish Technology Industries (2008), *ICT and Productivity Growth*, Helsinki: Federation of Finnish Technology Industries.

INSEAD (2012), *The Global Innovation Index 2012: Stronger Innovation Linkages for Global Growth*, Fontainebleau: INSEAD/WIPO.

Ministry of Communications and Transport (2012), *Internet in the Finnish Economy*, Helsinki: Ministry of Communications and Transport.

Ministry of Employment and the Economy (2008), *Proposal for Finland's National Innovation Strategy*, Helsinki: Ministry of Employment and Economy.

Ministry of Employment and the Economy (2012), *Evaluation of TEKES: Final Report*, Helsinki: Ministry of Employment and the Economy.

Ministry of Trade and Industry (2003), *Evaluation of the Finnish Innovation Support System*, Helsinki: Ministry of Trade and Industry.

OECD (2011), *OECD Science, Technology and Industry Scoreboard 2011*, Paris: OECD.

Ornston, Darius and Olli Rehn (2006), 'An old consensus in the "new economy": institutional adaptation, technological innovation, and economic restructuring in Finland', in J. Zysman and A. Newman (eds), *How Revolutionary was the Digital Revolution? National Responses, Market Transitions and Global Technology*, Stanford, CA: Stanford University Press, pp. 78–100.

Prime Minister's Office (2004), *Strengthening Competence and Openness: Finland in the Global Economy*, Helsinki: Prime Minister's Office, http://vnk.fi/julkaisukansio/2004/r05-strengthening-competence-and-openness/pdf/Strengthening_competence_and_openess_-_Finland_in_the_Global_economy.pdf.

Rouvinen, P. (2002), 'Finnish experiences in information society', presentation at Knowledge Economies in EU Accession Countries, World Bank Forum, Paris, 19–22 February, Helsinki: ETLA.

SITRA (2011), *Actions and Visions for Social Change: Sitra's Evaluation 2002–2011*, Helsinki: SITRA.

TEKES (2009), *Better Results, More Value. A Framework for Analyzing the Societal Impact of Research and Innovation*, Helsinki: TEKES.

TEKES (2012), *The Impact of TEKES and Innovation Activities*, Helsinki: TEKES.

Williamson, J. (2004), 'A short history of the Washington Consensus', paper commissioned by Fundación CIDOB for a conference 'From the Washington Consensus towards a new Global Governance', Barcelona, 24–25 September.

World Economic Forum (2012a), *The Europe 2020 Competitiveness Report: Building a More Competitive Europe, 2020*, Geneva: The World Economic Forum.

World Economic Forum (2012b), *Global Information Technology Report*, Geneva: The World Economic Forum.

14 US innovation strategy and policy: an indicators perspective
Christopher T. Hill

1. INTRODUCTION

For most of the second half of the twentieth century, the United States led the world in innovating new products, processes and systems, in developing and implementing innovation strategy and policy, and in gathering and publishing innovation indicators.

Over the past decade or so, the United States has lost its lead in each of these important domains. Rather than leading the world, the United States now seeks to maintain its position as one among many leaders and to catch up with other leading countries and regions of the world in several of these domains.

This chapter first describes and assesses US innovation strategy and policy, considering both their implicit and explicit characteristics. It then turns to a discussion of the state of innovation indicators research and analysis in the United States, including a few thoughts about how innovation indicators both inform and influence policy choices.

2. US INNOVATION STRATEGY AND POLICY

In this chapter, innovation strategy refers to the deep, underlying structure of societal choices about how best to accomplish broad national innovation goals. Innovation policy, on the other hand, refers to the set of specific public policies that are intended to influence the rate and direction of innovative activity and that seek to manage the consequences of new technological applications on behalf of society.

US Innovation Goals

In the United States, there is widespread agreement that innovation and change are, on the whole, good things. Even as Americans venerate the past and its links to the present, it is a rare person who opposes innovation and change *per se*. Innovation is understood to be a central feature of a dynamic, competitive and growing economy. Innovation is frequently called forth as a means to address or even resolve public problems and issues, ranging from national security to public health. Innovation is also understood to be critical to maintaining the privileged position of the United States in competition with other nations. And innovation is widely appreciated as a source of new ways for Americans to amuse, entertain and improve themselves.

Thus one can safely say that it is a settled goal of the United States to be a leading place where innovation happens and where its benefits are enjoyed.

Along with the goal of strong leadership in innovation comes a somewhat different and definitely more contentious goal of ensuring that the United States and its citizens and residents are protected from the important and undesirable consequences of the use of innovations.

Achieving either or both of these goals – an innovative society and a protected society – requires an array of policies within a broad set of strategies. These strategies and policies are our focus here.

US Innovation Strategies: Implicit and Explicit Elements

The implicit elements of US innovation strategy are deeply enmeshed in the core concepts and beliefs underlying the nation's history, culture and Constitution. They are rarely articulated directly in discussions of innovation strategy or policy, yet they condition attitudes toward what government should do and how. The implicit elements of US innovation strategy include:

- innovation largely originates in the private market sector, which should be supported and encouraged;
- market activity, both domestic and international, should be free of unnecessary encumbrances;
- education should be universal through the primary and secondary levels and should allow for flexibility and 'second chances';
- labor mobility in place and role, including immigration from other countries, is highly valued;
- initiative and entrepreneurship are key to the growth and development of both individuals and groups;
- governments (federal and state) have legitimate roles in both innovation and protection, but the roles are circumscribed by constitutional limits on the powers of each to act.

Nearly every debate and discussion about innovation strategy and policy in the United States takes place in the context of these implicit elements of innovation strategy. These implicit elements both support and constrain the range of viable innovation strategies and policies that might be considered by policy makers. Proposed policies that might be in conflict with one or more of the implicit elements of national strategy of the sort listed above are not likely to get a hearing, much less be adopted by the political process.

In discussions of innovation policy alternatives in the United States, it is common for someone to ask 'whether this [proposed policy] represents an appropriate government role'. As a logical matter, the person asking the question may not realize that 'appropriate' alone is not a well-defined criterion for decision. Appropriate only has meaning in the context of some agreed-upon standard. In the case of innovation strategy and policy, the implicit elements of innovation policy lie behind the determination of what is appropriate.

The explicit elements of US innovation strategy are considerably more familiar to students and practitioners of innovation strategy and policy than the implicit elements. The explicit elements include:

- research and development (R&D), wherever it is conducted, should be supported and encouraged because it is the central activity that enables and conditions innovation;
- strong intellectual property rights, especially patents, should be maintained because they are key to ensuring that investors in innovative activity can anticipate profiting from those investments and are, therefore, critical to the advance of technology;
- partnerships and other collaborations among firms in different sectors and between industry, universities and government should be facilitated, because synergies in innovation arise from the diverse mix of capabilities of each;
- both supply- and demand-side approaches to innovation should be employed; that is, innovative activity in general as well as to address specific defined societal challenges should be encouraged;
- when imposing social controls on the use of technologies, performance-based standards rather than design-based standards should be used whenever feasible.

The Obama Administration's Innovation Strategy

Just eight months after his January 2009 inauguration, President Obama issued a formal statement of his Administration's innovation strategy (Executive Office of the President 2009). The 22-page strategy document includes a rich array of commitments to act to strengthen US innovation, organized under three broad themes:

- invest in the building blocks of American innovation;
- promote competitive markets that spur productive entrepreneurship;
- catalyze breakthroughs for national priorities.

The first two categories follow a supply-side approach to innovation, providing resources and changing the 'rules of the game' under which innovation can flourish. The third category is unabashedly demand side, focusing on promotion of innovations to address identified national problems.

While the Obama strategy speaks to the importance of transparency and accountability in government, it does not address the state of or need for improved innovation indicators. In a few places, largely having to do with R&D investments, the strategy does call for specific measurable quantitative changes, such as its commitment to raise aggregate US R&D spending to 3 percent of GDP.

The 2009 Obama strategy document set forth an ambitious agenda of actions on many fronts to stimulate innovation generally and for specific purposes. Some of the actions – especially those related to short-term increases in R&D spending and certain forms of loan guarantees for commercialization of new technology – had already been realized in the American Recovery and Reinvestment Act (ARRA) of 2009, the so-called 'Stimulus Package', adopted in February 2009. Action on many of the other proposals, however, has been blocked by the Republicans in the House of Representatives and/or their colleagues in the Senate as part of the general Republican strategy of blocking passage of the President's policy initiatives.

In February 2011, the Obama Administration issued a revised national innovation strategy (National Economic Council 2011). The revised strategy goes along the same general lines as the first version with significantly greater detail in many areas and with changes in emphasis that reflect evolving concerns about innovation and closely related public policy topics. The revised strategy incorporates many dozens of specific program and budgetary initiatives, as well as changes in regulation of business and industry, all intended to stimulate and encourage innovation. The strategy document reflects an expansive perspective on what constitutes innovation policy, with major sections devoted to such matters as investment in physical and information technology infrastructure, production of clean energy, new agreements and enforcement of existing agreements on trade, manufacturing, intellectual property protection, cyber security, space development, educational reform and so on. Once again, while the revised strategy document includes projections of many policy outcomes or goals in quantitative terms, it does not make explicit reference to the challenges of measuring or developing indicators of the activities and outcomes it projects.

Other Sources of US Innovation Strategy and Policy

Public policy in the United States consists of more than the initiatives of the presidential administration, regardless of their level of ambition and complexity. Other actors, including the Congress, the courts and the individual state governments, are also key contributors of public policy regarding such matters as innovation.

Under a strict interpretation of the US Constitution, public policy making at the federal level is actually the responsibility of the Congress, not the President or his administration in the executive branch of government. For at least the last half-century, however, most of the initiatives for changes in public policy have come from the executive branch. Final action on those initiatives, as well as provision of funding when needed, however, remains in the hands of the Congress. It has been said about modern US governance that 'the President proposes, but the Congress disposes'. (The origin of this aphorism is not known.) It is this mechanism that has allowed the Republicans in the House and Senate to block many of President Obama's innovation-related initiatives. President Obama was able to side-step these blocking actions on some items of his innovation agenda by taking advantage of the unusually broad grant to the President by Congress of discretion over spending the stimulus funds that was incorporated in the ARRA to provide funds for one or two years for such purposes as R&D spending, technology commercialization loan guarantees and other related purposes.

Most of the US states have acted to encourage and stimulate innovation (SSTI 2011). Traditionally, states have had the responsibility for economic development in the United States, although the federal government has often been a partner with the states in such activity. Many aspects of innovation policy are state responsibilities within the economic development framework. In its report on state activities in 2011, SSTI notes that states were particular active in that year in such areas as higher education, research, tax incentives, regionally focused activities and investment incentives. In 2009, the states spent a total of approximately $1.2 billion on R&D, with about 75 percent of this amount coming from non-federal sources including the states themselves (NSF 2012a). When compared with total US spending on R&D in 2009 of just over $400 billion (NSF 2012b), it is apparent that the state role in R&D spending is relatively small. In other areas, including tax incentives and direct grants for investment, the state role is much more prominent.

3.   INNOVATION INDICATORS IN THE UNITED STATES

Systematic exploration of new innovation indicators in the United States dates back at least to the early 1980s (Hill et al. 1983). Hill and colleagues tested nearly three dozen possible new indicators of innovation to supplement the traditionally collected and reported data on R&D spending, the scientific and engineering workforce, patents applied for and awarded, and bibliometrics. Following relatively successful preliminary testing of candidate indicators by Hill, Hansen and colleagues, NSF fielded a trial survey of some of them. However, response rates to the indicator questions were unacceptably low and the effort was terminated after two rounds.

In 2002, the NSF commissioned a wide-ranging study by the National Research Council of measuring R&D investments in the United States (NRC 2005). In addition to its examination of the R&D statistics, the study committee reviewed the state of the art of innovation indicators in the United States, Europe, Canada and Australia. The committee made two recommendations for action by NSF leading to the establishment of a set of innovation indicators for the United States. It said:

> The panel recommends that resources be provided to SRS [Science Resources Studies] to build an internal capacity to resolve the methodological issues related to collecting innovation-related data. The panel recommends that this collection be integrated with or supplemental to the Survey of Industrial Research and Development. We also encourage SRS to work with experts in universities and public institutions who have expertise in a broad spectrum of related issues. In some cases, it may be judicious to commission case studies. In all instances, SRS is strongly encouraged to support the analysis and publication of the findings.
> . . .
>
> The panel recommends that SRS, within a reasonable amount of time after receiving the resources, should initiate a regular and comprehensive program of measurement and research related to innovation. (NRC 2005: 101)

Based on the NRC committee's recommendations, the NSF Division of Science Resources Studies (SRS, now NCSES, the National Center for Science and Engineering Statistics) embarked on an effort to incorporate a small number of questions regarding innovation in the annual survey of R&D expenditures in industry. This was done in connection with a broad revision of the entire industrial R&D survey. The new survey, now called BRDIS (Business Research and Development and Innovation Survey), was released in 2008 (NSF 2010a). Details about BRDIS are available at (NSF undated a). The current version of the BRDIS survey questionnaire is on line at www.nsf.gov/statistics/srvyindustry/about/brdis/surveys/srvy brdis_2009.pdf.

From the point of view of innovation indicators, the most important aspect of BRDIS is that it asks several questions designed to illuminate the firm's engagement in innovative activity and its success in that activity as measured by contributions of 'the new' to the firm's sales. It also probes widely into collaborative activities with other firms, academic institutions and government laboratories, as well as foreign entities. And it asks for the levels of R&D investment by lines of business, by state and by country, as well as in several specific areas of technology.

NSF has released key results regarding whether firms innovate from the first round of the new BRDIS survey, applicable to the year 2008 (NSF 2010b). The results show that about 22 percent of manufacturing firms introduced product and 22 percent introduced process innovations, whereas about 8 percent of firms in non-manufacturing introduced product and 8 percent introduced process innovations. The percentage of firms that introduced innovations varies substantially across industries within the major sectors. The results also indicate that firms that spent more money on R&D tended to be more likely to have introduced innovations. Unfortunately, in the first BRDIS survey, NSF did not ask for a breakdown of sales attributable to innovations, but it did so in the second round. Results from the second-round survey are not available as of this writing.

It is clear that NSF has embarked on an important new direction in querying business firms about their innovative activities and their results. Over the next several years, as experience is gained with BRDIS in both NSF and industry, increasingly valuable results are likely to become available. It is to be hoped that the rich array of data now being asked for can be fully exploited to gain new insights into where innovation happens in the US economy, how significant it is to firm performance, and how various institutional linkages and practices contribute to the success of firms' innovative activities.

Proceeding along a different track, the Secretary of the US Department of Commerce (DOC) convened an expert panel in 2006 to examine the possibilities for new innovation indicators (Department of Commerce 2008; Aizcorbe et al. 2009; Rose et al. 2009; ASTRA undated).

The DOC panel took a somewhat unusual approach to its consideration of innovation indicators. Rather than reconsider the kinds of firm-level data and information as the basis for indicators typical of previous innovation indicator studies, which NSF was beginning to test around the same time, the panel focused instead on how innovation might better be captured and reflected in the National Income and Product Accounts. In fact, the panel rather abruptly dismissed other approaches to indicators, saying:

Detailed innovation surveys such as the European Community's Community Innovation Survey are used by statistical organizations in [the] European Union and some other countries including Australia and Canada. Relatively new, and only tested among manufacturing firms in the U.S., the surveys collect information on different varieties of innovations, including 'new to the firm, new to the industry and new to the world.' They also collect extensive information on innovation expenditures (e.g., capital investment, training and marketing costs) and costs of protecting innovation (e.g., patent and copyright costs). However, such surveys are very costly and have encountered both definitional and response rate problems.

In addition to foreswearing further consideration of such indicators as those used in Europe, the panel made only passing mention of the activities of the NSF in collecting and publishing an array of innovation-related indicators through the reports of the National Center for Science and Engineering Statistics and the National Science Board's biennial document, *Science and Engineering Indicators*. The panel ignored, except by implication, the past efforts of the NSF in supporting both research on and testing of an array of potential innovation indicators, including its contemporaneous activity leading to the BRDIS survey discussed above. And the panel apparently disregarded any consideration of a wide array of possible micro-level indicators proposed to it by a study committee convened by the Alliance for Science, Technology and Research for America (ASTRA undated).

What the DOC panel did do was address in some depth the interpretation of Total Factor Productivity (TFP) data and possibilities for improving collection of the underlying data so as to help reveal the outcomes of innovation as reflected in trends in TFP. The panel also commented on the need and possibilities for collection of new data on investments in so-called 'intangibles', drawing in part on a background paper on the topic by Rose et al. (2009).

Going beyond its charter, the panel also called for new studies and analyses of the impact of government regulation and legislation on innovation. Such calls have been a staple of innovation policy studies for decades. Generally, studies find that the effects of regulation on innovation are highly contingent on the form of the regulation, the nature of the industry, other forces affecting the industry concerned, and how innovation is measured. Those effects can be both positive and negative. The notion that regulation can stimulate profitable innovation is often referred to in the economics literature as the 'Porter Hypothesis' (Porter and van der Linde 1995; Ambec et al. 2011; Wikipedia undated). However, the positive effects of regulation had been noticed much earlier (see, e.g., Hill et al. 1975; Ashford et al. 1979).

4. BARRIERS TO INNOVATION INDICATORS IN THE USA

In comparison with most European countries, Canada, Australia and others, the United States has not progressed as far in developing, testing and implementing a national system of innovation indicators. That this should be the case may be a bit puzzling, since the USA led the way in creating national systems of accounts, in measuring national investments in science and engineering, and in early research on indicators.

It is certainly not for a lack of interest in indicators, nor is it for the want of efforts to advocate for their adoption. Rather, the answer can be found in a set of cultural and political features of US society. These include a reluctance to impose costs of government data collection on respondents, a reluctance to share what is considered to be confidential information belonging to the firm, and a closely related political tradition of minimizing government in general.

It is an unfortunate coincidence that early interest in innovation indicators emerged around the same time that determined opposition to federally imposed data reporting requirements was also ascendant. The latter culminated in the passage by Congress of the Paperwork Reduction Act in 1980. This law gave the Office of Management and Budget in the Executive Office of the President the responsibility to oversee all federally sponsored data collection and created a strong presumption against new data reporting requirements. The same year saw the election of Ronald Reagan as president and the surprise victory of numerous conservatives to the US Senate, a combination that reflected in part a successful new 'small government' politics and that led to the use of the Paperwork Reduction Act authorities to impose severe limits on new and existing data collections.

An integral part of the opposition to federal reporting was industry's opposition to reporting about such sensitive topics as innovation, which invariably links closely to business strategy and competitive actions. Individually, of course, companies would like to have access to systematic data on the innovation performance of companies and especially of those in their lines of business. On the other hand, understandably, they would prefer not to have to share that kind of data about themselves. One of the keys to successful adoption of the new BRDIS survey discussed above was a major effort by NSF to solicit the views and inputs of the business community on the needs for and uses of the data to be collected and the manner of its collection (NSF undated b).

5.   RELATIONSHIP OF INNOVATION INDICATORS TO PUBLIC POLICY

The Political and Intellectual Setting

While it is not always apparent from American politics, nor is it universally true, it is generally the case that policy-making processes in the USA are data-driven. Interest groups of every persuasion muster numbers to justify their advocacy for, or opposition to, public policies. The administrative agencies of the federal government are under great pressure from a variety of sources to make decisions about both regulations and implementing actions that can be justified to the courts and in the court of public opinion by appeal to facts and evidence. In the government of the United States with its separation of policy-making powers between the Congress and the executive branch, each tries to convince the other and their political supporters of the rightness of their position by drawing on data.

In addition, policy makers, pundits and ordinary citizens live in a sea of statistics and data about everything from the batting averages of baseball players to the probabilities that life exists on other planets. Americans are accustomed to reading statistical reports every day about sports, the weather, the financial markets, public opinion and so on.

It is no wonder, then, that there is a desire among policy makers and those who would try to influence them for indicators of industrial innovation. They want to know 'how we are doing' and 'where we are headed' on innovation as much, or nearly so, as on high-school graduation rates or the number of gold medals won by the USA in the Olympic games.

The desire for performance data has only been reinforced by the passage of the Government Performance and Results Act of 1992 ('GPRA'), which requires federal agencies to collect data on their performance and their results, and to report those data to Congress and the public. As part of the general movement toward greater accountability in government, GPRA and subsequent actions emphasizing accountability and transparency have substantially elevated the importance of policy makers and government officials being able to demonstrate quantitatively that their actions have significant and positive consequences.

Innovation policy has not escaped the expectation for quantitative demonstration of needs and outcomes. Data on innovation are in demand. There is a problem, however. 'Innovation' does not lend itself to direct measurement. Unlike a barrel of oil, a ton of steel, or the number of university graduates in chemistry, we have no way to conceptualize or measure a unit of innovation. We know that innovation is generally good and that more of it would be better, but we have no way to measure how much we have (of course, innovation is not always good, indicators could also be useful in knowing how much 'bad' innovation might be happening).

Thus we must fall back on indicators of innovation – constructs that point to but are not the same as the measures of innovation we would like to have (Hill and Hansen 1988).

The Reciprocal Relationship of Indicators and Public Policy

The needs of policy makers shape the demands for innovation indicators. Conversely, the availability of innovation indicators tends to shape the demand for public policies. So, for example, policy makers frequently ask for an assessment of the competitiveness of US industry or specific industries compared with those of other nations. As it is usually understood, an important component of competitiveness is the success of firms in generating new technologies that gain significant shares of international markets – that is, the innovativeness of those firms or industries. At present, while many surrogate indicators can be examined – such as R&D expenditures, patents, numbers of employed scientists and engineers, and the like – there is no truly satisfactory answer to the question of the relative innovativeness of US versus foreign firms or industries.

Conversely, the mere fact that we can develop good indicators of R&D investments on a national, sectoral or industrial level leads policy makers to consider policy measures to encourage additional R&D spending at various levels, regardless of whether more R&D would necessarily lead to more innovation.

It will be interesting to see whether the availability of the new BRDIS-based indicators of the proportion of firms in an industry or sector that offer new products or processes to the marketplace will lead to policy interventions intended to help make a greater fraction of firms innovative. That is, will the new indicators, whose meaning is far from clear on an aggregate level, create a demand for policy innovations intended to affect them?

Policy makers are frequently told that one or the other industry or sector is becoming more, or perhaps less, innovative as compared with itself in past years, in comparison with other industries or sectors, or compared with those in other countries. Logically, they seek evidence of the comparative innovativeness as reflected in indicators. The evidence, again, often takes the form of R&D spending, patents applied for or granted, or balance of trade. None of these is a fully valid indicator of innovativeness, and some of them – such as patents applied for – are heavily influenced by firm practice and culture or by industry structure rather than by innovativeness *per se*.

In the national security arena, where a 'technological lead' is a cornerstone of US defense policy, it is especially important to be able to assess the state of technology and the ability of various countries to develop new technologies, especially breakthrough technologies, which might pose new national security threats to the USA and its allies. Once again, indicators of innovation are sought.

In addition to entirely new indicators that might provide a richer picture of the innovativeness of US firms and industries, policy makers often ask for more nuanced or finely detailed versions of existing indicators. For example, since it is widely understood that patents vary widely in their significance, policy makers might ask about patent performance based on some selection of the most important patents. This need has been met to some degree by the development of the so-called 'triadic patent', which is a patent applied for in the USA, the EU and Japan. The argument is that these sorts of patents represent concepts that are expected to have economic value in all of the world's major markets and are therefore the most significant. Policy makers also frequently ask for breakdowns of industrial R&D expenditures or patenting by state or substate region or by firms of various sizes, and so on. They also frequently ask about the state of innovation for specific technological fields, such as avionics, optoelectronics, nanotechnology, biotechnology, solid state physics and the like.

In summary, in the USA, policy makers are nearly always interested in more data, better measures, more detail, or greater granularity on a geographic, sectoral or technology basis. They would also like to have indicators, not just of the current state of innovation, but of the likely direction of innovation in the future. Furthermore, the availability of new innovation data almost always leads to policy initiatives intended to improve upon whatever is being indicated, even if the indicator is an inferior partial indicator of what is 'really' desired to be enhanced.

6.   CONCLUSION

The USA is unfortunately behind many competing countries in developing, testing and routinely gathering data on a variety of new innovation indicators. Even if no new indicators were developed in the USA, simply catching up with the state of the art of innovation indicator production around the world would greatly enhance its understanding of where it stands and where it is headed. Recent initiatives by the National Center for Science and Engineering Statistics in NSF, as well as those in the Department of Commerce, should improve the ability of policy makers to understand and act on innovation policy on a more informed basis over the next half-dozen years. The pace of improvement is glacial, however, owing to the need for each initiative to overcome institutional inertia in government and the skepticism and lackluster cooperation with data collection in the private sector.

REFERENCES

Aizcorbe, A.M., C.E. Moylan and C.A. Robbins (2009), 'Toward better measurement of innovation and intangibles', *Survey of Current Business*, January, 10–23, www.bea.gov/scb/pdf/2009/01%20January/0109_innovation.pdf.

Ambec, S., M.A. Cohen, S. Elgie and P. Lanoie (2011), 'The Porter Hypothesis at 20', Discussion Paper RFF DP-11-01, Washington, DC: Resources for the Future, January, www.rff.org/rff/documents/rff-dp-11-01.pdf.

Ashford, N.A., G.R. Heaton Jr and W.C. Priest (1979), 'Environmental, health and safety regulation and technological innovation', in C.T. Hill and J.M. Utterback (eds), *Technological Innovation for a Dynamic Economy*, Oxford: Pergamon Press, pp. 161–221.

ASTRA (undated), *Innovation Indicators for Tomorrow: Innovation Vital Signs Project 'Candidates' – by Framework Category*, Washington, DC: ASTRA, www.usinnovation.org/files/Innovation_Indicators807.pdf.

Department of Commerce (2008), Advisory Committee on Measuring Innovation in the 21st Century Economy, *Innovation Measurement: Tracking the State of Innovation in the American Economy*, Washington, DC: Department of Commerce, http://www.esa.doc.gov/Reports/innovation-measurement-tracking-state-innovation-american-economy.

Executive Office of the President (2009), *A Strategy for American Innovation: Driving Towards Sustainable Growth and Quality Jobs*, 20 September, Washington, DC: Executive Office of the President, www.whitehouse.gov/assets/documents/SEPT_20__Innovation_Whitepaper_FINAL.pdf.

Hill, C.T. and J.A. Hansen (1988), 'The measurement of technology and innovation', in J.D. Roessner (ed.), *Government Innovation Policy: Design, Implementation, Evaluation*, New York: St. Martin's Press, pp. 147–57.

Hill, C.T., J.A. Hansen and J.I. Stein (1983), *New Indicators of Industrial Innovation*, CPA83-14, Report to the National Science Foundation from the Center for Policy Alternatives, Massachusetts Institute of Technology, July. On file in the MIT library, library.mit.edu/F/?func=direct&doc_number=000190426&local_base=MIT01PUB.

Hill, C.T., E. Greenberg, D.J. Newburger and G.R. Whitaker (1975), *The Effects of Regulation on Technological Innovation in the Chemical and Allied Products Industries*, Report to the National Science Foundation, Office of R&D Assessment, Volume I, Executive Summary; Volume II, The State of the Art; Volume III, Abstracts and Literature List; February, Arlington, VA: NSF.

National Economic Council (2011), *A Strategy For American Innovation: Driving towards Sustainable Growth and Quality Jobs*, 4 February, Washington, DC: National Economic Council. www.whitehouse.gov/innovation/strategy.

NRC (2005), *Measuring Research and Development Expenditures in the U.S. Economy*, Panel on Research and Development Statistics at the National Science Foundation, Lawrence D. Brown, Thomas J. Plewes and Marisa A. Gerstein (eds). Committee on National Statistics, Division of Behavioral and Social Sciences and Education, Washington, DC: The National Academies Press, www.nap.edu/openbook.php?record_id=11111&page=R1.

NSF (2010a), 'Business R&D and Innovation Survey, survey description', on line at www.nsf.gov/statistics/srvyindustry, updated 25 May 2010.

NSF (2010b), NSF releases new statistics on business innovation', NSF11-300, October, Arlington, VA: NSF. www.nsf.gov/statistics/infbrief/nsf11300/.

NSF (2012a), 'State research and development expenditures total $1.2 billion in FY 2009',

US National Science Foundation, Report 12-324, July, Arlington, VA: NSF, www.nsf. gov/statistics/infbrief/nsf12324/.

NSF (2012b), 'U.S. R&D spending suffered a rare decline in 2009 but outpaced the overall economy', US National Science Foundation, Report 12-310, March, Arlington, VA: NSF, www.nsf.gov/statistics/infbrief/nsf12310/.

NSF (undated a), *Business R&D and Innovation Survey*, Arlington, VA: NSF, www.nsf.gov/ statistics/srvyindustry/about/brdis/.

NSF (undated b), *2008 BRDIS Business Expert Panel*, Arlington, VA: NSF, www.nsf.gov/ statistics/srvyindustry/about/brdis/panel.cfm.

Porter, M. and C. van der Linde (1995), 'Toward a new conception of the environment–competitiveness relationship', *Journal of Economic Perspectives*, **9**(4), 97–118.

Rose, S., S. Shipp, B. Lal and A. Stone (2009), 'Frameworks for measuring innovation: initial approaches', Science and Technology Policy Institute and the Athena Alliance, Working Paper #06, March, Washington, DC: Athena Alliance, www.athenaalliance.org/pdf/ InnovationFrameworks-STPI.pdf.

SSTI (2011), *Tech-based Economic Development and the States: Legislative Action in 2011*, Westerville, OH: State Science and Technology Institute, www.ssti.org/Publications/ tbedandstates2011.pdf.

Wikipedia (undated), *Porter Hypothesis*, www.en.wikipedia.org/wiki/Porter_Hypothesis.

PART VI

BEYOND THE HORIZON

15 Developing and using indicators of emerging and enabling technologies[1]

Leonid Gokhberg, Konstantin Fursov, Ian Miles and Giulio Perani

1. INTRODUCTION

Statistical frameworks have usually been regarded, with some justification, as like Minerva's owl, alerting us to important knowledge only at the end of the day. Statisticians have been understandably reluctant to introduce modifications to their systems whenever a major breakthrough in technology or economic organization is announced. But this has meant that it can take a very long time for indicators to catch up with important developments. Often observers – and decision makers – are left only with impressionistic claims or consultancy reports. This becomes particularly problematic when one is dealing with emerging technologies, especially those that have the potential to transform wide swathes of social and economic activity. Is it possible to construct statistical frameworks that will allow us to monitor and track developments in such technologies from an early stage?

Extensive experience has been gathered from the development of the ICT revolution over the last half-century. This has been very informative when it has come to establishing statistics and indicators capable of addressing biotechnology, another set of developments with far-reaching implications. Now, while the ICT revolution is still ongoing, and the biotechnology revolution is just beginning to demonstrate its scope, we are confronted with another field (or set of fields) of potentially pervasive significance – the emerging technologies collectively known as nanotechnology. The fact that many commentators talk of 'converging technologies' underlines the scale of the task.

However, it is vital to capture more of the critical developments at early stages, even if only imperfectly, for a number of reasons. One reason is that we will then be better equipped to identify and examine different rates of development that present themselves in different regions and sectors. This chapter considers the scope for capturing developments in technology at an early stage, rather than waiting for the applications of this technology to be so widespread that they can no longer be ignored. It is also an attempt to provide ideas for developing a general framework to measure the extent to which a technology has become an enabling technology, that is, an engine for production of goods and services across various economy sectors.

Such a framework can be built on the lessons learned from statistical work around ICT and biotechnology; indeed, this has already resulted in practical efforts to establish new frameworks. The chapter will review national experiences, and draw out the implications for further efforts around nanotechnology and emerging and enabling technologies (EETs) in general.

The Russian experience is particularly interesting, because this is a case where data production has been deemed necessary to inform decision making. It also demonstrates the scope for using technology foresight to orient statistical work, and suggests that a combination of improved statistical monitoring of ongoing developments, and foresight analysis of anticipated technology and technology applications, represents a powerful approach to achieving early footholds by way of indicators of emerging technologies in concrete circumstances. Foresight exercises are especially helpful when new, forward-looking classifications for technology areas and allied goods and services are to be provided in the absence of any standardized schemes and statistical evidence. The result in this case has been elaboration of established statistical systems, so that nanotechnology developments can be assessed, while not reorganizing the harmonized frameworks so extensively as to reduce the scope for conventional historical or cross-national comparisons (whether or not these included attention to nanotechnology-related issues). The chapter will outline the main requirements for such an approach to be effectively implemented and its results utilized; it concludes with proposals for future methodological and conceptual development.

2. EMERGING, ENABLING AND GENERAL-PURPOSE TECHNOLOGIES

There is widespread and increasing interest in the development of indicators for measuring EETs. Such indicators can be used for monitoring their arrival, development and subsequent diffusion, as well as their key social and economic impacts – all of these are topics that concern national and regional policy makers, and are often of interest to industrial actors, research institutions, education bodies and so on. The growing integration of new technologies into economic and social processes over the last 50 years has been accompanied by a growing understanding that the resources allocated for augmentation of knowledge, for evaluation of effects and consequences of experimental activities, and for support to innovation and diffusion need sophisticated analysis. One result has been efforts to establish relevant statistics, allowing for standardized and internationally harmonized measurement of science and technology (S&T) in terms of inputs (R&D and other expenditures and labour forces), outputs (scientific publications, patents, technology exports etc.), outcomes (diffusion of innovations) and to a limited extent impacts (productivity trends, for example). These can contribute to evidence-based S&T policy making at national and regional level.

Emerging technologies have been accepted as one of the pillars of future innovation-based economic growth. A number of surveys focusing on specific 'technological domains' have already been carried out in several countries, to identify and characterize certain S&T areas, to estimate their economic and social effects, as well as to explore public attitudes and perceptions (especially since some technologies, such as nuclear energy and genetic modification of organisms, have proved highly controversial). These studies were not just about well-established domains such as ICT and biotechnology, for which statistical measurement is conducted on a regular basis in many developed countries, but also on less harmonized areas, such as nanotechnology, 'green' technology or other types of 'advanced' or 'emerging' technologies.

The notion of 'emerging technologies' is widely employed, and is used here to focus our attention on developments that: (a) result from contemporary advances in a given field of knowledge; (b) are rapidly evolving; and (c) have high potential to result in inventions and innovations with significant societal and economic impacts. A set of technologies, or a growing technology area, is involved, with novel ways of applying scientific or technical knowledge for practical purposes to transform energy, matter or information. A well-known case is microelectronic technologies, which allowed for much more powerful and small-scale devices as compared to those based on thermionic valves. The new transformations, or ways of transforming things, that they offer are such as to be of considerable potential influence on the applicability of other, even well-established technologies. (For example, development of magnetic resonance imaging in medicine can reduce application of existing systems using X-rays.) Finally, these potentials are liable to produce – direct and indirect – economic and societal impacts of the emerging technologies on final users over the long term.

It is almost impossible to distinguish between different technologies when they are at the early stage of their life cycle (at least, with the use of traditional statistical surveys), as they appear to be uncategorized and chaotic where merely expectations and visions guide the field, rather than facts and prime examples 'out there' (Van Merkerk and Smits 2008). One of the problems here is that several competing technological solutions to common problems can always be found but one or other wins out. As they are therefore different from the later stages of technology development owing to the absence of transparent and structured relations between actors, there could also be 'false starts' when the eventual technology regime is quite different from the first attempts to institute it. The Web and Videotex competition in the mid-1990s is an exemplar case in this regard (Carey and Elton 2009). Another problem is methodological. The new developments tend to be assimilated into existing statistical categories until their significance is more definitively established. Thus the general definition of emerging technologies above has to be set against existing and standardized definitions of the most common technological domains in which particular examples or cases, representing nationally relevant rising technology areas or particular priorities in technology development, should be taken into consideration, at least for a certain reference period. In particular, emerging technologies should be distinguished from so-called 'enabling technologies', considered as already-available inventions or innovations that are likely to be applied in a foreseeable period of time and to drive radical change in the capabilities of a user in its use of other technologies. Allied irreversibilities that emerge in the ongoing activities of researchers, policy makers and organizations engaged in knowledge production create a need for agenda-building processes (Van Merkerk and van Lente 2005), when spontaneous and open socio-cognitive patterns are to be limited by user needs and expectations, policy issues and national interests. Examples are EU key enabling technologies,[2] and official lists of S&T priority areas in Russia and the USA. It should be noted that some enabling technologies may not be emerging, in the sense that they involve upgrading and more fully exploiting a known technology, but for many of them it is a bit of a struggle to make them commercializable.

Finally, when new enabling technologies have the potential to become widely used across the entire economy or a core technology has a substantial and pervasive effect across the whole of society, it is often termed a 'general-purpose technology' (GPT). This stage is characterized by more sustainable relations between various actor-networks involved to share beliefs that the GPT is spawning innovations in multiple technological areas. Previous research has suggested that a GPT must have at least three attributes: pervasiveness, an innovation spawning effect, and scope for improvement (Helpman and Trajtenberg 1994). Some authors add a fourth element to the definition of a GPT, that of wide dissemination (Lipsey et al. 1998), although this element is often considered a logical consequence of the other three attributes. Taking these criteria as a reference point, researchers (e.g. Youtie et al. 2008) show that new and growing areas such as bio- and nanotechnologies have a chance to be followed by a sequence of events in which a major technological innovation is preceded by a number of smaller incremental inventions that expand the range of applicability of the core technology, bringing them to the group of GPTs such as electricity, ICT and others that have been previously documented as major breakthroughs.

At least three classes of emerging technologies can be identified:

1. 'Revolutionary' technologies, based on major advances in knowledge in some field of science (and applied science), with potential for wide applicability because they propose new approaches to providing solutions to problems widely encountered in social and economic processes – Freeman and Perez's heartland technologies, such as electrification, microelectronics and genomics (Freeman and Perez 1988). Often several related breakthroughs work synergistically – software, optronics, microelectronics, for example.
2. 'Convergent' technologies, where dramatic advances in technological knowledge across several such fields are applied in combination – as in the NBIC technologies (nano, bio, ICT and cognitive technologies), where development in each of the sub-areas is heavily reliant on development in the others, but where the underlying fields of knowledge are from domains with little prior relationship.[3]
3. Problem-oriented technologies, such as 'green' technologies or 'advanced manufacturing methods', that are identified more on the basis of the set of problems that they address than of the core knowledge on which they are built (as in the first two groups). Often there may be a critical breakthrough around which many other solutions cluster – such would be the case if one achieved readily commercializable breakthroughs in, say, renewable energy production or energy efficiency across a wide spectrum of products. Until this is clearly the case, however, the emerging technology label is applicable on account of the devotion of substantial concerted efforts to achieving what is hoped will be far-reaching impacts from development of a multiplicity of partial solutions to the set of problems that has been identified here.

Current classifications of emerging technologies focus most attention on a few technological areas – and these may be defined in several, sometimes contradictory, ways. Biotechnology is a good case in point, being still in its specific segments considered an 'emerging' technology but also influenced by a process of 'convergence' – and as having the potential of 'enabling'

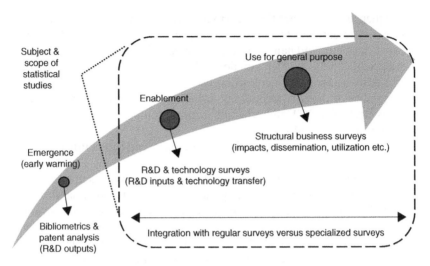

Subject &
scope of
statistical
studies

Use for general purpose

Enablement

Structural business surveys
(impacts, dissemination, utilization etc.)

Emergence
(early warning)

R&D & technology surveys
(R&D inputs & technology transfer)

Bibliometrics &
patent analysis
(R&D outputs)

Integration with regular surveys versus specialized surveys

*Figure 15.1   Measuring emerging, enabling and general-purpose
technologies: scope of statistics*

other technologies to be applied in several fields having 'general-purpose'
implications. Basically, by 'biotechnology' a quite large technological area
is meant, where specific 'sub-domains' (including some overlapping with
the 'nanotechnology' domain) can have different features.

In order to develop the framework in a structured and coherent way,
it is important to denote the subject and the scope for statistical studies
(Figure 15.1). On the one hand it is important to distinguish the moment
when (a) a specific technology starts to 'emerge' and (b) when it becomes
relevant for measurement in statistical terms such as 'scientific productivity' and technology creation, diffusion and use, and production of
technology-enabled goods and services.

The identification of the moment of technology emergence is strongly
connected to the provision of a common definition and general classification principles that can help to describe the nature of the area uncovering
one or more of its 'sub-components' and reflecting distinctive features.
Various analytical exercises based on the analysis of bibliometric and
patent data can be quite helpful in solving the task. Some examples of
analysis and reporting of emerging technology indicators that can help
to monitor 'hot research areas' and reveal how multidisciplinary, transla-
tional networks are evolving can be found in OECD (2010: 28–9). As for
the strategies of bibliometric analysis, at least three basic methodological
approaches can be identified. The first one is to visualize the structure
of knowledge and key emerging trends. It is based on keyword analysis

(mainly on first appearance and life cycle of the keywords used to describe scientific articles) and helps to identify growing research areas and emerging topics as well as the disciplinary structure of the whole of knowledge (Chen 2006; Cobo et al. 2011; Morel et al. 2009; Van Raan 1996). The second approach is focused on analysis of research areas already accepted by the scientific community as likely to contribute to future development. It is based on citation indexing of publications produced in a particular research area and allows identifying certain research clusters (Shibata et al. 2008). A similar approach is applied in patent analysis (Daim et al. 2006). Finally, the third approach evidently combines both the previous strategies and detects fast-growing research areas in the entire field of knowledge and depicts the life cycles of research fronts (Guo et al. 2011, Upham and Small 2010). One more strategy is based on linking of patents to scientific literature through co-citation analysis (OECD 2010: 36). It provides an indication of the type of scientific knowledge certain types of innovation, for example 'green innovation', draw on. These mapping tools become a kind of early warning system that helps to identify areas of high R&D potential and can also be used productively as a shared source of data providing basis for more detailed analysis and expert sounding.

The question of statistical measurement focuses on the relation of a technology field with existing institutionalized units, such as fields of science (scientific disciplines), sectors of R&D performance and so on, as well as existing S&T policy frameworks (e.g. priority settings and funding instruments). It brings statistics to the field, identifies the scope for measurement and highlights the need for elaboration of classification approaches and an indicator system for measuring inputs, outputs and impacts of EETs within the existing structure of national statistical surveys. It is common to find that such technologies cross several established disciplines and fields of knowledge. The complex interdisciplinary character of such areas is one reason why methodologies to detect and describe them are particularly challenging, with measurement approaches still in the testing phase. One typically has very limited knowledge about the main sources of growth and potential application of EETs. Policy makers require verifiable and comparable data, based on consistent methodology and harmonized approaches, and presented in a timely and useful fashion. Statisticians, meanwhile, lack standard definitions and classifications for the growing areas, and have to deal with relatively rare populations, and incomplete knowledge of outputs and impacts. It should be admitted that no single methodology can meet the abovementioned challenges; rather a multifactorial suite of databases, surveys, forecasting and foresight approaches, and case studies provides a mosaic representation of activities, players, linkages and issues within the field. The importance of such a measurement mix for statistical description of EETs requires rethinking available approaches to the development of an operational definition and classification of technologies for statistical purposes; looking at the best national practices in knowledge measurement will be important for learning and for inspiration.

3. APPROACHES TO THE DEVELOPMENT OF AN OPERATIONAL DEFINITION OF TECHNOLOGIES FOR STATISTICAL PURPOSES

The development of approaches to describe S&T and innovation processes as proper categories goes back to the 1920s when national policy-making organizations in the USA, Canada and later Great Britain started campaigns to measure costs of national research laboratories and compute 'national research budgets'. The word 'research' became central to these studies. Although it had been measured, the question 'what is research?' was originally left to the questionnaire respondent to decide (Godin 2005). It took several decades before research activities came to be defined precisely for statistical purposes and first adopted in a form of internationally accepted methodological guidelines by OECD member countries in Frascati (Italy) in 1963. Since then the OECD *Frascati Manual* (OECD 2002) became a major methodological source focusing on definitions, classifications and methodologies for measuring the expenditures and human resources devoted to R&D.

The discussion on the construction of an operational definition of technology begins with the introduction of the OECD *Oslo Manual* in 1992 that was initially aimed at providing approaches to measuring the use and planned use of technologies (Gault 2010: 39–43). Despite the fact that technological innovation was taken as a central notion and an object for statistical observation the manual included no discussion on the concept of 'technology'. Technology in the wide sense was intended to capture both hardware and software aspects, as well as including productive knowledge, or production capabilities, more generally. The OECD was following a Schumpeterian view that radical innovations were motivated by a concern for dynamics at the level of industrial organization, so these guidelines were dealing only with new 'products and processess, which are technological innovations proper' (OECD 1992: 28). The second edition of the *Oslo Manual* (OECD/Eurostat 1997) inherited the semantic uncertainty of the term, especially when used in multilingual contexts, and in terms of outlining an analytical framework for the manual. The technological aspect played a major part in the then *Oslo Manual's* definition of innovation: it only concerned technological product and process innovations – those that must be 'technologically' new or improved. However, there is a certain amount of ambiguity: 'the term "technological" is not defined as such: it therefore has shades of meaning which can vary from one country to another, and even from respondent to respondent within the country' (Gimel 2003: 4). Technological development was concerned with processes leading to value-added outputs and measurable changes in it, such as increased productivity or sales (OECD/Eurostat 1997: 47, 52–5). In both cases it dealt with the respondent's understanding of the measurement issues similarly to an early stage of R&D data collection, as mentioned above. In the third edition of the *Oslo Manual* the word 'technological' was removed from the definitions 'as the word raises a concern that many services sector firms would interpret "technological" to mean "using high-technology plant and equipment" and thus not applicable to many of their product and process innovations' (OECD/Eurostat 2005: 17). Technological product and process innovations are no longer the subject of the manual. Focus is now placed on the close concepts of 'new or significantly improved product or process' and include only 'implemented' products and processes that are 'introduced on the market' or 'brought into actual use in the firm's operations' (ibid.: 47).

Only two of the OECD manuals actually consider how the concept of 'technology' can be defined for statistical purposes: one for compiling technology balance of payments (TBP) (OECD 1990), and the *Handbook on Economic Globalisation Indicators* (OECD 2005a). The *Patent Statistics Manual* (OECD 2009a) shows how technologies can be classified. These manuals interpret the concept of 'technology' in its basic meaning of 'technical knowledge'. More specifically, while the *Patent Statistics Manual* recommends use of the standard international patent classification to identify relevant technological areas, the *TBP Manual* points out that the concept of 'technology' should be qualified in terms of 'utilisation' (i.e. 'potential use' and economic value, as for patents in general), 'scope of application' (generality versus specificity), and 'novelty and exclusivity'. Thinking about 'technology' as a combination of definite pieces of technical knowledge, or 'techniques', may be useful in creating statistical frameworks for emerging technologies. In the *Handbook on Economic Globalisation Indicators* the technology definition is based on Mansfield's study (1983) and defined as a 'stock of (physical or managerial) knowledge which makes it possible to make new products or new processes', which includes 'implying the constant addition of new knowledge to existing knowledge that may make the existing knowledge totally or partially obsolete' (OECD 2005a: 166). As this knowledge is quite heterogeneous, the *Handbook* proposes measuring it in embodied forms of tangible and intangible goods (equipment, software etc.) and incorporated in patents, licences, know-how or technical assistance, external databases (Internet), published research findings, knowledge acquired through takeovers or mergers, or through cooperation with other firms or sectors (ibid.). A supplementary distinction lies in identifying high-tech sectors and products. The former is based on an R&D intensity criterion; the latter supplements a sectoral classification by including additional criteria either answering countries' national specifics or using the UN Standard International Trade Classification for cross-country comparisons at the international level.

Even a quick overview of different fields of study shows that the concept of 'technology' is unclear, potentially used with several different meanings and potentially misleading.[4] The main problem lies in the widespread use of the concept that (in addition to the basic definition of being the 'practical application of knowledge'[5]) includes references to specific techniques (i.e. the 'self-assembly' nanotech technique for microprocessors), single devices (i.e. transistor technology), as well as to 'assemblage of different techniques' (i.e. 'laser' technology), technological domains (i.e. 'biotechnologies'), or complex technological systems (i.e. the 'aircraft gas turbine')[6] and also to potential applications of 'technologies' (i.e. 'green technologies').

The concept of 'technology' is also affected by a serious risk of misunderstanding when used in different cultural and linguistic contexts. It can be clarified by comparing its meaning with that of a complementary word such as 'technics'. According to the OECD *TBP Manual*, this problem exists in the French language[7] but it seems even more relevant for the German and Russian languages.[8] An analysis of these potential inconsistencies in the understanding of the concept of technology may prevent further difficulties in developing a generally agreed system of technology classification.

The current use of the 'technology' concept is spreading as a result of its large success in the US culture. Following its early adoption in the mid-nineteenth century (when, for instance, the Massachusetts Institute of Technology was established by following the German tradition of the 'Polytechnic' schools), the concept of technology evolved in parallel with the Second Industrial Revolution, usually referred to as the 'Technological Revolution' (Landes 2003; Smil 2005). On the basis of the increasing awareness of the potential of new technical applications of science to change the economic and social structure of the Western countries, as well as strongly influencing the everyday lives of their citizens, the concept of technology gathered momentum and began to be used to identify the 'pervasiveness' and 'dominance' of machines on various aspects of our lives, at least in comparison with the previous age.

Deriving from the concept of 'Technik', largely used by German sociologists and economists, the 'American' concept of technology has been, since the end of the nineteenth century, strongly associated with the economic and social effects of the practical application of scientific findings in industrial and applicative processes (Schatzberg 2006). It soon became apparent that the diffusion of 'new technologies' was shaping a new social structure by influencing habits, cultures, economic relationships and social infrastructures (Marx 2010).

Two main lessons can be drawn from the analysis of the problems of definition related to the evolution of the concept of 'technology' in the USA and in most of the Western countries. First, this concept has become practically all-encompassing in its common usage, and its inclusion in a statistical framework must be given a clear definition, stressing the need for a full exploitation for statistical purposes of related terms and concepts (e.g. knowledge, technique(s), process, domain(s) etc.). Second, it should be stressed that a technology is more a social phenomenon than a scientific or technical one. It should also be mentioned that a technology development in itself can be identified in terms of 'social relationships' and with reference to its ability to establish them (e.g. see Gault 2011: 4–5). In this perspective, a technology exists since it can have a clear social and/or economic impact. A logical consequence is that the term 'emerging technologies' is rather controversial in the sense that if a 'technology' can be identified, it means that such technology has already 'emerged' and some evidence of it can be found in specific social processes.

For present purposes the general definition of technology contained in the OECD *Measuring Productivity* manual (OECD 2001) and subsequently in the *OECD Glossary of Statistical Terms* (OECD 2008) can be applied. Both appeal to the general definition, formerly introduced by Griliches (1987), and suggest that 'technology refers to the state of knowledge concerning ways of converting resources into outputs' (OECD 2008: 536) and appears 'rather in its disembodied form (such as a new blueprint, scientific results, new organizational techniques) or embodied in new products (advances in the design, quality of new vintages of capital goods and intensive inputs)' that link them to innovation and productivity measures (OECD 2001: 8).

To be consistent with these findings, a revision of the current system of technological classifications (or, to some extent, 'para-classification') should be proposed. The point here is whether definitions such as 'enabling technologies' or 'general-purpose technologies' or 'advanced technologies' can be effectively used in a statistical framework, or if some innovative approach is needed in order to avoid a potential confusion among these quite similar – and partially unclear – definitions.

For the purposes of this chapter, technology is considered as ways of knowledge application in which humans can effect transformations of the world (of things, of materials, of energy, of symbols, of organisms). Moreover, emerging technologies are then taken to mean application of new knowledge, or knowledge that is itself 'emerging' (i.e. underdeveloped) to create new or improved ways of transforming the world, where these transformations are ones that are, or are likely to be, those of widespread social and/or economic significance. Then there are the heartland (core) technologies – those components or devices that fundamentally accomplish these transformations: power stations, grids, electric motors, microprocessors, computers and several other important techniques such as nanotechnology tools. When the transformations are ones that are (or can be) very widely employed, and when the new technologies offer radical improvements in the price, performance or other desirable characteristics of these transformations, one can take a look at new heartland technologies that may trigger technological revolutions. There can be components (e.g. microprocessors), platforms and symptoms (computers, the Internet, social media etc.), and techniques (e.g. text processing) that are widely used.

In any case, identification of emerging technologies (or 'techniques') requires using specific methodologies, drawing on the definition proposed earlier, and taking into account the particular problems associated with converging and problem-oriented technologies. For example, the NBIC technologies mentioned above pose problems due to the convergence of activities and knowledge from widely dispersed domains; specific methodological guidelines will be required for their measurement and it may be that only general recommendations on how to deal with them can be included in the overall statistical framework at present. The problem-oriented contenders for the title of emerging technologies may, in the absence of new heartland technologies, have to be measured almost exclusively in terms of social and economic impacts given that they are linked more in terms of these impacts than in terms of their industrial or technological origins.

4.   TOWARDS THE 3D CLASSIFICATION OF TECHNOLOGIES

The main statistical frameworks are not designed to support analysis of the knowledge economy and society as well as current technological development. Although the introduction of groupings for bio- and nanotechnology R&D[9] into current versions of NACE and of the North American

Industry Classification System (NAICS) is an important breakthrough in this regard, there is still lack of internationally standardized and commonly used classifications and data collection by technology area with respect to technology-specific information, of relevance for analysis in the fields of bio- and nanotechnology as well as in new materials and ICT (Veugelers 2007: 43). In current statistical practice industries are classified in terms of sectors (ISIC, NACE) for which data on employment and expenditures are collected; jobs are classified in terms of occupations (ISCO) and educational qualifications in terms of programmes (ISCED); product classifications (CPA) cover goods and services – but the groups here are largely derived from the sectors used in NACE. Typically the references to technology are relatively indirect ones – a set of firms that manufactures computers or a set of jobs that produces software, for example, can be identified, but the particular underpinning technologies are usually only sketchily outlined, with newer methods and tools rarely being visible (see Box 15.1). It creates an even greater problem when measuring biotechnology that lacks a core 'sector' that can be immediately identified for the purpose of collecting data (Box 15.2). Research fields are classified in various ways (e.g. the *Frascati Manual* (OECD 2002) 'Fields of Science and Technology' (FOS)), and scientific journals can be considered according to fields of study. Perhaps most relevant to the discussion, patents are grouped according to a technology area in line with the International Patent Classification (IPC). This classification system can refer to quite detailed technology developments, but patent data are rarely integrated into economic accounts. In principle, such data can be used to explore which sectors or regions are generating technological knowledge in particular fields.

For certain technology areas (e.g. bio- and nanotechnologies) some countries use national *ad hoc* classifications (e.g. technology areas, types of goods and services etc.), so as to generate information on industrial activity, skill shortages and related topics surrounding new technologies.

The most relevant problems reported by countries are related to:

(a) methodological issues, in particular to technology (or emerging technology) detection and classification;
(b) the selection of a proper level of aggregation (a single technology, a (intermediate) technology domain, or a larger technology area);
(c) identification of statistical units and sampling, understanding by respondents and achieving a relevant response rate.

In addition, it is widely reported that there are problems in gaining attention and support from policy makers, national business or professional associations when it comes to the statistical measurement of technologies.

BOX 15.1   MEASUREMENT APPROACHES IN ICT
STATISTICS

The ICT revolution was analysed in so-called 'neo-Schumpeterian' terms (e.g. Freeman and Perez 1988), as techno-economic paradigm change involving a revolutionary heartland technology. The new ICTs are seen as representing more than just a further step in the steady evolution of information activities (Machlup 1962; Porat 1977), and in the slow process of application of technologies of all types to information processing (Beniger 1986). A vast range of changes in the use of information is under way as a result of the cheapening of programmable information-processing power, through the use of microelectronics. Since the ICT revolution has largely been based upon the cheapening and increased performance of the core technology of microelectronics, it might seem reasonable to focus on devices that use this heartland technology – but what then about the software required to realize the utility of ICT, the services that are created? And if anything using microelectronics is classified as an ICT device (rather than, say, an ICT-enabled device), this would mean that as more and more products come to incorporate silicon chips (not only computers, phones, audiovisual products and robots, but also cars, household appliances, devices used in stores and hospitals, even 'smart buildings' and 'smart grids'), all of these might be classified as if they were equally ICTs.

One solution introduced in Miles (1991) is to discriminate between:

(1) Heartland ICT components (silicon chips, etc. – scope should be left for future developments in defining these: for instance, optronics might well at some point displace microelectronics from its leading role in ICT. The functions that are affected are more important than the specific materials that achieve this).

(2) The core ICT products, such as computers and telecommunications equipment and services, which provide general-purpose information-processing functionality as their main output.

(3) ICT-using products, which may incorporate dedicated chips and embedded computers, or be controlled through telecommunications or other means, but whose main

functionalities will often involve effecting physical, chemical or biological changes (e.g. moving things, maintaining them, changing people's physical health status etc.). Note that this definition would assign robotics and similar automated processes and equipment to this category.

(4) Non-ICT-using products, which may or may not be embedded within systems which include other elements that are ICT-using, and may or may not have been produced with ICT assistance (e.g. a tin of food in a supermarket may have been produced through the use of robotics, and may carry a bar code which enables automated check-out in a supermarket that uses ICT – but it is not itself ICT).

The 'ICT revolution' features the development of potentials in category (1), and the application and diffusion of these potentials in categories (2) and (3) (where there may be many 'swarms' of innovation). Greater shares of category (4) would be expected to be produced and delivered through ICT-using systems. Furthermore, the economy as a whole becomes more ICT-intensive, which is not to say that everything is ICT. The sort of distinction between ICT products and ICT-enabled products outlined above became embedded in the statistical classifications used by the OECD, in particular, although the various studies this organization commissioned on the information economy more broadly also take into account the specific information and communication products and services enabled through new ICTs – digital content, e-commerce, social media and the like.

According to the *Guide to Measuring the Information Society* (OECD 2011), activity in manufacturing products of a candidate activity is identified as ICT in cases where they are intended to process and communicate information, as well as to transmit and display it, or to use electronic processes to detect, measure and/or record physical phenomena, or to control a physical process. In service activities, the products of a candidate activity must be intended to enable the processing and communication of information by electronic means. This definition has allowed statisticians to use existing structural business statistics, such as employment, turnover, wages and salaries, and added value to access the size and the structure of the ICT sector (Gokhberg and Bøegh-Nielsen 2007).

BOX 15.2   MEASUREMENT APPROACH IN BIOTECHNOLOGY STATISTICS

Biotechnology development refers to the social and economic impacts of developing technologies that allow life to be manipulated at the level of genes. It consists of a group of related technologies with applications in many different economic sectors – agriculture, forestry, aquaculture, mining, petroleum refining, environmental remediation, human and animal health, food processing, chemicals, security systems – and in many industrial processes. It is the range of current and potential applications, together with their economic, environmental and social impacts, that creates policy interest in obtaining high-quality indicators for biotechnology.

The first attempts to measure biotechnology focused on R&D activities in the late 1980s. Early measurement showed rapid increases in R&D spending, almost doubling every second year (Rose 1997). This was a sign that businesses were adopting biotechnology. Then, in the late 1990s, statistical offices of some OECD member countries (Canada, New Zealand and France) initiated their first dedicated surveys of biotechnology activities in the industrial sector. The main focus of these surveys was firms that were actively engaged in the use of biotechnology for R&D, innovation and production purposes (Rose and McNiven 2007).

First measurement experiences demonstrated that, unlike ICT or other technologies, biotechnology lacks a core 'sector' that can be quickly identified and surveyed. This has created major challenges for developing comparable biotechnology indicators. These include national differences in the definition of biotechnology and the fields of application of biotechnology, and of a biotechnology firm. To address these issues, over the past seven years the OECD has coordinated work by national experts to improve definitions and survey methodologies (OECD 2007: 227). The Ad Hoc Working Group met five times between 2000 and 2004. It established a statistical definition for biotechnology and proposed ways of applying the definition in R&D surveys, dedicated biotechnology surveys and a patent classification. It also proposed a list of potential indicators, collection guidelines, classification schemes, and model questionnaires and surveys (OECD 2005b).

According to the OECD recommendations, a single definition describes biotechnology as 'the application of S&T to living
organisms as well as parts, products and models thereof, to alter
living or non-living materials for the production of knowledge,
goods and services' (OECD 2009b: 9). This definition is supplemented by a so-called list-based definition, accepted by member
countries in 2008 and including several biotechnology techniques
in such sub-areas as DNA/RNA, proteins and other molecules,
cell and tissue culture and engineering, process biotechnology
techniques, gene and RNA vectors, bioinformatics and nanobiotechnology (OECD 2005b: 9). In addition to these definitions a
number of criteria for identification of biotechnology-related firms,
products and processes was elaborated. That allowed introducing a conceptual model and general measurement approach
bringing together key biotechnology activities, techniques and
elements of probable end uses of biotechnology products (mostly
beyond the scope of the proposed approach) into existing statistical frameworks (OECD 2005b).

One possible classification approach is aimed at avoiding most of the diff-
culties experienced with current 'classifications' by considering three basic
criteria that should be used to identify the main features of any 'technology' or 'technique':

(a) the field(s) of science on which its development has been based (sci-
    entific base or origin);
(b) the industries (goods and services) where it is actually applied
    (application);
(c) the socioeconomic dimensions most influenced by its diffusion and
    adoption (impact).

Following this proposal, some technologies will be classified only in
terms of their scientific base (e.g. putatively 'emerging' technologies or
techniques that have not yet found any specific application). In contrast,
those technologies that are already diffusing into the economy could be
more effectively classified also in terms of the industries where they are
applied (e.g. extracting, manufacturing or service technologies) or in
terms of expected societal impact ('energy-saving' or 'green' technologies).
This approach should allow for providing the statistical framework with
a robust classification base (as only official statistical classifications, and

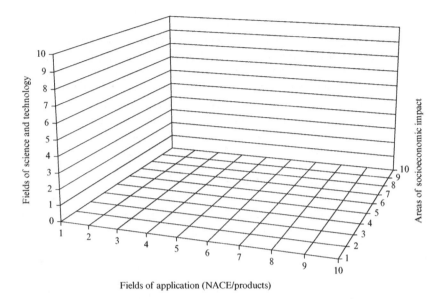

Figure 15.2   A 3D visualization of an integrated system of classification for technologies

thus the data organized on their basis, will be used in this context, at least at the initial stage). It should also be able to deal with demand by users – mainly by policy makers – for evidence on the results of their investments in S&T.

By taking into account that the current classifications have, as a major shortcoming, the limitation of considering only a single aspect of technology development, it should be stressed that the proposed classification approach allows for a 'multidimensional' classification of technical knowledge that could be further developed in the future along two main lines of activity: improvement of the existing statistical classifications; and testing of a new multidimensional classification of technologies.

Figure 15.2 portrays the three dimensions that can contribute to a more inclusive classification system. The main conventional statistical classifications used currently in the international S&T statistics domain are brought together: the Frascati FOS classification, the classification of economic activities adopted at the international level (either NACE or ISIC, which can be broken down by product groups by applying the related classifications used in the statistics on production), and the Frascati classification of Socio-Economic Objectives (SEO). Adoption of these classifications does not imply that these will be the ultimate categories in the new statistical framework: they could certainly be improved. For example, the FOS classification still relies on traditional boundaries among scientific fields, and provides few options to deal with multidisciplinarity. SEO classification shows that there is a general need to invest resources in evaluating and reorganizing classifications currently used in accordance with ongoing social and economic changes, and, moreover, to develop new ones – more suited to the new socioeconomic configurations that are emerging and, it is hoped, more helpful for the measurement of technology and technological activities that underpin this. At the same time, using existing classifications helps at least to reflect most recent technological advancements by levelling such multidisciplinary horizontal areas as ICT, bio- and nanotechnology within the conventional frameworks, similar to more traditional fields of science. In another case, new technologies are shaping new industries (for example one can see the rapid emergence of various web-related industries, from ISPs and server farms, to web design and mobile web services), and the current classification of economic activities may not always reflect these quite recent changes.

The sorts of data that could go into the cells of this 3D matrix should be described. For example, economic accounts would conventionally primarily deal with money (the value of inputs and outputs) or with people (the number of workers [or FTE workers] engaged here). But other data sets could be brought to bear, perhaps through satellite accounting or similar – for example the wave of studies of the diffusion of robotics across manufacturing, or PCs/Internet across the whole economy, yields data that could be fitted into such cells (e.g. the share of enterprises using ICT, per capita ICT investment).

Another possible path of development, missing from the current framework, is the occupational and educational levels (ISCO and ISCED) that demonstrate the need for new competencies for technology development/processing. Going further still, one can see the accounting matrix extending into social accounting: the situation of the household economy, where some SEOs are instantiated, and where money and time are spent consuming (and often producing with the aid of) new technologies. Quite a few information society statistics examine this sort of thing – and social accounting matrices (SAMs) can be used to depict digital divides and the like.

Returning to the discussion of the identification and characterization of EETs, further development of such approaches should be a by-product of the actual statistical activity. The indicator system that will emerge from the new statistical framework will assist the elaboration of criteria to distinguish the moment when a specific technology starts to 'emerge', when it becomes relevant for measurement in terms of 'scientific productivity' and of technology creation, diffusion and use, which goods or services will be enabled (or affected otherwise) by relevant changes as a result of its application (potency), and which changes in the social and economic system will be caused by its diffusion. These are the criteria that – in connection with a common definition and general classification principles that can assist in describing the nature of new technology, uncovering one or more of its 'sub-components' and reflecting distinctive features of it – can help to identify the dynamic position of each single technology in the 3D matrix by highlighting its process of evolution from one position to another.

5.   RECOMMENDATIONS ON SURVEY STRATEGIES AND KEY INDICATORS

Measuring EETs is a challenging task, dealing with growing potential innovations caused by results of technological development extending across various economic sectors. The existing rhetoric highlights the future success of technologies under development, while the *de facto* high level of the expectations is portrayed with the low range of indicators of technology-related activities. It should be noted that, in general, national statistical offices as well as research organizations have not actively participated in the elaboration of statistical data to provide evidence of EET development. These activities are locally addressed and commonly based on the integration of limited indicators (questions) into regular surveys.[10] On the one hand, this allows to identify a population of organizations engaged in technological development and, on the other hand, to exploit the potential of existing measurement frameworks. Thus regular innovation surveys may be amended to include questions about the use of particular techniques or technologies; even the Labour Force Survey has been used as a vehicle to carry out enquiries about employee use of new ICTs, and categories reflecting new ICT consumer goods have been added into household expenditure surveys and so on.

Specialized regular surveys of more established technology domains, such as ICT or biotechnology, have been established in several countries. In some cases, topics that were at one time the focus of much attention have dropped somewhat from visibility, and so a wave of surveys of uptake of office automation and industrial robotics in the 1980s has largely subsided (although the 1990s and the first decade of the 2000s saw waves of new interest on topics such as Internet use and e-commerce). A few similar projects were started with the aim of an in-depth analysis of biotechnology.[11] Some *ad hoc* surveys were addressed to distinct technology areas.[12] Among the variety of projects related to the analysis of trends in nanotechnology development and using different qualitative and quantitative indicators, there are few examples of statistical observations as such. The forms and extent of data collection in the field of nanotechnology are also very diverse: from censuses of organizations (Israel, the USA and Canada) or individual researchers undertaking projects in nanotechnology (Mexico) to the study of public opinion (the USA, Japan, Russia and most EU countries) and assessment of personal experience of using nanotechnology-enabled products (Australia). In some cases, statistical questionnaires include indicators of innovative activity and industrial output (Russia), and some patent and bibliometric indicators (Belgium, France, Italy, Germany and Sweden). In most cases such studies are initiated by government agencies and carried out within the national nanotechnology initiatives or major programmes with the participation of manufacturing companies, non-profit organizations, universities and research centres.

Since a technology area (domain) is taken as an object for statistical observation, its identification and measurement require developing indicators, charaterizing economic inputs, outputs and impacts from their development and use. The EETs form a specific field in different areas of S&T. Moreover, the cycle of EET development is integrated into the S&T system, which lends itself well to a systemic analysis. One way in which the S&T system can be presented involves the depiction of a system comprising education, research and innovation subsystems. They are introduced into an environment and receive input from this environment. The three subsystems use this input to create and produce technological outputs. If successful, new scientific knowledge and the EET that result from it are applied to create goods and services. The goods and services resulting from the new scientific knowledge and EET will be distributed, marketed, consumed and used. Finally the distribution, marketing, consumption and utilization activities of the new scientific knowledge and EET will have an impact on the environment. The sustainable development indicators will tell whether this impact is positive or not.

The EET indicator system can be superimposed on the overall S&T system. The EET indicator system is divided into six major categories that form the main elements of the S&T system: context, input, procedure, output, growth of knowledge and technological progress and, lastly, impact (Table 15.1). Activities that cross over from one category of indicators to another enable a global view of the development cycle of the EET. It is important to analyse and therefore to measure these activities. The indicators of incentive, utilization, creation and development, and then consumption, dissemination, and marketing of EETs also have to be developed.

Table 15.1   Emerging and enabling technology indicator system

Contextual indicators
Economic, social, political and ecological environment, incentive structures

Input indicators	Process indicators	Output indicators	Impact indicators
Sources (financial, personnel, knowledge and technological) and public funding	Collaboration, partnership, HRST mobility and skills, technology transfer	Tacit knowledge (graduates, diplomas and certificates), codified knowledge and disembodied technologies (scientific publications, patents and their citations, licences, know-how etc.), embodied technologies and innovations (technological advances, new and advanced products and processes)	Direct impacts (sales, employment, market shares, final user adoption etc.), economic, social and other indirect impacts (CO_2 savings, energy efficiency and other sustainable development indicators and responses to global challenges)

Indicators on the cycle of development of EETs
IPR and technology commercialization, technology dissemination, utilization
    and consumption in industry, public sector and households

This indicators system can be applied to all EETs or to particular techno-logical areas (ICT, biotechnology, nanotechnology, energy, environment, health etc.). This model recognizes existing and growing institutional structures and actors that generate, transmit and use S&T knowledge by engaging in different activities. Given levels represent key stages of knowledge flows, taking into account their measurable forms and various inputs. At the same time outputs lead to a wide range of direct outcomes and indirect longer-term impacts connected in turn to key policy issues and global challenges. Since the model describes the flow of S&T knowledge through the system, it also addresses environmental issues that provide a general context of EET development. In particular, output indicators can be partial measures of impacts while impacts can influence the social and economic objectives, creating incentive structures for generating new knowledge, and developing and disseminating new technologies, as the cycle begins again.

6. DEVELOPING A MONITORING SYSTEM FOR EETS – THE RUSSIAN EXPERIENCE WITH NANOTECHNOLOGY STATISTICS

In most cases efforts to statistically measure technology at the national level have mainly been limited to three broad technological domains: ICT, biotechnology, and more recently nanotechnology, adopting existing OECD and Eurostat definitions and methodological guidelines. Although the nanotechnology case is not that widely spread, and lacks international harmonization, the Russian experience is particularly interesting, due to the high and clear demand for statistical evidence from decision makers (Gokhberg et al. 2011, 2012).

In Russia the beginning of an ambitious programme of nanotechnology development and, accordingly, statistical monitoring of this field, was laid by a presidential initiative ('The Development Strategy for Nanotechnology') adopted in 2007. It defined the need for a system of integrated information and analytical support to R&D in nanotechnology to enable more efficient use of the financial and organizational resources in interdisciplinary research, with the aim of creating a competitive domestic supply of and market for nanotechnology-enabled products. On the other hand, practice of implementation of the existing R&D initiatives and co-financing projects in the field of nanotechnology demonstrated different approaches to the understanding of activities related to nanotechnology. These emphasized the importance of organizing a unified system of statistical measurement based on common concepts and drawing on the experience of leading international organizations for standardization and statistics.

The work started with the elaboration of an operational definition of nanotechnology, which reflected its distinctive features and could be used in statistical surveys, as well as for policy making in S&T and innovation. Current national practices of statistical studies of EETs as well as OECD recommendations on indicators and measurement of ICT and biotechnology (OECD 2009b, 2011) involve creating core and list-based definitions of the phenomenon under study to identify more clearly the subject of the survey, which in turn improves the quality of filling out statistical questionnaires and ensures the collection of complete and accurate information. This principle was taken to elaborate operational definition and classifications of nanotechnology.

A core definition for the Russian statistical system was developed as an umbrella concept to 'distinguish a set of methods and techniques for the analysis, design, and manufacture of nanostructures, devices, and systems, including targeted control and modification of the shape, size, interaction, and integration of the constituent elements of the nanoscale level, which brings improvements or additional performance and/or consumer properties to the resulting products' (Alfimov et al. 2010: 11). This definition took into account the integrated scientific and technological nature of the phenomenon of the targeted molecular manipulations and emphasized their decisive influence on the properties of the products created, and the market innovation status.

In the course of the work, a general definition of nanotechnology was completed featuring seven major areas of nanotechnology. They comprise the 'list-based definition' and form the basis for a local classification of nanotechnology areas. Besides, a grouping of the product types related to nanotechnology has been proposed, to be applied in the analysis of the degree of penetration by nanotechnology of the product. All together they formulated a kind of a 3D classification system to be used for statistical purposes. This represents a sophisticated move on from the ICT classification, and can be characterized as such.

The targeted goal of the classification system (Figure 15.3) determined a number of methodological principles to be taken into consideration. The 'principle of consistency and independence' of the three classifications integrated into a system suggests that together they cover the entire

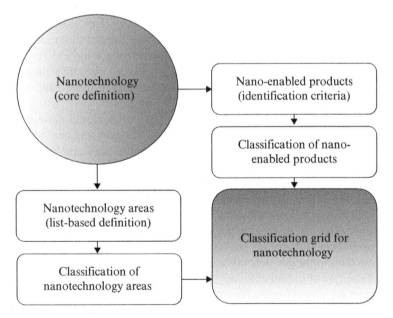

Figure 15.3   A classification grid for nanotechnology measurement in Russia

innovation cycle, from R&D to manufacturing of products. This requires the formation of a consistent terminology and criteria for classification, reflecting the existing technology–product–market structures, and the integrity of the system *vis-à-vis* independence of specific classifications. This means a flexible system dealing with functionalities rather than the specific tools and techniques used at one point in time. The 'principle of harmonization and compatibility' answers the requirement for harmonization with basic international standards (ISO, ISIC/NACE etc.), correspondence to regular statistical practices for S&T and innovation measurement, and compatibility with national standard classifications. The 'principle of openness and dynamism' implies the use for statistical and standardization purposes of diverse information and data sources, including statistical surveys, lists of actual and prospective research and technology areas, patent groups and nanotechnology-enabled products. The classification then allows to cover groups of already available nanotechnology-related goods and services as well as providing room for further expansion to emerging market niches. In addition to these principles the classification system required the development of a qualitative approach based on grouping products by types depending on the scale of the technology input that allowed taking an overview of nanotechnology as a research area and as a cross-industry activity.

Developing Specialized Supporting Classifications

In contrast to the core definition, the list-based definition is a more operational one, because it presents the object of observation in ways that are quantifiable for statistical purposes. To develop classification of nanotechnology areas the latter were considered primarily as a research field; and, indeed, much of the activity at this point is R&D, even though commercial applications appear with increasing frequency. The first step was for a group of experts to identify seven nanotechnology areas on the basis of various national and international technical standards. Taking into account the multidisciplinary nature of nanotechnology, the following areas have been identified:[13]

A *nanomaterials* include as a research object a nanoscale ensemble of atoms or molecules with at least one dimension smaller than 100 nm and are structurally distinguishable from the surroundings;

B *nanoelectronics* brings together a group of technologies related to the study of physical principles of operation and development of architectures and manufacturing nanoscale electronic devices and functional devices based on them;

C   *nanophotonics* includes technologies related to the production of nanostructured devices for generation, amplification, modulation, transmission and detection of electromagnetic radiation, as well as the research methods aimed at understanding physical phenomena that determine the functioning of nanostructured devices and processes in the interaction of photons with nanoscale objects;

D   *nanobiotechnology* is a research area related to the strategic use of biological macromolecules and organelles for the construction of nanomaterials and nanodevices;

E   *nanomedicine* is regarded as a practical application of nanotechnology for the diagnosis, monitoring, targeted drug delivery, as well as of rehabilitation and reconstruction of biological systems of the human body, using nanostructures and nanodevices;

F   *methods and tools for the research and certification of nanomaterials and nanodevices* include initial infrastructure for nanotechnology such as analytical, measuring and other equipment designed for manipulation of nanoscale objects as well as for control and standardization of the properties of nanomaterials and nanodevices;

G   *technologies and specialized equipment for experimental and industrial production of nanomaterials and nanodevices* combine technological and engineering techniques associated with the development of processes and specialized equipment for the manufacturing of elementary nanoproducts.

The second step then involved the classification of groups of specific technologies highlighted by experts as related to the nanotechnology research area, classified according to the extracted technology areas. For each of the seven selected areas a number of positions, consisting on average of three to five technology sub-areas, has been proposed. For example, the area of nanomaterials included five sub-areas, characterizing its various types by the level of complexity and methods of design and experimental development.

Finally, a third step was the validation of this draft classification by representatives of a wider S&T community to (1) assess the coverage of the proposed list of technology groups within the selected areas, (2) clarify proposed terminology and definitions, and (3) evaluate the consistency of the elaborated areas.

A specialized classification of nanotechnology-enabled products has been developed to measure manufacturing activities in nanotech-related industries.

It should be noted that both international and domestic practices of statistical surveying offer different interpretations of what is a nanotechnology-enabled product. A narrow interpretation suggests that only nanomaterials and nanodevices are treated as primary nanotechnology products. Following a wider approach, nanotechnology-related output includes conventional products that contain nanomaterials as integral components or that have been produced with the use of nano-enabled processes. The approach proposed for Russian statistics uses a block structure of the classification. Goods and services related to nanotechnology, depending on the latter's contribution to the composition of the final product, can be grouped for the statistical observation purposes into the following types:

I   *nanoproducts* are the artificially created nanoscale components (nanoparticles, nanomaterials and nanosystems) that could be used for manufacturing other product categories with new or improved properties, functions and performance;

II   *conventional products containing nanocomponents* are those integrating elementary nanoproducts in any proportion that determine their new or significantly improved functional and consumer properties;

III   *goods and services based on technological processes using nanotechnology* involve the use of nanotechnology as a part of the overall process that contributes to a significant improvement in their performance, but contain no nanoproducts as an integral part;

IV   *tools and equipment for nanotechnology* are a specific category bringing together the equipment required to perform various operations on the atomic and molecular levels in order to obtain, modify, produce, measure and control the properties of nanoproducts.

The block structure of the nanotechnology-enabled products classification allows adopting the abovementioned grouping principles for the further analysis of different nanotechnology markets as well as providing opportunities for complementing other statistical classifications and, thus, further comparisons with other types of statistical information (e.g. on R&D expenditure, production output etc.).

The methodological approach adopted in the early phases of establishing this area of statistics was largely aimed at upgrading existing surveys by incorporating new indicators for nanotechnology. The subsequent phases involve the design of various specialized surveys to cope with the fundamental novelty of this area for both national and international statistical practices. In this case, nanotechnology statistics in Russia were based on rigorous statistical methods rather than on *ad hoc* questionnaires, as happens in many countries. The earmarked classification of nanotechnology-related areas and nanotechnology-enabled products allowed extending the National Classification of Products by Types of Economic Activities (NCP) to be used in regular surveys.

The distribution of goods and services related to nanotechnology and manufactured in the entire economy, along the NCP classes, resulted in the identification of product groups notable for either similarities or differences according to certain selection criteria such as use of advanced nanomaterials and/or nano-enabled processes and their influence on the technical or consumer characteristics of the final product.

Such an approach provides Russian statistics with a multi-level classification, taking into account the cross-cutting nature of nanotechnologies. It makes it possible to relate nanotechnology to the structure of national economic activities. Furthermore, the grouping of goods and services in their relation to nanotechnology, depending on the specifics of allied manufacturing processes, supports the measurement of output, not only as total sales of nanotechnology-enabled products, but also by distinguishing their types and application categories for analytical purposes.

ACKNOWLEDGEMENTS

The authors would like to thank Fernando Galindo-Rueda (OECD) and Elisabeth Pastor (Swiss Federal Statistical Office) for their valuable contributions to the discussion and for providing materials.

NOTES

1. This chapter summarizes the key results of a study on developing a conceptual and methodological approach to statistical measurement of emerging, enabling and general-purpose technologies, carried out within the framework of the Basic Research Program of the National Research University Higher School of Economics (Moscow, Russia) in 2011–12.
2. According to the EU definition, key enabling technologies (KET) are knowledge- and capital-intensive technologies associated with research and development (R&D) intensity, rapid and integrated innovation cycles, high capital expenditure and highly skilled employment. Their influence is pervasive, enabling process, product and service innovation throughout the economy. They are of systemic relevance, multidisciplinary and trans-sectorial, cutting across many technology areas with a trend towards convergence, technology integration and the potential to induce structural change. KETs can assist technological leaders in other fields to capitalize on their research efforts. These KETs are nanotechnology, micro- and nanoelectronics, advanced materials, photonics, biotechnology, along with advanced manufacturing technologies as a cross-cutting application (EC 2009).
3. The concept of technology convergence and the NBIC abbreviation seems to be first employed in Roco and Bainbridge (2002). However, further studies of S&T develop-

ment demonstrated that its various rhetorical uses are connected to earlier policy discourse around nano-convergence (Schummer 2010).

4. 'Early on I found out that words were a problem in technology . . . Many of the ones used most heavily – "technology" itself, "innovation", "technique" – have overlapping and often contradicting meanings . . . "Technology" has at least half-a-dozen major meanings, and several of these conflict' (Brian Arthur 2009: 5).

'In common parlance, nonetheless, when we refer to one of these complex systems as a technology, the material component more often than not serves as the tacit referent. But, that restricted sense of the word, as in the case of the railroad, can be ambiguous and misleading' (Marx 2010: 574).

5. Four main meanings are provided by the *Merriam-Webster Dictionary*:

   (1) the practical application of knowledge especially in a particular area;
   (2) a capability given by the practical application of knowledge;
   (3) a manner of accomplishing a task especially using technical processes, methods, or knowledge;
   (4) the specialized aspects of a particular field of endeavor.

6. 'A jet engine (or more generally, any technology) consists of component building blocks that are also technologies, and these consist of subparts that are also technologies, in a repeating (or recurring) pattern' (Brian Arthur 2009: 38–9).

7. 'In French, . . . two separate concepts [are used]: "technique" is defined as a body of methodical processes based upon scientific knowledge that are used in production, and "technologie" as the study of techniques, tools, machines and materials' (OECD 1990: 10).

8. 'In German and other European languages, a distinction exists between "Technik" and "Technologie" that is absent in English, as both terms are usually translated as "technology"' (Schatzberg 2006: 487–8). In Russian, similarly, 'technics' usually means hardware equipment, while 'technology' is mostly applied to processes.

9. It should be noted, then, that codes for bio- and nanotechnology R&D still do not allow relevant analyses since, for example, pharmaceuticals are listed as a separate category under the aggregate 'manufacture of chemicals and chemical products'.

10. From the perspective of a research analyst, a mirror strategy envisions collecting and matching secondary data from different sources. See, for example, Hullman (2006).

11. Canadian experience provides a good basis for further discussion on the topic and is documented in a series of working papers on the Canadian Biotechnology Use and Development Survey (Byrd 2002; McNiven 2001a, 2001b, 2002; McNiven et al. 2003; Traoré 2003).

12. Among one of the latest initiatives the *Swiss Cleantech Report* (Federal Department of Economic Affairs etc. 2011) should be mentioned.

13. For details of the definitions and approaches, see Alfimov et al. (2010).

REFERENCES

Alfimov, M., L. Gokhberg and K. Fursov (2010), 'Nanotechnology: definitions and classifications', *Nanotechnologies in Russia*, **5**(7–8), 8–15 (in Russian).

Beniger, James R. (1986), *The Control Revolution: Technological and Economic Origins of the Information Society*, Cambridge, MA: Harvard University Press.

Brian Arthur, William (2009), *The Nature of Technology*, New York: Free Press.

Byrd, Craig (2002), 'Profile of Spin-off Firms in the Biotechnology Sector: Results from the Biotechnology Use and Development Survey – 1999', Statistics Canada Working Paper ST-02-04, http://www.statcan.ca/english/research/88F0006XIE/88F0006XIE2002004.pdf.

Carey, J. and M.C.J. Elton (2009), 'The other path to the web: the forgotten role of videotex and other early online services', *New Media & Society*, **11**(1–2), 241–60.

Chen, Chaomei (2006), 'CiteSpace II: detecting and visualizing emerging trends and transient patterns in scientific literature', *Journal of the American Society for Information Science and Technology*, **57**, 359–77.

Cobo, M.J., A.G. Lopez-Herrera, E. Herrera-Viedma and F. Herrera (2011), 'An approach for detecting, quantifying, and visualizing the evolution of a research field: a practical application to the fuzzy sets theory field', *Journal for Informetrics*, **5**, 146–66.

Daim, T.U., G. Rueda, H. Martin and P. Gerdsri (2006), 'Forecasting emerging technologies: use of bibliometrics and patent analysis', *Technological Forecasting and Social Change*, **73**, 981–1012.

EC (2009), *Preparing for Our Future: Developing a Common Strategy for Key Enabling Technologies*, Communication from the Commission to the European Parliament, the Council, the European Economic and Social Committee and the Committee of the Regions, Brussels: Commission of the European Communities.

The Federal Department of Economic Affairs and the Federal Department of the Environment, Transport, Energy and Communications (2011), *Swiss Cleantech Report*.

Freeman, Christopher and C. Perez (1988), 'Structural crises of adjustment: business cycles and investment behaviour', in Giovanni Dosi, C. Freeman, R. Nelson and L. Soete (eds), *Technical Change and Economic Theory*, London and New York: Pinter Publishing, pp. 38–66.

Gault, Fred (2010), *Innovation Strategies for a Global Economy*, Cheltenham, UK and Northampton, MA, USA: Edward Elgar Publishing.

Gault, Fred (2011), 'Social impacts of the development of science, technology and innovation indicators', UNU-MERIT Working Paper, 2011-008.

Gimel, F.L. (2003), 'Definitions. General features from the Oslo Manual Revision', in *OECD/ Eurostat Workshop on the Oslo Manual Revision, SDE-13/2003/LDG/amm*, Paris: OECD.

Godin, Benoit (2005), *Measurement and Statistics on Science and Technology: 1920 to the Present*, London: Routledge.

Gokhberg, Leonid and Peter Bøegh-Nielsen (eds) (2007), *Information Society Statistics in the Russian Federation: Harmonization with International Standards*, Moscow: State University – Higher School of Economics.

Gokhberg, L., K. Fursov and O. Karasev (2012), 'Nanotechnology development and regulatory framework: the case of Russia', *Technovation*, **32**(3–4), 161–2.

Gokhberg, L., I. Kuznetsova, K. Fursov and V. Dalin (2011), 'Statistics of nanotechnology in Russia: formation of a new area', *Issues of Statistics*, **9**, 3–20 (in Russian).

Griliches, Zvi H. (1987), *R&D, Patents, and Productivity*, Chicago, IL: The University of Chicago Press.

Guo, H., S. Weingart and K. Borner (2011), 'Mixed-indicators model for identifying emerging research areas', *Scientometrics*, **89**(1), 421–35.

Helpman, E. and M. Trajtenberg (1994), 'A time to sow and a time to reap: growth based on general purpose technologies', NBER Working Paper 4854, Cambridge, MA: National Bureau of Economic Research.

Hullman, Angela (2006), *The Economic Development of Nanotechnology: An Indicators Based Analysis*, Brussels: European Commission, DG Research.

Landes, David (2003), *The Unbound Prometheus: Technical Change and Industrial Development in Western Europe from 1750 to the Present*, New York: Cambridge University Press.

Lipsey, R.G., C. Bekar and K. Carlaw (1998), 'What requires explanation?', in Elhanan Helpman (ed.), *General Purpose Technologies and Economic Growth*, Cambridge: MIT Press, pp. 14–54.

Machlup, Fritz (1962), *The Production and Distribution of Knowledge in the United States*, Princeton, NJ: Princeton University Press.

Mansfield, Edwin (1983), 'Long waves and technological innovation', *The American Economic Review*, **73**(2), 141–5.

Marx, Leo (2010), 'Technology: the emergence of a hazardous concept', *Technology and Culture*, **51**(3), 561–77.

McNiven, Chuck (2001a), 'Biotechnology use and development, 1999', Statistics Canada Working Paper ST-01-07, http://www.statcan.ca/english/research/88F0006XIE/88F0006 XIB2001007.pdf.

McNiven, Chuck (2001b), 'Practices and activities of Canadian biotechnology firms: results from the Biotechnology Use and Development Survey – 1999', Statistics Canada Working Paper ST-01-11, http://www.statcan.ca/english/research/88F0006XIE/88F0006 XIB2001011.pdf.

McNiven, Chuck (2002), 'Use of biotechnologies in the Canadian industrial sector: results from the Biotechnology Use and Development Survey – 1999', Statistics Canada Working Paper ST-02-03, http://www.statcan.ca/english/research/88F0006XIE/88F0006 XIE2002003.pdf.

McNiven, C., L. Raoub and N. Traoré (2003), 'Features of Canadian biotech innovative firms: results from the Biotechnology Use and Development Survey – 2001', Statistics Canada Working Paper ST-03-05, http://www.statcan.ca/english/research/88F0006XIE/8 8F0006XIE2003005.pdf.

Miles, Ian (1991), 'Measuring the future: statistics and the information age', *Futures*, **23**, 915–34.

Morel, C.M., S.J. Serruya, G.O. Penna and R. Guimaraes (2009), 'Co-authorship network analysis: a powerful tool for strategic planning of research, development and capacity building programs on neglected diseases', *PLOS Neglected Tropical Diseases*, **3**(8), 1–7.

OECD (1990), *OECD Proposed Standard Method of Compiling and Interpreting the Technology Balance of Payments Data*, Paris: OECD.

OECD (1992), *OECD Proposed Guidelines for Collecting and Interpreting the Technological Innovation Data – Oslo Manual*, OCDE/GD (92)26, Paris: OECD.

OECD (2001), *Measuring Productivity: Measurement of Aggregate and Industry-Level Productivity Growth*, Paris: OECD.

OECD (2002), *Frascati Manual: Proposed Standard Practice for Surveys on Research and Experimental Development*, Paris: OECD.

OECD (2005a), *Handbook on Economic Globalisation Indicators*, Paris: OECD.

OECD (2005b), *A Framework for Biotechnology Statistics*, Paris: OECD.

OECD (2007), *OECD Science, Technology and Industry Scoreboard 2007*, Paris: OECD.

OECD (2008), *OECD Glossary of Statistical Terms*, Paris: OECD.

OECD (2009a), *OECD Patent Statistics Manual*, Paris: OECD.

OECD (2009b), *Biotechnology Statistics*, Paris: OECD.

OECD (2010), *Measuring Innovation: A New Perspective*, Paris: OECD.

OECD (2011), *Guide to Measuring the Information Society*, Paris: OECD.

OECD/Eurostat (1997), *OECD Proposed Guidelines for Collecting and Interpreting Technological Innovation Data – Oslo Manual*, Paris: OECD.

OECD/Eurostat (2005), *Oslo Manual: Guidelines for Collecting and Interpreting Innovation Data*, 3rd edn, Paris: OECD .

Porat, Mark U. (1977), 'The information economy: definition and measurement', US Department of Commerce, Office of Telecommunications, OT Special Publication 77-12(1), Washington, DC: US Government Printing Office.

Roco, M.C. and W.S. Bainbridge (eds) (2002), *Converging Technologies for Improving Human Performance: Nanotechnology, Biotechnology, Information Technology and Cognitive Science*, Washington, DC: NSF/DOC.

Rose, Antoine (1997), 'Biotechnology research and development (R&D) in Canadian industry: a portrait of large performers in 1997', *Science Statistics*, **24**(2), Ottawa: Statistics Canada.

Rose, Antoine and Chuck McNiven (2007), 'Biotechnology: from measures of activities, linkages and outcomes to impact indicators', in OECD, *Science, Technology and Innovation Indicators in a Changing World: Responding to Policy Needs*, Paris: OECD, pp. 215–30.

Schatzberg, Eric (2006), 'Technik comes to America: changing meanings of technology before 1930', *Technology and Culture*, **47**(3), 486–512.

Schummer, Joachim (2010), 'From nano-convergence to NBIC-convergence: "The best way to predict the future is to create it"', in Mario Kaiser, Monica Kurath, Sabine Maasen and Christoph Rehmann-Sutter (eds), *Governing Future Technologies: Nanotechnology and the Rise of Assessment Regime, Sociology of the Sciences Yearbook 27*, London and New York: Springer.

Shibata, N., Y. Kajikawa, Y. Takeda and K. Matsushima (2008), 'Detecting emerging fronts based on topological measures in citation networks of scientific publications', *Technovation*, **28**, 758–75.

Smil, Vaclav (2005), *Creating the Twentieth Century: Technical Innovations of 1867–1914 and Their Lasting Impact*, Oxford and New York: Oxford University Press.

Traoré, Namatié (2003), 'Bioproducts development by Canadian biotechnology firms: findings from the 2001 Biotechnology Use and Development Survey', Statistics Canada Working Paper ST-03-13, http://www.statcan.ca/english/research/88F0006XIE/88F0006XIE2003005.pdf.

Upham, Phineas S. and Henry Small (2010), 'Emerging research fronts in science and technology: patterns of new knowledge development', *Scientometrics*, **83**, 15–38.

Van Merkerk, Rutger O. and Ruud E.H.M. Smits (2008), 'Tailoring CTA for emerging technologies', *Technological Forecasting and Social Change*, **75**, 312–33.

Van Merkerk, Rutger O. and Harro van Lente (2005), 'Tracing emerging irreversibilities in emerging technologies: the case of nanotubes', *Technological Forecasting and Social Change*, **72**(9), 1094–111.

Van Raan, Anthony F.J. (1996), 'Advanced bibliometric methods as quantitative core of peer review based evaluation and foresight exercises', *Scientometrics*, **36**(3), 397–420.

Veugelers, Reinhilde (2007), 'Developments in EU statistics on science, technology and innovation: taking stock and moving closer to evidence-based policy analysis', in OECD, *Science, Technology and Innovation Indicators in a Changing World: Responding to Policy Needs*, Paris: OECD, pp. 33–47.

Youtie, J., M. Iacopetta and S. Graham (2008), 'Assessing the nature of nanotechnology: can we uncover an emerging general purpose technology?', *Journal of Technology Transfer*, **33**, 315–29.

16 Foresight and science, technology and innovation indicators
Dirk Meissner and Alexander Sokolov[1]

1. INTRODUCTION

Technology foresight as one of the key areas of forward-looking activities over the last two decades has become a tool with a significant influence on science, technology and innovation (STI) policies in many countries worldwide, with a much longer tradition in Japan and a few other countries. Since the early 1990s foresight has been evolving from an instrument to assess future prospects of individual research areas to an integral part of STI policy formulation and implementation. Luke Georghiou singles out five generations of foresight (Georghiou et al. 2008: 15–16) that vary from mainly forecasting that refers to the internal dynamics of technology to a wide mix of activities aimed at either structures of actors within the STI system or the STI dimensions of the broader social or economic context.

Foresight can affect the innovation performance of a country through different channels. In the present globalization context in the industrialized nations it is accepted that an explicit and coherent STI policy is essential for economic and social development. Foresight studies affect STI policy strategy decisions by supporting priority setting. They create, in addition, crucial networks and interactions between participants in the national system of innovation and contribute to the acceptance of new developments and to the consideration of all of the technological potentials (Martin 1995).

Since foresight, and STI indicators, are both aimed at informing and improving policy making, they naturally have much in common, are interdependent and complement each other.

The interrelations between foresight and STI indicators are many. On the one hand, indicators are extensively used in foresight to provide data on STI trends, thus stimulating experts' creative thinking and solidifying their judgements. On the other hand, foresight exercises contribute to highlighting new areas of concern for STI policy that can and should be addressed by statistical measurement and emerging research areas with a great innovation potential that needs more detailed statistical analysis.

Between these two extremes, there are many other fields where the two areas are closely related.

Another topic of increasing interest is the search for suitable practically proven indicators available for measuring and assessing foresight studies as such, for example in terms of management but also with respect to their eventual impact in either a direct or indirect way on the national innovation system (NIS) and on long-term economic performance. Hence there is an urgent need to develop and apply a coherent and consistent set of indicators suitable for monitoring the effectiveness and efficiency of foresight studies from a process perspective and that can contribute to measuring their impact.

This chapter introduces three major dimensions of interrelations between foresight and STI indicators: (1) use of indicators in the course of foresight studies; (2) building particular STI indicators to monitor and measure foresight activities; and (3) the contribution of foresight to complementing existing indicators and developing new ones.

2.   FORESIGHT AND ITS MANIFESTATIONS

According to Ben Martin's classical definition, foresight is a 'process involved in systematically attempting to look into the longer-term future of science, technology, the economy and society with the aim of identifying the areas of strategic research and the emerging generic technologies likely to yield the greatest economic and social benefits' (Martin 1995: 142). Currently, foresight is used as a set of instruments to support and improve decision making.

Usually foresight studies also contribute to knowledge creation, absorption and diffusion. They see the technological regime in a broad sense, for example describing and anticipating varying scenarios surrounding actual technological trends (Malanowski and Zweck 2007: 1806). Hence it can be assumed, if not concluded, that foresight studies have a significant impact on the design of national innovation systems but also on national innovation performance in a long-term perspective.

Foresight envisages an open and interdisciplinary discussion and communication culture, facilitating the exchange between actors from policy administration, industry, science and society, fostering the interaction between them as well as supporting networking and the implementation of results. In principle these studies follow systemic, integrative approaches with different instruments and methods, and aim at matching diverging interests and achieving consensus between all parties, thus requiring commitment of key stakeholders. More general groupings of foresight exercises address different aims, territorial needs, outputs and the results attained (Gavigan et al. 2001; Molas-Gallart et al. 2002; Keenan 2003; Cuhls 2003; Meissner 2013a).

Foresight does not aim to predict a predetermined future but through the involvement of players and decisions taken 'today', it allows participants in foresight studies to actively shape the future, but to a modest degree only. Current foresight exercises quite often involve a wide range of stakeholders, thereby opening the minds of participants to new possibilities for the future (Cachia et al. 2007; Sokolov 2013). They constitute powerful assistants in planning and managing uncertainty levels. Foresight offers possibilities to identify and take advantage of opportunities; to investigate and understand the nature of risks inherent in the innovation process; and to develop reaction to mitigate problems once they start to unfold (Santo et al. 2006).

Foresight studies can take many different shapes. Lempert et al. (2003) suggest grouping such studies into the following categories: top–down versus bottom–up; explorative versus normative; quantitative versus qualitative; and expert-based versus assumption-based. Another approach by Popper proposes the 'foresight diamond' (see below), which builds on the ability to gather and process information, for example evidence, expertise, interaction and creativity (Popper 2011). Other approaches towards grouping foresight studies are centred around particular fields of the foresight study (Tran and Daim 2008; Godwin and Wright 2010; Höjer and Mattsson 2000; Bishop et al. 2007; Bradfield et al. 2005; van Notten et al. 2003; Ringland 1998; Voros 2006) or on the use of methodologies (Popper 2008; Keenan and Popper 2007).

Traditionally the application of indicators to predict the future from modelling (often with the use of time series) is based on the assumption that the general system will remain unchanged and therefore further development will be of a deterministic nature. This is valid for well-defined systems reflecting physical laws, but is misleading when it is related to innovation. Since innovation is a non-linear process based both on creativity and on innovative use of existing goods/services, foresight activities are more productive when they are not just aimed at predicting indicators on the basis of existing models (trends extrapolation and other such methods) but try to articulate new problems to be resolved, to reveal new trends and to construct relevant categories to be addressed by policy makers.

Given this context, the key questions for this chapter are as follows: 'How can foresight use existing indicators to become more efficient and more effective?'; 'What can foresight contribute to making the system of STI indicators more relevant to existing and emerging policy concerns?' and 'How can foresight and STI indicators, together, provide valuable background for decision makers?'

3. THE USE OF INDICATORS IN THE FORESIGHT PROCESS

Foresight has been increasingly considered as a systematic process. It consists of five interconnected and complementary phases (Miles 2002; Georghiou et al. 2008: 45): pre-foresight; recruitment; generation; action; and renewal. At each of these phases STI indicators can be used as a valuable source of information.

At the pre-foresight stage, the overall goals of the project are set, including rationale, thematic domain, territorial scale, time horizon and expected outcomes. At this stage analysis of STI indicators helps to more precisely identify major issues to be addressed by the study and create a background for further actions.

During the succeeding recruitment stage, bibliometric and patent analysis is used for the identification of key experts and institutions to be involved in the exercise. For this purpose, analysis of the dynamics of publications and mapping the development of and interconnection between research areas as well as assessments of new (interdisciplinary) research areas based on STI indicators are of high relevance for foresight studies. Participation of the best specialists (highly cited researchers, inventors, innovators etc.) is a key success factor for any foresight project.

Following the pre-foresight and recruitment stages, the generation phase covers a number of activities aimed at extracting expert knowledge and building a shared vision by anticipating possible futures and selecting desirable ones. Thus detailed description of research fronts is the core of this phase. Involvement of experts at this stage allows the early identification of issues, the elaboration of scenarios and the discussion and interpretation of results (Wehnert and Jörß 2009). This phase is related to analysis of existing codified knowledge (e.g. expressed in the form of STI indicators), extraction and codifying of tacit knowledge, and generating on this base new knowledge related to the future.

In the action phase the new knowledge generated through foresight activities is used for prioritization and policy making in the field of STI. Revising policy instruments requires developing new instruments to measure their efficiency, which leads to a demand for new STI indicators.

The renewal phase is focused on monitoring and evaluation of the foresight results, although sometimes this evaluation is not an easy exercise and requires specific approaches as well as a system of relevant indicators (see the discussion below).

Foresight methodology includes many qualitative, quantitative and semi-quantitative methods. Traditionally, foresight was mainly built on qualitative methods based on expert judgements, but during the last

CREATIVITY
EXPLORATORY METHODS

SF
WILD CARD
SCENARIO VIGNETTE
GENIUS/EXPERT FORECAST
BACKCASTING   ROLE PLAY/GAMING
TEEPSE ANALYSIS SWOT BRAINSTORMING
ROADMAPPING   DELPHI   SCENARIO WORKSHOP
PREDICTION MARKET   WEB-BASED CROWDSOURCING
RULE-BASED FORECAST   RELEVANCE TREES   CITIZEN PANEL
MULTI-CRITERIA ANALYSIS   MULTIPLE PERSPECTIVE ANALYSIS   SURVEY
EXPERT PANEL   *SYSTEM DYNAMICS/SIMULATION*   CONFERENCE/WORKSHOP
KEY TECHNOLOGIES   MORPHOLOGICAL ANALYSIS   POLLING/VOTING
IMPACT ANALYSIS DATA/TEXT MINING   STAKEHOLDER ANALYSIS
CROSS-IMPACT/STRUCTURAL ANALYSIS   *BENCHMARKING*
SMIC   INTERVIEW   LOGIC CHART   *SEGMENTATION*
INDICATOR/INDEX   REGRESSION ANALYSIS
EXTRAPOLATION   PATENT ANALYSIS
BIBLIOMETRICS   SCANNING
LITERATURE REVIEW
WEAK SIGNAL
SNA

EXPERTISE
ADVISORY METHODS

INTERACTION
PARTICIPATORY METHODS

EVIDENCE
EXPLANATORY METHODS

LEGEND
QUALITATIVE
QUANTITATIVE
SEMI-QUANTITATIVE

Source: Popper (2011).

Figure 16.1   The foresight diamond

decade a clear trend towards inclusion of evidence-based methods can be observed. The foresight diamond (Figure 16.1) includes such methods as modelling, trend extrapolation, patent analysis, analysis of statistical indicators as well as a number of methods that include quantitative analysis as an integral part. Two examples are the Delphi method and roadmapping.

Indicators for measuring and monitoring foresight studies comprise a fairly new field of science and are also rather new when it comes to practical application. Such indicators need to go far beyond the established evaluation and impact measurement of STI policy measures. Moreover, they need to take into consideration the many different forms in which foresight studies appear. Also foresight usually has a very broad target audience and involves a large number of stakeholders with their own expectations on the implementation and use of the results. Hence the impact of foresight studies is in theory assumed to be very strong once all stakeholders support both the actual process and the result implementation. However, practical experience shows that the implementation of the results achieved is far more difficult and challenging than the process itself, for example running the study.

A completely different picture arises when it comes to indicators used in the course of foresight studies. Such indicators are designed for various purposes, for example to describe technology development paths, to determine technology development priorities, to detect societal needs and requirements, among others. Thus foresight studies are used as an instrument to prepare countries for meeting future challenges such as contributing to enhanced industry–science relationships, the cooperation and coordination of administrative and political institutions and actors, and providing a useful tool for research strategy development by many different actors, for example research institutions, universities and public funding agencies. In addition, foresight studies are increasingly used as radar by industry to identify societal feelings and development trends (Vishnevskiy et al. 2013).

Furthermore, indicators arising from foresight studies need to take special characteristics into account, for example with respect to the long-term focus and the time horizon varying according to the topic discussed (in most cases between 10 and 30 years). Also such studies apply an open and interdisciplinary discussion and communication culture, facilitating the exchange between actors from policy administration, industry, science and society, fostering the interaction between representatives from science, technology, economy, culture and social as well as supporting networking to strengthen the implementation of results. In principle these studies follow systemic, integrative approaches with different instruments and methods, and aim to match diverging interests and achieve consensus between key stakeholders.

Foresight exercises usually have long time horizons (10 to 50 years or more) and take a broad view of environment, organization and strategies, commonly resulting in scenarios that in turn usually contribute to stakeholder learning, stimulate imagination and enhance aspiration (Bezold 2010). The ultimate goal of national foresight projects is to coordinate research and innovation agendas across public and private organizations, industrial and service sectors, and academic disciplines by developing new alliances between the producers and the consumers of knowledge. These projects take into account and make visible the processes by which research agendas and priorities are established, the degree and nature of autonomy in the practices of scientists and engineers, the relations of academic disciplines to one another and to industrial knowledge, and the ends to which S&T are directed (Rappert 1999).

4. INDICATORS FOR MONITORING AND EVALUATION OF FORESIGHT

Features of Foresight Studies – Implications for the Evaluation of Foresight

Foresight studies are not at all, or only in very few cases, aligned to the strategic agenda of their initiator. Moreover, especially weak signals currently gaining importance in foresight practice are left aside from the integration into the organization's strategies (Battistella and De Toni 2011).

Grim (2009) introduced a Foresight Maturity Model (FMM) including six major elements that characterize the essentials of foresight studies: leadership, framing, scanning, forecasting, visioning and planning. The framework aims to provide organizations with a tool to assess their current position in the future orientation of their competences and practices. The FMM aims to evaluate and monitor the competences and capabilities of organizations not only to design and conduct foresight studies but also to prepare the organizations themselves for future requirements and challenges (Grim 2009). Hence the leadership indicator aims to convert the foresight into practical action on an ongoing basis, the framing dimension focuses on the degree to which the right issues are identified and solved, and scanning refers to the immediate environment of the organization. The forecasting competences are the central element of the model, visioning is meant to develop future visions and finally planning expresses the ability of organizations to develop tools that support the implementation of the generated vision. With the help of the FMM, the maturity of the organization in foresight terms can be determined at five levels: *ad hoc*, aware, capable, mature, world-class. Another increasingly common feature of foresight studies is the inclusion of future application potentials expressed as market potential (although it is often difficult to determine).

The acceleration of innovation in most STI fields has led to the phenomenon that new product groups are entering markets for the first time even before their physical fundamentals are fully understood (Malanowski and Zweck 2007). Thus the identification of application fields and potential markets for technologies is characterized by higher uncertainty than ever as the applications of technologies might change in the course of their maturity. For evaluating and monitoring foresight studies, indicators are needed that measure the long-term accuracy of the identified application and market fields, for example the percentage of change in applications. Also indicators for evaluation need to reflect the changes in technology application that might occur over time due to societal change associated with the embedding of the technology in the society.

Furthermore, the technology is characterized by inherent uncertainty when it comes to actual large-scale industrial application. Technological attractiveness as determined by foresight studies is by no means a guarantee that the technology is applied in the identified fields, but foresight also needs to consider the particular conditions that must be met in order to ease the feasibility of technology application (related industries, infrastructures, skilled labour etc.) (TFAMWG 2004). Quantitative methods are increasingly used for building integrated STI indicators that offer numerous opportunities for foresight (Haegeman et al. 2012). The most popular quantitative methods use bibliometric and patent indicators and Internet-based tools, allowing for the integration of data. Bibliometric studies have been widely used as a valuable source of data for foresight, allowing the identification of emerging research fields that can offer disruptive technologies in five to ten years ahead. Innovation forecasting models commonly use frequency analysis of keywords in scientific publications. Incremental and radical innovations can be distinguished through the analysis of emerging clusters with respect to citations and keywords for a particular technology field. Another area for using bibliometric and patent data is to distinguish between groups of technologies and vice versa for cross-impact analysis to identify relationships between technologies.

Foresight studies have both a direct and an indirect impact. Direct impacts refer to information about the extent and the features of future situations, the future environment and/or possible future partners or competitors, for the benefit of organizational processes such as decision making, strategy design, formulating new perspectives on growth, building new alliances and allocation of management capacity for the stakeholders. Indirect impacts express the culture of the stakeholders and the implications of that culture for the future. Foresight studies also enable and incentivize stakeholders to think about what is important in the present, about biases in current reflections and other perspectives that are currently not considered (van der Steen et al. 2011).

One major outcome of national foresight studies used to be as a supporting tool for priority setting in public national R&D spending. However, there remains a great debate about the appropriateness of foresight results for priority setting, especially those that express a predictable but still uncertain future. Thus in the design of foresight studies special attention needs to be given to the role of national policy in coordinating organizations, the participants involved in the development of future scenarios, and the extent to which these scenarios can contribute to setting public research priorities (Rappert 1999).

The need for *ex ante* assessment of foresight exercises stems from the requirement to check all possible impact dimensions and to evaluate the likelihood of their realization and their strengths, while *ex post* impact assessments are able to evaluate the efficacy and the efficiency of the foresight projects by measuring and monitoring their performance (i.e. data-gathering and reporting strategies) and practices to review the foresight (Blind 2004).

New developments in S&T detected by foresight studies often challenge the existing research agendas, or call for the redirection of research and technology roadmaps and agendas (Meissner et al. 2013). Changes and dynamics in S&T can be identified and traced by different indicators. These indicators must allow for the comparison between S&T fields, countries, organizations and over time. Currently the most common indicators for such comparison are publications in scientific journals and patents (Moed et al. 2004). The former indicators help to visualize the ongoing trends in basic research, whereas publication and patent indicators cover the change in applied R&D.

Evaluation of Foresight Indicators

Georghiou and Keenan (2006) distinguish three classes of evaluation criteria. First, they discuss the efficiency of implementation, second, the impact and effectiveness, and third, the appropriateness of the foresight exercise. The efficiency of implementation concentrates mainly on the procedural perspective, for example organization and management. Typical indicators developed during evaluation are the background and the competences of the people involved, the degree of support to expert panels, the link to decision makers but also the appropriateness and efficiency of methods used. Impact and effectiveness indicators reflect the immediate outputs and outcomes. According to Georghiou and Keenan, outputs measure only activity; for example they count quantitative data such as numbers of participants in meetings or surveys, reports disseminated, meetings held, website hits and so on, but there is no real assessment of the short- and long-term impact of these. Moreover, these indictors have an inherent potential to lead to misinterpretation and misunderstanding as they do not express novelty, size, significance and sustainability. The appropriateness indicators reflect a scenario-type style of evaluation centred around the 'what if . . .' questions, for example highlighting alternative scenarios (Georghiou and Keenan 2006).

The evaluation of foresight exercises also needs to take into account the dynamics of the project, for example be conducted in real time or immediately after to ensure that the findings are not distorted by hindsight or obscured by loss of data (Georghiou and Keenan 2006).

According to Saritas and Oner (2004), there is a lack of translating future requirements into R&D projects and initiatives. In the course of most foresight exercises topic statements are formulated and assessed using different instruments that place more emphasis on action rather than on theoretical understanding of the underlying science. Hence evaluation indicators need to be developed that take account of this gap.

Basic Definitions and Characteristics of Indicators

The structure and composition of foresight studies raises another challenge. Two types of foresight studies have to be considered: (1) with a clear focus on selected themes and a narrow scope consisting of one project; and (2) with a broader scope that includes several projects. Indicators used for monitoring or evaluating foresight studies thus need to consider the interdependencies of different projects that make up a broad foresight study. Therefore indicators need to consider not only the single projects but also the whole project portfolio (Meissner 2013b). Thus indicators to measure and monitor foresight studies can be grouped into three major areas:

- measurement and monitoring objective;
- time horizon; and
- resource orientation.

Measurement and monitoring objective
In principle, three major perspectives are measured and monitored:

- monitoring and steering of the foresight study (process perspective);
- measuring the impact of the foresight study – long-term impact measurement, multiple impacts on diverging surroundings; and
- near-time evaluation of foresight studies.

Process indicators   During foresight studies bibliometric indicators are often used to determine the importance of selected trends in different facets or to assess the national or institutional strengths and weaknesses.

Evaluation perspective   Typically foresight studies are initiated, issued and financed by public bodies and funds. Thus in most countries evaluation is an integral part of foresight, and in the first instance it aims at testing the effectiveness and efficiency of the study. To some extent evaluation indicators also reflect the (mainly short-term) impact achieved with the foresight study. Evaluation of foresight studies (as projects) refers to two dimensions:

- Effectiveness – 'doing the right things' – is measured by long-term indicators and addresses the question of whether the goals and ambitions of the foresight study were achieved once the study is complete. That includes building an inventory of all activities taking place, matching these with the original scheduled activities and determining whether the activities have contributed to the goals. Such analysis will give the evaluators of the study reliable information.
- Efficiency – 'doing the things right' – is measured through assessment of the value achieved from the input of resources, for example the ratio of input and output indicators. Input indicators need to mirror not only the actual financial resources spent but also take into account the non-financial investments, especially the time and know-how of experts other than the project team used for conducting the study. Usually external experts are not reimbursed for most of the working time they provide to the foresight study team; hence quantifying these efforts in a reliable and solid way is critical. The problem in determining these values lies in the fact that no direct cost can be attributed to the study, nor is there an existing market mechanism which would provide a market price.

Impact perspective   Impact indicators are designed to measure the impact caused by the foresight study. Such impacts can be of a direct as well as an indirect nature. Direct impacts refer to actions taken as a consequence of the foresight study and related results. For example, such impacts are redesigned or restructured research portfolios and adjusted and adapted research funding programmes. Indirect impacts refer more to qualitative impacts that arose from the study. Examples are effects that arise from networking and also from communication and media activities.

Time horizon

A second dimension for grouping indicators relates to the time horizon on which the indicators focus. These are leading, lagging and learning (accordingly *ex ante*, *ex post* and monitoring indicators) and, finally, resource-oriented indicators, for example input, output and process indicators.

Leading (ex ante)   Leading indicators summarize expected framework conditions and match them with the potential impacts of a foresight study.

Leading indicators follow the exploration of a current trend derived from past experiences or from qualitative assessment of experts. A combination of both methods (trend exploration and expert assessments) is a possible methodology. Hence *ex ante* indicators look towards the future and predict potential developments in different ways. Leading indicators are thus considered to be indicative but not necessarily accurate. They require regular updates of the information base on which the indicator is built. Changes of the leading indicators in the course of time are interpreted as upcoming changes in the real situation. Commonly, leading indicators are used in economics and business. There are many examples of leading indicators, one of which is The Conference Board Leading Economic Index® (LEI) for the USA. It uses ten data series to reduce volatility and is produced for the USA and other countries (www.conference-board.org/data/bcicountry.cfm?cid=1).

Lagging (ex post)   Lagging indicators oriented towards describing the past are often used to assess whether the foresight study was done efficiently, for example whether the things were done right. With a reasonable time lag the effectiveness of foresight studies can be evaluated, although caution is required here since foresight studies on average have a 10–20-year time horizon. First, effectiveness cannot be reliably assessed before the study has reached its full impact. Second, after a long period of time, the real contribution of a foresight study towards any impact generated is difficult to evaluate since, in the meantime, many factors may influence trends and developments. Despite these limitations, *ex post* evaluations of foresight offer a significant learning potential to draw from the experiences gained in studies carried out and already completed.

Learning (monitoring)   The main function of these indicators is to provide near-time (real-time) information about the ongoing project (foresight study), thus providing an information base for project management and for leaders to react in near time. Besides the information function for immediate reaction, these indicators provide a valuable information source for learning in the sense of continuous improvement and further development, and adjustment of methodologies and processes.

Sometimes learning and monitoring indicators are also referred to as near-time, interim or controlling indicators.

Resource orientation
Evaluation and measurement studies always take into account the resources and processes that eventually lead to certain results.

Input   Measuring the input into foresight studies is a precondition for building and interpreting many related performance and monitoring indicators, but also for enabling benchmarking with other foresight studies. It has become practice in operational management to compare various foresight studies for different purposes. Input indicators include financial resources invested, but there is also a qualitative dimension in terms of the composition of human resources and their experience.

Output   The output of a foresight study can take many different forms. Since results of foresight studies are not tradable goods, their value is difficult to determine in quantitative ways. The difficulties continue to grow with the long-term orientation of the outputs, for example regardless of which output is considered, the common feature is that issues and matters with a long time perspective are contained and explored in these documents. Typical outputs of foresight studies are scenarios, technology roadmaps, forecasts, analysis of trends and drivers, research and other priorities, policy recommendations and lists of key technologies. It is not advisable to gather the number of outputs, but rather the quality and newness of the content of the output. Quality is of relevance but it is difficult to measure in quantitative terms.

Process   Process indicators are closely related to monitoring indicators. However, they are useful for *ex post* evaluation of the foresight study and especially for determining its efficiency. Process indicators combine major quantitative as well as qualitative indicators.

Table 16.1 shows that different indicator types are, to a varying extent, suitable for measuring different objects.

Effectiveness and efficiency of foresight studies are often assessed by the

Table 16.1   Suitability of indicators to measure different objectives

		Measurement perspective		
		Process	Evaluation	Impact
Indicator type	Leading (*ex ante*)	↓	→	↑
	Lagging (*ex post*)	→	↑	↑
	Learning (monitoring)	→	↑	→
	Input	↓	↑	→
	Output	↓	↑	↑
	Process	n/a	↑	→

Note: ↑ Fully suitable; → partially suitable; ↓ not suitable.

estimation of impacts such as Delphi participation rate;[2] thematic panels' feedback, accomplishment of the formally set goal in terms of specifying research areas. Data are usually collected via (empirical) evaluations and international comparisons. These are especially reviews of project management, personal and formal information obtained from client and stakeholders, as well as comparisons with key indicators of projects in other regions and countries.

The quality of foresight studies can be measured using additional constructed indicators such as survey participation rate, share of rejected participations, time needed for completion of the foresight study compared with time scheduled, resources needed for completion of the foresight study compared with resources scheduled (person days/person months) as well as resources needed for completion of the foresight study compared with resources scheduled (financial budget).

To monitor and evaluate ongoing foresight projects, typical indicators used are the accuracy of keeping milestones and deadlines for outputs, the share of workshop participants not appearing and the on-time completion of different projects (see Table 16.2).

While the individual indicators have some specific characteristics, developing and building a set of indicators for different purposes raises additional challenges. Despite the original purpose of indicator selection and development, a few underlying basic principles need to be taken into account. Indicators comprising a measurement or evaluation system need to be mutually exclusive but collectively exhaustive.

Impact Dimensions of Foresight Studies

Foresight studies have various impacts in different time horizons (see Table 16.3). The most significant impacts are usually considered to be of long term rather than showing immediate effects (Meissner 2013a). However, caution is recommended when it comes to measuring their real contribution to a given impact in the long term. This is mainly due to the fact that in the course of time the framework conditions are likely to change. Thus it is hardly possible to assess the total contribution of foresight studies and their respective results to the changed situation.

In particular, comprehensive foresight studies produce results that concern different ranges of the society and are relevant for policy development in a broad social context. However, it is appropriate to note that the emphasis on policy influence is likely to move the foresight study results in a politically correct direction. Such behaviour has been observed especially for those countries that conducted foresight studies for the first time. With studies focused on certain ranges, the effects are likewise only meas-

Table 16.2   Criteria for assessing effectiveness, efficiency and quality of foresight studies

Effectiveness	Efficiency	Quality indicators
Project management procedures	Project management and monitoring, followed up by review	Participation rate surveys
(Empirical) evaluation	Personal and formal information obtained from client and stakeholders	Share of rejected participation
International evaluation	Assessment of change in basic research culture, without indicators	Time needed for completion of foresight study versus time scheduled
Indicators of impact and the Delphi participation rate	Comparing with cost of similar projects in other countries	Resources needed for completion of foresight study versus resources scheduled (person days/ person months)
Thematic panels' feedback	Project management and monitoring, followed up by review	Resources needed for completion of foresight study versus resources scheduled (financial budget)
Accomplishment of the formally set goal in terms of specifying research areas	Personal and formal information obtained from client and stakeholders	
	Comparing with cost of similar projects in other countries	

urable over sector-specific policies. Foresight studies are often characterized as having little intrinsic value, with a small or absent involvement of policy decision makers, and a perception that the foresight study provides only informative frameworks.

Foresight has a lasting positive impact on the innovation performance of countries when it facilitates the cooperation of the initiators with major stakeholders in the early stages of the study. A foresight study often combines a top–down approach at the beginning and a bottom–up one at later stages. The necessary acceptance of the expected results is thus part of the objective from the beginning.

Table 16.3   Impact of foresight studies

		Impact type and time horizon			
		Direct		Indirect	
		Short-term	Long-term	Short-term	Long-term
Main domains of impact	Science	Interaction/ inspiration with non-science	New/ adapted research priorities/ fields	Horizon expansion	Industrial and inter- disciplinary spillovers
	Economy and society	Awareness building	Improved techno- logical know-how	Increased productivity	Targeted R&D investments, improved competi- tiveness and innovative- ness of countries/ nations
	Policy	Application thinking	Priority setting, NIS shaping	Increased problem awareness	Increased general satisfaction

Foresight improves communication and cooperation between participants of different sectors and disciplines. Interdisciplinary thinking is strengthened and a common language is developed. Besides common indicative visions of the future, new targeted innovation policy measures can be developed from a solid base. Such harmonization of participants within NIS is essential for the exhaustion of the new (technological) potential and in particular for states with fragmented innovative systems. Foresight studies contribute, by the inclusion of the public, to the strengthening of the acceptance of the technology and innovation among stakeholders and society. However, national foresight studies are also a political process during which, perhaps, entrenched views influence the results (Cuhls 2003).

Foresight is to be understood as a continuous process from the initial goal definition to implementation. However, it is essential that implementation is considered in the early planning stage. Foresight studies are not finished when the results are presented; rather they begin, again and again, with an increasing impact over a long learning process.

5. HOW FORESIGHT CAN CONTRIBUTE TO STI INDICATORS

One of the peculiar features of foresight is its focus on extracting and integrating tacit knowledge (Meissner 2013b). The many opportunities for the use of STI indicators to facilitate this process were discussed above. Foresight has a great potential to complement STI indicators. Below some of the most promising areas of such complementarity are discussed.

Identification of Emerging Areas of Research

Most foresight studies in the field of STI are aimed at identification of key research areas and key technologies, with the highest promise of economic and social return to be addressed by the national or regional governments. Since they are related to future issues, an opportunity is created to take a closer look at emerging areas of research, such as nano-, bio- and cognitive technologies. The new fields of S&T identified through foresight can both contribute to existing statistical classifications and nomenclatures by introducing new research fields or innovative goods and services. On the other hand, there is room for new indicators to be measured in the framework of statistical surveys. For example, there are many new issues in the field of information and communication technologies that are poorly covered by statistics, while being among the key topics discussed within forward-looking activities, such as Web 2.0, cloud computing, social networks and semantic search.

Fast progress in the emerging S&T areas requires new instruments for measuring them. The foresight community can be addressed in this respect as a source of new indicators that should be used in the planned surveys and a tool to elaborate a future time-line for introduction of those indicators into statistical practices.

In the OECD Blue Sky II Forum (OECD 2007), several challenges for STI statistics were discussed. One of them was a new context for STI indicators – globalization, fast changes in STI, and technological shifts towards emerging economies. Since foresight integrates judgements of a wide range of stakeholders, including researchers, business people and government officials, it makes it possible to identify promising areas of innovation activities and key factors that will reflect the future role of particular research areas so that the STI statistics can be better prepared to meet the future demands of policy makers.

Global Challenges

A key issue for forward-looking activities is to address the global challenges: globalization, climate change, energy, an ageing population,
scarcity of basic resources, migration, food and water security, health
and well-being and sustainable development.[3] In Boden et al. (2010) three
major groups of global challenges are considered. They are the need to:
change the current ways in which essential natural resources are used;
anticipate and adapt to social changes; and foster more effective and transparent governance. STI, on the one hand, plays a crucial role in designing
relevant responses to meet the challenges and, on the other hand, constitutes some of the particular challenges themselves. The convergence of
conventional technologies and the emergence of new (multidisciplinary)
fields of research create a potential for great impact on all dimensions of
life. Foresight provides tools for the identification of early (weak) signals
of changes to come, thus outlining a future policy agenda and introducing
new indicators to measure the results of future policy making. Among the
issues to be tackled by foresight and STI indicators are the impact of convergent technologies on various sectors of the economy and new modes of
research (such as web-based labs distributed over different countries, open
innovation, and research collaboration across countries and disciplines).

Industry–Science Linkages and Multidisciplinarity of Research

Measuring linkages between the science community and industry has been
one of the most urgent issues for STI statistics (see, e.g., OECD 2007:
38). It covers such issues as cooperation, co-publication and co-patenting
between research institutions and companies, university–industry relations and spin-off companies. Another dimension in this respect is
increasing multidisciplinarity of research and innovation. Foresight, in its
essence, is a participatory process that involves all types of stakeholders
and thus creates new linkages in the 'triple helix'. On the other hand it can
be used to identify new types of linkages and to assess key characteristics
of emerging research networks (Nugroho and Saritas 2009).
    Statistical time series are often used as a key source of information for
economic models. At the same time the underlying assumptions do not
necessarily reflect real processes and causal relationships between the
indicators used in the model. The value of conventional models deterio-
rates with rapidly advancing technologies and increasingly complicated
systems of policy tools. Foresight contributes to both deeper-expert-
based analysis of trends and correlations within existing models and to
the identification of new (not necessarily directly related to STI) drivers

of changes and relationships between them to be included in the models. John Marburger notes that 'we need models that stimulate social behavior and that feeds into macroeconomic models . . . that we can exercise to make intelligent guesses at what we might expect the future to bring and how we should prepare for it' (OECD 2010: 31).

Foresight provides a number of instruments allowing for the contribution of added value to existing models. Among other methods, there are scenario workshops where experts select the most important and most unpredictable variables to design relevant scenarios and indicators that can be used to show policy makers which scenario is taking place.

6. OUTLOOK – HOW FORESIGHT AND STI INDICATORS WILL BE INTEGRATED IN THE FUTURE

R&D is becoming a globally sourced commodity, especially by multinational companies. For these companies foresight is a useful tool to identify new areas of application and to get insights into expected national STI priority fields. Hence a major application for the results of foresight studies will be the influence of these results on R&D policy priorities, which in turn will require statistical measurement in support of sound indicators.

R&D priority fields identified and assessed in such a way also deliver valuable information for governments but also for private investors, for example companies and financial investors, since the assessment of these fields and applications in turn allows to measure the value of R&D projects and portfolios. Eventually the combination of the calculated value of these R&D fields and applications allows the overall assessment of the innovation pipeline, especially of companies.

Moreover, foresight is a tool that has the potential to deliver results for the prospective development of the higher education sector, such as the design of future-oriented curricula of universities to meet prospective demand for skills. Foresight is likely to evolve as an instrument to identify the key skills/competences needed to work with emerging technologies and hence for revising existing nomenclatures for professions and programmes of professional education. In that respect, methodologies addressing weak signals and their implications for change will develop. In addition, foresight will go much beyond the established fields and horizons of investigation but will include policy fields complementary to STI policy. Hence foresight will be used as an instrument for the identification of future needs and policy issues and, as a consequence, will highlight the need for new indicators. In the short term the need for the substantial validation of trends identified and described with the help of foresight studies will be met. Such validation will eventually lead to building classifications and nomenclatures for emerging technology areas. The close interrelation of foresight, indicators and policy making requires building an integral system that will be able to identify future issues of concern, elaborate efficient policy tools (with a shared responsibility between different government agencies – a policy mix) and have a set of indicators able to measure progress and the effects. Eventually foresight mapping is likely to become one source for developing new STI indicators that are also well suited to correspond to the emergence of more sophisticated scenarios, for example indicators that reflect the shift to particular scenarios and can be used to identify and to describe key drivers (the most important and the most unclear).

The emergence of the foresight diamond (Figure 16.1) and its increased application also calls for more evidence-based methods, especially the integration of the qualitative and the quantitative. Such a new generation of indicators requires a move towards net-based indicators that are also capable of reflecting the increased use of web-based tools for the purpose of foresight. Such indicators are required to reflect new methods such as data mining and semantic search. In addition, the process perspective needs complementary indicators that describe the importance and functioning of networks within foresight.

NOTES

1. This chapter was prepared with the kind support of the National Research University, Higher School of Economics, Basic Research Fund.
2. For details, see NISTEP (2010) and Loveridge et al. (1995).
3. Global challenges have been extensively discussed during recent years by international organizations (see OECD 2010 and the Millennium projects – www.millennium.org).

REFERENCES

Battistella, C. and A.F. De Toni (2011), 'A methodology of technological foresight: a proposal and field study', *Technological Forecasting and Social Change*, **78**, 1029–48.
Bezold, C. (2010), 'Lessons from using scenarios for strategic foresight', *Technological Forecasting and Social Change*, **77**, 1513–18.
Bishop, P., A. Hines and T. Collins (2007), 'The current state of scenario development: an overview of techniques', *Foresight*, **9**(1), 5–25.
Blind, K. (2004), *The Economics of Standards: Theory, Evidence, Policy*, Cheltenham, UK and Northampton, MA, USA: Edward Elgar.
Boden, M., C. Cagnin, V. Carabias, K. Haegeman and T. Konnola (2010), *Facing the Future: Time for the EU to Meet Global Challenges*, EUR 24364 EN, Luxembourg: Publication Office of the EU.

Bradfield, R., G. Wright, G. Burt, G. Cairns and K. Van Der Heijden (2005), 'The origins and evolution of scenario techniques in long range business planning', *Futures*, **37**(8), 795–812.

Cachia, R., R. Compañó and O. Da Costa (2007), 'Grasping the potential of online social networks for foresight', *Technological Forecasting and Social Change*, **74**, 1179–203.

Cuhls, K. (2003), 'From forecasting to foresight processes – new participative foresight activities in Germany', *Journal of Forecasting*, **22**, 93–111.

Gavigan, J., F. Scapolo, M. Keenan, I. Miles, F. Farhi, D. Lecoq, M. Capriati and T. Di Bartolomeo (2001), *FOREN (Foresight for Regional Development Network): A Practical Guide to Regional Foresight*, Brussels: European Commission Research Directorate General, STRATA Programme, http://foresight.jrc.ec.europa.eu/documents/eur20128en.pdf.

Georghiou, L. and M. Keenan (2006), 'Evaluation of national foresight activities: assessing rationale, process and impact', *Technological Forecasting and Social Change*, **73**, 761–77.

Georghiou, L., J.C. Harper, M. Keenan, I. Miles and R. Popper (eds) (2008), *The Handbook of Technology Foresight: Concepts and Practice*, Cheltenham, UK and Northampton, MA, USA: Edward Elgar.

Godwin, P. and G. Wright (2010), 'The limits of forecasting methods in anticipating rare events', *Technological Forecasting and Social Change*, **77**(3), 355–68.

Grim, T. (2009), 'Foresight Maturity Model (FMM): achieving best practices in the foresight field', *Journal of Futures Studies*, **13**(4), 69–80.

Haegeman, K., E. Marinelli, F. Scapolo, A. Ricci and A. Sokolov (2013), 'Quantitative and qualitative approaches in FTA: from combination to integration?', *Technological Forecasting and Social Change*, **80**(3), 386–97.

Höjer, M. and L.G. Mattsson (2000), 'Determinism and backcasting in future studies', *Futures*, **32**(7), 613–34.

Keenan, M. (2003), 'Identifying emerging generic technologies at the national level: the UK experience', *Journal of Forecasting*, **22**, 129–60.

Keenan, M. and R. Popper (2007), *RIF (Research Infrastructures Foresight). Practical Guide for Integrating Foresight in Research Infrastructures Policy Formulation*, Brussels: European Commission.

Lempert, R.J., S.W. Popper and S.C. Bankes (2003), *Shaping the Next One Hundred Years: New Methods for Quantitative Long-Term Policy Analysis*, Santa Monica, CA: The RAND Pardee Center, http://www.rand.org/pubs/monograph_reports/2007/MR1626.pdf.

Loveridge, D., L. Georghiou and M. Nedeva (1995), *United Kingdom Foresight Programme*, Manchester UK: PREST, University of Manchester.

Malanowski, N. and A. Zweck (2007), 'Bridging the gap between foresight and market research: integrating methods to assess the economic potential of nanotechnology', *Technological Forecasting and Social Change*, **74**, 1805–22.

Martin, B.R. (1995), 'Foresight in science and technology', *Technology Analysis and Strategic Management*, **7**(2), 139–68.

Meissner, D. (2013a), 'Results and impact of national foresight-studies', in D. Meissner, L. Gokhberg and A. Sokolov (eds), *Science, Technology and Innovation Policy for the Future: Potentials and Limits of Foresight Studies*, Berlin: Springer, forthcoming.

Meissner, D. (2013b), 'Indicators for foresight studies', in D. Meissner, L. Gokhberg and A. Sokolov (eds) *Science, Technology and Innovation Policy for the Future: Potentials and Limits of Foresight Studies*, Berlin: Springer, forthcoming.

Meissner, D., M. Cervantes and V. Roud (2013), 'Innovation policy or policy for innovation?', in D. Meissner, L. Gokhberg and A. Sokolov (eds), *Science, Technology and Innovation Policy for the Future: Potentials and Limits of Foresight Studies*, Berlin: Springer, forthcoming.

Miles, I. (2002), *Appraisal of Alternative Methods and Procedures for Producing Regional Foresight, Report*, prepared by CRIC for the European Commission, DG Research, STRATA-ETAN Expert Group Action, Manchester, UK: CRIC.

Moed, H.F., W. Glänzel and U. Schmoch (eds) (2004), *Handbook of Quantitative Science and Technology Research*, Dordrecht, The Netherlands: Kluwer Academic Publishers.

Molas-Gallart, J., R. Barrè, M. Zappacosta and J. Gavigan (eds) (2002), *A Trans-National Analysis of Results and Implications of Industrially-Oriented Technology Foresight Studies (France, Spain, Italy & Portugal)*, JRC/IPTS-ESTO Study, Brussels: Joint Research Centre, http://bookshop.europa.eu/en/a-trans-national-analysis-of-results-and-implications-of-industrially-oriented-technology-foresight-studies-pbLFNA20138/? CatalogCategoryID=OloKABstRQYAAAEj1JEY4e5L.

NISTEP (2010), *The 9th Science and Technology Foresight, Contribution of Science and Technology to Future Society*, NISTEP Report No. 145, Tokyo: NISTEP.

Nugroho, Y. and O. Saritas (2009), 'Incorporating network perspectives in foresight: a methodological proposal', *Foresight*, 11(6), 21–41.

OECD (2007), *Science, Technology and Innovation Indicators in a Changing World. Responding to Policy Needs*, Paris: OECD.

OECD (2010), *The OECD Innovation Strategy. Getting a Head Start on Tomorrow*, Paris: OECD.

Popper, R. (2008), 'How are foresight methods selected?', *Foresight*, 10(6), 62–89.

Popper, R. (2011), 'Wild cards and weak signals informing and shaping research and innovation policy', paper presented at the Fourth International Seville Conference on Future-Oriented Technology Analysis (FTA): FTA and Grand Societal Challenges – Shaping and Driving Structural and Systemic Transformations, Seville, 12–13 May.

Rappert, B. (1999), 'Rationalising the future? Foresight in science and technology policy co-ordination', *Futures*, 31, 527–45.

Ringland, G. (1998), *Scenario Planning: Managing for the Future*, Chichester and New York: Wiley.

Santo, M., G. Coelho, D. dos Santos and L. Filh (2006), 'Text mining as a valuable tool in foresight exercises: a study on nanotechnology', *Technological Forecasting and Social Change*, Volume 73(8), 1013–27.

Saritas, O. and A. Oner (2004), 'Systemic analysis of UK foresight results – joint application of integrated management model and roadmapping', *Technological Forecasting and Social Change*, 71, 27–65.

Sokolov, A. (2013), 'Foresight in Russia: implications for policy making', in D. Meissner, L. Gokhberg and A. Sokolov (eds), *Science, Technology and Innovation Policy for the Future: Potentials and Limits of Foresight Studies*, Berlin: Springer, forthcoming.

TFAMWG (Technology Futures Analysis Methods Working Group) (2004), 'Technology futures analysis: toward integration of the field and new methods', *Technological Forecasting and Social Change*, 71, 287–303.

Tran, T. and T. Daim (2008), 'A taxonomic review of methods and tools applied in technology assessment', *Technological Forecasting and Social Change*, 75(9), 1396–405.

van der Steen, M., M. van Twist, M. van der Vlist and R. Demkes (2011), 'Integrating futures studies with organizational development: design options for the scenario project "RWS2020"', *Futures*, 43, 337–47.

van Notten, P.W.F., J. Rotmans, M.B.A. van Asselt and D.S. Rothman (2003), 'An updated scenario typology', *Futures*, 35, 423–43.

Vishnevskiy K., O. Karasev, D. Meissner and E. Vetchinkina (2013), 'Integrated roadmaps for technology forecasting and application potential assessment – the case of applying nanotechnology to water treatment', in D. Meissner, L. Gokhberg and A. Sokolov (eds), *Science, Technology and Innovation Policy for the Future: Potentials and Limits of Foresight Studies*, Berlin: Springer, forthcoming.

Voros, J. (2006), 'Introducing a classification framework for prospective methods', *Foresight*, 8(2), 43–56.

Wehnert, T. and W. Jörß (2009), 'Integration of qualitative and quantitative methodologies for European energy foresight', EFONET 2009. www.efonet.org.

17 Measuring innovation in the public sector
Carter Bloch

1. INTRODUCTION

There is now a vast amount of experience on the measurement of innovation in businesses, as is clear from this handbook. However, public sector organizations, and for that matter also public services in general, have been neglected in these efforts. This has gradually begun to change in recent years with the growing perception that public sector innovation is vital for meeting many of the social and economic challenges faced today. As a result, there is a need for tools to measure public sector innovation.

Based on these needs, there has been an increase in work within public sector innovation measurement. This work has had to grapple with difficult issues concerning both the nature of public sector innovation and statistical measurement. These recent studies have made significant progress both in identifying what can be measured and in shedding more light on the challenges that lie ahead towards the development of internationally comparable indicators.

To set the stage, this chapter briefly examines related literature and key factors that have influenced measurement, focusing on what distinguishes the public sector from businesses. It then reviews measurement work within the area. Earlier work consists mainly of a relatively small number of individualized studies, many of which were structured as innovation competitions. However, recent efforts to develop indicators of public sector innovation on a more systematic basis have added significantly to the stock of experience in this area. The chapter examines what types of indicators have been developed, identifying which measures appear to have worked well and what challenges remain for future work.

2. WHY MEASURE INNOVATION IN THE PUBLIC SECTOR?

The increased interest in public sector innovation measurement stems from an increased recognition of the importance of public sector innovation itself. This is probably due to a number of factors. One is necessity. The public sector is under increasing pressure from a number of sides – rising costs, increasing demands from citizens and businesses, demographic changes, environmental issues and globalization pressures – that can increase the difficulty of maintaining high levels of welfare services. The need for change to adapt to these pressures has only become more visible following the recent financial crisis and subsequent worsening of government budget deficits. The basic message from all this is that the public sector must do more for less. Another factor is opportunity. An effective and innovative public sector can contribute greatly to the performance of businesses. At the same time it constitutes an important market for businesses – one that may be used as a tool to promote business innovation through procurement. In addition, recent theoretical and qualitative studies have helped raise attention in the public sector and its potential contribution to innovation and growth. Most noteworthy among these is the EU-funded PUBLIN project (Koch et al. 2005; Koch and Hauknes 2005). Other works include papers from the UK Cabinet Strategy Unit (Mulgan and Albury 2003; Kelly et al. 2002) and from Nesta (Mulgan 2007; Harris and Albury 2009).

From the increased interest in innovation follows naturally the need for data. In order to be able to improve knowledge and understanding of the rate and degree of innovation in the public sector, as well as its incentives, processes and impact, there is a need for systematic and comparable data. This was one of the key recommendations of the above-mentioned PUBLIN project (Koch et al. 2005) and has been stressed in a number of countries and in international organizations such as the OECD and the supranational EU.[1]

Establishing that there is a need for data is, however, the easy part. Determining which specific types of indicators will be most useful is more difficult, and requires careful examination of user needs. A number of questions are relevant here, and the answers may vary across countries. For example, which topics dominate national discussions concerning public innovation? Value for money and user satisfaction? The role of the public sector as an enabler of business innovation and public–private cooperation? Issues of transparency and trust in government? Need for new solutions that can help maintain or improve levels of service in the face of cost cuts and demographic changes? Better quantitative measures of public sector performance? Identifying main obstacles and drivers of public sector innovation? Which parts of the public sector have the greatest interest? An understanding of which topics are most important will help guide indicator development. This is, however, an ongoing process that cannot simply be completed up front; both trial and error in actual use of initial indicators and the quality of the data collected will be important for indicator development and understanding user needs.

3.   A CONCEPTUAL BACKGROUND – HOW DOES INNOVATION IN THE PUBLIC SECTOR DIFFER FROM THAT IN THE BUSINESS SECTOR?

An initial step in developing measures of public sector innovation is address-ing conceptual issues such as what an innovation is in the public sector and how to characterize innovation processes. An additional and equally important step concerns statistical issues, such as populations and statisti-cal units. These are outlined in the next section. This section addresses con-ceptual issues concerning the nature of public sector innovation.[2]

One possible approach in conceptualizing public sector innovation would be to see it in complete isolation from the business sector, essen-tially starting from scratch in considering how to go about measuring it. However, this would ignore both the extensive amount of experience that has been gained from measuring innovation in the business sector and the fact that some degree of comparison of public and private sector innovation is inevitable. Hence an alternative approach is to take busi-ness sector innovation as a reference point and consider how the public sector might differ from the business sector and how this might influence measurement.

A fundamental feature that is typically first to be pointed out when comparing the public and private sector is that most public sector organizations lack a market and thus also market incentives to innovate. Connected to this, public sector objectives are broad and often go beyond improving the direct performance or output of the organization itself. For example, objectives may also include improving the 'performance' of others; that is, enabling innovation among citizens, business suppliers or other public sector institutions. Public sector objectives may also be con-flicting. For example, public sector organizations are under pressure to cut costs and at the same time improve or provide new services or reach new users. Given limited resources, aims to target specific groups or to comply with regulations may come at the expense of other stakeholders.

The nature of public services is also important here in a number of respects. A number of features of services in general also apply to public service providers, such as intangibility, simultaneity of production and consumption,[3] and the central role of worker competences and user interaction. At the same time, there are also differences between services provided by private businesses and by public sector organizations. This is particularly the case for collective or 'public-good' services that have to do with administration, monitoring and policy/regulation development.

Public sector organizations are typically part of a complex organiza-tional structure that affects, both directly and indirectly, how organizations operate and innovate. Individual organizations thus typically do not have full autonomy over their decision making. A potential implication of this is that external actors (in particular policy and other public organizations) will play a larger role in enabling innovation in individual public sector organizations than for a business.

An additional feature that is relevant here is the heterogeneity of public sector organizations, across different levels of both government and sectors (each with different types of outputs). In terms of level of government, or types of institutions, there will be differences in kinds of activities or services they provide. Policy-making institutions (ministries) are arguably very distinct from other institutions, as are their main 'products', that is, policies. Agencies and the administrations of regional and local governments will, for the most part, be less involved with the provision of services, but will have a large amount of process and organizationally oriented activities. However, there are probably many agencies or other entities in central government that provide services directly to users, be they citizens, businesses or other public sector organizations. And, finally, there is the group of frontline delivery institutions (e.g. schools and hospitals) that are directly involved in the provision of public services to users. In terms of sectors, the greatest differences here are in terms of objectives and measures of outputs, where both will have some elements that are specific to individual sectors. However, there may also be a number of other aspects that vary across sectors, such as effects of innovations, barriers, specific organizational issues or types of collaboration.

4.   STATISTICAL ISSUES

In order to collect data on innovation among public sector organizations, a number of standard statistical issues need to be addressed, such as determining the target population, statistical units, and methods of classification of units.[4] To a large degree, the establishment of a survey methodology for data collection of this type among public sector organizations is uncharted territory. There are few examples of other types of surveys on which innovation surveys can draw.[5] This section outlines the main issues, which will then be revisited below when reviewing recent work.

As its title indicates, the primary focus of this chapter is the public sector as opposed to public services, although much of the discussion here could be considered relevant for both. While there are no commonly accepted definitions of the public sector or public services, the following are fairly representative.

The **public sector** comprises the general government sector plus all public corporations including the central bank. (OECD 1997)

Public services: 'General-interest services' are services considered to be in the general interest by the public authorities and accordingly subjected to specific public-service obligations. They include non-market services (e.g. compulsory education, social protection), obligations of the State (e.g. security and justice) and services of general economic interest (e.g. transport, energy and communications). (EU-glossary; http://europa.eu/scadplus/glossary/general_interest_services_en.htm)

The concepts public sector and public services differ in that the public sector is defined in terms of ownership and control (essentially the SNA sector General Government plus other publicly owned or controlled entities), while public services are defined in terms of their functions or activities. The public sector implies an exclusive focus on organizations that are part of government or publicly owned. An alternative focus on public services would essentially follow the same approach as used for the business sector, where organizations are classified by their economic activity (in this case being the main activities classified or considered as public services). This approach would then include both publicly and privately owned institutions that provide public services.

Taking the public sector as a starting point in determining the target population, there is the question of whether any sectors or groups should be excluded (as is typically done in business innovation surveys). Among the possible subsectors that could be considered for exclusion from the target population are: social security funds, public corporations, non-profit institutions in market services, non-profit institutions in non-market services, higher education institutions, government research institutions, defence services and religious services. The target population can be further delineated to include a smaller group of activities or functions, for example based on a small set of main public sectors. However, narrowing down the target population requires a classification of units, which is a challenge in itself (see below).

A survey sample is drawn from the frame population, which may differ from the target population. It may include units that no longer exist or that are no longer part of the target population. In addition, the frame may not include all units that are part of the target population. In practical terms, the most likely source for frame populations of the public sector is a business register. However, there is a general lack of experience in drawing samples of public sector units from business registers.

An additional issue is identifying the desired statistical unit. According to the *Oslo Manual* (OECD/Eurostat 2005: Para. 231): 'Ideally, innovation data should be compiled (and collected) at the organizational level for which decisions on innovation activity are made. Taking into account how innovation activities are usually organized, the enterprise is in general the most appropriate statistical unit.' However, for the public sector there are varying degrees of autonomy, which may mean that greater flexibility is needed in determining the ideal statistical unit. For example, the ideal observation unit may in some cases be the establishment unit. Some relevant examples here are schools, or breaking down large municipalities by activity. Related to this is the question of how similar the distinction between enterprise and establishment units is in business registers for different countries.

Yet another issue is how to classify units. Two possible methods are by type of economic activity using ISIC/NACE classifications or by Classification of Functions of Government (COFOG). ISIC/NACE has the advantage that it is available in business registers and is also used for the business sector. However, initial studies give the impression that the great majority of enterprise units are found within a single two-digit industry, public administration services. COFOG, on the other hand, is used for many public sector statistics; however, data on this classification are typically not available in business registers.

5. APPROACHES TO MEASURING PUBLIC SECTOR INNOVATION

A number of possible approaches can be followed in measuring public sector innovation. This section outlines the main types of approaches that, however, should not be considered mutually exclusive as some of them can be combined. The first could be called the *Oslo Manual* approach; that is, that measurement follows the same principles used for the *Oslo Manual* in terms of how innovations, innovation activities and other key concepts are defined and in terms of the use of the subject approach. Given that this is essentially the approach followed in the most recent work, it is also the primary focus of this chapter.

A second approach is the 'object approach', which can either focus on innovation projects or on individual innovations. There are a number of early examples of this approach for business innovations, and also some examples for public sector innovations through surveys based on innovation award competitions. The advantage with this approach is that many aspects of innovations such as objectives, effects and linkages can vary greatly across different innovations within the same organization. In addition, respondents are probably more able to answer questions on a single innovation than on innovation in general over a two–three-year period.

Surveys can also focus on a specific sector or type of organization, where many questions are formulated to be specifically applicable to the organizations in question. An example is an OECD project to measure innovation in schools.[6] This approach could of course be combined with a more general *Oslo Manual* approach by including sector-specific modules in a generalized questionnaire.

It was mentioned above that organizational aspects may be more policy relevant for the public sector than for businesses. This can motivate the development of surveys in order to create a benchmarking or management tool for individual organizations. Two examples of this approach, the Korean Government Innovation Index (Korean Ministry of Government Administration and Home Affairs 2005) and the Nesta Public Sector Innovation Index (Hughes and Baker 2011), are described below.

An alternative to covering organizational units is a two-tiered approach. The most common example here is employer–employee surveys of organizational changes, such as those outlined in the MEADOW guidelines (MEADOW Consortium 2010). However, such an approach can also be used to cover the organizational unit and individual projects or innovations.

A final approach would be to utilize existing data, either supplemented by the addition of a small set of questions concerning innovation or solely on the basis of existing data. This can be done at different levels of aggregation. Some examples of aggregate-level work on the basis of existing data is the OECD *Government at a Glance* (OECD 2009b) and output measurement and productivity analysis of the UKCemGa.[7]

6. EARLY AND RECENT STUDIES OF PUBLIC SECTOR INNOVATION

Much of the earliest work on the measurement of public sector innovation was not in the form of actual innovation surveys, but instead innovation competitions among public sector organizations. As part of these competitions, participating organizations were required to fill out a (typically open-ended) questionnaire on the individual innovation being nominated for the award. While the initial purpose was not to generate innovation data, the data have since been analysed and used to create indicators. Borins (2006) discusses a number of innovation award programs[8] conducted in the USA, Canada and other Commonwealth countries in which nominees are required to fill out an innovation survey questionnaire.

An early attempt at measuring public sector innovation through an actual survey was undertaken by Statistics Canada in 2000 (Earl 2002).

The study, which was part of a Survey of Electronic Commerce and Technology 2000 and essentially a supplementary module, inquired about the introduction of organizational and technological changes in both public sector organizations and private businesses. They found that very high shares of public sector organizations had implemented these changes, even among the smallest administrations. These results are quite similar to those found in recent studies, despite the use of very different definitions of innovation.

Other examples of *ad hoc* innovation surveys include two surveys conducted in the UK by the National Audit Office and the Audit Commission. The National Audit Office (2009) survey examines innovation in central government, covering organizations' own conceptualization of innovation, and on how the organization innovates, including culture and capabilities, risk management and the role of selected barriers and incentives. The Audit Commission study of local authorities in England (Audit Commission 2007) covers attitudes to innovation, the role of organizational structure and staff, barriers and enabling conditions, and learning activities. It also highlights a number of specific examples of innovations in local government.

The Korean Government Innovation Index (GII)[9] was developed as a management tool that uses an innovation survey to generate internal data. The GII survey focuses mainly on management and organizational capability for innovation, which creates diagnostic index measures that are used to analyse and benchmark public sector organizations. The GII thus represents an alternative type of survey, where the focus is less on the creation of aggregated indicators and instead on creating composite index measures for individual benchmarking. This general idea of an innovation management tool was also applied by Nesta in the UK towards the development of a public sector innovation index. However, the topics covered by the Nesta survey (described below) were fairly different from the GII.

The studies described above were either *ad hoc* surveys or were devoted to a specific purpose such as an innovation award or a management tool. In contrast, three recent studies, the Nordic MEPIN project, the EU Innobarometer 2010 and the Nesta Public Sector Innovation Index, have been directed more towards the development of internationally comparable statistics.[10] The Nordic MEPIN project (Measuring Public Innovation in the Nordic Countries, www.mepin.eu) developed an initial measurement framework for conducting public sector innovation surveys and implemented a pilot survey of innovation among public sector organizations in the Nordic countries (Bugge et al. 2011; Bloch 2011). The EU's Innobarometer 2010 was devoted to innovation in public administration

(Gallup Organization 2011). A survey was conducted among 4063 public administration organizations in 29 countries across Europe using a questionnaire that draws partly on the MEPIN survey. And, as mentioned above, as part of the Public Sector Innovation Index, Nesta commissioned a pilot survey of innovation across two parts of the public sector: the National Health Service (NHS) and local government. The survey draws both on Nesta's Private Sector Index survey questionnaire, the MEPIN survey and the EU Community Innovation Survey (CIS) for businesses (Hughes and Baker 2011).

A Review of the MEPIN, Nesta and Innobarometer Studies

Given that these last three studies constitute the state of the art at this point in time, the surveys are described here in greater detail. Of the three studies, the Nordic MEPIN has been most focused on development and testing aspects, since the creation of a framework and guidelines was the main objective of the project. The two other studies share a number of elements with MEPIN, both building on and modifying questions used in the MEPIN study and drawing on other sources. For a more detailed description of these studies, the reader is referred to the above-mentioned reports.

Innovations and Other Concepts

The frameworks on which these studies were based are very much influenced by the *Oslo Manual*. A number of concepts or topics essentially follow the *Oslo Manual* approach, typically with minor modifications to make them more appropriate for the public sector. This includes the definitions of innovations and innovative novelty, innovation activities, objectives and effects of innovations, linkages-related aspects such as information sources for innovation and innovation cooperation, and hampering factors. At the same time, some additional topics were included, such as innovation drivers, innovation strategy and organization, and innovative public procurement. This section focuses on the definition of innovations and the newer topics included in the surveys. Information on the construction of other measures can be found in the reports for the individual studies.

The innovation concept used in these studies was fairly closely aligned with *Oslo Manual* definitions. While there were some differences in the actual wording used, all three studies essentially followed the same approach here. As an example, the definitions of innovation used in the MEPIN study are shown in Box 17.1. As can be seen, the four types are quite similar to the *Oslo Manual* definitions (OECD/Eurostat 2005),

BOX 17.1   DEFINITIONS OF INNOVATION USED
            IN THE MEPIN STUDY

An **innovation** is the implementation of a significant change in
the way your organization operates or in the products it provides.
Innovations comprise new or significant changes to services and
goods, operational processes, organizational methods, or the way
your organization communicates with users.

Innovations must be new to your organization, although they can
have been developed by others. They can either be the result of
decisions within your organization or in response to new regulations or policy measures.

A **product innovation** is the introduction of a service or good that
is new or significantly improved compared to existing services
or goods in your organization. This includes significant improvements in the service or good's characteristics, in customer access
or in how it is used.

A **process innovation** is the implementation of a method for the
production and provision of services and goods that is new or significantly improved compared to existing processes in your organization. This may involve significant improvements in, for example,
equipment and/or skills. This also includes significant improvements in support functions such as IT, accounting and purchasing.

An **organizational innovation** is the implementation of a new
method for organizing or managing work that differs significantly
from existing methods in your organization. This includes new or
significant improvements to management systems or workplace
organizations.

A **communication innovation** is the implementation of a new
method of promoting the organization or its services and goods,
or new methods to influence the behaviour of individuals or others.
These must differ significantly from existing communication
methods in your organization.

Source: Bloch (2010).

where marketing innovations are instead formulated as communication innovations, and the wording is slightly modified in an attempt to better reflect the nature of public sector activities. The main motivations behind this approach were that many existing definitions of public sector innovation[11] are essentially based on the same characteristics as the *Oslo Manual* and cognitive testing suggested that these definitions fit well with the perceptions of public sector organizations (Annerstedt and Björkbacka 2010). Initial results with very high shares of innovative public organizations (see below) can, however, be interpreted as questioning whether businesses and public sector organizations share the same perception of what an innovation is.

Innovation drivers can be people, organizations or other factors that push organizations to innovate. What is, however, of more specific interest with respect to the public sector is 'political drivers', as they provide some information on how much autonomy individual public sector organizations possess in making decisions on innovation activities. Among the political drivers covered in the studies were mandated budget increases or reductions, new laws or regulations, changes implemented in higher-level organizations, mandated introduction of new online services, and new policy priorities.

The question of autonomy is part of a broader question concerning to what extent public sector organizations are geared towards innovation. Questions on innovation strategy and management have sought to shed light on how the innovation process is organized in public sector organizations.[12] Among the topics included were:

- Specific goals/targets for innovation activities
- An innovation strategy included in the overall vision or strategy of the organization
- Development department/section
- Innovation activities organized as projects, steered by a dedicated group
- Evaluations of the innovation processes conducted regularly
- Managers give high priority to developing new ideas or new ways of working
- Managers support trial-and-error testing of new ideas
- Top management is active in leading the implementation of innovations
- Members of staff devote part of their time to development/ innovation projects
- Staff incentives to identify new ideas and take part in their development

● Users involved in the design or planning of new or improved services.

The issue of public procurement has been approached in slightly different ways in each study. The MEPIN survey asks whether organizations make purchases that encourage the development of products or processes that do not yet exist or require new features, and whether selected procurement related activities are used to promote innovation.[13] Results were, however, somewhat mixed for this question (Bugge et al. 2011). The Innobarometer includes four questions on procurement: which types of services or goods are tendered; which actors are consulted with in preparing the tender; how innovation is weighed against cost when considering tenders; and whether any tenders have resulted in innovations or other important impacts.

Selecting the Population Frames

The starting point for the MEPIN surveys was the populations of enterprise (or legal) units within the general government sector. Selected units in a number of countries were excluded by manual sorting, based on an assessment of their relevance for this pilot study. Universities and units within defence were typically excluded from all countries. Some of the Nordic countries also included selected direct service providers in their samples (where these are typically classified as establishment-level units). Norway, Denmark, Sweden and Iceland included hospitals and Denmark and Iceland included schools in their samples.

The 2010 Innobarometer focused exclusively on public administration organizations with ten or more employees. The survey included all EU countries plus Norway and Switzerland, 29 countries in all. Sampling sizes depended on country size with four classes: 400 units for large countries; 100 for medium-sized countries; 50 for small countries; and ten units for the smallest countries. Selection of units was based on business registers and continued until the target number of responses was reached in each country. This gave a total number of 4063 responses, which also includes a smaller number of non-profit institutions and private businesses.

The Nesta survey in the UK focused on two areas of government, surveying NHS trusts (hospitals or groups of hospitals) and local authorities (municipalities). In both cases, organizations were requested to participate in the survey, and those that agreed were surveyed by telephone. About 16 per cent (64 units) of trusts and 31 per cent (111 units) of local authorities participated in the survey.

7. KEY MEASUREMENT ISSUES

Recent studies have made considerable headway towards the development of internationally comparable measures of public sector innovation. The development work that has been undertaken and the survey results provide a solid basis that can be built upon in further work. At the same time it should be kept in mind that these are initial pilot studies designed to test measurement frameworks. While the results provide a useful impression of what has worked well and what has been less successful, no issues can be considered to be laid to rest based on these first results. In addition to this, there are of course questions about whether these pilots neglect key issues of importance for understanding public sector innovation, or whether other approaches might have been better. This section examines selected measurement issues that are motivated by these recent studies.

A first issue concerns the definition of innovation. In all three recent studies, shares of public sector organizations with innovations are very high, more than perhaps was expected and substantially higher than shares for businesses. For example, from the MEPIN study, shares with product innovations ranged from 44 per cent in Sweden to 72 per cent in Denmark, and the EU-27 average (for service innovations) in the Innobarometer study was around 66 per cent. Shares in the Nesta survey are even higher at around 90 per cent. There is a need for a better understanding of what factors are driving these results and better methods of characterizing or distinguishing innovations.

While further testing is needed to do this, a number of potential factors can be identified. One possible factor is that public sector organizations may interpret the concept of innovation differently from businesses, particularly concerning changes that are either borderline in terms of meeting the criteria for an innovation or perhaps also changes that should not be considered as innovations. A second factor is that public sector organizations are typically larger than businesses. Given that large units are found to be more likely to be innovative, this would be expected to push innovative shares upwards. Another factor could be that low response rates may introduce a bias in the results. For example, the MEPIN study was a voluntary survey where, with the exception of Iceland, response rates were under 50 per cent.[14] Finally, there may be a large number of innovations that are driven by political mandates or by broad governmental changes or changes elsewhere in the public sector.

A second issue is the measurement of innovation expenditures, where great difficulties were encountered in recent studies. The MEPIN study followed an *Oslo Manual* approach in asking for expenditures on innovation activities, although intervals were used instead of actual amounts.

The Nesta survey adopted an 'intangibles' approach, covering five types of expenditures (which may or may not be directly related to the development or implementation of an innovation): staff training, external consultants, new equipment or software, research, and design or design services. Neither of these approaches was able to produce satisfactory results, with high non-response rates indicating that respondents experienced great difficulty in answering the questions. Provided there is interest in further pursuit of quantitative measures of innovation expenditures, it is unclear which direction is most advisable based on these results. However, a next step might be to examine in more detail what types of expenditure data public sector organizations are typically able to report on.

A third issue concerns the survey methodological aspects, such as the target population, statistical units and classifications. The main challenges involved here have already been outlined above. For example, what classification should be used in order to delineate the population? How well does the enterprise unit appear to function as the ideal statistical unit? What is the quality of business registers with respect to public sector units? And are all these issues similar across countries? Of the three recent studies, only the MEPIN study has attempted to construct a population frame for the entire public sector. While the experiences of the MEPIN study offer a number of examples that are potentially applicable in a broader international context, piloting across a much wider range of countries is needed in order to get a better idea of what work is needed and what approaches are most applicable across a broader range of countries.

A much-discussed issue concerning the measurement of public sector innovation is the heterogeneity of public sector organizations. Is it possible to conduct a harmonized survey across such a wide range of organizations? Each of the three recent studies uses what could be characterized as a 'generic' survey that is applicable across subsectors. The general impression from these studies when examining results across subgroups for individual countries is that a generic approach is feasible. However, this does not mean that a differentiation of questionnaires may not be useful in some cases. In particular, for specific groups of institutions, such as hospitals or schools, it would be valuable to include modules of questions that target specific aspects relevant to the group in question. This approach with 'sector-specific' modules has, however, not yet been used. An alternative approach would be to completely tailor a survey to a specific subgroup, which, however, would sacrifice generalizability across sectors.

An issue related to this is the lack of output measures. Measuring output for any individual public sector group is a very difficult task in itself, but there are some possibilities for homogeneous groups such as schools or hospitals. In contrast, no general measures exist of outputs for the public sector. At the same time, a key area of interest in measuring public sector innovation is what its impacts are on the organization's activities. While there is no question that this is one of the most difficult aspects of public sector innovation to measure, there is at least a fairly strong motivation to continue examining this aspect.

8.   CONCLUSION

This chapter has reviewed work to date on the measurement of innovation in the public sector. As discussed, recent work has accomplished much, but additional experience and testing are needed in order to arrive at a measurement framework with a sufficient degree of international comparability. Broadly speaking, there are two directions for further work, involving a wider set of countries in this measurement work and further examination of many of the issues that have been explored in recent work. For both of these, international coordination by, for example, the OECD and Eurostat will be important. While the Innobarometer 2010 survey covered a large number of countries, this was a telephone survey based on limited samples. A larger-scale pilot survey that is more representative of the entire public sector, perhaps carried out by official statistical offices, would be very beneficial in establishing internationally comparable statistics. Likewise, additional testing work is needed to further explore a number of issues, among these the definition of innovation and the quality of business registers.

NOTES

1. See, e.g., OECD (2010), European Commission (2010), Danish Agency for Science, Technology and Innovation (2008), UK Department of Business, Innovation and Skills (2008).
2. See also Mulgan and Albury (2003), Halvorsen et al. (2005), Hartley (2005) and Bugge et al. (2010).
3. However, there are exceptions to this. For example, many services are provided as assets or stocks, e.g. IT, public libraries, parks, hospitals, and environmental services.
4. For a more detailed discussion of many of these issues, see Mortensen (2010).
5. Surveys of ICT usage, which are regularly conducted among businesses in most OECD countries, are also implemented for the public sector in some countries (among these, the Nordic countries, Canada and New Zealand).
6. See OECD (2009a) for an overview of the project.
7. See http://www.ons.gov.uk/ons/guide-method/ukcemga/index.html. See also Atkinson (2005) for a discussion of the main issues involved in measuring public sector output and productivity.

8.   USA: Ford-KSG awards; Canada: IPAC awards; and countries of the Commonwealth: CAPAM awards.
9.   This short description of the Korean GII is based on PowerPoint presentations by the Korean Ministry of Government Administration and Home Affairs (2005) and Yoon (2006).
10.   This is perhaps only partly the case for the Nesta Public Sector Innovation Index; while its questionnaire seeks to achieve comparability with the other two studies, the main purpose of the survey is to create the Index.
11.   Some examples are Mulgan (2007): 'The simplest definition is that public sector innovation is about new ideas that work at creating public value. The ideas have to be at least in part new (rather than improvements); they have to be taken up (rather than just being good ideas); and they have to be useful.' And the UK Audit Commission (2007): 'practices undertaken by organizations in order to improve the product or service they provide, characterised by: Change – step-change and impact; Novelty – new to the organization in question; Action – completed, not just an idea'. See also Bloch (2010).
12.   These factors can also be related to measures of knowledge management practices that have been developed and tested for businesses. See, e.g., OECD (2003).
13.   Innovative procurement is defined as purchases that encourage the development of products or processes that do not yet exist or require new features.
14.   This is partly due to the fact that only one reminder was sent out under data collection. See Bugge et al. (2011).

REFERENCES

Annerstedt, P. and R. Björkbacka (2010), 'Feasibility study of public sector organizations', *MEPIN (Measuring Public Innovation in the Nordic Countries) Project*, Copenhagen: Danish Agency for Science, Technology and Innovation.

Atkinson, A. (2005), *Atkinson Review of Measurement of Government Output and Productivity for the National Accounts: Final Report*, Basingstoke, UK: Palgrave Macmillan.

Audit Commission (2007), *Seeing the Light: Innovation in Local Public Services*, London: UK Audit Commission.

Bloch, C. (2010), 'Towards a conceptual framework for measuring public sector innovation', *MEPIN (Measuring Public Innovation in the Nordic Countries) Project*, Copenhagen: Danish Agency for Science, Technology and Innovation.

Bloch, C. (2011), 'Measuring Public Innovation in the Nordic Countries – Final Report', *MEPIN (Measuring Public Innovation in the Nordic Countries) Project*, Copenhagen: Danish Agency for Science, Technology and Innovation.

Borins, S. (2006), *The Challenge of Innovating in Government*, Washington, DC: IBM Center for the Business of Government.

Bugge, M., J. Hauknes, C. Bloch and S. Slipersæter (2010), 'The public sector in innovation systems', *MEPIN (Measuring Public Innovation in the Nordic Countries) Project*, Copenhagen: Danish Agency for Science, Technology and Innovation.

Bugge, M., P.S. Mortensen and C. Bloch (2011), 'Report on the Nordic Pilot Studies – Analysis of Methodology and Results', *MEPIN (Measuring Public Innovation in the Nordic Countries) Project*, Copenhagen: Danish Agency for Science, Technology and Innovation.

Danish Agency for Science, Technology and Innovation (2008), *Strategy for Promoting Innovation in the Public Sector (in Danish)*, Copenhagen: Danish Agency for Science, Technology and Innovation.

Earl, L. (2002), 'Innovation and change in the public sector: a seeming oxymoron', Statistics Canada Working Paper, Catalogue No. 88F0006XIE No. 01, Ottawa: Statistics Canada.

European Commission (2010), *Europe 2020 Flagship Initiative – Innovation Union*, SEC (2010)1161, Brussels: European Commission.

Gallup Organization (2011), *Analytical Report – Innovation in Public Administration*, Report commissioned by the DG Enterprise and Industry of the European Commission, Brussels: European Commission.

Halvorsen, T., J. Hauknes, I. Miles and R. Røste (2005), *On the Differences between Public and Private Sector Innovation*, Publin Report D9, Oslo: NIFU STEP Studies in Innovation Research and Education.

Harris, M. and D. Albury (2009), 'Why radical innovation is needed to reinvent public services for the recession and beyond: The innovation imperative', The Lab Discussion Paper March 2009, London: Nesta.

Hartley, J. (2005), 'Innovation in governance and public services: past and present', *Public Money & Management*, **25**, 27–34.

Hughes, A. and C. Baker (2011), *Public Sector Innovation Index – The Findings from our Pilot Project Measuring Innovation in the Public Sector using a Survey Approach*, Report produced by Ernst & Young for Nesta, London: Nesta.

Kelly, G., G. Mulgan and S. Muers (2002), *Creating Public Value – An Analytical Framework for Public Service Reform*, London: Strategy Unit, Cabinet Office, UK.

Koch, P. and J. Hauknes (2005), *On Innovation in the Public Sector*, Publin Report D20, Oslo: NIFU STEP Studies in Innovation Research and Education.

Koch, P., P. Cunningham, N. Schwabsky and J. Hauknes (2005), *Innovation in the Public Sector – Summary and Policy Recommendations*, Publin Report D24, Oslo: NIFU STEP Studies in Innovation Research and Education.

Korean Ministry of Government Administration and Home Affairs (2005), 'Government Innovation Index – model and diagnosis', PowerPoint presentation, Seoul: Korean Ministry of Government Administration and Home Affairs.

MEADOW Consortium (2010), *The MEADOW Guidelines, Meadow (MEAsuring the Dynamics of Organisations and Work) Project*, 6th EU FP, Brussels: European Commission.

Mortensen, P.S. (2010), 'Survey methodology for measuring public innovation', *MEPIN (Measuring Public Innovation in the Nordic Countries) Project*, Copenhagen: Danish Agency for Science, Technology and Innovation.

Mulgan, G. (2007), *Ready or Not? Taking Innovation in the Public Sector Seriously*, Nesta Provocation 03, London: Nesta.

Mulgan, G. and D. Albury (2003), *Innovation in the Public Sector*, London: UK Cabinet Office.

National Audit Office (2009), *Innovation Across Central Government*, London: National Audit Office.

OECD (1997), *Measuring Public Employment in OECD Countries*, Paris: OECD.

OECD (2003), *Measuring Knowledge Management in the Business Sector – First Steps*, Paris: OECD.

OECD (2009a), 'Measuring innovation in education and training', OECD Discussion Paper, Paris: OECD.

OECD (2009b), *Government at a Glance*, Paris: OECD.

OECD (2010), *The OECD Innovation Strategy: Getting a head start on tomorrow*, Paris: OECD.

OECD/Eurostat (2005), *Oslo Manual – Guidelines for Collecting and Interpreting Innovation Data*, Paris: OECD.

UK Department of Business, Innovation and Skills (2008), *Innovation Nation*, London: Department of Business, Innovation and Skills.

Yoon, J. (2006), 'Government Innovation Index (GII): concept, development and application', PowerPoint presentation, Seoul: Korean Ministry of Government Administration and Home Affairs.

18 Indicators for social innovation
Geoff Mulgan, Kippy Joseph and Will Norman

1. INTRODUCTION

Over the last few decades, much work has gone into attempting to measure what is sometimes called social, public or civic value – the value created by NGOs, social enterprises and social ventures, and the related value associated with social programmes and policies. Much of this assessment is by its nature retrospective. But it has also become important to assess and even measure future value, the potential social impact of new ideas, ventures and programmes, and more broadly the socially innovative capacity of different societies.

It is widely accepted that 50–80 per cent of economic growth comes from innovation in its widest sense – the creation and use of new knowledge – and this awareness has spurred improvements in the measurement and assessment of innovative capacity in the economy.[1] There is probably a comparable relationship between social innovation and social progress, although there are even fewer accepted measures to test this assumption. There are also links between economic innovation and social progress on the one hand, and social innovation and economic growth on the other. Research by William Nordhaus (2003), for example, has shown that health gain accounts for as much of the gain in human welfare over the last century as economic growth. But we still lack robust theories, let alone measures, that can map the ways in which societies seek and adopt novel ideas to address challenges such as those associated with ageing populations, youth unemployment, social conflict and climate change.

The acuteness of the fiscal crises faced by many countries explains why many are turning their attention to public sector productivity, with growing recognition that the only plausible ways to increase productivity sustainably will involve much more intensive and systematic innovation.[2] Data for public services show productivity to be at best stagnant, and perversely, OECD data show that the countries that spend the most on health suffer more rather than less mortality, and even that those that have increased spending most have experienced the poorest improvements in mortality (Reeder 2011). In education too there is little correlation between spending and results. In short there is an urgent need for much more disciplined innovation to drive up productivity.

For philanthropists the pressures are less acute. But they too want to know where their money can achieve the biggest impact, whether by backing the spread of already-proven models, or by encouraging creative experiment in new ones.

Yet at the moment there are few usable indicators to guide decision makers. There are no reliable measures of spending on social innovation; no indicators of its scale; and no measures of its impact. The field is roughly where the world of R&D was in the middle of the last century, before the sustained attention of governments, foundations, economists and statisticians started to fill in the gaps.

There is now a great deal of experimentation under way to raise standards of measurement and evaluation. As always with indicators, the greatest challenge is to be clear about what they are for. Five different goals can be distinguished:

1. to measure the scale and nature of innovation activity at the level of nations, regions or enterprises in order to generate more knowledge about its dynamics;
2. to measure innovative capacity, within nations, regions, sectors or organizations;
3. to account to stakeholders, and in particular funders, investors and commissioners allocating scarce resources between organizations;
4. to guide managers allocating scarce resources within organizations; and
5. to assess the impact of actions on broader social and economic outcomes.

Not surprisingly, these require rather different approaches: a family of related approaches with some shared architecture needs to evolve, rather than a single indicator of social innovation. Ideally a common architecture should share some conceptual underpinnings, and some consistent language, while also allowing sufficient flexibility to fit widely divergent goals.

2.   THE LANDSCAPE OF TOOLS AND APPROACHES

Many available tools have been used to help measure social innovation and could be adapted. These can be broadly classified into those that measure the specific impact of a particular initiative, those that measure broader social outcomes, a smaller number that aim to measure levels of innovation, and an emerging field looking to measure civil society activity.

Tools to Measure Impact

The majority of the tools available are designed to measure the impact of particular projects and programmes, the third of the goals outlined above. There is a large number of specific tools, of which the different variations can be clustered into broadly similar approaches:

- Cost–benefit analysis (and its variant, cost-effectiveness analysis) remains the most widely used family of tools. Cost–benefit analysis has been applied particularly in transport (where it is often linked to environmental appraisals) and for big capital projects (where it is notorious for underestimating costs) (Flyvbjerg et al. 2003).
- Another common approach uses methods that seek to monetize social value by asking people what they would pay for a service or outcome ('stated preference methods').[3] Another set of methods, coming from economics, focuses on the choices people have actually made in related fields ('revealed preference').[4] The burgeoning field of environmental economics has spawned methods for measuring everything from wetlands to emissions, usually using a combination of these revealed and stated preference methods.
- Social impact assessment methods have been in use since the 1960s, trying to capture all the dimensions of value that are produced by a new policy or programme. These attempt to estimate the direct costs of an action (e.g. a drug treatment programme), its probability of, and the likely impact on future crime rates, hospital admissions or welfare payments. Within the non-profit world, social return on investment (SROI) methods (first developed by REDF)[5] translated the methods of the social impact tradition into the language of rates of return. There are many variants in use around the world. The EU's €2 billion 'EQUAL Programme', for example, advocated use of SROI and encouraged countries to develop variants, such as Finland's methods for assessing social enterprises.[6]
- NGOs and foundations have used many similar methods to assess social impact, all variants of the social impact model.[7] These include the Acumen Fund's Best Available Charitable Option (BACO) ratio methodology (Acumen Fund 2007), various methods developed by the Center for High Impact Philanthropy (CHIP)[8] and 'blended value' methods (associated with Jed Emerson).[9]
- Within the public sector a parallel body of work has looked at the public value created by public agencies and policies (see, e.g. Moore 1995); these methods have been looking at the value associated with public policy.[10] They have been used by organizations such as the

British Broadcasting Corporation (BBC) to explain what they do and the value they offer the public (Coyle 2010).

- Within any particular field there will also be many specific methods. A Young Foundation study of methods for measuring value in the built environment, for example, identified nearly 30 in use (Mulgan et al. 2006). Some were designed to guide investors, and some for developers, running the gamut from methods using artificial neural networks and 'hedonic' price models to fuzzy logic methods and, for the eager, 'auto-regressive integrated moving averages methods' and 'triple bottom line property appraisal methods'.[11]

Tools to Measure Broad Social Outcomes

There are also many indicators that can be used to measure broader social impacts.

- Measurements of QALYS and DALYS (quality and disability adjusted life years) have become a common way to judge health policies and clinical interventions (e.g. showing that smoking cessation programmes are far more cost-effective than most drugs). Health has also developed other measures including PROMs (patient reported outcome measurements),[12] EQ-5D (a measure of health status)[13] and the Health Utility Indexes developed at McMaster University[14] to track how people feel.
- In education, 'value-added' measures assess how much individual schools 'add' to the quality of pupils they take in – some schools might achieve very good exam results simply because of the quality of their intake (Ray 2006).
- Within academia creative new methods are being used. One approach draws on surveys of life satisfaction and income to judge social projects and programmes by how much extra income people would need to achieve an equivalent gain in life satisfaction. An imaginative study of a regeneration scheme employed this method and showed that modest investments in home safety, costing about 3 per cent as much as home repairs, generated four times as much value in terms of life satisfaction (Dolan and Metcalfe 2008).
- Many accounting methods are used at the level of national governments and regions. France's 'bilan sociétal' requires companies employing over 300 people to report on how their work affects society using a set of 100 indicators.[15] Italy has a similar 'bilancio sociale'.[16] Others have measured time. For example, Australia's

statistics office estimates unpaid work at around 48 per cent of GDP (Willis 2005).

- The OECD's 'Beyond GDP' programme, started in 2004, has mobilized many of the world's finest statisticians and economists to develop better indicators of social progress and well-being,[17] bearing fruit in the Stiglitz Commission's work for President Sarkozy in France which has led to a radical overhaul of GDP measures (Stiglitz et al. 2009). The UK has now introduced a large-scale survey on well-being, while the OECD's Wikiprogress website now offers a huge range of indicators, and allows users to customize indices.

Tools to Measure Innovation

The methods used to measure social innovation itself are less developed. There are adaptations of the survey techniques used for business – usually asking managers to comment on innovation investment and activity. However, traditional measures of innovation, which tend to focus on science and technology, are not able to account for all the innovation that is taking place. In practice much innovation is taking place through developing new contractual relationships, novel combinations of existing technology and processes (Nesta 2007, 2009). The *Oslo Manual*, widely recognized as a standard framework for business innovation measurement (OECD/Eurostat 2005), makes the key distinction between product (good or service), process, marketing and organizational innovation. In many ways the process and organizational innovations come closest to encapsulating social innovation.

The direction of travel of broader innovation measures has relevance to social innovation, as it moves away from the narrow emphasis on R&D spends and counting patents. These approaches are beginning to be applied in the social field. The Measuring Public Innovation in the Nordic countries (MEPIN) survey, for example, reviewed product, process, organizational and communications innovation across the public sector organizations (see Chapter 17 by Carter Bloch, this volume). It captures data about the number of staff involved, prevalence of ICT-led innovation, information channels for innovation, and use of procurement practices to drive innovation (Bugge et al. 2011). The European Commission is supporting much more extensive work on measures of public sector innovation, starting with a pilot European Public Sector Innovation Scoreboard which will, it is hoped, bear fruit before long. There are also more reflective survey tools that can be used within organizations to ask employees about their perceptions of how open the organization is to new ideas and their development.

Tools to Measure Civil Society

A very different body of work is under way on the measurement of civil society activity – pioneered by figures such as Lester Salamon at Johns Hopkins University. This is obviously not a measure of social innovation, since much social innovation happens within the public sector and in business, and much civil society activity is not innovative. But it is bringing a sharper statistical insight into patterns of activity among NGOs and social enterprises that used to be rather difficult to discern. Some of these data point to the size of the sector. By the end of the twentieth century, a study in 26 countries for which data were available showed that non-profit organizations accounted for only 6.8 per cent of the non-agricultural workforce (Salamon et al. 2007). The EU estimates that 11 million work in the broadly defined social economy (CIRIEC 2007) and another study showed that in the USA in the middle of the first decade of the 2000s charities alone employed nearly 10 million paid workers and engaged just under 5 million full-time equivalent volunteer workers, equivalent to about 10 per cent of the total workforce (Salamon and Sokolowski 2006). Other estimates show that including estimates of the value added by volunteers, non-profits accounted for an average of 5 per cent of GDP in the countries for which satellite account data are available (Salamon et al. 2007).[18] Related measures capture the size of social enterprises, the cooperative and mutual sector and traditional charity. Some of the survey tools make it possible to assess rates of start-up, survival rates and growth rates. The rise of a field of social investment is also bringing with it much more analysis of the capital needs of the sector, and more classic market analyses looking at patterns of demand.[19]

3. LIMITATIONS OF THE CURRENT TOOLS

So how useful are any of these indicators? The short answer is that the collection of data has not yet had much impact on decision making or action. The main reasons relate to those surrounding any kind of indicator. Indicators are most useful when they connect to a plausible model of causation, such that changes in one indicator may lead to changes in others. Without theories, indicators risk becoming just clutter. However imperfect they are, measures of R&D spending and patents at least connect to plausible theoretical claims, such as those claiming that R&D spending will contribute over time to economic growth.

By contrast, there is no settled theory of social innovation. The field of social innovation is theoretically underdeveloped, with few, if any, accepted concepts or causal relationships.[20] This is of course related to the lack of indicators since there are no usable data sets or time series to draw on to test hypotheses. There is a great deal of interesting theoretical work feeding into social innovation, including from innovation studies, the study of entrepreneurship, complexity theory, the theories of techno-economic paradigms as well as resilience theories of sociology-ecological systems, and others. The proliferation of academic centres attending to social innovation also means that much more brainpower is being applied to the field than before. But for now there are few frameworks to make use of data, and little agreement about fundamental issues such as how much social change is driven by entrepreneurial individuals, by movements, teams or networks, or for that matter by political parties and governments. Why do some ideas travel well and others poorly? Will there be any common patterns as to where the most influential ideas come from? Can the experimental methods of natural science be transplanted to social change? Do social innovations scale in the same way as business innovations, or does the path better mirror how novel change manifests in ecological systems?

The next challenge is that social science simply is not robust enough to make any firm predictions about what causes will lead to what effects, and thus about the potential value or use of particular social innovations – far too many variables are usually involved. The state of evidence on crime reduction shows that well-implemented policies can cut reoffending rates by a few per cent. But there are no actions that can reliably achieve the much larger impact claimed by some NGOs (possibly because the truly exceptional NGOs really are exceptional – the qualities that make them so good cannot easily be replicated). Indeed there are not really any 'laws' in social science or economics in the way that there are in physics.[21] Even in a field such as medicine, which has much stronger evidence than social action, bitter experience shows that it is only wise to believe that x causes y when many research studies using varied methods have all pointed in the same direction. Even many influential randomized control trials (still seen as the gold standard of evidence) have been dramatically overturned by subsequent research. Many would love the social field to be more like natural science, where evidence would definitely tell you that if you invested $10 million or $100 million in a particular programme it would have predictable effects. There is a strong case for introducing a much more orchestrated experimental approach into fields such as education. But even with a much greater pool of evidence it will still be hard to be certain about causation simply because of the sheer number of variables involved in social issues. Molecules obey the laws of physics; the people involved in social projects generally have minds of their own.

Another important limitation is that in many of the most important fields for social action – such as crime, childcare or schooling – the public are divided over values as well as value. For most people, for example, there is an intrinsic virtue in punishing criminals regardless of the costs and benefits of alternatives to prison. Psychologists have shown the prevalence of what is called 'altruistic punishment', our willingness to sacrifice a great deal to see others punished. As a result the standard social value assessments of more progressive approaches to crime risk missing the point: they are describing one view of crime, and often provide important insights about the folly of current programmes, but they cannot pretend to reflect the views or values of society.

Even without these problems, the monetized values generated by cost–benefit analysis (CBA), social return on investment (SROI) and other methods generally have very large variances, and are highly sensitive to the particular weights given to estimates of costs and paybacks. They can point in the round to potential paybacks – but they are rarely useful for making decisions at the margins, in the way that ROI methods can. Revealed preference and stated preference methods are also notoriously unreliable. They confuse rigour and precision: because they try to provide precise numbers, they end up being less rigorous about the means of deriving them (a point increasingly recognized by REDF and others in the SROI field).

Methods such as SROI generally apply discount rates taken from commercial markets. But it is not clear why social organizations should adopt time preferences from commercial markets that radically devalue the future: a 5 per cent discount rate values $100 after 30 years at $35.85 today, and after 50 years at $7.69. An alternative might be to copy governments that try to reflect both time preferences and, in the more sophisticated versions, take account of the fact that extra income in the future will be worth less than income today because future populations will be richer (the UK Treasury currently applies a 1.5 per cent rate to reflect time preferences and 2 per cent to reflect these income effects). But even this is misleading. A closer analysis of discount rates shows that very different ones apply in different sectors. In health, many countries apply a very low or zero rate, on the grounds that today's young people should not be disadvantaged relative to the old. Governments ignore discount rates in their investment in education and defence technologies. In climate change a furious debate has raged about what discount rates should apply – again in part a moral argument about what weight to give to future generations. Often governments – and foundations – behave more like a guardian or steward who is charged with sustaining or growing capital, rather than the strictly rational consumers of economic theory who always value present consumption more than future consumption. This makes it somewhat ironic to find many foundations routinely applying discount rates from commercial markets when it comes to social returns.[22]

These problems explain why, despite often complex architectures of analysis, the great majority of methods are both unreliable and largely unused.

4.   A POTENTIAL ROUTE FORWARD TO DEVELOP A FAMILY OF RELATED METHODS

So what should be done? Are these problems inevitable? Is it just impossible to measure social value in a meaningful way, and therefore impossible to measure social innovation?

It is possible both to measure and map social innovation activity, and to link this to the measurement of outcomes achieved or not achieved. The indicators of social innovation activity are likely to include the following elements:

- measures of investment: these will start off as self-reported, but may over time become more reliable, as has happened with commercial R&D investment;
- measures of activity, such as numbers employed, or time committed;
- subjective assessments of innovation culture: surveys of staff perceptions of how open the organization is to ideas, its capacity to adopt and adapt;
- managerial assessments of numbers of new goods and services, and their share of turnover.

None of these is perfect but it is possible that over time some of them will become more reliable and start building up a more detailed composite picture of activity across different types of organization and sector. The bigger challenge is to link measures of innovation activity or investment to value or impact achieved.

Measuring Social Value

A good starting point is to be clear what value is, and what it is not. Although economics has made many mistakes in measurement, it offers some important lessons for the social field. For much of human history economists believed that value was an objective fact. Aristotle thought that there was a 'just price' for everything. Karl Marx thought that value came from labour. Neoclassical economics argued instead that the only meaningful concept of value sees it as coming from the interaction of demand and supply in markets. Something is valuable only if someone is willing to pay for it.

This blunt approach upset many: it implies that there may be no economic value in a beautiful sunset, an endangered species or a wonderful work of art. But it liberated economics and allowed it to become a much more useful discipline, observing real behaviour rather than trying in futile ways to find a hidden reality.

The time is ripe for the social field to take an equally simple starting point as the precondition for progressing to a more sophisticated but also useful approach. In commercial markets value comes from the interaction of consumer demand and willingness to pay, and the willingness of businesses to provide goods and services. In the social field, too, value comes from the interplay of 'effective demand' and 'effective supply'. Effective demand implies that someone is willing to pay for a service or an outcome. That someone may be a public agency, a foundation or individual citizens. Effective supply implies that there is a capacity to provide the service or outcome at a reasonable price.

In some fields there are mature links between supply and demand: for example public willingness to pay through taxes for policing, or primary schools, connects to governments' ability to supply these things in familiar ways. Donors' willingness to finance children's charities in the developing world, or local churches, is also stable and mature in these senses. In these fields it is not hard to analyse social value, connecting what funders want and what providers know they can provide.

In other fields the links are missing. There may be available supply but insufficient demand – because the public, foundations or politicians do not see the need as sufficiently pressing (in some countries drug treatment or sex education would fall into this category). It is useful to note that mostly it is proxies for demand that operate in place of real demand, as in the case of school districts determining the expenditure for the implementation of new pupil programmes or foundations choosing investment of risk capital in novel promising ideas, rather than aggregated student and parent demand around new programming. In other cases there may be demand but inadequate supply at a reasonable cost (for example of methods for cutting obesity). Or there may be profound disagreement about the facts or what needs to be done (think of migration in the USA, for example).

Both sides of the equation may be complex or fragmented. In many areas of social policy demand for the better results that come from more holistic approaches is split across many different public agencies, from welfare to prisons, as well as NGOs. Equally the supply may be fragmented: help for homeless people, for example, may depend on the contribution of many different agencies, providing therapy, alcohol treatment, skills and housing.

And with a systems lens, it is clear that the opportunity for innovation to effect significant lasting change is dependent on ripeness and readiness across scales, from the individual, community and organizational levels straight through to the institutional arrangements like legal and political systems. Each of the most promising social innovations requires a unique combination of entrepreneurship, established or institutional connectors, sufficient financing and other ways that windows of opportunity line up to translate into systems-level impact. This kind of impact or change rarely occurs from the scaling of one specific idea or organization, and is most certainly not something that can be predicted or controlled. Just as pressing social problems are complex and have interdependent solution requirements, corresponding responses that address them tend to be multifaceted and well diffused.

But the key point is that for value to be meaningful it has to be an aspect of the relationship between demand and supply. The demand may come from a foundation wanting to promote carbon reduction, or the spread of Christianity, or human rights, or from a government wanting to save money. But there is no objective measure of value that is separate from these expressions.

Practical work designing assessment tools for services funding innovation has shown that these insights can be used to shape everyday tools. In practice, any tools need to address at least three dimensions of assessment.

1. The assessment of outcomes achieved: in some fields such as health there are well-established quantitative measures such as QALYS, employment rates or education value added.
2. Economics: how much does the idea cost, how much does it save, and over what time horizon?
3. The practicalities of implementation and risk: however good the idea, can it be implemented in practice? Will powerful interests block it? Are there the capacities in place to put it into effect?

Finally, for funders we can add a fourth dimension: how well does the activity fit with the strategic priorities of the funder, whether it is a government or a foundation?

All four dimensions tend to be important to real-world decision making (Figure 18.1). The four cannot easily be added up into a single number, since they are based on a combination of some hard data and much more qualitative judgements.

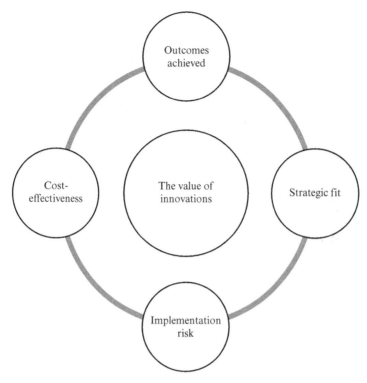

Figure 18.1   Four dimensions of evaluation

If there is to be a shared architecture for measuring or assessing social value *ex ante*, frameworks of this kind are essential. For measuring value *ex post*, implementation risk no longer matters.

Several critical points emerge from this approach. The first is that the value of these tools is that they help to structure a discussion, and later a negotiation, between a funder and a provider. The second is that because there are no objectively right answers to the questions, it matters a great deal if the people involved in trying to make estimates can review each other's work and help to make assessments more consistent and reliable. Again the formal tools are only useful to the extent that they help a community to learn from experience about the difficult task of making decisions with uneven and limited data. Statistical measures are feedback tools, and their use depends largely on how well developed the broader systems of learning are. The third is that the tools are most useful if they help both funders and practitioners to think creatively about the links between inputs and outcomes: for example, how to reap the very different economies of scale, scope, flow, penetration or prevention.

It then soon becomes clear that different structures of value exist in different fields. In some fields, such as in health in the UK, it is relatively straightforward because there is a single purchaser, which has great power relative to the overall health system. But in most fields where social innovation is occurring, this is not the case. Indeed every field has a different structure of value that has to influence what is measured and by whom. For example, in education, some value accrues directly to the learner (in the form of future earnings), while some accrues to the family or the wider community. Over several decades researchers have tried to distinguish the individual and social returns from different types of education. Vocational education has a different structure from generic skills. Some skills may be not only specific to an industry, but also to a location (e.g. particular language skills). A programme providing intensive support to a chaotic drug user will have a more complicated structure of value, creating some value for the individual (both financial and in terms of well-being), value to the community (for example from lower crime) as well as value for a wide range of public agencies (from hospitals, whose emergency services will be less used to police, prisons and welfare agencies).

Serious assessments of value need to start with making sense of the structure of value. But there are some simpler starting points. It is legitimate for a funder to set out what it wants to fund (for example, care for prisoners' families or action to prevent HIV/AIDs infection), and then to hold NGOs to account for what they achieve. And it is legitimate for an NGO to set out what it wants to achieve, and then to showcase what it has done, perhaps with the help of a third party. Some rough and ready measures of social impact may help managements decide to shift their resources and energy from one activity to another. However, these are bound to be sketches and should not pretend either to a spurious scientificity, or to be objective.

Within sectors, measures are expected that will increasingly emerge from peer commentary and review, whether in explicit wiki formats or through other measures of crowd-sourcing. For funders the most useful source of ideas about how to assess a project for homelessness will be other projects concerned with homelessness. Likewise, projects addressing loneliness among the elderly will often learn most from similar projects, and find out how they cope with such tricky issues as the measurement of subjective well-being or the cost savings that result at hospitals. Accumulating more good examples, with relevant comparisons, will make it possible to develop more intelligent communities of practice, balancing the generic needs of measurement with necessarily more sector- and context-specific combinations of elements.

5. CONCLUSIONS

There is a great deal of activity in the field of measurement of social innovation. But it remains an underdeveloped field. It can and should learn lessons from business, but should not be naïve. The world has learned the hard way that even in commercial markets concepts such as profit are not the objective facts they appear to be in economics text-books. Instead, measurement tools are tools for discovery, and should be used to support discussion and negotiation between people wanting to finance social goods and those wanting to provide them. They are useful if they bring choices and trade-offs to the surface, less so if they disguise them.

For decision makers in urgent need of tools, devices are required that bring to the surface the key facts rather than simplifying them into a single number. In particular, tools are needed that cover the four key dimensions of assessment: will the right outcomes be achieved? Is the action cost-effective? Does it have a strategic fit with the priorities of the funding bodies? And is it likely to be implementable?

Within these we suggest some simple presentation devices for investment organizations. Visually and conceptually we can think of a circle representing the direct monetary value of innovation, included in a circle representing the indirect monetary value, included in circles representing other types of impact and value (Figure 18.2).

Suggestions have been made as to how the rather different field of innovation measurement could evolve, with greater use of tools for assessing cultures of innovation, measuring innovation spending and activity, and showing the proportions of goods and services in different fields that are 'new to market'. However, indicators do more than just monitor and measure. They have agency of their own; they can have a mobilizing effect, bringing attention to specific issues, allowing people to share information, provoking institutional action and so on (Davis and Kingsbury 2011). Indicators for social innovation are required to ensure that new approaches are effective, but also to ensure that the field continues to grow and develop.

Indicators are, of course, dynamic; like any technology, they change. The indicators for social innovation will be modified by users and develop in response to users' needs (Gault 2011). In the early stages of evolution indicators are likely to produce data that are crude and even misleading. It is easy to conclude that no data are better than misleading data. However, this is a necessary stage to be navigated through as the field develops more comprehensive, reliable and meaningful indicators, and a sophisticated body of users able to understand what they mean.

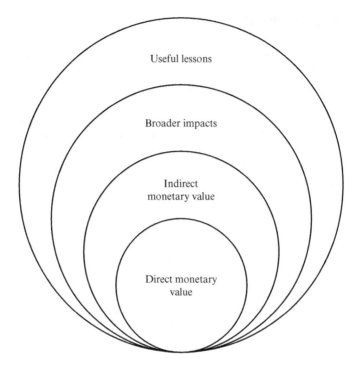

Figure 18.2   Value and outcomes of innovation

NOTES

1. The Nesta Innovation Index is one such method, endorsed by the OECD, the US Department of Commerce and the UK Office of National Statistics. A pilot in 2009 has been followed with more recent data sets, including 2012. The index measures business investment in innovation, covering not just traditional R&D but also other aspects of innovation such as software and organizational development.
2. The public sector productivity estimates produced over the last few years by the UK Office of National Statistics are, to the best of our knowledge, the most serious effort to address the many complex measurement issues faced by services such as criminal justice and eldercare.
3. These also try to estimate what non-users might value, whether through 'altruistic use' (knowing someone else might like it); 'option use' (having the opportunity to do something); 'bequest use' (leaving something for the future), and 'existence use' (satisfaction that things exist even if you do not enjoy them personally).
4. 'Travel cost method' is one example that looks at the time and travel cost expenses that people incur to visit a site as a proxy for their valuation of that site. Because travel and time costs increase with distance, it is possible to construct a 'marginal willingness to pay' curve for a particular site.
5. REDF (The Roberts Enterprise Development Fund) is a San-Francisco-based venture philanthropy organization that creates jobs and employment opportunities for people facing the greatest barriers to work: www.redf.org.

6. The Social Value Added Working Group of the EQUAL National Thematic Network for Social Entrepreneurship is developing the 'SYTA method' (SYTA-malli) of assessing the economic and the content-related outcomes of a social enterprise's activities: www.syta.fi.

7. For a more detailed survey of methods used by NGOs see Melinda Tuan's review (2008) for the Gates Foundation.

8. For more information about the Center for High Impact Philanthropy, see www. impact.upenn.edu.

9. For more information about blended value, see www.blendedvalue.org.

10. For example an opinion poll that suggests that citizens would like government to spend more money on services but fails to indicate public willingness to pay for this course of action does not constitute evidence that higher spending will increase public value.

11. These include 'multi-criteria' analysis methods such as Value in Design (VALID) or Design Quality Indicators (DQI); 'stated preference' models; and an array of choice modelling and hedonic methods, quality-of-life metrics, environmental impact assessments, environmental footprints, Placecheck, Local Environmental Quality Survey (LEQS) and landscape area characterisation methods. These and others are described in more detail in a literature review undertaken by the Young Foundation for the Commission for Architecture and the Built Environment (CABE) (Mulgan et al. 2006).

12. For further information, a range of reports is available at Patient Reported Outcomes Measurement Group, http://phi.uhce.ox.ac.uk/oldpubs.php.

13. EQ-5D is a standardized measure of health status developed by the EuroQol Group in order to provide a simple, generic measure of health for clinical and economic appraisal. It provides a simple descriptive profile and a single index value for health status that can be used in the clinical and economic evaluation of healthcare as well as in population health surveys. For more information, see Rabin and de Charro (2001) and www.euroqol.org.

14. For further information, see http://fhs.mcmaster.ca/hug/.

15. www.rsenews.com/public/dossier_social/bilan_societal.php?rub=2.

16. http://www.bilanciosociale.it/.

17. For more information about the Beyond GDP programme, see www.beyond-gdp.eu.

18. Varying from a high of 7.3 per cent in Canada to a low of 1.3 per cent in the Czech Republic (Salamon et al. 2007).

19. Boston Consulting Group and the Young Foundation (2011), was the first of a series of more in-depth market analyses of social investment.

20. The literature is expanding rapidly. See, for example, Nicholls and Murdock (2012).

21. Indeed, economics has no laws comparable to the laws of physics. Even apparently firm laws, such as that demand falls when prices rise, have many significant exceptions.

22. For a fuller analysis of discount rates, the roles of 'exponential' and 'hyperbolic' rates, and why their level tends to reflect social structures and the strength of social bonds, see the chapter on value in Mulgan (2009).

REFERENCES

Acumen Fund (2007), *The Best Available Charitable Option*, New York: Acumen Fund, www.acumenfund.org/uploads/assets/documents/BACO%20Concept%20Paper%20final_B1cNOVEM.pdf.

Boston Consulting Group and the Young Foundation (2011), *Lighting the Touchpaper: Growing the Market for Social Investment in England*, Boston, MA: Boston Consulting Group and London: The Young Foundation.

Bugge, M., P. Mortensen and C. Bloch (2011), *Measuring Public Innovation in Nordic*

Countries: Report on the Nordic Pilot studies, MEPIN, http://www.mepin.eu/documents/public/News/MEPIN_%20Nordic_pilot_study.pdf.

CIRIEC (International Centre of Research and Information on the Public, Social and Cooperative Economy) (2007), *The Social Economy in the European Union: Summary of the Report Drawn up for the European Economic and Social Committee*, Brussels: European Economic and Social Committee.

Coyle, D. with C. Woolard (2010), *Public Value in Practice: Restoring the Ethos of Public Service*, London: BBC Trust, www.bbc.co.uk/bbctrust/assets/files/pdf/regulatory_framework/pvt/public_value_practice.pdf.

Davis, K. and B. Kingsbury (2011), *Indicators as Interventions: Pitfalls and Prospects of Supporting Development Initiatives*, New York: Rockefeller Foundation.

Dolan, P. and R. Metcalfe (2008), 'The impact of subjective wellbeing on local authority interventions', unpublished manuscript.

Flyvbjerg, B., N. Bruzelius and W. Rothengatter (2003), *Megaprojects and Risk: An Anatomy of Ambition*, Cambridge: Cambridge University Press.

Gault, F. (2011), 'Social impacts of the development of science, technology and innovation indicators', Working Paper, Maastricht Economic and Social Research and Training Centre on Innovation and Technology, UNU-MERIT, http://www.merit.unu.edu/publications/wppdf/2011/wp2011-008.pdf.

Moore, M. (1995), *Creating Public Value: Strategic: Management in Government*, Cambridge, MA: Harvard University Press.

Mulgan, G. (2009), *The Art of Public Strategy: Mobilising Power and Knowledge for the Common Good*, Oxford: Oxford University Press.

Mulgan, G., G. Potts, J. Audsley, M. Carmona, C. de Magalhaes, L. Sieh and C. Sharpe (2006), *Mapping Value in the Built Urban Environment: A Report to the Commission for Architecture and the Built Environment (CABE)*, London: The Young Foundation.

Nesta (2007), *Hidden Innovation: How Innovation Happens in Six 'Low Innovation' Sectors*, London: Nesta.

Nesta (2009), *The Innovation Index: Measuring the UK's Investment in Innovation and its Effects*, London: Nesta.

Nicholls, Alex and Alex Murdock (eds) (2012), *Social Innovation: Blurring Boundaries to Reconfigure Markets*, London: Macmillan.

Nordhaus, W. (2003), 'The health of nations: the contribution of improved health to living standards', in K. Murphy and R. Topel (eds), *Measuring the Gains from Medical Research: An Economic Approach*, Chicago, IL: University of Chicago Press.

OECD/Eurostat (2005), *Oslo Manual: Guidelines for collecting and interpreting innovation data*, Paris: OECD.

Rabin, R. and F. de Charro (2001), 'EQ-5D: a measure of health status from the EuroQol Group', *Annals of Medicine*, **33**(5), 337–43.

Ray, A. (2006), 'School value added measures in England: a paper for the OECD Project on the Development of Value-Added Models in Education Systems', London: Department for Education.

Reeder, N. (2011), *Public Service Productivity in the UK: What Went Wrong? What Could Go Right?*, London: Young Foundation, www.youngfoundation.org/files/images/Productivity_in_UK_public_services.pdf.

Salamon, L. and W. Sokolowski (2006), 'Employment in America's charities: a profile', *Nonprofit Employment Bulletin*, **26**, Johns Hopkins Center for Civil Society Studies, www.ccss.jhu.edu/pdfs/NED_Bulletins/National/NED_Bulletin26_EmplyinAmericas Charities_2006.pdf.

Salamon, L., M. Haddock, W. Sokolowski and H. Tice (2007), 'Measuring civil society and volunteering: initial findings from implementation of the UN Handbook on Nonprofit Institutions', Working Paper No. 23, Johns Hopkins University, Center for Civil Society Studies.

Stiglitz, J., A. Sen and J.-P. Fitoussi (2009), *Report by the Commission on the Measurement of Economic Performance and Social Progress*, www.stiglitz-sen-fitoussi.fr/.

Tuan, M. (2008), *Measuring and/or Estimating Social Value Creation: Insights into Eight Integrated Cost Approaches*, Seattle, WA: Gates Foundation, www.gatesfoundation.org/learning/Documents/WWL-report-measuring-estimating-social-value-creation.pdf.

Willis, J. (2005), 'Financing transitional labour markets: factoring in unpaid work – do we need a universal basic income?', refereed paper presented to the 'Transitions and Risk: New Directions in Social Policy' Conference, Centre for Public Policy, University of Melbourne, 23–25 February.

PART VII

CHALLENGES

19 Innovation indicators and measurement: challenges
Fred Gault

1. INTRODUCTION

Innovation indicators are part of the policy process and measurement activities provide the statistics that become the indicators. This handbook has covered many of the issues related to measuring the activity of innovation, producing and presenting the indicators, and, then, using them. In Part VI, some evolving subjects were presented. In this chapter the first section addresses issues that are ongoing in indicator production and use. Then there is a discussion of developments anticipated in the short and in the longer term.

Language and Governance

Throughout the handbook, there has been reference to the language used to discuss indicator development by the community of practice that is part of the process, and it is clear that the language will continue to evolve, to add words and rules of grammar. A common language supports clarity of thought, improves communication and avoids confusion. This dependence on common language is not peculiar to the *Oslo Manual* and the innovation discourse.

One of the more striking precedents is the King James Bible, which came into being when King James, assuming the throne of England in 1603, found a number of bibles in use that hindered the discussion of theological matters that, at that time, were of considerable importance, certainly to the King. In 1604 he convened the Hampton Court Conference, provided clear instructions and the result was published in 1611, just over 400 years ago. The book solved the immediate problems of the King, and went on to transform the English language (Bragg 2011). Language matters.

The King James Bible also provides an example of governance (Davis et al. 2012), from the top down, which contrasts with the consensus and bottom–up approach to the creation of the *Oslo Manual* by the OECD Working Group of National Experts on Science and Technology Indicators (NESTI). The NESTI process is open, builds on evidence, and requires consensus before a manual can be recommended for publication and use. As discussed in Chapter 2, in the EU, the 'most recent *Oslo Manual*' is part of a regulation and there is a different governance structure dealing with the use of the manual in the conducting of the EU Community Innovation Survey (CIS) in member states. CIS and CIS-like surveys are a means of implementing the rules in the *Oslo Manual*.

Communities of Practice

Innovation indicators and measurement involve five communities of practice with, in some cases, overlapping membership. They are: the rule makers; the implementers of the rules; producers of the data; analysts of the data; and the policy analysts who use the indicators and analytical insights from the other communities of practice.

The NESTI community – making the rules

NESTI has already been discussed above and in Chapters 1 and 2. Members of NESTI, in collaboration with Eurostat, produce and revise the *Oslo Manual*. The manual, by regulation in EU countries, then governs the surveys that are used to implement the rules, CIS and CIS-like questionnaires.

The CIS community – implementing the rules

As Chapters 3, 4 and 8 have shown, implementing the *Oslo Manual* (Chapter 2) is not a simple task if the surveys, conducted in different countries in different languages, are to produce results that are comparable over time and that can be compared, with confidence, across jurisdictions. And there are different ways of doing innovation surveys. They can be repeated cross-sectional surveys that support trend analysis and micro-data analysis but that cannot deal with the demonstration of causal links between a policy intervention and a possible outcome. For that, as was discussed in Chapter 6, a panel survey is required and, even then, there are difficulties in demonstrating causal relationships. Whether an innovation survey is combined, or not, with a survey of R&D is a question addressed in Chapter 7 and there are arguments for and against doing this.

The CIS is revised every two years by a group of experts convened by Eurostat. New questions undergo cognitive testing and a collaborative project on cognitive testing involving Eurostat and the OECD ensures that the questions produce results that are internationally comparable.

The producer and the analytical communities – learning from the data

Once the surveys are in place, they produce statistics, some of which may be used as innovation indicators, such as the propensity of a firm to innovate in a particular industry or in a region, or the percentage of total turnover (revenue) in the last year resulting from the introduction of new or significantly improved products over the last three years. Many other indicators are possible, some of which have been discussed in Chapter 11, including the *OECD Science, Technology and Industry Scoreboard* (OECD 2011) with over 180 indicators and the *Innovation Union Scoreboard (IUS)* (EC 2011). In addition, in CIS 2010 (Chapter 1: appendix), there are 27 questions, some with multiple sub-categories, all of which could provide innovation statistics, and some of which could be used as indicators and presented, for example, by industry, by region, or by degree of novelty of the innovation. Finding combinations of statistics that, through cross-tabulation, yield useful indicators for policy purposes is a policy-dependent exercise, but there are core indicators common to most applications (Chapter 11). CIS data can also be linked to economic and social data from other sources, providing even more indicators of innovation.

One of the ways that data quality is assured and valuable insights are gained is through use of the data on innovation gathered through surveys, from administrative sources or by other means. The analysis of the data by those who produce it is an important part of this process, although it is not done in all organizations that produce data and is discouraged in some. In addition to data quality monitoring, producers who work with their own data are able to talk to analysts from outside their organizations about the strengths and weaknesses of the data and of the sources from which the data are derived.

Gaining access to microdata for analytical purposes is deliberately not easy as the data producer is bound, in many cases by law, to protect the confidentiality of the respondent that provided the data. Eurostat provides secure access to microdata from CIS, and some statistical offices have procedures for gaining such access. If access can be gained, there are two approaches to the analysis.

Researchers who wish to understand the national or regional aspects of innovation can be granted access to the relevant data sets and allowed to do the appropriate econometric analysis, assuming the data can support it. For international comparisons, the OECD has run a microdata analysis project (OECD 2009) where the first step was agreement on an econometric model. Then researchers in each of the participating countries gained access to the data and ran the model. The results were published in OECD (2009). The use of innovation survey microdata for economic analysis is intrinsically important, but it is also part of data quality assurance. Mairesse and Mohnen (2010) provide a comprehensive review of the use of innovation survey data for economic analysis.

An underlying requirement for this work is the availability of a researcher database that contains the final data, after editing and imputation, and the metadata that define each variable in the data set and the extent to which the variable has been populated with imputed data as opposed to data resulting from measurement. This is necessary if access to the data is to be facilitated as it is very difficult to work with the production database which is used as part of the survey process.

However, researcher databases are expensive and additional costs are incurred in training researchers in their use and then reviewing the outputs to ensure that there has been no breach of confidentiality. It is the protection of confidentiality that leads some statistical offices to allow regression coefficients to be removed from the secure site, but not tabulations, which remain the province of the statistical office. There is a reason for this. Each tabulation of aggregates from a database reveals more information about the microdata. A series of tabulations can then reveal the identity of a respondent if there are no measures in place to prevent this, one of which is knowing about every tabulation made from the database.

The communities of practice dealing with data production and analysis are valuable components of the process of producing, understanding and using data and indicators of innovation. A fifth community of practice is made up of the policy analysts.

The policy community – using the indicators and the analytical insights

The policy community, those responsible for developing, implementing, monitoring and evaluating policy initiatives, has made limited use of indicators of innovation, and one of the findings of Chapter 11 was that scoreboards use few indicators that result from the direct measurement of innovation. This may change and, if it does, the preferred outcome would be a policy community that was able to make intelligent use of indicators of innovation while understanding the limitations of the measurement process. Chapters 12, 13 and 14 illustrate some of the challenges to using direct measures of innovation, and their analysis, in the policy process.

Chapter 13 raises the danger of using 'old' indicators in a current context to guide or monitor policy. This issue has been raised by Marburger (2007: 32), who observed that 'in the face of rapid global change, old correlations do not have predictive value' and by Freeman and Soete (2007: 272): 'the link between the measurement of national STI[1] activities and their national economic impact, while always subject to debate, . . . has now become so loose that national STI indicators are in danger of no longer providing relevant economic insights'. The use of innovation indicators must take account of the context of change. The number of kilometres of railways in a country may once have been an indicator that informed policy and in the context of social goals and industrial development provided the policy maker with the knowledge needed to change the system. The lesson that those responsible for innovation indicators and measurement, and the policy community that uses the indicators, must adapt is very clear from Chapter 13.

Innovation Indicators

This handbook has concentrated on direct measurement of the activity of innovation, giving rise to indicators of the activity. However, there is a long history of using other indicators as proxies for indicators of innovation, reviewed next, and that is followed by a short discussion of data quality measures. Quality assurance is important for all statistical indicators, not just those of innovation, but it is particularly important for a field that is still developing. Finally, ten essential properties of indicators are introduced.

What are the indicators?
Before there were behavioural measures of innovation found in CIS, or in technology use surveys, analysts used R&D, patents and publications as proxy indicators of innovation. These indicators have advantages: they are readily available and they are understood by the policy community. However, there are disadvantages.

As has been repeatedly mentioned, more firms innovate than do R&D, so to argue that R&D is a proxy for innovation rules out many firms, especially SMEs. Large firms have a higher propensity to do R&D and to innovate, and the propensity to do R&D is greater in some industries that dominate the R&D statistics. A correlation between R&D performance and the activity of innovation will be present for large firms, but this has implications for the use of such analysis in policy, especially policy directed at SMEs. Not all academics are driven by influencing the policy process, but the readers of this handbook should be prepared to ask questions about any analytical work that uses R&D as a proxy for innovation.

The same caution applies to patents and to publications; the emphasis is on caution as both can produce useful indicators. Nagaoka et al. (2010) provide a review of patents and their use as indicators of innovation. The caution is based on the fact that not all firms protect their intellectual property with patents and not all firms publish in the peer-reviewed literature. The propensity to do either is size dependent and, for patents, there are significant sectoral differences. While indicators based on patents and publications have limitations as indicators of the activity of innovation, they have many other uses, including detecting emerging technologies (Chapter 15) and supporting foresight analysis (Chapter 16).

Co-publication statistics demonstrate collaboration between sectors and regions, and the propensity of some fields of science to collaborate more than others. The OECD is collaborating with SCImago research group (http://scimaps.org/) to report on key trends and country differences in scientific production, excellence and collaboration. However, innovation indicators, while linked to the science system, are fundamentally different because of the connection to the market (or potential users).

Before leaving publication analysis there is a variation on the theme of analysing peer-reviewed papers that involves examining the titles of books on technology over a period to determine the impact of technological change (Alexopoulos 2011). It is noted here as another initiative that may, in time, contribute to the development of innovation indicators.

Quality of innovation statistics
Indicators are expensive, especially reliable, timely and relevant indicators, and the justification for that expense is in their use. Indicators that are not used are not indicators. This introduces the question of data quality. Statistics Canada (2002) uses six dimensions in its quality assurance framework: relevance; accuracy; timeliness; accessibility; interpretability; and coherence. Achieving these objectives is a necessary part of producing indicators that can be used. However, the objectives are interrelated. Accurate, accessible and coherent indicators may be of no relevance if they are released the day after the policy debate they were expected to inform has taken place.

Desirable properties of innovation indicators
In 2010, the EU Commissioner for Research and Innovation called for 'headline indicators for innovation in support of the Europe 2020 strategy'. A high-level panel was convened and, in the course of its deliberations, it proposed ten essential properties of indicators, acknowledging that these were desirable but difficult to achieve (EC 2010). The ten properties are that the indicators: be simple and understandable; be sizeable and direct; be objective; be presently computable; be stable; be internationally comparable; be decomposable; have a low susceptibility to manipulation; be easy to handle technically; and be sensitive to stakeholders' views. A detailed explanation of these properties can be found in EC (2010) and an agenda for the development of indicators is given in the next section.

Current and Ongoing Activities

This section has reviewed the importance of language, codified in the *Oslo Manual*, for discussing the activity of innovation and the governance structure that gives rise to the *Manual*. It has made reference to the five overlapping communities of practice involved in innovation indicators and measurement. It has looked briefly at proxy indicators and data quality guidelines and a set of ten desired properties of indicators. All the activities described are part of the ongoing work of producing innovation indicators based on measurement and they would continue even if there were no changes in the indicators produced or new ways of using them. However, there is change. The next section deals with change in the short term.

2. THE SHORT TERM

In the short term, the ongoing work just outlined is part of the agenda of the community of practice responsible for the *Oslo Manual* that includes the OECD, Eurostat, and experts in member and observer countries of the OECD, member states of the EU and other countries. Elements of an agenda for indicator development can be found in OECD (2007, 2010a) and are summarized in OECD (2010a). They are to:

- improve the measurement of broader innovation and its link to macroeconomic performance;
- invest in high-quality and comprehensive data infrastructure to measure the determinants and impacts of innovation;
- recognize the role of innovation in the public sector and promote its measurement;
- promote the design of new statistical methods and interdisciplinary approaches to data collection; and
- promote the measurement of innovation for social goals and of social impacts of innovation.

There is also the community of practice that implements the rules, an example of which is the Eurostat group that prepares the CIS and develops the survey over time. The current version of the CIS 2010 questionnaire is reproduced in the appendix to Chapter 1. However, there are areas that need more attention.

Organizational and Marketing Innovation

The third edition of the *Oslo Manual* extended the definition of innovation to include industrial organization and practices, and market development or the development of new markets, but they are not yet probed to the same degree as product and process innovation in the CIS (Chapter 1: appendix). This can be seen by comparing the questions at the front of the questionnaire on product and process innovation with those later in the questionnaire on organizational innovation and marketing innovation.

There may be a limited market for the answers to these questions in a world where R&D policies outweigh innovation policies. However, understanding organizational and marketing innovation is part of understanding the activity of innovation, and that discussion should be held. In the case of organizational innovation, Chapter 10 provides a guide to current work that illustrates how firms learn. Going back to Lundvall (1992), learning is part of the activity of innovation and it is still not part of the standard practice of innovation measurement and indicator development. There is also the issue of how knowledge flows within the innovation system and how those flows influence the activity of innovation.

There is a substantial literature on organizational learning (Dierkes et al. 2001), on the learning economy (Archibugi and Lundvall 2001) and on the dynamics of the knowledge economy (Dolfsma and Soete 2006). However, the findings from this literature are not having a substantial influence on the discussions of the communities of practice that are responsible for innovation indicators and measurement.

There is some work on organizational innovation and business practices, but there is comparatively little on marketing innovation.[2] While more is needed now, in the longer term the 'market' part of the innovation definition in the *Oslo Manual* will become more a matter for discussion, and a better knowledge of market development as part of the activity of innovation will help. It would take few changes to CIS and similar surveys to collect information that applied to all components of the definition of innovation.

Innovators that are Not R&D Performers

Innovation indicators for firms that do not do R&D are becoming more available and they raise different policy needs for these firms. As mentioned in Chapter 1, these firms do not benefit from R&D tax credits or direct support to R&D, but they may need support through voucher schemes that allow them to access knowledge in local colleges or universities, or management and networking support, or support for staff training or for visiting staff experts in areas needed by the firm such as management, finance or human resource development. Some of these services are provided by venture capital firms, some by banks, but there is a case for looking at the public services available to non-R&D-performing innovative firms.

Table 19.1   *Breakdown of the population of innovative firms*

Innovative firms	Non-R&D performers	R&D performers	Comment
SMEs	SMEs using organization and marketing change to gain competitive advantage	Spinoffs from universities and research labs. High-tech start-ups	Domain of Schumpeterian creative destruction (Mark I)
Large firms	Some service firms and firms in the extraction industries innovating through organizational change	All industries with firms engaged in Schumpeter Mark II creative accumulation	Domain of Schumpeterian creative accumulation of knowledge (Mark II)
Comment	Problem solvers using available knowledge from doing, using and interacting	Formal knowledge creation leading to new products or processes	All firms that innovate

Source: Author.

As mentioned in Chapter 1, the distribution of R&D performance is quite different from that for the activity of innovation. R&D performance is dominated by a few large performers in a few industries; innovation is more pervasive and can be found in the large number of SMEs that do no R&D. These are quite different from the SMEs that do R&D, which may be high-tech spinoffs from firms or universities. The proposal is that the indicators be presented in such a way as to suggest different policy approaches. A first step could be the provision of the percentage break-down of innovative firms by size and performance of R&D, or not, and by industry or by region. This is illustrated in Table 19.1, where the two Schumpeterian domains of creative destruction (Mark I) and creative accumulation (Mark II) are introduced. Soete (2006) provides a discussion of the two domains and they suggest different approaches to analysis and to policy.

As SMEs account for at least 95 per cent of firms, and they play a role in job creation, there are many policies to support entrepreneurship, start-ups and R&D performance in small businesses. SMEs act in a competitive arena with limited resources. Small firms, with limited resources, can make just one mistake in their business strategy and they are finished, victims of creative destruction. Ideally, the people involved in the failed business go on to create new firms, having learned from the mistake. Large firms can make more than one mistake and they can accumulate knowledge as a result, this is part of the corporate accumulation of knowledge by the firm that prevents the large firm from making the same mistake again. The policy domain is different for large firms as they may use their accumulated knowledge to dominate the market and to reduce competition, but they may also create jobs and wealth, the taxes on which support public services.

Returning to Table 19.1, while core indicators are needed for all firms that innovate, additional and different indicators are needed to support the understanding of innovation in small and large firms and in those that do and do not do R&D. The present gap is information on large firms and their affiliates, and on how knowledge flows within the firm and to and from other parts of the innovation system.

Use and Planned Use of Technologies and Practices

Technologies and practices are part of the processes of the firm: transformation and delivery; organizational change and use of business practices; and market improvement or new market development. As such, they are an integral part of the activity of innovation.

As Chapter 15 makes clear, work is being done on developing indicators for emerging and enabling technologies, and this raises a question about earlier work on the use and planned use of technologies (and practices). The work on foresight in Chapter 16 is also part of this discussion as it deals with where technologies (and practices) may be going, how they could be used, and the possible consequences. Foresight also builds a community of practice, a network, that can influence the trajectories of the technology identified.

Using a technology as part of the production process is only an innovation if it is new to the firm. All firms, as part of their capital investment, buy and use technologies. However, what may be interesting are the other ways of adopting technologies. One is by buying and modifying the technology to suit the needs of the firm. Another is adoption by developing the technology by a firm that cannot find the needed technology on the market. The last two cases are examples of user innovation by firms (Chapter 5). From a CIS perspective, the firms that modify or develop technologies are process innovators, as are the firms that buy off-the-shelf technology that is new to the firm. Earlier work has shown that in Canadian manufacturing firms, of those that are adopting advanced technologies, about 20 per cent adopt by modifying and about 20 per cent adopt by developing the technologies. While these are significant figures, the question is the policy relevance of identifying the activity of user innovation and probing further to find out how the firms dealt with the intellectual property gained as a result of the user innovation. Some of this has been addressed in Gault and von Hippel (2009).

As technology modifiers tend to be smaller than technology developers, and to be less likely to do R&D, the same policy questions arise as were raised above when discussing innovative firms that are not R&D performers. The work on technology use and the development of related indicators described in Chapter 15 should continue, taking note of the questions about user innovation in firms in Chapter 5, but with consideration of the policy relevance of the indicators produced. Ideally it should lead to guidelines for measurement and interpretation of the results in the longer term.

Chapters 2 and 15 make reference to the way the OECD dealt with technology use, by separating the subject from the *Oslo Manual* in the third edition and starting what became the Working Party on Indicators for the Information Society (WPIIS) in 1997 to deal with information and communication technologies (ICTs) and their applications. Also, NESTI created an *ad hoc* group for biotechnology statistics until the measurement programme was established (www.oecd.org/sti/biotechnology/indicators) and also provides input to work on statistics for nanotechnologies.

Chapter 10 deals with measures of the dynamics of organizations and the place of work practices. Becker (2008) discusses organizational routines, Lam (2005) organizational innovation, and Foray and Gault (2003) the measurement of knowledge management, a set of business practices. The approach to the measurement of the use and planned use of business practices is similar to that used for the measurement of the use and planned use of technologies, and there are the same expectations that firms will buy and modify their business practices or develop practices in the absence of their availability on the market. This is an area where more work is needed to produce robust indicators of how firms function and how that influences innovation.

Indicators of Knowledge Flows

A full set of indicators would support a better understanding of the system of innovation, and that includes information on the actors, their activities and linkages, the outcomes of the activities and the linkages, and the longer impacts of the outcomes. Data on linkages provide evidence of flows between actors that can be uni- or bi-directional and that may involve the transfer of energy, material or finance, of knowledge or people. Energy, material or finance can be quantified by physical or financial measures. People can be counted and their characteristics identified. Knowledge flow is more complicated.

Knowledge can be codified and exchanged through many media. It can be tacit and transferred by moving people or teams that hold the knowledge and it can be embedded in technology or practices. The measuring of knowledge flows and knowledge markets, as part of the innovation system, is both a short- and a long-term objective that builds on the chapter on linkages in the *Oslo Manual* (OECD/Eurostat 2005: 75).

An OECD project on Knowledge Networks and Markets (KNM) has been examining the types of knowledge flows used by firms and organizations with a view to producing a taxonomy leading to a common language for discussing KNM. An output expected from the project is a set of indicators of knowledge flows (www.oecd.org/sti/knowledge).

Platforms for Innovation

The current example of platforms for innovation is the production of applications (Apps) for existing products such as the iPhone. The Apps would not diffuse rapidly were it not for the App store to promote them, and the large number of devices on which they can be used. The advantage of a platform is that the innovator needs knowledge only of the interface to the devices supported by the platform. Given that knowledge, the innovator can design a new or significantly improved product and bring it to market, and anyone can participate in the activity of innovation. There is a place here for new innovation indicators that take account of the environment, or the framework conditions under which the innovation is developed. The App is not the only example. Readily available molecules provide a platform for innovation in biotechnology and infrastructure of any kind invites innovators to take advantage of it. Chapter 13 provides the example of healthcare as a platform in Nordic countries where new hospitals will support the testing by firms of new products or practices that might then be made available to potential users, subject to the appropriate regulations. This is a good example of taking what could be perceived as a problem, an ageing population (Gault 2010: 106, 119), and turning it to advantage, given that significant public money will have to be spent on activities related to the ageing population in any case. The building of a widely accessible platform for innovation may reduce the cost of healthcare in the long run, while providing increased tax revenues from innovative firms. As with the App, the challenge is to develop innovation indicators that include the platform as a facilitator of innovation.

Diffusion of Existing Indicators and their Understanding

As measures of the activity of innovation develop, there is a need for more diffusion of indicators based on direct measurement of innovation

(Chapter 11) and their use. Rather than comparison of country aggregates, there is a need for more breakdowns by industry and by region within countries if the indicators are to be used to influence policy. In federal countries, such as the USA, the states lead in industrial policy and that is the level at which innovation indicators could be used.

At the OECD Blue Sky II Forum in 2006, John Marburger argued that the minister of research/education/technology/innovation should receive advice comparable to that received by the equivalent of the minister of finance/economy, based on complex and intimidating models such as those used by economists (Marburger 2007). As part of this, he advocated the creation of a new social science, the science of science and innovation policy (SciSIP). SciSIP will be discussed further in the next section.

Since 2006, as the OECD developed the Innovation Strategy (OECD 2010b), the target of influence has begun to shift to the equivalent of the minister of finance/economy. The reason is that this minister controls resources and makes decisions that affect other departments of government. In the short term there is a case for producing indicators that mean something to those who control financial decisions at all levels of government – municipal, state/province and federal levels – as a result making the use of evidence, supported by indicators, more common at all levels of government than it currently is.

Other Indicators of Innovation?

Headline indicator of innovation

The High-Level Panel convened by European Commission Directorate General (DG) Research and Innovation (EC 2010) was charged with finding a headline indicator for innovation to complement the ratio of gross domestic expenditure on R&D (GERD) to GDP, the GERD/GDP ratio, which has been produced and tracked for the last 50 years and is used for target setting. As noted in Chapter 14, the target in the Obama innovation strategy is 3 per cent and that is also the target for the EU, with 2 per cent coming from the business sector.

This is a challenge as it is difficult, if not impossible, to measure the cost of innovation whereas R&D is a measure of the expenditure on R&D performed in the reference year in the firm, no matter how funded (OECD 2002). The statistic that can be produced for innovation is the propensity to innovate by a firm in a given industry. To produce this statistic, the population of firms in the industry must be known, and for this a reliable business register is required. However, the question that then arises is whether knowing that 20 per cent of firms in one industry innovate and 60 per cent do so in another is helpful for policy purposes without additional information about the activity of innovation, such as the level of novelty, the sources of information for innovation, or the relevance of collaboration. Consider also that no country uses the propensity to do R&D in an industry as an indicator as it would be very small. R&D is a rare event.

The High-Level Panel looked at five indicators: hourly labour productivity; patent applications weighted by GDP; percentage of employment in knowledge-intensive activities; share of fast-growing (or young?) and innovative firms in the economy; and the contribution of innovation-related trade in manufactured goods to the balance of trade goods. In the end, two options were offered. Option A was a list of three indicators: patent applications weighted by GDP; percentage of employment in knowledge-intensive activities; and the contribution of innovation-related trade in manufactured goods to the balance of trade in goods. Option B was fast-growing innovative firms.

As this handbook has focused on direct measures of innovation, leading to innovation indicators, option B will be considered as it is closest to a direct measure of innovation, depending upon how it is implemented.

Measuring the presence and the economic and social contribution of fast-growing innovative firms is part of the broader subject of business demographics and its change with time, giving rise to evidence of business dynamics. To measure business demographics requires a business register and the following of the same rules in every country that is part of the indicator project. The report of the High-Level Panel notes that EU regulation (EC) No. 177/2008 provides a common framework for statistical purposes but suggests that further legislation is needed, which may move this topic into the long-term rather than the short-term category.

Assuming a good business register, making use of or linked to tax data, for example, firms with and without employees, by industry and by region, can be tracked over time. What is required in a good register is the ability to register in a timely manner the birth and deaths of firms (and of establishments within firms). Deaths can result from mergers and acquisitions, and so can births, depending on how the surviving entity is registered. Given this, information industries at any level of industrial classification can be classified according to their growth and their volatility. Both matter.

Consider an industry in which some firms are growing rapidly, based on employment, and some are shrinking rapidly. This volatile industry will differ from one in which there are rapidly growing firms and few in decline, or the reverse. The report of the High-Level Panel notes that the employment resulting from high-growth firms will reflect the framework conditions of the innovation system such as the availability of financial services, education and the orientation of economic institutions towards entrepreneurship. The employment would also indicate structural change as it happened. These are important points and they are part of entrepreneurship studies.[3]

The question to be resolved is where innovation enters the picture as not all of these high-growth firms will be covered by CIS and not all will be innovative. Growth does not necessarily require innovation, and innovation can also contribute to the decline of the firm if the market does not respond positively to the new or significantly improved product it is offered. A possibility is to measure high-growth firms in industries where there is a higher propensity for firms to innovate, based on CIS findings.

From the perspective of this handbook, the reader is encouraged to watch the progress of this indicator, the possibility of setting targets for the share of employment in an industry (or region) of high-growth firms, and the extent to which these firms are truly innovative.

Productivity growth as an indicator of innovation

This handbook has focused on direct measures of innovation through surveys, but it has considered other indicators that may be correlated with innovation, such as the headline indicators just discussed. Hall (2011), in a report prepared for the High-Level Panel on measuring innovation, looked at productivity growth as an innovation indicator. The conclusion was that multi-factor productivity (MFP) growth, as measured in a growth-accounting approach, could serve as an indicator of innovation. The paper goes on to discuss the data issues and the influence of business cycles on the results. Hall (2011) also reviewed firm-level productivity and innovation analysis based on the Crépon, Duguet and Mairesse (CDM) model (Crépon et al. 1998) and noted that there was a positive relationship between innovation in firms and their growth, based on revenue, and that it appeared to be due primarily to product innovation.

A Council of Canadian Academies expert panel on business innovation made use of an MFP approach in its assessment of innovation in Canada (CCA 2009) and explored shortcomings of Canadian industry. While there are data challenges in doing MFP analysis within a country, and more so for international comparisons, the MFP statistics could be used as an indicator of the activity of innovation.

The US Conference Board[4] is developing a new database on total factor productivity (TFP, synonymous with MFP), both in the advanced industrial economies and in many developing countries. To date, the TFP series are available only for 1990 onward, although there are plans to extend them back in time.

Public Sector Innovation

As Chapter 17 demonstrates, considerable work is now ongoing measuring 'innovation' in the public sector. One approach is to use a CIS approach for surveying the public sector units of observation, but there is still the question of how to deal with the definition of innovation and what 'market' means in this context. There has been a suggestion, mentioned in Chapter 5, that the phrase 'introduced on the market' in paragraph 150 of the *Oslo Manual* (OECD/Eurostat 2005: 47) be replaced by 'made available to potential users' (Gault 2012), but that is not for a short-term discussion as it will be a matter for consideration for the revision of the *Oslo Manual*, discussed in the next section. Meanwhile, the measurement work and the production of indicators should continue, in the same way that the original experimental work on innovation was done in the 1980s, before any internationally agreed guidelines are proposed.

The importance of gaining experience of measuring 'innovation' in the public sector is that it will contribute to a better understanding of innovation in the business sector, especially if there is more attention to knowledge flows and institutional learning, and to the interaction of the public and private sector in ways that influence innovation, such as procurement policy, regulation coming from the public sector, and technologies and practices coming from the business sector.

Developing standards and guidelines for measuring public sector innovation activities and interpreting the results goes beyond NESTI and the *Oslo Manual* as there is a new Observatory of Public Sector Innovation established at the OECD. The Observatory aims, systematically, to collect, categorize, analyse and share innovative practices from across the public sector, through an online interactive database. This is an opportunity for the Directorate for Science, Technology and Industry (DSTI) to collaborate with the Directorate for Public Governance and Territorial Development.

Public Sector Procurement as a Promoter of Private Sector Innovation

One aspect of public sector activity that could have a more direct impact on innovation in the private sector is procurement. If governments are prepared to set the performance standards for goods and services that it procures and leave to the bidding firms how those standards are to be met, there is an incentive for innovation and for indicators that identify the public sector as a source of information for innovation or of collaboration. The CIS team preparing CIS 2012 is considering asking specifically about innovation related to procurement contracts and if that is approved it will be the start of indicators of innovation that highlight the involvement of public sector procurement.

3. THE LONGER TERM

Looking beyond two or three years from the publication of this handbook, there are a number of activities that will affect indicators of innovation and measurement. Some of these are discussed here.

OECD Blue Sky Forum

In 2016, the third OECD Blue Sky Forum, Blue Sky III, is anticipated and its purpose, as with the previous two (Chapter 1), will be to look at new indicators for science, technology and innovation (STI), better use of existing STI indicators and new uses for existing indicators that have not been included in STI analysis.

In 2006, 250 people from 25 countries gathered in Ottawa to consider the same agenda and the outcome of that Forum provided input to the OECD measurement agenda (Chapter 9) and influenced the OECD Innovation Strategy (Chapter 12). The same outcome from Blue Sky III is anticipated and the issues raised in this handbook form part of the agenda. These include more indicators of the innovation system to provide a better understanding of how the system works, or does not, and new ways of gathering data on innovation at a time when response rates to traditional surveys are declining and some governments are reducing survey activity.

Also feeding into this will be the recommendations of the US National Academies Panel on *Improving Measures of Science, Technology and Innovation* (National Research Council 2012), which will appear in the final report of the panel in 2013. The work of this Panel is broader than innovation indicators and measurement, but innovation, especially given the new measurements of innovation through the Business R&D and Innovation Survey (BRDIS) of the NSF National Center for Science and Engineering Statistics (NCSES), will have a prominent place.

In Canada, the Council of Canadian Academies (CCA) Panel on Socio-economic Impacts of Innovation Investments will also have reported and some of its recommendations will bear on innovation indicators and measurement. More broadly, the CCA Panel on *The State of Science and Technology in Canada 2012* (CCA 2012) uses a variety of indicators discussed in this chapter to provide an evidence-based assessment.

The *Oslo Manual*

The *Oslo Manual* (OECD/Eurostat 2005) was last revised in the three-year period 2003–05 and it extended the definition of innovation and emphasized the systems approach to understanding innovation implicit in earlier editions. As the third edition approaches its tenth anniversary, there is a case for a fourth edition. One of the issues is how to deal with intangible investment as part of innovation. In national accounting, software was capitalized in the 1993 revision of the SNA (EC 1993) and R&D in SNA 2008 (EC et al. 2009). Firms also invest in training, brand development and other firm-specific activities such as their place in knowledge networks and value and supply chains. From a measurement or indicators approach, the question is which innovation activities should be measured, with the implicit assumption that they may give rise to innovation when they connect to the market. The most established is the performance of R&D, but there are others, and the number is growing as the understanding of the innovation system grows.

Intangibles play a key role in the growth-accounting approach of Corrado et al. (2009) to measure the contribution of innovation activity to productivity at national level (Hall 2011), and there is work on this link at the OECD and in a number of countries, including the USA (Aizcorbe et al. 2009). Recognizing the importance of knowledge-based capital (KBC), the OECD has launched a two-year project, 'New Sources of Growth: Intangible Assets', to explore the link between investment in intangibles and growth (OECD 2012), and, more specifically, between intangible investments and innovation expenditures. On a broader front, measuring intangibles is a key part of the analysis of sustainable development (World Bank 2011).

It is also clear from the implementation of the *Oslo Manual*, mainly through the CIS, that there is still much to learn about how an innovation system functions and that knowledge is needed if policy makers are going to be able to propose policy interventions that will achieve their socio-economic objectives. This makes Eurostat, as the manager of CIS, a key player in the revision of the *Oslo Manual*.

Consumers Who Change or Create Goods or Services

Chapter 5 introduced the consumer as a 'user innovator' and made a case for more attention to be given to this activity in official statistics on innovation. The problem from the *Oslo Manual* perspective is that consumers are not innovators as they do not produce products and introduce them to the market, but this does not mean that their effect is not present in existing statistics on innovation collected through CIS and similar surveys.

It is important to distinguish the consumer as a 'user innovator' from the consumer as a co-innovator, or collaborator, or as a source of information for innovation. All innovation surveys show the client or customer as a significant source of information for innovation and as a cooperation partner. This, however, is not 'user innovation'. Chapter 5 discusses ongoing work to establish the magnitude of this transfer from consumer to producer, and the result may provide a case for identifying the transfer in CIS and possible private and public sector encouragement for such transfers.

A 'consumer innovator' may decide to start a business and become an entrepreneur. Identifying the magnitude of this activity is also an objective considered in Chapter 5. The new firm would be in scope for an innovation survey but might not enter the sample unless it had 5 or 10 or 20 employees, depending on the country conducting the survey. There are many policies for entrepreneurs and start-up firms. The interesting statistic will be the percentage of 'consumer innovators' that start a firm.

Not all 'consumer innovators' have commercial interests; they may prefer to transfer their knowledge to a peer group or community of practice, and this is not captured anywhere in official statistics. There has been discussion on how to include this activity in innovation as defined in the *Oslo Manual* (Gault 2012), but this would require a revision of the definition in the current manual. As a revision of the *Oslo Manual* is anticipated, it is a matter of establishing the magnitude of the transfer of knowledge and its economic and social importance. The policy issue here is supporting a culture of innovation that may or may not lead to commercial outcomes, but supporting such a culture may increase the possibility of the next world-class innovation emerging in the country supporting an innovation culture.

Social 'Innovation'

Social innovation deals with new answers to social problems and seeks to improve the welfare of individuals and communities. The *Oslo Manual* approach to innovation in the business sector requires the measurement of the delivery of a new or significantly improved good or service to the market, or of better ways of getting the goods or services to the market.

Social problems are complex as they are embedded in a complex social system with many actors engaged in activities and interacting to achieve desired outcomes. The business innovation system is also complex, and both the business innovation system and the social system are dynamic, non-linear in their response to interventions, and global. In other words, neither is easy to understand to the point where advice can be given with any certainty to a policy maker about which interventions will achieve the desired objectives.

Nonetheless, social innovation matters as it changes the well-being of people and communities, and there are many groups in many countries working on the subject, developing measurement techniques and collecting data. The subject of social innovation, perhaps because of its diversity, has yet to give rise to the equivalent of the *Oslo Manual*, or a community of practice engaged in rule making such as NESTI.

Chapter 18 brought together three organizations, the National Endowment for Science, Technology and the Arts (Nesta), the Rockefeller Foundation and the Young Foundation, which work on social innovation to provide a review of the subject and the place of measurement and indicators. Many of the challenges in Chapter 18 are found elsewhere in the handbook, and there is reference to indicators having agency and moving people and organizations to do things that were not originally anticipated. In a social environment, the development of indicators carries with it a social responsibility not found in all indicator development.

Social innovation overlaps in some cases with public sector innovation (Chapter 17). However, the measurement of public sector innovation is much closer to the process that gave rise to the *Oslo Manual* and continues to support its revision. The subject of social innovation has been brought into a handbook on innovation indicators and measurement to show that there are other views and other demands that arise when people and communities try to solve problems to improve their own welfare. This can also be seen as an extension of the thinking on user innovation in Chapter 5. The reader is encouraged to follow the subject and the work of many organizations around the world working on social innovation.[5]

The Science of Innovation Policy

This is not a handbook on innovation policy, but it is through the implementation of innovation policy that indicators are used for monitoring, evaluation and benchmarking (Gault 2010). Policy issues, as seen in Chapters 12, 13 and 14, are wide-ranging, and policies are difficult to implement. This raises a question of why there is not more work on understanding innovation policy.

John Marburger called for a science of science and innovation policy (SciSIP) (Marburger 2007) and the US National Science Foundation has solicited proposals on a number of occasions giving rise to a community of academics that have a greater understanding of the policy issues, but Hill (Chapter 14) makes it very clear that moving from understanding the issues to the making of policy and then implementing that policy is a difficult process. However, learning how this is done matters as it involves understanding how the innovation system works so that the indicator and measurement communities can respond with the indicators needed to inform the policy debate. The birth of a social science that tries to understand policy, and innovation systems, is a very long-term activity (Gault 2011).

4. CONCLUSION

This handbook appears at a time when innovation indicators and measurement are being discussed in a number of countries and international organizations. There is the OECD measurement agenda (OECD 2010a), which is part of the OECD innovation strategy (OECD 2010b) and there is the research agenda associated with the call for a headline indicator of innovation in Europe (EC 2010). This thinking, within the communities of practice responsible for innovation indicators and measurement, has a long history and the knowledge of the subject was first codified in the 1990s, under the direction of Robert Chabbal (OECD 1992: 3), with the support of the Nordic Fund for Industrial Development. More recent history can be found in the work of many of the authors cited in this chapter and in Arundel et al. (2006), Colecchia (2007), and Chapters 2, 3 and 12.

The handbook has reviewed much of the work on innovation indicators and measurement that is happening in 2013 and it has examined emerging topics that could form part of the innovation measurement discussion in the near future, including innovation in the public sector and social innovation, and how they may be related to innovation in the business sector, which is the province of the *Oslo Manual* (OECD/Eurostat 2005). In the not-too-distant future the *Oslo Manual* will be revised and the OECD will convene the third of its series of Blue Sky Forums on indicator development for science, technology and innovation. The handbook is meant to be a guide to these developments as well as a tool for understanding what is now measured, how the statistics become indicators, and how they are used.

Finally, this handbook has dealt with innovation that alters wealth accumulation and distribution, and forces people to think about doing things differently. Acemoglu and Robinson (2012: 430) note that 'sustained economic growth requires innovation and innovation cannot be decoupled from creative destruction, which replaces the old with the new in the economic realm and also destabilizes established power relations in politics'. This leads to a broader discussion of the framework conditions needed to advance innovation, which is well beyond the scope of a handbook on innovation indicators and measurement, but more appropriate to a handbook on innovation policy and its implementation written by policy makers at the political level and by senior civil servants who have implemented policy.

NOTES

1. STI: science, technology and innovation.
2. The EC Directorate for Research and Innovation has initiated a study within the INNO Grips project to examine organizational and marketing innovation. There is also interest in indicators of these innovation activities.
3. See Atrostic (2008) on related US data and Haltiwanger (2011) on firm dynamics.
4. www.conference-board.org/data/economydatabase/.
5. There are many such organizations, but a review of the organizations of the authors of Chapter 18 is a start, and there is the Centre for Social Innovation in Vienna (www.zsi. at), the OECD Local Economic and Employment Development (LEED) programme, the OECD LEED Trento Centre for Local Development in Trento, Italy and the Center for Social Innovation at the Stanford Graduate School for Business.

REFERENCES

Acemoglu, Daron and James A. Robinson (2012), *Why Nations Fail: The Origins of Power, Prosperity and Poverty*, London: Profile Books.
Aizcorbe, A.M., C.E. Moylan and C.A. Robbins (2009), 'Toward better measurement of innovation and intangibles', *Survey of Current Business*, January, 10–23.
Alexopoulos, Michelle (2011), 'Read all about it! What happens following a technology shock', *American Economic Review*, **101**, 1144–79.
Archibugi, Daniele and Bengt-Åke Lundvall (2001), *The Globalizing Learning Economy*, Oxford: Oxford University Press.
Arundel, Anthony, Alessandra Colecchia and Andrew Wyckoff (2006), 'Rethinking science and technology indicators for innovation policy in the twenty-first century', in Louise Earl and Fred Gault (eds), *National Innovation, Indicators and Policy*, Cheltenham, UK and Northampton, MA, USA: Edward Elgar, pp. 167–97.
Atrostic, B.K. (2008), 'Measuring U.S. innovative activity: business data at the U.S. Census Bureau', *Journal of Technology Transfer*, **33**, 143–71.
Becker, Markus C. (2008), *Handbook of Organizational Routines*, Cheltenham, UK and Northampton, MA, USA: Edward Elgar.
Bragg, Melvyn (2011), *The Book of Books: The Radical Impact of the King James Bible 1611–2011*, London: Hodder and Stoughton.
CCA (2009), *Innovation and Business Strategy: Why Canada Falls Short, The Expert Panel on Business Innovation*, Ottawa: The Council of Canadian Academies.
CCA (2012), *The State of Science and Technology in Canada 2012*, Ottawa: The Council of Canadian Academies.
Colecchia, Alessandra (2007), 'Looking ahead: what implications for STI indicator develop-

ment?', in OECD, *Science, Technology and Innovation Indicators in a Changing World: Responding to Policy Needs*, Paris: OECD, pp. 285–98.

Corrado, C.A., C.R. Hulten and D.E. Sichel (2009), 'Intangible capital and U.S. economic growth', *Review of Income and Wealth*, International Association for Research in Income and Wealth, **55**(3), 661–85.

Crépon, B., E. Duguet and J. Mairesse (1998), 'Research, innovation and productivity: an econometric analysis at the firm level', *Economics of Innovation and New Technology*, **7**, 115–56.

Davis, K.E., A. Fischer, B. Kingsbury and S. Merry (eds) (2012), *Governance by Indicators: Global Power Through Quantification and Rankings*, Oxford: Oxford University Press.

Dierkes, Meinolf, Ariane Berthoin Antal, John Child and Ikujiro Nonaka (2001), *Handbook of Organizational Learning & Knowledge*, Oxford: Oxford University Press.

Dolfsma, Wilfred and Luc Soete (2006), *Understanding the Dynamics of a Knowledge Economy*, Cheltenham, UK and Northampton, MA, USA: Edward Elgar.

EC (2010), 'Elements for the setting up of headline indicators for innovation in support of the Europe 2020 strategy', Report of the High Level Panel on the Measurement of Innovation established by Ms Máire Geoghegan-Quinn, European Commissioner for Research and Innovation, Brussels: European Commission, DG Research and Innovation, http://ec.europa.eu/commission_2010-2014/geoghegan-quinn/hlp/documents/20101006-hlp-report_en.pdf.

EC (2011), *Innovation Union Scoreboard 2010: The Innovation Union's Performance Scoreboard for Research and Innovation*, Brussels: European Commission.

EC, IMF, OECD, UN and World Bank (1993), *System of National Accounts 1993*, Brussels/Luxembourg, New York, Paris, Washington, DC: EC, IMF, OECD, UN and World Bank.

EC, IMF, OECD, UN and World Bank (2009), *System of National Accounts, 2008*, New York: United Nations.

Foray, Dominique and Fred Gault (2003), 'Measurement of knowledge management practices', in OECD, *Measuring Knowledge Management in the Business Sector: First Steps*, Paris: OECD, pp. 11–28.

Freeman, Christopher and Luc Soete (2007), 'Science, technology and innovation indicators: the twenty-first century challenges', in OECD, *Science, Technology and Innovation Indicators in a Changing World: Responding to Policy Needs*, Paris: OECD, pp. 271–84.

Gault, Fred (2010), *Innovation Strategies for a Global Economy: Development, Implementation, Measurement and Management*, Cheltenham, UK and Northampton, MA, USA: Edward Elgar and Ottawa: IDRC.

Gault, Fred (2011), 'Developing a science of innovation policy internationally', in Kaye Husbands-Fealing, Julia Lane, John Marburger and Stephanie Shipp (eds), *Science of Science Policy: A Handbook*, Stanford, CA: Stanford University Press, pp. 156–82.

Gault, Fred (2012), 'User innovation and the market', *Science and Public Policy*, **39**, 118–28.

Gault, Fred and Eric von Hippel (2009), 'The prevalence of user innovation and free innovation transfers: implications for statistical indicators and innovation policy', MIT Sloan School of Management Working Paper no. 4722-09, Cambridge, MA: MIT.

Hall, Bronwyn H. (2011), 'Using productivity growth as an innovation indicator', Report for the High-Level Panel on Measuring Innovation, Brussels: European Commission, DG Research and Innovation.

Haltiwanger, John (2011), 'Job creation and firm dynamics in the U.S.', Working Paper, Maryland: University of Maryland.

Lam, Alice (2005), 'Organizational innovation', in Jan Fagerberg, David C. Mowery and Richard R. Nelson (eds), *The Oxford Handbook of Innovation*, Oxford: Oxford University Press, pp. 115–47.

Lundvall, Bengt-Åke (ed.) (1992), *National Systems of Innovation: Towards a Theory of Innovation and Interactive Learning*, London: Pinter Publishers.

Mairesse, Jacques and Pierre Mohnen (2010), 'Using innovation surveys for econometric analysis', in Bronwyn H. Hall and Nathan Rosenberg (eds), *Handbook of the Economics of Innovation*, Amsterdam: North-Holland, pp. 1129–55.

Marburger, John (2007), 'The science of science and innovation policy', in OECD, *Science, Technology and Innovation Indicators in a Changing World, Responding to Policy Needs*, Paris: OECD, pp. 27–32.

Nagaoka, Sadao, Kazuuki Motohashi and Akira Goto (2010), 'Patent statistics as innovation indicators', in Bronwyn H. Hall and Nathan Rosenberg (eds), *Handbook of the Economics of Innovation*, Amsterdam: North-Holland, pp. 1083–27.

National Research Council (2012), *Improving Measures of Science, Technology and Innovation: Interim Report, Panel on Developing Science, Technology and Innovation Indicators for the Future*, eds R.E. Litan, A.W. Wyckoff and K.H. Fealing, Committee on National Statistics, Division of Behavioral and Social Science and Education, and Board on Science, Technology and Economic Policy, Division of Policy and Global Affairs, Washington, DC: The National Academies Press.

OECD (1992), *Technology and the Economy: The Key Relationships*, Paris: OECD.

OECD (2001), *Science, Technology and Industry Review, Special Issue on New Science and Technology Indicators*, No. 27, Paris: OECD.

OECD (2002), *Frascati Manual: Proposed Standard Practice for Surveys on Research and Experimental Development*, Paris: OECD.

OECD (2007), *Science, Technology and Innovation Indicators in a Changing World: Responding to Policy Needs*, Paris: OECD.

OECD (2009), *Innovation in Firms: A Microeconomic Perspective*, Paris: OECD.

OECD (2010a), *Measuring Innovation, A New Perspective*, Paris: OECD.

OECD (2010b), *The OECD Innovation Strategy: Getting a Head Start on Tomorrow*, Paris: OECD.

OECD (2011), *OECD Science, Technology and Industry Scoreboard 2011*, Paris: OECD.

OECD (2012), *New Sources of Growth: Knowledge-Based Capital Driving Investment and Productivity in the 21st Century, Interim Project Findings*, Paris: OECD.

OECD/Eurostat (2005), *Oslo Manual, Guidelines for Collecting and Interpreting Innovation Data*, Paris: OECD.

Soete, Luc (2006), 'Knowledge, policy and innovation', in Louise Earl and Fred Gault (eds), *National Innovation, Indicators and Policy*, Cheltenham, UK and Northampton, MA, USA: Edward Elgar, pp. 198–218.

Statistics Canada (2002), *Statistics Canada's Quality Assurance Framework*, Catalogue No. 12-586-XIE, Ottawa: Statistics Canada.

World Bank (2011), *The Changing Wealth of Nations: Measuring Sustainable Development in the New Millennium*, Washington, DC: World Bank.

Index

accountability 336, 342
accounting methods 232, 310, 311, 355, 367, 423–4, 458
Acemoglu, D. 461
Act for Enhancing Research and Development Competences (2008) 198
action phase, of foresight 384
ad hoc classifications 361
ad hoc groups 50, 301, 364, 451
ad hoc surveys 368, 410
adaptability, organizational 252, 258
adaptive capabilities 248, 309
adhocracy 253
advanced technologies 45, 351, 359, 450
advanced technology surveys (Canada) 50, 123–4
Advisory Board (NESTI) 241
African Intergovernmental Committee on Science, Technology and Innovation Indicators 51
ageing population 249, 328, 398, 420, 452
aggregate measures, economic performance 232–5
Aghion, P. 306
Åkerblom, M. 73, 76–8
altruistic punishment 427
American Recovery and Reinvestment Act 2009 (US) 336, 337
analytical publications 224–5
Annual Economic and Fiscal Report (Japan) 207
Annual Report on the Japanese Economy (Japan) 198
Apps 452
Aristotle 428
arrival cities 10
Arthur D. Little 63
Arundel, A. 90, 116, 279, 294, 461
Asia 205, 305, 306, 314

Alliance for Science, Technology and Research for America (ASTRA) 340
The Atlantic Century 292
Audit Commission 410
Australia 46, 88–105, 91, 236, 303, 313, 338, 341, 369, 423–4
autonomy 387, 406, 408, 413
average partial effect (APE) 166
award programs 409

Basic Plan of Developing National Official Statistics (Japan) 200, 210
basic scorecards (KAM) 293
Becker, M. 451
benchmarking 104, 217, 283, 286, 290, 292–3, 393, 409
Best Available Charitable Option (BACO) 422
best practice 65, 80, 89, 219, 248, 279
Beyond GDP programme 424
bias 65, 79, 140, 142, 143, 169, 170, 181, 187, 237, 255, 257, 258–9, 388, 415
bibliometrics 224, 227, 236, 338, 354, 369, 384, 388, 390
bilan sociétal 423
bilancio sociale 423
biotechnology 50, 57, 236, 304, 353–4, 361
biotechnology statistics 219, 227, 349, 364–5, 451
Biotechnology Statistics (OECD) 221
'blended value' methods 422
block structure classification 375
Blue Sky Forums 47, 83, 221–2, 227, 240–41, 303, 397, 453, 457
Blue Sky indicators project 227–8, 311
Boden, M. 398
Bogdandy, A. von 5
Bogotá Manual 51
Borins, S. 409
brain drain 302